Praise for *In Search of Beauty*

18TH CENTURY ENGLISH AND DUTCH GLASS

"As a museum director, I am delighted to meet collectors who, like Jay Kaplan, have acquired deep knowledge of the field in which they collect. Moreover, Jay has had the taste and resolve to add only significant specimens to his collection. That Jay focused on acquiring important examples of 18th century English Glass is evident in the enviable collection he formed. Indeed, his approach should be a model for other serious collectors to follow."

—Dwight Lanmon, retired Director, The Corning Museum of Glass;
former Director Winterthur Museum, Garden and Library

"Jay Kaplan assembled a most impressive collection of English glass. I am in full admiration of his enthusiasm for the subject together with his desire to share his knowledge with others. It is testament to the esteem in which he is held by fellow collectors that the name Kaplan is now closely associated with the best of 18th century glass."

—Simon Cottle, Director of British and European Glass, Bonham's
and formerly Head of Glass at Sotheby's, London

"While I have always greatly admired Jay's 18th Century English wine glasses, it is fascinating to learn from this book the circumstances of his finding and buying each glass, and the thoughts that went through his mind at the time. This is an insight to how a great collection was formed by a great collector and those who helped to guide him in his quest."

—Dr. Richard Mones, Glass Collector, Doctor of Medicine

"The thrill of acquiring a beautiful glass comes through time and again. Patiently put together, it became a sumptuous collection. Kaplan is intelligent in that he is very much aware that his Search for Beauty took him to very knowledgeable scholars who knew and loved glass. Not surprisingly they became his close friends. Bravo!"

—Simon Wain-Hobson, Glass Collector, Professor of Virology, Institut Pasteur, Paris

"Jay Kaplan did not only collect glass; glass became a way of life for him. He always loved to be around fine glass, and to be with glass-people, like fellow collectors, glass-curators, experts and dealers from all over the world. Jay assembled a truly outstanding collection of glass, thanks to the fact that each glass was selected with the utmost knowledge, taste, love, care and sometimes even courage."

—The Frides Laméris family, Frides Lameris Kunst en Antiekhandel, Amsterdam

MOSTLY AMERICAN ART

"Jay Kaplan, a master of the art of living, allows us to join him in his long love affair with art: the pursuit, the capture, and best, the art of living with art. He speaks of the artists represented over time in his collection--Bellows, Pene du Bois, Hartley, Luks, et al as friends, as are the contemporary artists whose work has graced his home. His reminiscences invite us to share his delight in artists, collecting and the world of art."

—Ruth R. Perlin, Associate Director (Retired), Center for the Study of Modern Art
The Phillips Collection

"In the midst of a demanding law practice, Jay Kaplan became a true connoisseur of American art, focusing on an important niche period, the early 20th Century. His book is both a memoire and an art history; it gives insight to how the author acquired a depth of knowledge and, at the same time, developed a "good eye." This book is a rewarding piece of research which constantly engages the reader. With this book, Jay joins Washington's creative inner circles."

—Lenore D. Miller, Director, University Art Galleries and Chief Curator
The George Washington University

"Jay Kaplan has been a lifelong admirer of the great American realist painters Robert Henri and George Bellows. His memoir recounts a singular life inspired by Henri's clarion call to his students (including Bellows) during the first decades of the twentieth century: art for life's sake!"

—Charles Brock, Associate Curator of American and British Paintings
National Gallery of Art

CHINESE ART

"Jay Kaplan shares a fascinating history of how his collection of Chinese art began modestly, and evolved into a museum-quality collection. In all parts of this book, he brings to life not only the beautiful art in his collection, but also his experiences with scholars and other collectors."

—Iris Miller, Adjunct Professor, School of Architecture and Planning
The Catholic University of America

GENERAL

"For Jay Kaplan, collecting is more than a hobby: it is a passion. He finds delight in the entire process: the discovery, the acquisition, and the possession of beautiful works of art. Each stage is brought alive in this easy to read and most enjoyable memoire. And through it all, he made many friends with other collectors, dealers, and museum people. I feel it most fortunate to be numbered among them."

—Stephen Pohlman, Collector and International Entrepreneur

In Search of Beauty

In Search of Beauty

Memoir of an Art Collector

By Julius Kaplan

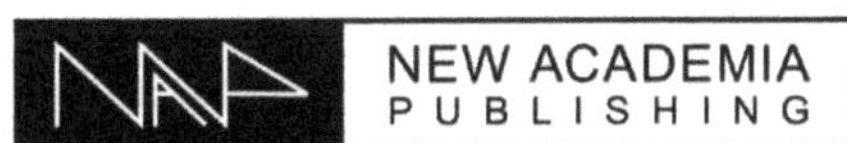

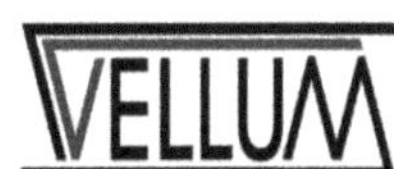

Washington, DC

New Academia Publishing, 2019

Printed in the United States of America

Library of Congress Control Number: 2019948163
ISBN 978-1-7330408-7-7 paperback (alk. paper)
ISBN 978-1-7330408-8-4 hardcover (alk. paper)

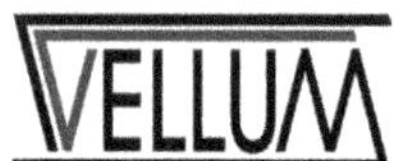

An imprint of New Academia Publishing

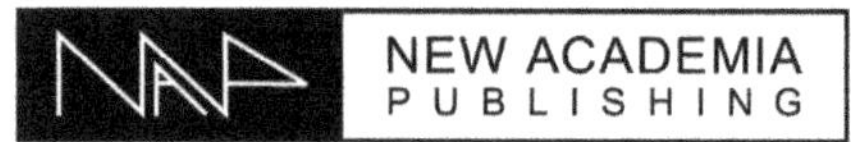

4401-A Connecticut Ave., NW #236
Washington DC 20008
info@newacademia.com
www.newacademia.com

Designed by Deanna Luu, International Arts & Artists

This book is dedicated to:

Marilyn Yalom

and

Irvin D. Yalom*

*See Author's Note (pg 194)

Table of Contents

Foreword

One of the interesting things about Jay Kaplan as a person and as a collector is the simultaneous presence of finely focused and diversely directed interests, together with an important tendency to think outside the box. When I directed the National Jewish Museum in the 1990s, and Jay came onto my board, he immediately had an impact on our fund-raising capacity and our programmatic direction by suggesting means for the first and ideas for the second that ruffled the stodgy feathers of many of our Board members—but who, however, ended up enthusiastically embracing his proposals, which in fact worked exceedingly well. Our shared love of culture and preference for projects that are challenging helped cement a friendship that has remained intact in the more than two decades since that brief era. What was true of Jay as a supporter and collaborator for the museum is more emphatically true for his role and that of his wife, Ann, as collectors.

If his initial direction was finely focused on American figurative painters of the Robert Henri circle—which remains a passion—his collector brachiation has swung him not onto different branches, but diverse trees in the forest of art. One moves with him from glass (and his focus within that realm into the specific sub-realm of 18th -century English and Dutch glass) to Judaica (and specifically, the esoteric realm of travelling Hanukkah menorot), and from Indian miniatures and Chinese art—of three specific periods, mind you—to English place-card holders, and into a wide array of contemporary media and styles.

To peruse the pages of this narrative is to be carried on a wonderfully idiosyncratic journey though significant parts of the history of art, through areas that are typically left entirely apart from each other. The journey is led by a guide who writes both with humor and seriousness while interweaving a personal story with a well-cultivated discussion and analysis of the works that have passed through his hands over the years.

As someone who has visited the Kaplan home many times and enjoyed both its hospitality and many intriguing conversations about the works of art that adorn its walls and fill its display cases, I could hardly feel more at home in reading through a volume that resonates with the descriptive sound-patterns and recapitulates the remembered content of many of those visits. I am drawn for opposite reasons to the discussion of, say, the Judaica—because it brings me back to what I wrote, twenty years ago, in a small catalogue of the collection—and that of the glass and English place-card holders (because I knew nothing of such things, or even that they existed).

I love the engagement of modern and contemporary object, too and—well, to be fair, there is not really anything here to which I am not drawn, because of my own interests and how they are met by Jay's engaging text. This is not a book for the artistically faint-hearted, but one to be relished by anyone who enjoys the twists and turns of a delightfully distinguished and entertaining intellectual and aesthetic voyage.

Ori Z Soltes
Professor of Art and Comparative Religion, Georgetown University.
Author of *Tradition and Transformation: Three Millennia of Jewish Art and Architecture.*

Preface

I have had a lifelong love of art. Indeed, as a youth, it was my goal to become a museum curator, or perhaps, even a museum director. My mother had different ideas. She let it be known, in her distinct Yiddish accent, "Mein boy, you vill be a doktor or a lawyer. Genug." "But Mother, I do not like blood." "So you vill be a lawyer." I ended up being an international lawyer, and, fortunately, I loved it. *But I never abandoned my search for beauty.* Whenever I had to travel to some foreign countries on clients' cases, I not only prepared carefully for the legal cases, but I also educated myself about the art and culture of the places to be visited, as well as what items of beauty might possibly be available for purchase.

I had, from my early days, a strong acquisitive instinct. This first led me to collect Chinese ceramics, then, English and Dutch 18th-century glass, American and other paintings of the early 20th century, and contemporary studio glass. Along the way, I also picked up antique miniature Hanukkah menorahs, Gandharan art of the 2nd/ 3rd centuries AD, English Victorian and Edwardian place card holders, and even antique and modern martini glasses, et al. All are discussed in this book with accompanying illustrations.

I believe that one of the great joys of collecting is how it invariably "opens doors" to the worlds of other collectors, dealers, museum curators and directors, allowing friendships to arise and knowledge to be shared. This was certainly so in my case. In this book, I relate, not only the friendships formed as a result of my collecting, but also the knowledge I gained of the histories and cultures of the places where the art was produced.

Since many of the art related experiences described in this book grew out of my law practice, a brief over view of my academic background and legal experience is in order.

EDUCATION

I received my B.A. from Wesleyan University in Middletown, Connecticut. I majored in art and did a distinction thesis on Robert Henri, an American artist and art teacher. (Henri had a defining impact on our choice of artists to collect.) I then went to law school at the University of Chicago ("Chicago") where I earned my law degree and was elected an editor of the *Law Review.* I also earned a Master's of Comparative Law degree from Chicago in French law. As part of that program, I studied and taught comparative law at the University of Grenoble, France.

PROFESSION

I worked for the Kennedy Administration as an attorney in the then newly formed Agency for International Development (AID) in the Department of State. Shortly after the death of President Kennedy, I left AID and three other young lawyers and I formed an international law firm with initial offices in Bangkok, Saigon, Santo Domingo, and Washington, D.C. The firm grew nicely and we added offices in Asia, the Middle East, Latin America, and the United States. During most of my career with the firm, it was called Kaplan Russin and Vecchi. Before fully retiring from the practice of law, I spent several years as "Of Counsel" with Messrs. Cadwalader, Wickersham, and Taft in their Washington, D.C. offices. Throughout my career, I specialized in International Law. This international practice required a great deal of travel and brought me into contact with many of the things I collected. (For more about my legal career see my fist book, *"Secrets and Suspense: International Law Stories."*)

As a result of my odyssey in search of beauty, my wife and I acquired numerous works of art between 1960 and 2010. In this book, I share the stories behind my favorite ones. I have had a number of these works professionally photographed. Other photographs were found in our family scrapbooks or on the internet.

I had no inherited wealth, and my wife's inheritance was modest. I thus had to make an early decision whether to buy art or put my earnings into securities to assure a comfortable retirement. I decided on the former, based on the simple theory that a beautiful work of art was more pleasing to look at than a stock certificate. I also hoped the work of art would appreciate as much as stocks and bonds. But this meant that when it came time to retire, it was necessary to sell some things from our collections. We were fortunate to do well on the sales of our art. Of course, the objects sold are no longer in our home. I have nevertheless included some of them in this book along with our other collections.

I had one advantage over many other collectors: I had the good fortune of having married a woman of keen intelligence and a great eye. Her name is Ann Lanyon Kaplan.

CHAPTER 1

Mostly American Paintings

1.1 | INTRODUCTION AND SUMMARY

In the 1970's and 1980's American paintings of the early 20th century were somewhat out of fashion, and relatively low prices prevailed. American collectors had, for the most part, become enamored of non-representational art. This facilitated our ability to acquire important American realist paintings of the early 20th century. Our first major acquisition was a 1909 George Bellows landscape done in Zion, New Jersey. The Bellows was followed by two paintings done in 1932: a still life of flowers by Marsden Hartley and a Guy Pene du Bois portrait of his daughter. From my mother-in-law we acquired a late 1920's John Graham portrait of his wife Elinor, who was my mother-in-law's friend. The remaining American paintings described in this chapter are George Luks' *Boy with a Blue Cap*, Grigory Gluckmann's portrait of a woman *à la Japonese*, Vasclav Vytlacil's abstract painting No. 47, and an American fauvist painting of fruit by Jerome Blum.

In addition to these American artists, we acquired several beautiful European paintings. These include a watercolor by the German/Dane artist, Emil Nolde, entitled *Rough Sea with Steamboat*(1941), and a 1909 neo-impressionist landscape entitled *L'Ile des Pécheurs* (Fishermen's Island) by the French artist Henri Le Sidaner. This was perhaps my favorite painting. Before going to bed, I would frequently sit and examine the painting for a while with a glass of Calvados in hand. I helped put together a New York show of works by the Russian artist, Nicholas Tarkhoff, and I was rewarded with his 1901 painting entitled *Boulevard en mouvement à la Mi-Carême*.

The reason for my attraction to the early 20th Century American art was, in a word, Robert Henri. I majored in art at Wesleyan University, where, in 1956, I wrote a senior thesis on Henri who was an important American painter, and an equally important teacher of artists. He began his career in Philadelphia as an illustrator in the late 19th century, where he attracted a group of four other illustrators who met regularly to discuss art. These artists became known as the "Philadelphia Four": William Glackens, George Luks, Everett Shinn and John Sloan. By 1900, Henri and several of his Philadelphia colleagues had moved to New York, where he took up painting oil on canvas. But rather than paint impressionist paintings, then in vogue, he painted more realistic art that sought

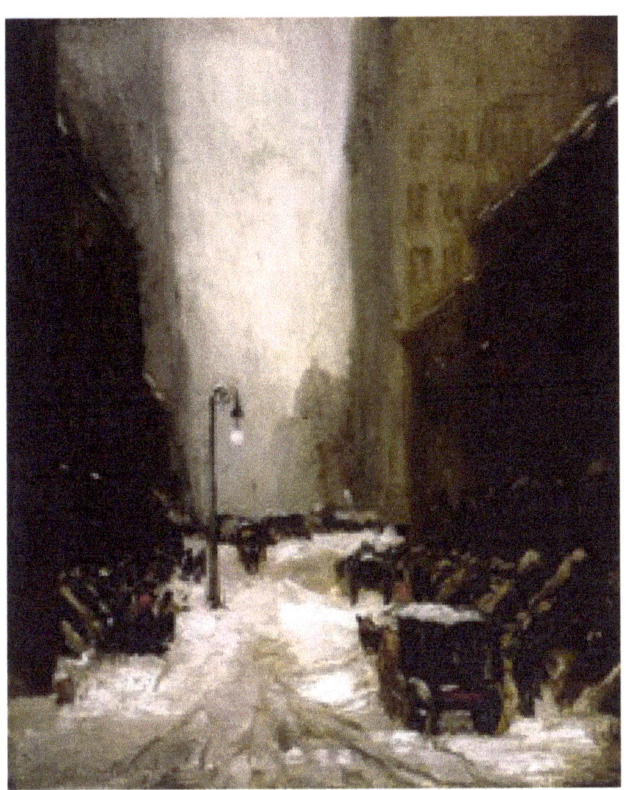

Illustration 1: Robert Henri, *Snow in New York*, 1902. Oil on canvas, 32 × 25 13/16 inches. National Gallery of Art, Chester Dale Collection, 1954.4.3.

out the less genteel subjects in the modern American city. My favorite Henri street scene is in the collection of the National Gallery of Art (NGA). It is called *Snow in New York* (1902), oil on canvas (Illustration 1).

In 1902, Henri became a teacher at the New York School of Art. Among his long list of students who became well known are Bellows, Pene du Bois, and Stuart Davis. With some of his former students, he formed a group of eight painters, later known as "The Eight," who put together a now famous show at the Macbeth Galleries in 1908. Their work soon became known as the Ashcan School of American Art. The Eight consisted of Henri, *the Philadelphia Four*, and three other artists: Maurice Prendergast, Ernest Lawson, and Arthur B. Davies.

It was my dream as a student to someday own a work by at least some of these students of Henri. As you will see below, I succeeded in owning works by Henri students Bellows, Luks, and Pene du Bois. After retiring from the practice of law, I started a short-lived art business, where I was involved, *inter alia*, in the purchase and sale of paintings by Henri students' Everett Shinn and George Luks. Let us now examine some of the major paintings in our collection.

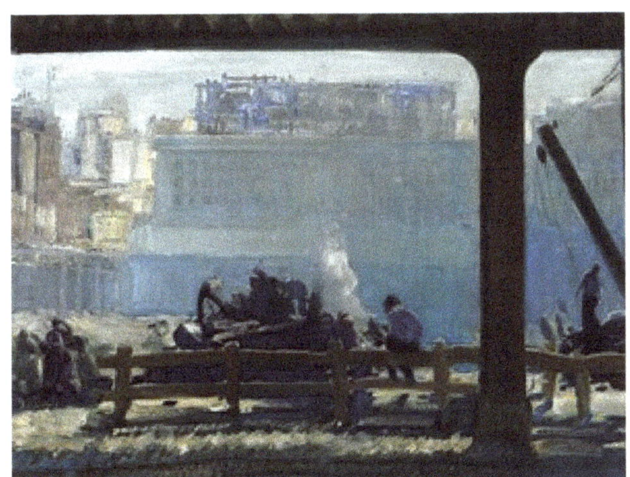

Illustration 2: George W. Bellows, *Blue Morning*, 1909. Oil on canvas, 34 x 44 inches. National Gallery of Art, Chester Dale Collection, 1963.10.82.

1.2 | GEORGE WESLEY BELLOWS (1882-1925)

In 1961 I went to work with the new Kennedy Administration in Washington, D.C., and became a frequent visitor of the NGA. Its collection contained a number of important paintings by Henri's student, George Bellows, and I would make it a point on each trip to visit his paintings. At first, I was most attracted to his famous paintings of boxers. I then gravitated towards his 1909 paintings of the construction site for Pennsylvania Station, and one painting in particular, *Blue Morning*, 1909 (Illustration 2).

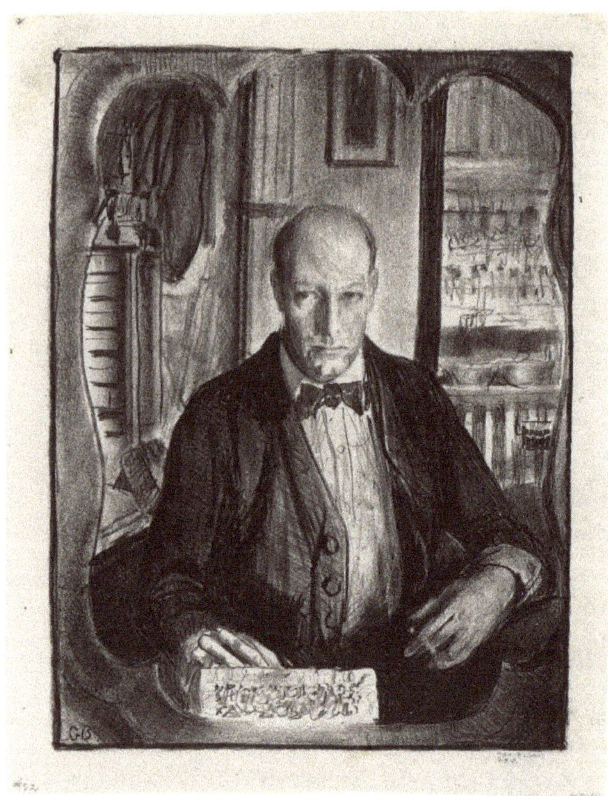

Illustration 3: George W. Bellows, *Self-Portrait*, 1921. Lithograph on paper, 10 1/2 × 7 7/8 inches. National Portrait Gallery, Smithsonian Institution, NPG.84.187.

Blue Morning is the last of four paintings that Bellows executed from 1907 to 1909 depicting the construction site of the Pennsylvania Station railroad terminal in New York City.

I had no ambition of ever owning a Bellows (Illustration 3). They were, to my mind, for museums, and not for neophyte collectors of modest means. Then, one day in 1976, I looked at a catalogue of Weschler's Auctioneers in Washington, D.C., and was excited to see that a 1909 Bellows oil painting on canvas, entitled *Jersey Woods*, was to be sold at a forthcoming auction. Ann and I immediately went there to examine the painting. It was a snow scene, 25 ½ by 29 ½ inches, and it was indeed lovely (Illustration 4).

I asked Mr. Weschler about the provenance of the painting. He said that it had been consigned by Hirschl & Adler, a well-known and highly regarded New York art dealer. Coming from that dealer, I thought it highly likely that the attribution to Bellows was correct, but I was hardly an expert. I went back to Mr. Weschler and asked him if his auction house would guarantee the authenticity of the painting. He answered in the affirmative. That certainly encouraged me to bid, and the estimated price was less than I would have expected. Ann also admired the painting and concurred in my bidding (up to a certain amount). We bid on the painting and succeeded in buying it for a wee bit less than our budgetary maximum.[1]

We decided it would be wise to insure our new painting, but to do so, we would need a certificate of authenticity. I turned to a renowned local art expert, one I will name LK. Weeks later LK came back to us explaining that she unfortunately could not authenticate the painting as a Bellows. The best she could do was certify that it was "attributed to Bellows." She had consulted many experts on Bellows' paintings, including N.V. Allison, a gallery in New York that has expertise in Bellows. They all agreed that it looked like a Bellows. However, LK pointed out that it was signed "BELLOWS"

1 Almost 30 some years after purchasing the painting, when we were planning to sell it, I learned from an art dealer (who in turn had learned from X-rays secured by a potential purchaser) that a portion of the painting had been restored. Moreover, in the opinion of the dealer, the restoration of the dirt road in the lower right corner was not well done. When I bought the painting, Weschler's Auction House did not offer a condition report, and I was too inexperienced to ask for one (or cause one to be done). I am most grateful to them for this, since, had they provided one, we may have been discouraged from buying the painting, and we would not have been able to enjoy living with the Bellows for all these years. Interestingly, when the painting was on public display in museum shows around the country, during which it was reviewed by experts, no one ever commented upon this small area of restoration. I now suspect that dealers in American art and other cognoscenti of New York always knew about this restoration, and thus stayed away from the auction at Weschler's. That is perhaps how we were able to buy it at a very reasonable price.

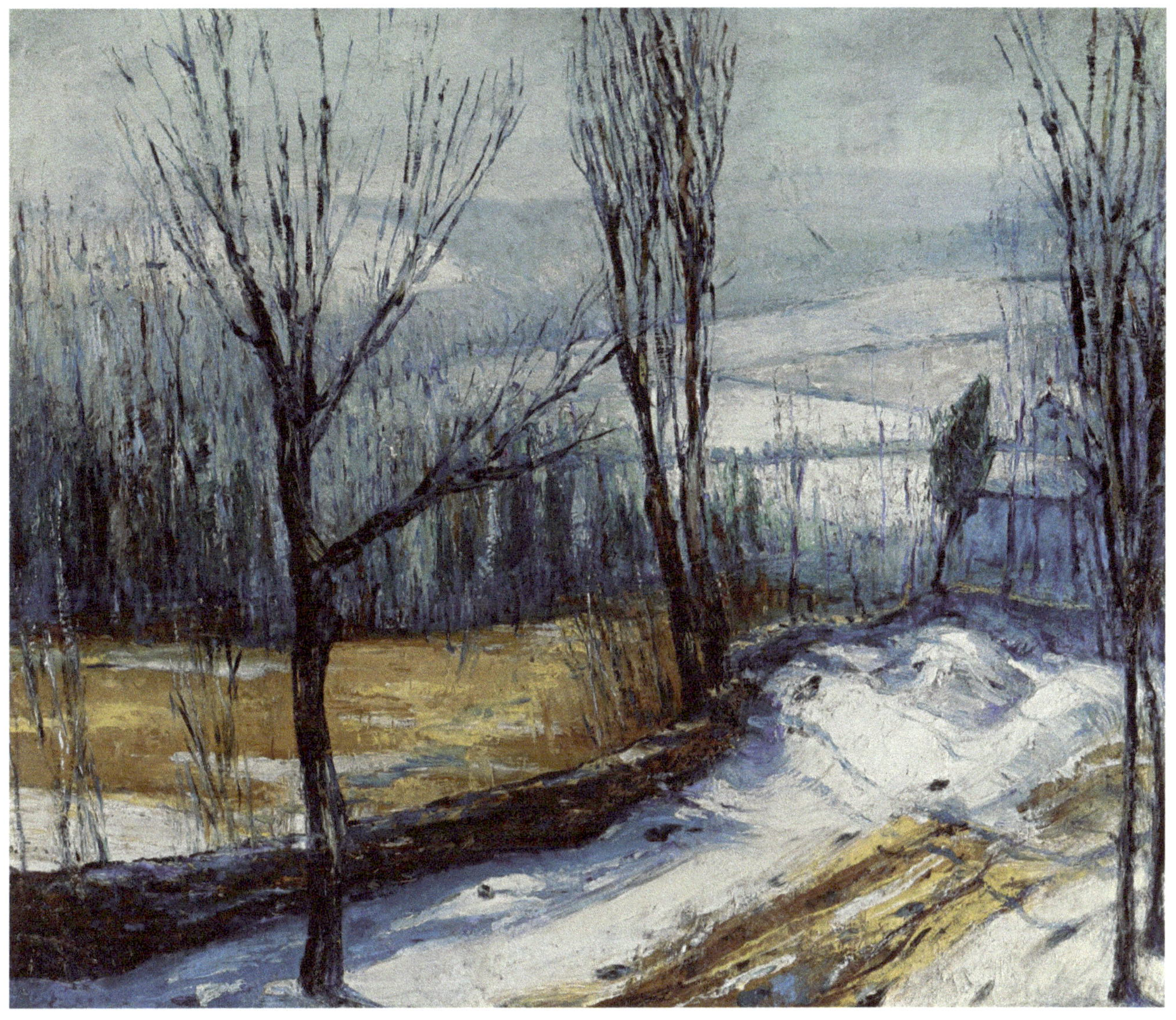

Illustration 4: George W. Bellows, *Jersey Woods*, 1909. Photo by Reid S. Yalom.

in capital letters, and she understood that the artist always signed his paintings in the lower case, usually with his first as well as his family name.

I was, to say the least, shocked and disappointed. The first thing I did was run to the Library of Congress, with a magnifying glass in hand, and examine dozens of books with illustrations of Bellows's paintings. To the extent possible, I studied all of the signatures, though it was difficult to read them in most of the illustrated paintings. But of those I could read, the signatures were indeed in lower case.

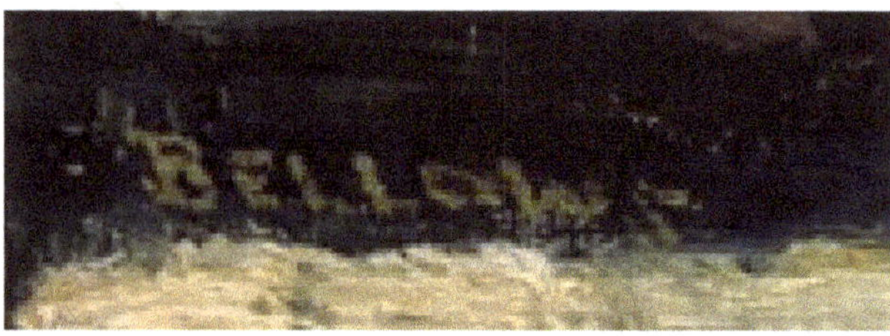

Illustration 5: Bellows' signature in majuscule on *Blue Morning* (1909). Photo by the author.

When I was next in the NGA, I went, as usual, to visit *Blue Morning*. I looked carefully for the artist's signature, and was ecstatic when I saw that it was signed "BELLOWS" - in majuscule, identical to the signature on our painting. On my next trip to New York, I found another Bellows painting, entitled *Kids* (1909), which was also signed in majuscule! For some reason, Bellows chose to sign some of his 1909 paintings this way. Here is the Bellows signature on the bottom of *Blue Morning* (Illustration 5).

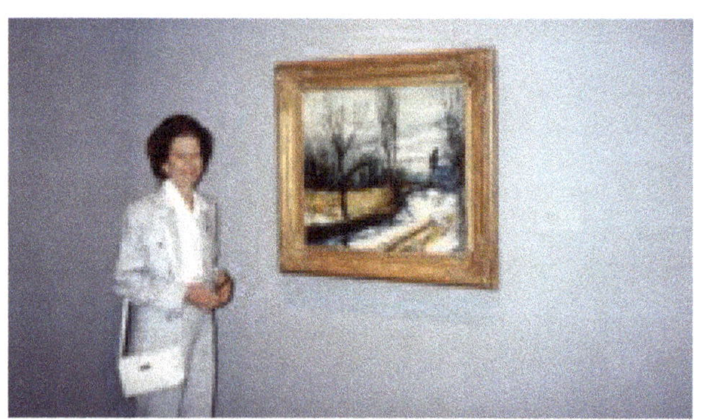
Illustration 6: Ann with Bellows' *Jersey Woods* in the 1998 exhibition *George Bellows: Love of Winter* at Columbus Ohio Museum.

Despite my success in finding other Bellows with similar signatures, the definitive authentication of *Jersey Woods* as a genuine Bellows came only in 1997, when the Norton Museum of Art invited us to lend the painting to a major Bellows show they were arranging, called *Love of Winter*. The show was also shown at the Newark Museum and in the Columbus Museum of Art. Other lenders included the Brooklyn Museum, the Metropolitan Museum of Art, the Museum of American Art of the Pennsylvania Academy of Fine Arts, the Museum of Fine Arts, Boston, the National Gallery of Art, the Philadelphia Museum of Art, the Whitney Museum of American Art, and Yale University Art Gallery, and other major museums and collectors. The lead article in the catalogue, which included commentary on *Jersey Woods*, was written by John Wilmerding. From 1977 to 1983 he served as senior curator at the National Gallery of Art and as Deputy Director under J. Carter Brown from 1983 to 1988. He, thereafter, served as Christopher Sarofin Professor of American Art at Princeton. In the catalogue he noted that *Jersey Woods* and several other Bellows paintings were done in the winter of 1909 in Zion, New Jersey.

I offer a picture of Ann standing next to "Jersey Woods" at the Columbus Museum of Art showing of *Love of Winter* (Illustration 6). Several memorable experiences emerged from our visit to the Bellows show at the Norton Museum. The most notable was a dinner given by William Koch, who was then on the museum's board of directors. It was held in his spacious and elegant Palm Beach home. The home was facing the ocean, but his property extended for blocks to the Inland Waterway, and was lined with sculptures by the Mexican artist, Fernando Botero. The dinner was to thank those of us who lent paintings to the show. William is the twin brother of David Koch. David and their brother Charles, are known as "The Koch Brothers," owners of Koch Industries (the second largest privately-owned company in the United States). William, however, broke away from "The Koch Brothers," and became a solo businessman, collector, and sailor.

When we entered the Koch home, I saw a friend who was a major dealer in American paintings in New York. He came up to me and said, "Jay, let's do an inventory of the art in the living room." We went from painting to painting, and my friend gave his estimate of the value of each as we circled the room. By the time we were called to dinner, we had reached $450 million. My favorite painting was a large Modigliani of a woman lying nude on a sofa. It hung over Koch's mantelpiece. A similar painting by Modigliani sold at Sotheby's in May 2018 for $157.2 million.

During the pre-dinner reception, several waiters were serving Russian Beluga caviar from kilo tins. Their companion waiters were serving Dom Perignon champagne, while another was serving oysters. When I was about to try one of the oysters, Bill Koch came up to me and said, "I hope you enjoy these oysters. They come from a farm in New England. When we first tasted their wonderful oysters, we were so delighted that we simply bought the whole farm." I ate one and it was indeed delicious.

The dinner was magnificent. The wines served, an array of noble Burgundies and one 1983 Chateau Margaux, were extraordinary. Afterwards, I complimented Bill Koch on the dinner, and the wines. I also mentioned that I was impressed that he served a 1983 Margaux in lieu of a 1982, since virtually everyone assumes that 1982, which was a great year for Bordeaux, was superior to 1983's – which it was except for the wines from Margaux. (I happen to know this only because a friend of mine, the late Alexis Lichine, owned a chateau in Margaux where he made Chateau Prieure-Lichine wines, and he told me, when I visited him in 1987, that the 1983 vintage was his best in 10 years.)

Bill said, "Jay, if you are that interested in wine, I must show you my wine cellar."

While walking to his cave, the chef came out of the kitchen. Bill introduced him to me, and I told him that the meal he had prepared for us was the best meal I have had since I last ate at the restaurant Le Taillevent in Paris. (Le Taillevent was then a Michelin three-star restaurant.) He asked me when that was. I replied, "About three years ago." He smiled and said, "*Quelle coincidence*! I was then the sous chef at Le Taillevent!"

While we continued on to the cave, Bill asked me if I'd noticed the label on the white wine. I replied that I had not. He took me to the section of the wine cellar where he kept his white wines, and pulled out a bottle of Le Montrachet. It had the word "Matador" stamped on its label. I asked, "What does the word Matador signify?" He responded, "That was the name of my boat when I won the Americas Cup in 1992!" He gave me a bottle as a souvenir. We then came to his large collection of Chateau Petrus, an extremely expensive wine from Bordeaux. Bill said, " You must admit that the 1982 Petrus is better than the 1983." I replied, "This is the closest I have ever been to a 1982 Petrus." He took a bottle from the shelf vintage, and said, "Please take this bottle as a little house present." I

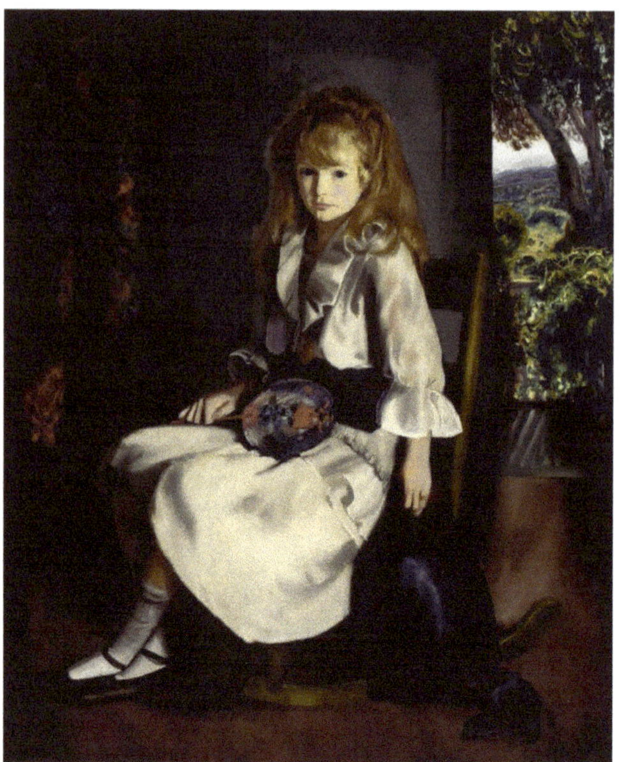

Illustration 7: George W. Bellows, *Anne in White*, 1920. Oil on canvas, 60 × 50 1/2 × 4 inches. Carnegie Museum of Art, Patrons Art Fund, 25.7.

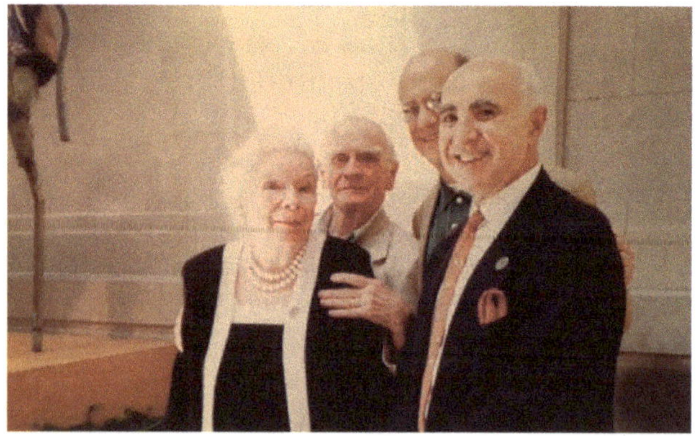

Illustration 8: Anne, her family, and me, 1997.

replied, "That is way too much! I cannot accept such an extravagant gift." I then paused while a new idea began to materialize. I said, "On second thought, I will accept your generous gift if, on your next trip to Washington, D.C., you pay me a visit, and we open my last bottle of 1961 Chateau Latour." (1961 was an extraordinary vintage and Chateau Latour is a top Bordeaux wine.) He replied, "It's a deal." Bill Koch has not to date come to my house to share my rare 1961.

Another memory from the Norton show was when I found myself standing next to another lender, Ben Ali Haggin, whom I had previously met in New York. We were standing in front of his painting which was also painted by Bellows during the Zion period. I said to him, "Ben, I guess that we are now both Zionists." He smiled and replied, "That's fine, Jay, but do not tell that to my Imam!"

The show traveled from Palm Beach to the Newark Museum, and then to the Columbus Museum of Art. We also went to both of the openings, and to the receptions hosted by the museum directors. Since Bellows was born in Columbus, the Museum had many paintings by the artist, in addition to those in the show.

At the reception in Columbus, Ann whispered to me, motioning towards an elderly woman, "I think she is Bellows' daughter, Anne." I confessed that, although I had seen several Bellows' paintings of his daughter Anne as a child, I could not tell if this woman was his daughter. We went over to introduce ourselves, and she responded, "My name is Anne Bellows." We spent the rest of the evening chatting with her about her father, and she told us a cute story from her youth. One evening, they were having the American artist John Sloan over for dinner. That morning, Bellows had sold a painting. Apparently, Sloan had not yet sold a painting. She said that several times before dinner, her father told her, "Say nothing about the sale of my painting to Mr. Sloan. Poor John, he is a great artist, but he has not yet sold a painting." I still marvel over Ann's ability to recognize Bellows' daughter from the paintings he had done of her about 70 years earlier (Illustration 7). Compare the 1920 painting of Anne with the photograph of Anne, her family, and me in 1997 (Illustration 8).

As a result of the Bellows shows, our painting was reproduced in *American Art Review*, August 1998, and in *New Jersey's Sourland Mountain* by T.J. Luce. Mr. Luce gives a description of the hardships Bellows, his roommate, Eugene O'Neill (Yes, the young writer who would become one of America's greatest playwrights) and Ed Keefe, a young painter, suffered while living in O'Neill's father's country house in Zion, New Jersey. "There was no heat, and only one broken down double bed and a sagging spring propped up on wooden boxes. They flipped coins over who would get the bed. O'Neill and Keefe won, leaving Bellows to sleep on the spring." It certainly did not adversely affect the quality of Bellows' Zion paintings, which are, in my opinion, among his best snow scenes.

According to the art curator of Lehigh University Art-Gallery: "During their short stay in Zion, Bellows became so entranced with the winter landscapes he saw that he felt compelled to paint snow scenes again and again, applying thick, juicy layers of paint directly with his palette knife and using his knife to shape and scratch back into the paint surface for its textural effect. Bellows used a bold palette of colors, laying in the jewel-like blues of the snow next to patches of rich amber tan for maximum contrast and impact."

Lehigh University owns a Bellows' Zion painting (Illustration 9). You may recognize the little house where Bellows and his friends lived, as well as the rock fence and the snow-covered road, from *Jersey Woods*. My favorite Bellows snow scene from the show was *Palisades*, also 1909. It is in the Art Institute of Chicago. Its owner was Dan Terra (Illustration 10).

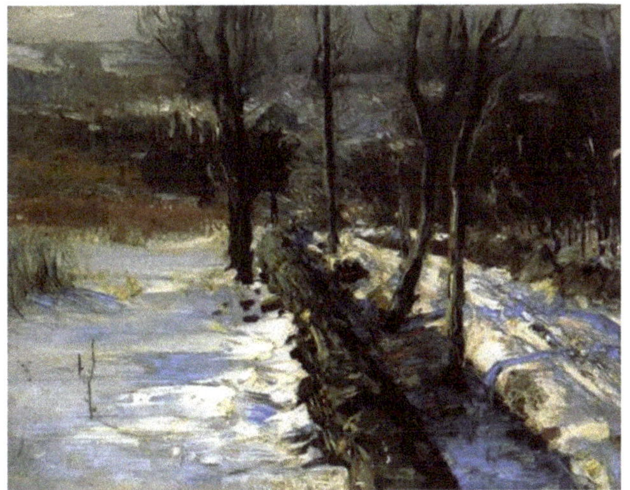

Illustration 9: George W. Bellows, *Winter in Zion*, 1909. Oil on canvas, 22 × 28 inches. Lehigh University Art Galleries, Gift of Mr. & Mrs. Ralph L. Wilson.

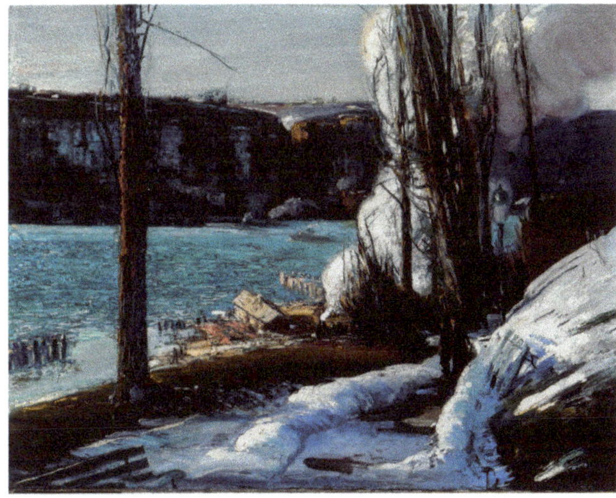

Illustration 10: George W. Bellows, *Palisades*, 1909. Oil on canvas, 30 × 38 1/8 inches. Photo courtesy of Terra Foundation for American Art. Terra Foundation for American Art, Daniel J. Terra Collection, 1999.10.

I met Dan Terra at the show, and we later became quite friendly. I once invited Dan and his wife, Judith, to our home for dinner. Dan was seated at the dinner table with a view of *Jersey Woods* in the living room. In the middle of the meal, Terra announced, "Jay and Ann, if a certain Bellows painting in your living room happens to disappear, worry not. I will take good care of it." Terra thought that his *Palisades* was likely painted in the same week as *Jersey Woods*.

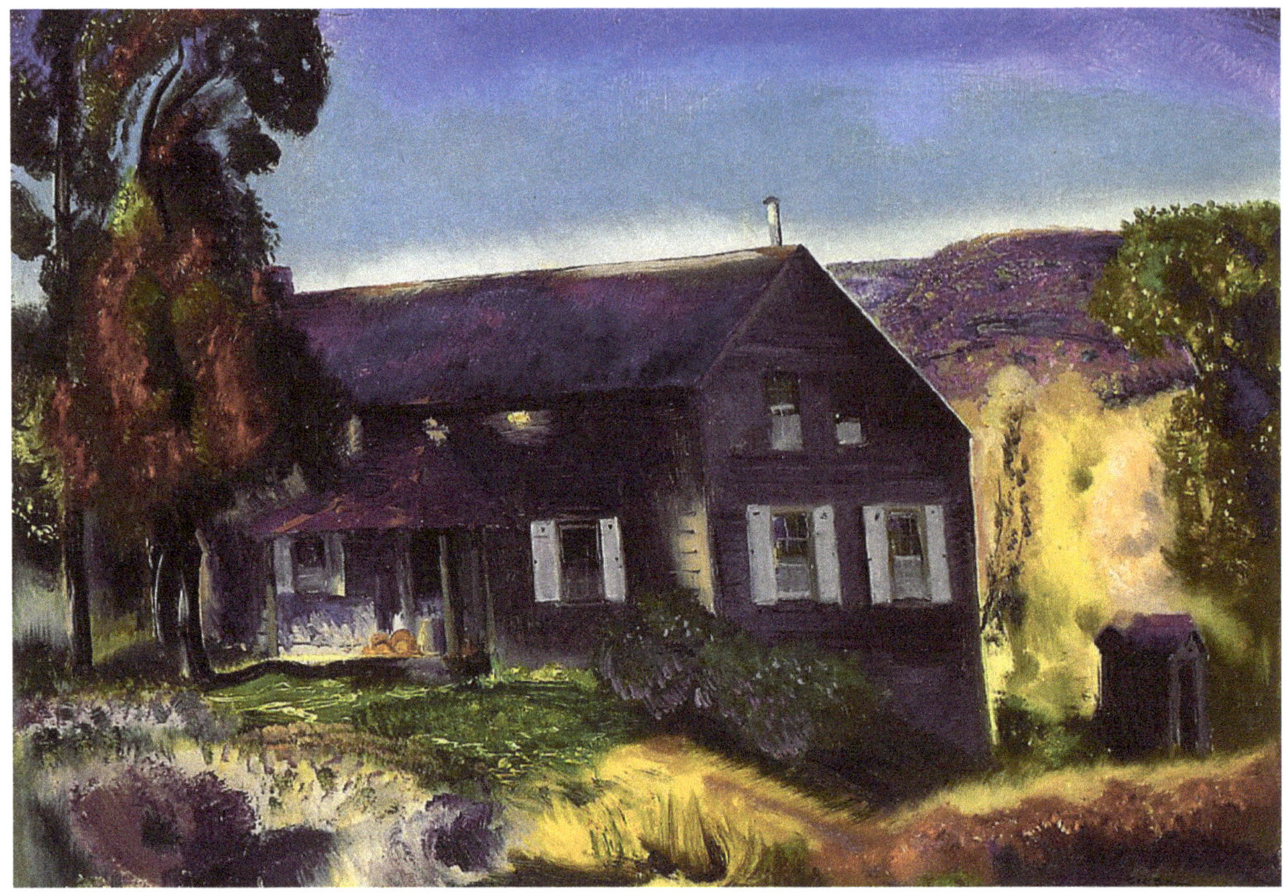

Illustration 11: George W. Bellows, *Black House*, 1924. Oil on board, 24 × 16 inches. Photo by Collisart. Julius and Ann Kaplan Collection.

There came a time when we had to sell our Bellows. As part of the purchase price, the buyer paid us a certain sum of money, plus ownership of a smaller, less important, but lovely, Bellows entitled *Black House,* circa 1924 (Illustration 11).

According to Majorie B. Searl and Ronald Netsky in *Bellows, Leaving for the Country*: "The magical light, presented in so many of Bellows' landscapes, appears here [in *Black House*]in the foliage and in the form of a bright glow on the horizon. Majestic hills in the background are back-lit with orange and yellow." Both they and I were struck by the sky, which ranges from white to light green, to grey blue, and finally to dark blue.

In addition to his paintings, I much admired Bellows' lithographs. I bought four of them to decorate my law office when I was with Cadwalader, Wickersham and Taft. My favorite of the lithographs is *Artists Judging Works of Art* (Illustration 12).

The lithograph depicts a crowd of mostly animated artists expressing their views of a painting on display. John Sloan is seen on the left with his hand in the air, apparently to express a point. Robert Henri sits on a chair in the front right, apparently in despair. Bellows stands in the back calmly overseeing the others' displays of emotion.

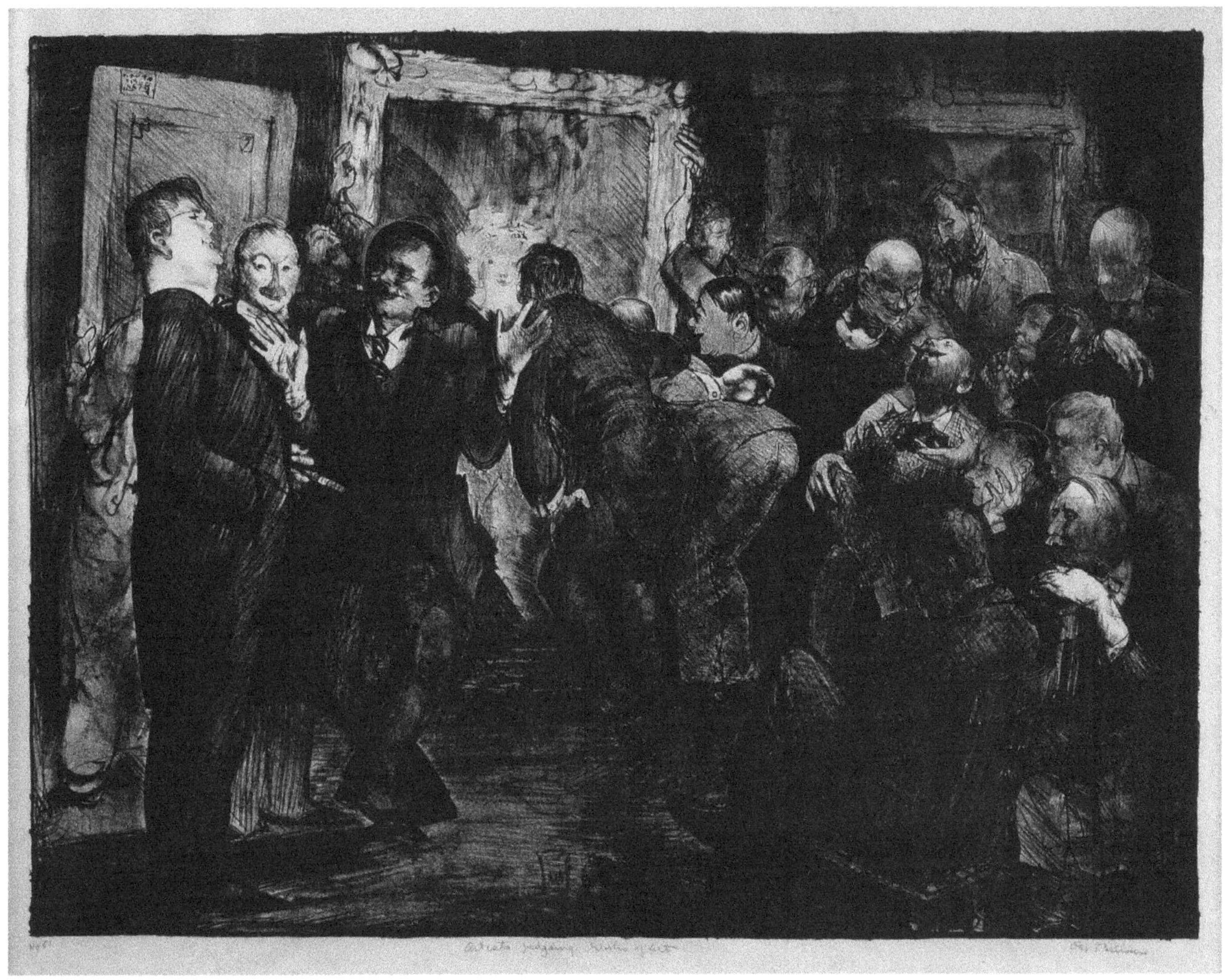

Illustration 12: George W. Bellows, *Artist Judging Works of Art*, 1916. Lithograph, 14 1/2 × 19 inches. Photo by Gregory R. Staley. Julius and Ann Kaplan Collection.

Glenn Peck of H.V. Allison Galleries, in his monograph entitled "Bellows," commented on this lithograph as follows: "The lithograph expresses the artist's skepticism of the jury system used by the major academies to select works for their exhibitions. The juries were generally composed of conservative members who hesitated to show new styles of painting and often excluded works of merit that did not correspond to the academic standards. Bellows was often chosen for such juries and attempted to assign young artists a place in the exhibitions."

Bellows died in 1925 at the tender young age of 43. In the catalogue of the major 2012 Bellows Show at the NGA, Metropolitan Museum of Art, and Royal Academy of Arts, an intriguing observation is made about his early demise, as follows: "Because Bellows was at midlife when he died, his career still full of potential, we are compelled to address a question that can never be answered: what would this immensely talented artist have accomplished had he lived another forty-two years and died in 1967...?" I am willing to speculate that, given some of his almost expressionistic skies in

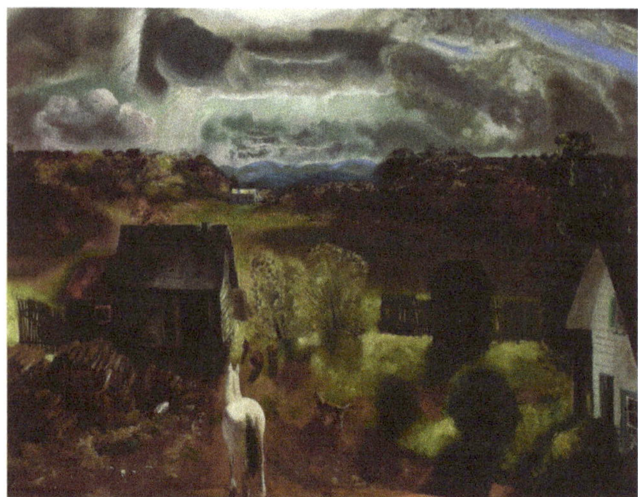

Illustration 13: George W. Bellows, *The White Horse*, 1922. Oil on canvas. Worcester Art Museum, 1929.109.

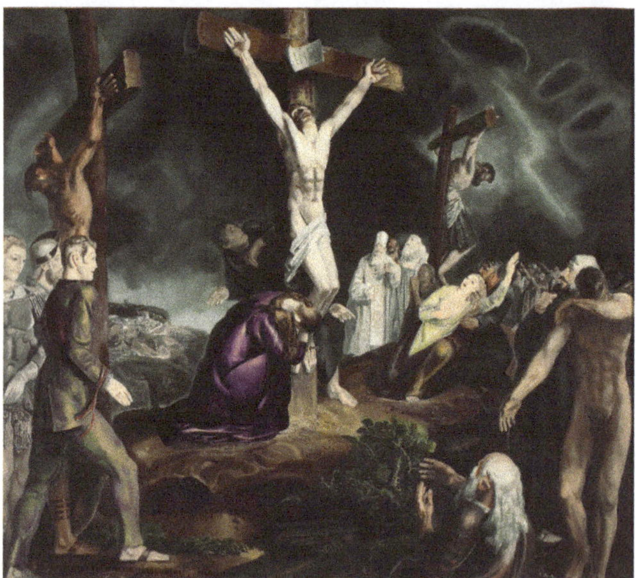

Illustration 14: George W. Bellows, *The Crucifixion*, 1923. Oil on canvas, 59.5 × 65.5 inches. Thrivent Collection of Religious Art.

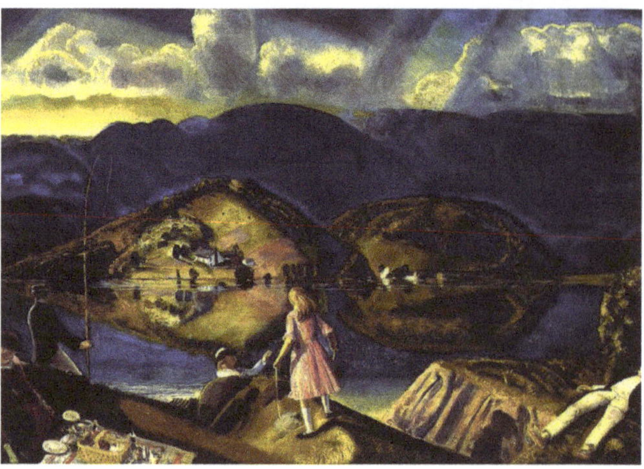

Illustration 15: George W. Bellows, *The Picnic*, 1924. Oil on canvas, 30.13 × 44.25 inches. Collection of the Maryland State Archives, MSA SC 4680-10-0003.

his late paintings such as *The White Horse* (1922), NGA (Illustration 13), *Crucifixion* (1923), Portland Museum of Art (Illustration 14) and *The Picnic* (1924) Baltimore Museum (Illustration 15), he could well have become even more expressionistic. Let us examine the sky in these three paintings. They are much more animated than in his earlier outdoor paintings, where the skies were, as a general rule, calm and benign.

It is reasonable to assume that had he lived a full life, Bellows' art, like most artists in the United States, would have been influenced by the Great Depression. American artists either continued painting as they had in the 1920's or they were influenced by social realism and regional movements. But this changed dramatically in the 1940's, 1950's, and 1960's when American art took its primacy, and artists who painted realistically in the 1920's and in the 1930's, felt free to turn to expressionism, and even abstract expressionism.

Given this post 1940's *zeitgeist*, I take the position that Bellows' dramatic, almost expressionistic skies as exemplified in the identified paintings of 1922-24, were a precursor to his future paintings. I argue that a self-confident, mature, and successful Bellows in the 40's on would have had the sense of freedom of expression to explore doing, not just the sky, but the entire canvas in an expressionistic manner.

Of course, you may disagree!

Paintings by Bellows are in many important museums of art, including the NGA, the Art Institute of Chicago, the Brooklyn Museum, the Cleveland Museum of Art, the Metropolitan Museum of Art, the Museum of Fine Arts, Boston, the Pennsylvania Academy of Fine Arts, Philadelphia, the Smithsonian American Art Museum, the Whitney Museum of American Art, Yale University Art Gallery, the Columbus Museum, Ohio, and other American Museums

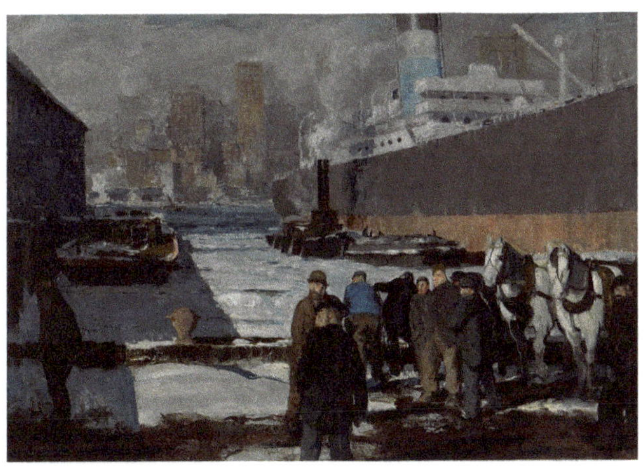

Illustration 16: George W. Bellows, *Men of the Docks*, 1912. Oil on canvas. Dimensions 45 × 63.5 inches. National Gallery of Art. Bought with a grant from the American Friends of the National Gallery, made possible by Sir Paul Getty's fund, and by a donation from Mark Getty KBE, 2014.

There is also a major Bellows painting in the National Gallery, London. It is Bellows' *Men of the Docks* (1912) (Illustration 16). The museum paid $25,500,000 for it. It was sold by Randolph College in Virginia, after years of litigation seeking to prevent the college from selling it. The students and American museum leaders protested the sale, condemning the practice of a university deaccessioning artwork to raise funds for other operations.

I took a keen interest in the sale of the painting, since Randolph College was my wife's college (though it was an all-girls college named Randolph Macon Women's College when Ann was there) and we now go almost yearly to London, and often stay at the Athenaeum Club on Pall Mall, which is very close to the National Gallery. I always drop by to say "Hello" to *Men of the Docks*.

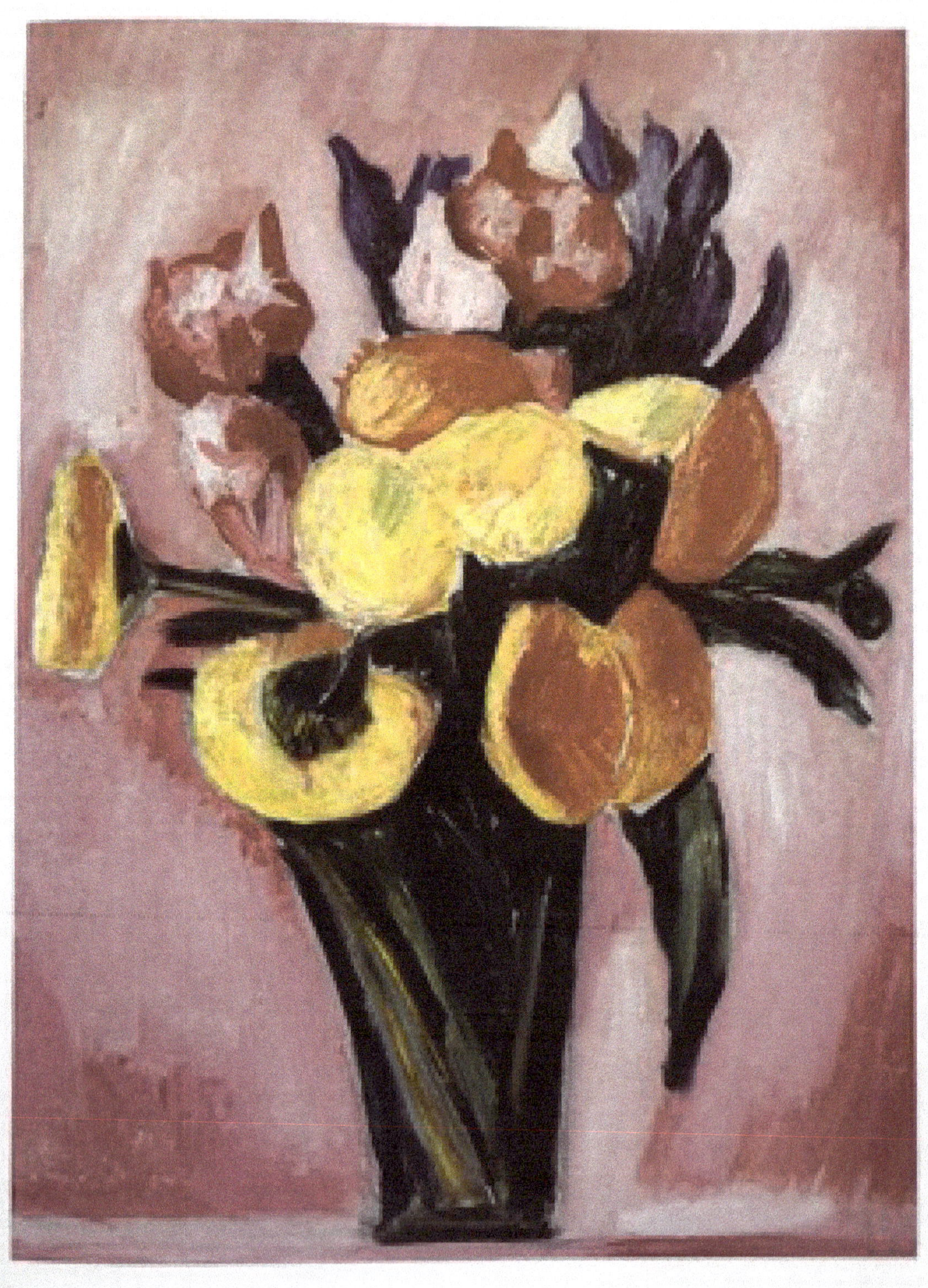

Illustration 17: Marsden Hartley, *Flower Still Life*, 1932. Photo by Collisart. Julius and Ann Kaplan Collection.

1.3 | MARSDEN HARTLEY (1878-1930)

In 1988, Ann and I went to New York in search of an American painting that would hold its own hanging close to *Jersey Woods*. After looking in numerous galleries, we saw a beautiful, and very strong, still life by the American modernist Marsden Hartley, entitled *Flower Still Life* (1932) (Illustration 17). Unfortunately it was priced well beyond our means.

At the time, I subscribed to the auction catalogues on American art at Sotheby's and Christie's. About two months after our New York trip, I was perusing the Sotheby's catalogue, when I spotted what appeared to be the very same Hartley we had seen in the gallery, but at a much lower price estimate, and happily at a price we could afford.

I called the gallery and inquired whether the painting in the catalogue was the same one we had seen. I received an affirmative response. I asked, "But why are the estimated prices in the catalogue so much lower than the price you were charging?" They responded, "Upon examination, there were too many restorations for us to continue to offer the painting."

I decided there and then to ask my friend and gallery owner, Sam Rosenfeld, to examine the painting. He did so, and concluded that the painting was in excellent condition. The Sotheby's sale was just before Christmas. I went to New York to bid on the painting, and was able to buy it at its lowest estimated price, which was less than 50% of the price being asked by the gallery. I did not tell Ann about the purchase, or even that I was going to bid. Indeed, I hid the painting until Christmas Eve. Then, after Ann fell asleep, I snuck downstairs and hung the painting with a Christmas ribbon on it as a holiday greeting to Ann.

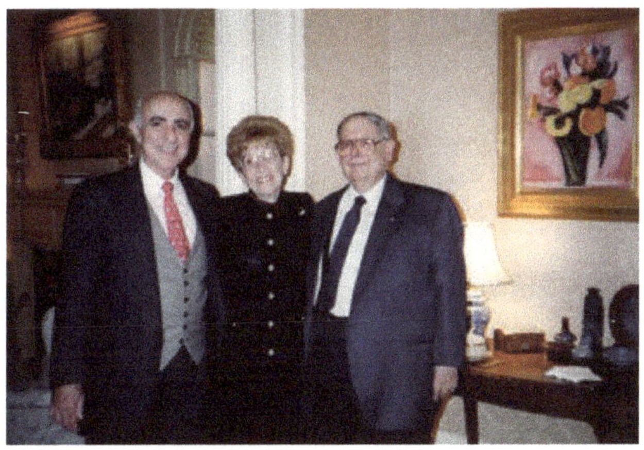

Illustration 18: The author, Jean and Manny Sulkes, with a view of Hartley, *Flower Still Life* (right), and Bellows, *Jersey Woods* (over the mantle)

Shortly afterwards we had a visit from my sister Jean, and her husband, Manny. A picture was taken of us standing in the landing where we ultimately hung the Hartley. You can see it hanging behind my brother-in-law, to his left. You can also get a glimpse of our Bellows behind me, hanging over the mantle in the living room (Illustration 18).

The Hartley was exhibited in the Worcester Art Museum in 1909 and in Boston's Museum of Fine Arts in September in 1966.

In a review of a major Hartley show at the Wadsworth Atheneum in 2003, Roberta Smith, art columnist of the *New York Times* wrote, "Marsden Hartley is one of the great artists and certainly one of the most intriguing art historical subjects of all times...He was something like a cross between Van Gogh and Oscar Wilde: his paintings, his personality and his life are all immensely embraceable, capable of captivating large and specialized audiences alike."

Allow me to provide a quote on Hartley's personality. In the introduction to *Marsden Hartley* by Gail R. Scoff, the author writes: "One afternoon in the 1920's critic Herbert Seligmann was viewing the pictures at Alfred Stieglitz's intimate gallery, 'A tall figure entered,' he later recounted, 'culminating in a lean, aquiline, bare, almost Roman head, the face deeply furrowed and vertically lined, a man of luxury, it seemed, for he wore a fur collared overcoat and carried a gold-headed cane.' The Ambassador of Poland, perhaps, I thought to myself. It was in fact, Marsden Hartley—elegant even though he might be starving."

Hartley was born in Maine in 1877, just four years before Bellows. He got his art education at the Cleveland School of Art, then moved to New York in 1892 to study painting at the New York School of Art under William Merritt Chase, an important American impressionist. (Chase and Henri were then the two instructors at the school.) He next attended the National Academy of Design. In 1922, Hartley moved to an abandoned farm in his home state of Maine. There, he produced his first serious works, which came to the attention of Alfred Stieglitz, the art dealer who was also a famous photographer (and the husband of Georgia O'Keefe). Stieglitz had a gallery, called 291, in New York and provided Hartley with his first solo exhibition in 1909. Stieglitz became a dear friend, and supporter of Hartley. When Hartley went to Europe, Stiglitz introduced him to a number of European modernists, including Cezanne, Picasso and Matisse. Each had a meaningful impact on the young Hartley.

In Europe, Hartley gravitated towards Germany, where he stayed from 1913 to 1915. My favorite paintings of his are the ones he made in Berlin, which was then a significant art city. Hartley there befriended Wassily Kandinsky and Franz Mark. Franz Mark introduced him to German expressionism which Hartley incorporated in his *oeuvre*. His best Berlin paintings, in my view, were those inspired by German military pageantry. In Berlin, Hartley befriended a Prussian lieutenant, Karl von Freyburg, who was killed in the Great War, and this had a strong impact on the artist. Freyburg and Harley apparently maintained a homosexual relationship. References to Freyburg were a recurring motif in Hartey's Berlin oeuvre. This can readily be seen in *Portrait of a German Officer* (1913) (Illustration 19) and *Painting No. 47* (1914-15), which is in the collection of the Hirshhorn Museum and Sculpture Garden, Smithsonian Institution, Washington, D.C. (Illustration 20). Note in the paintings that there is a box in yellow ochre with the initials "K.y.F." The initials obviously stand for Karl von Freyburg. You will also see the number 24 in both paintings. That number symbolizes the age of Freyburg when he died.

One of the reasons I like this latter painting so much is that I knew Joe Hirshhorn, the initial benefactor of the Hirshhorn Museum, and owner of the painting. He and his second wife, Olga, lived but a block from us in Washington, D.C. I once saw the painting in their home before it was removed to the museum, and I became attracted to it. I met Mr. Hirshhorn through his son, Gordon, who was a classmate of mine at Wesleyan University.

Allow me to regale you with a story related to Gordon and me. When I arrived at Wesleyan in 1952, I was assigned to a single room, which made me rather lonely and unhappy, this being the first time I was ever away from home. Shortly after I moved into my room, there was a knock at my door. It was Gordon. I had no idea that he was the son of a billionaire. He said that he and I were the only two

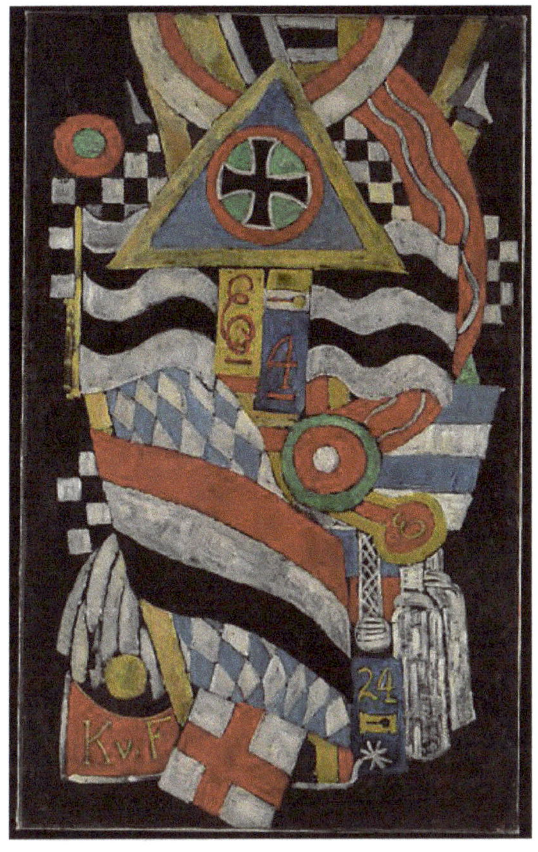

Illustration 19: Marsden Hartley, *Portrait of a German Officer*, 1914. Oil on canvas, 68 1/4 × 41 3/8 inches. Metropolitan Museum of Art, Alfred Stieglitz Collection, 1949, 49.70.42.

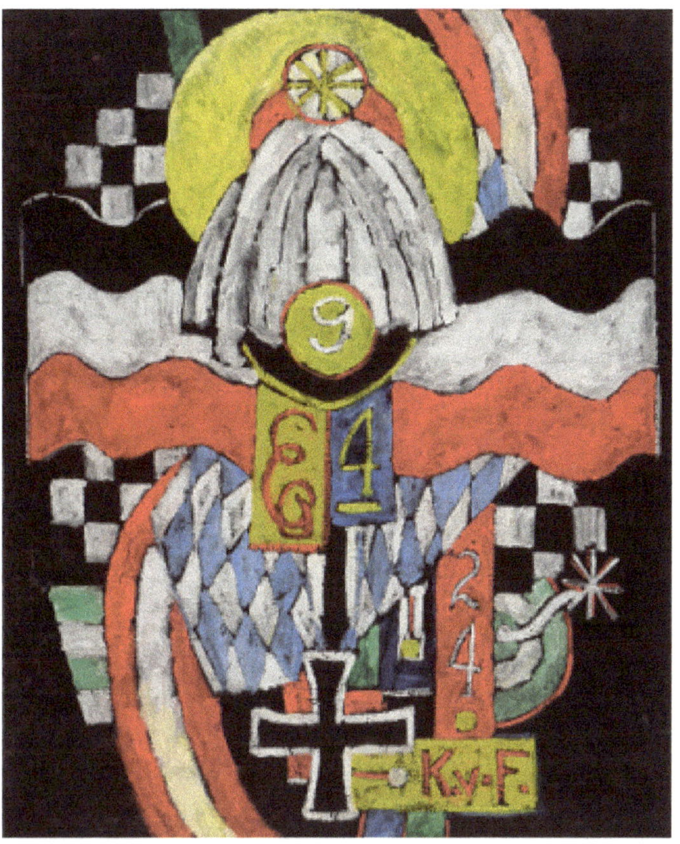

Illustration 20: Marsden Hartley, *Painting No. 47*, 1914-1915. Oil on canvas. 39 1/2 × 31 5/8 inches; framed: 47 × 38 7/8 × 2 9/16 inches. Hirshhorn Museum and Sculpture Garden Collection, Smithsonian Institution, Washington, DC, Gift of Joseph H. Hirshhorn, 1972. 72.148.

students assigned single rooms, so we are, in a way, "roommates." He suggested that we go to a local drug store and have a hamburger, and get to know each other.

After consuming our hamburgers, Gordon futilely searched his pockets for money, but had to confess that he left his money in his room. I paid for the hamburgers. A few weeks later he urged me to join him for another trip to the drug store since he said that there was a story about his father in *Fortune* magazine and he wanted to buy a copy of the magazine. I was floored when I saw in the article that his father, Joseph Hirshhorn, had earned hundreds of millions of dollars in Canadian uranium mines, and he had a son who was a student at Wesleyan University! At this point, Gordon recalled that the last time we were in the drug store, I had paid for his hamburger. He went for his wallet. I stopped him, saying I liked the idea of a Hirshhorn owing me money.

Thirty years later my secretary came into my office with a large silver tray with a silver cover over it, which she placed on my desk. I took the cover off and found a hamburger and a note that read, "I guess that we are even now! Please give me a call. Gordy"

When I called him, he told me that his father needed some help in D.C. regarding the naming of his proposed museum. "Apparently, a lot of Congressmen do not like the idea of a major building on the Mall with a conspicuously Jewish name attached to it." I turned to a friend who was a big-time lobbyist, and he helped take care of the problem

Back to Hartley. In early 1916, Marsden Hartley returned from Europe. He went directly to Maine. But after only a short period of time there, he decided to go to New Mexico, as did many other American artists of the period. He spent about five years in Taos. Notwithstanding the death of his lover, he was drawn back to Europe and stayed there from 1921 to 1930, where he painted still life's that were clearly inspired by George Braque and Juan Gris. He then painted landscapes similar to those he saw in New Mexico. He wrote frequently to his friend and mentor, Stieglitz, about these Taos-inspired works. After this stay in Europe, he was ready to return definitively to Maine, which he did, and where he painted some of his best and strongest works. It was while he was in Maine that he painted our *Still Life with Flowers*, along with many others: strong rocky landscapres, seascapes, country people, and other floral scenes. Many writers suggest that many of his Maine paintings were decidedly homo erotic.

Paintings by Marsden Hartley are in the permanent collections of many museums, including the Art Institute of Chicago, the Cleveland Museum of Art, Detroit Institute of Arts, Los Angeles County Museum of Arts, Metropolitan Museum of Art, Whitney Museum of American Art, Philadelphia Museum of Art, The Hirshhorn Museum and Sculpture Garden, The Smithsonian Museum of American Art, the National Gallery of Art, et al.

1.4 | GUY PENE DU BOIS (1884-1958)

After acquiring the Marsden Hartley, we had two strong American paintings in our living room, but we needed a third to complement the first two. We visited the galleries of New York and ended up once again at Hirschl & Adler. The first painting they showed us was Guy du Pene du Bois' *Yvonne in Landscape*, (1932). Yvonne was the artist's daughter. We both admired it very much. They showed us countless other paintings but we decided to buy the Pene du Bois (Illustration 21). I was drawn to it in part because Pene du Bois was a student of Robert Henri.

Pene du Bois was born in the U.S. to French parents. In 1899 he began his artistic training at the New York School of Art, where he studied under William Merritt Chase, as did Hartley. His early work generally depicted the culture and society around him: cafés, theaters, and in the twenties, flappers. However, when Henri became a teacher at the school in 1903, he began to paint the real world as it was in all of his harshness, reflecting Henri's instructions to his students to venture out of the studio, and into the city, to paint life as it was.

Pene du Bois was a writer as well as a painter. In 1906, he worked as an illustrator and cartoonist for the *New York American*. In 1908, he began writing art criticism, and he later became the editor of *Arts and Decoration*. He also became a journalist and wrote for the *New York Post*. In 1940 he wrote an autobiography entitled *Artist Say the Silliest Things*. In short, he loved writing almost as much as he loved painting.

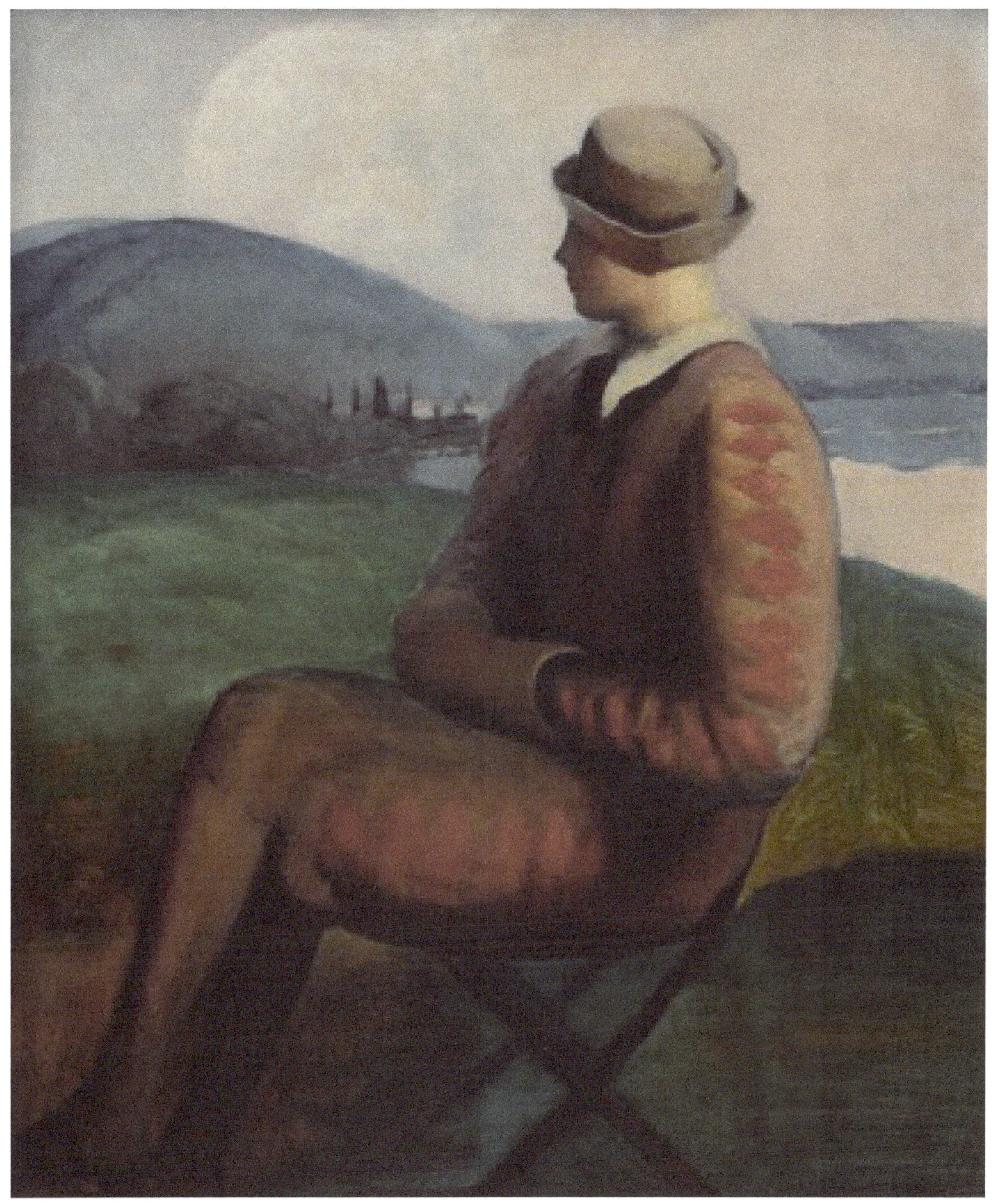

Illustration 21: Guy Pène du Bois, *Yvonne in a Landscape*, 1926. Oil on board, 21 1/4 × 17 1/4 inches. Photo by Collisart.

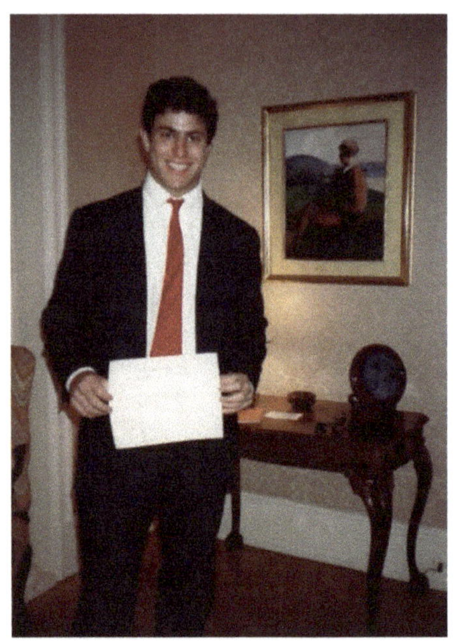

Illustration 22: Our son Lael standing in front of Dubois' *Yvonne in Landscape* with his chess certificate.

I was particularly interested in Pene du Bois, not only for his fine painting, but also because of his critical role in the short, but historically significant, *Armory Show* of 1913, which introduced many important avant guard European artists to the U.S. Penn du Bois not only contributed paintings to the show, he also handled the exhibition's publicity, publishing a special edition of *Arts and Decoration* that highlighted the show. The *Armory Show* was held from 17 February to March 15, 1913 in the 69th Street Armory in New York City.

It was originally planned to feature American artists alone, but with the election of Arthur B. Davies, a member of Henri's Ash Can School, the whole show changed. Davies invited many European artists to lend paintings to the show. This was the first major showing in America of European "Modernism." The exhibition had paintings by European Impressionists, Symbolists, Postimpressionists, Fauves, and Cubists. The contemporary American art scene was shaken to its core. It never recovered.

Guy Pene du Bois' work is in the permanent collections of numerous museums, including the Smithsonian American Art Museum, the NGA, the Phillips Collection, the Brooklyn Museum, the Whitney Museum of American Art, the Pennsylvania Academy of Fine Arts, et al.

1.5 | HENRI LE SIDANER (1862-1939)

With the Bellows over our mantle, flanked by the Hartley and the Pene du Bois, we realized that the wall opposite the Bellows, where we kept our sofa, was disturbingly weak. Once again we returned to Hirshl & Adler where we were shown two excellent candidates for the space. One was by another Henri student, George Glackens, and the other was a large, almost pointillist-painting by a French artist, Henri Le Sidaner. It was entitled, and depicted, the *L'ile des Pecheurs* (Fishermen's Island) in Lake Maggiore, Italy.

L'ile des Pecheurs was indeed a beautiful and arresting painting by a highly skilled and esteemed painter. It depicted Fisherman's Island at dawn, as seen from another island on Lake Maggiore. On the water between the island and the viewer was a subtle flickering of light on the undulating waves from the otherwise darkened buildings on the island. We sought the advice of our friend, artist Joan Danziger, who strongly recommended that we buy it. Joan lauded, in particular, the artist's skillful use of the color aqua marine (which she said was exceedingly difficult to work with). We bought the large painting of *L'ile des Pecheurs*. It is, in my judgment, a truly magnificent painting that draws the viewer in, and around, the depicted island (Illustration 23).

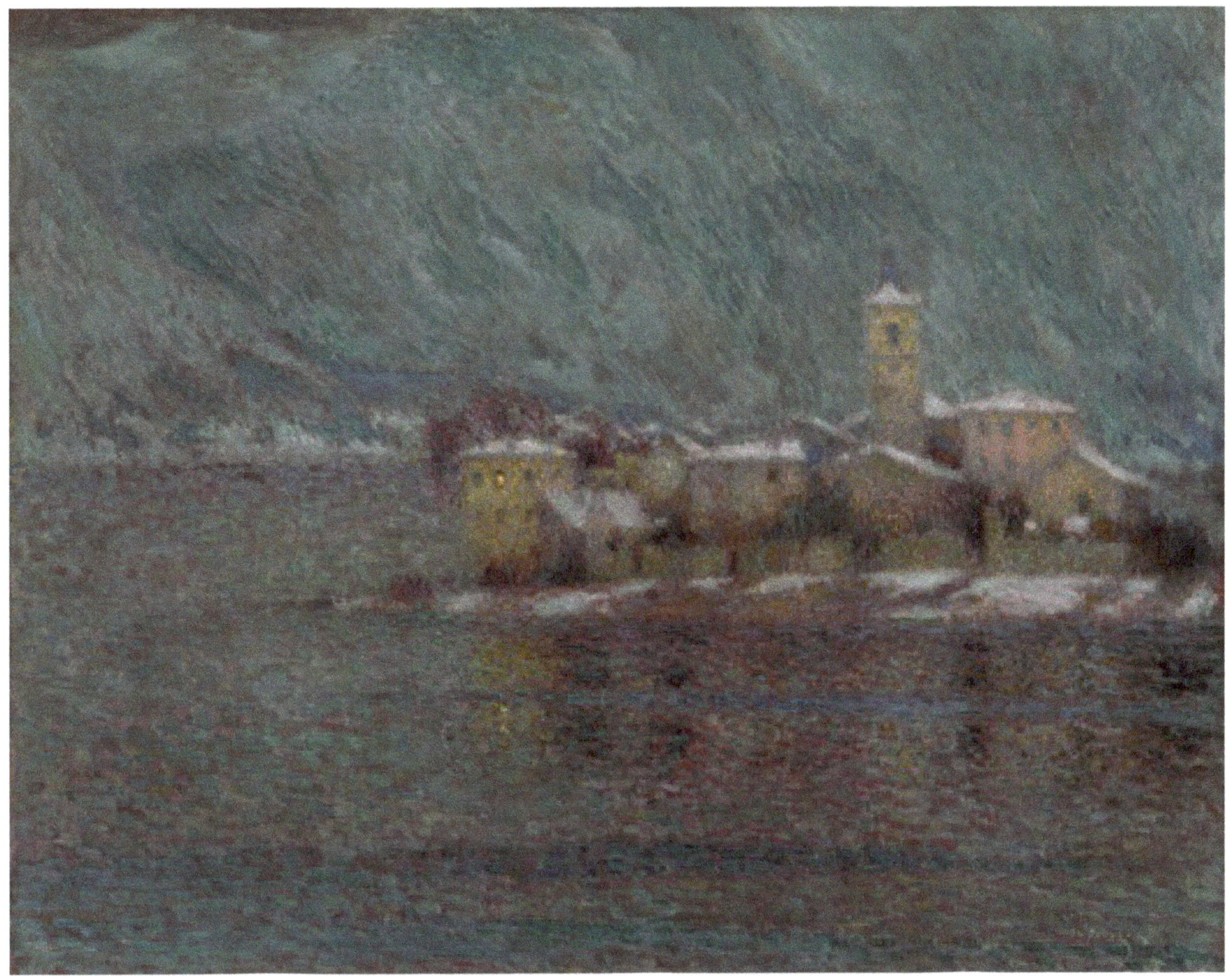

Illustration 23: Henri Le Sidaner, *L'il des Pecheurs,* 1909. Photo by Collisart. Julius and Ann Kaplan Collection.

On my next train trip through Italy, as I was making my way from Milan to Geneva, I got off the train near Lake Maggiore and hired a boat to take me around the lake. I sought to find the exact spot where the artist was situated when he painted the canvas. We found an island right across from Lake Maggiore with a view almost identical to that of the painting. I got off the boat and soon realized that Le Sidaner had to have painted it above ground level. I looked up and saw a building behind me. I went up to the second floor, with a picture of our painting in hand. I explained to the tenant that I wanted to look out of his window facing the Fishermen's Island, to see if this was where the artist painted our picture. He graciously allowed me to do so, and as I looked out of his window, I realized that I was at the exact spot where Le Sidaner had painted our painting! I must confess that was most exciting for me.

Henri Eugene Augustin Le Sidaner was born to a French family in Port Louis, Mauritius. In 1870 he and his family settled in Dunkirk. Le Sidaner received most of his training in art from l'Ecole des

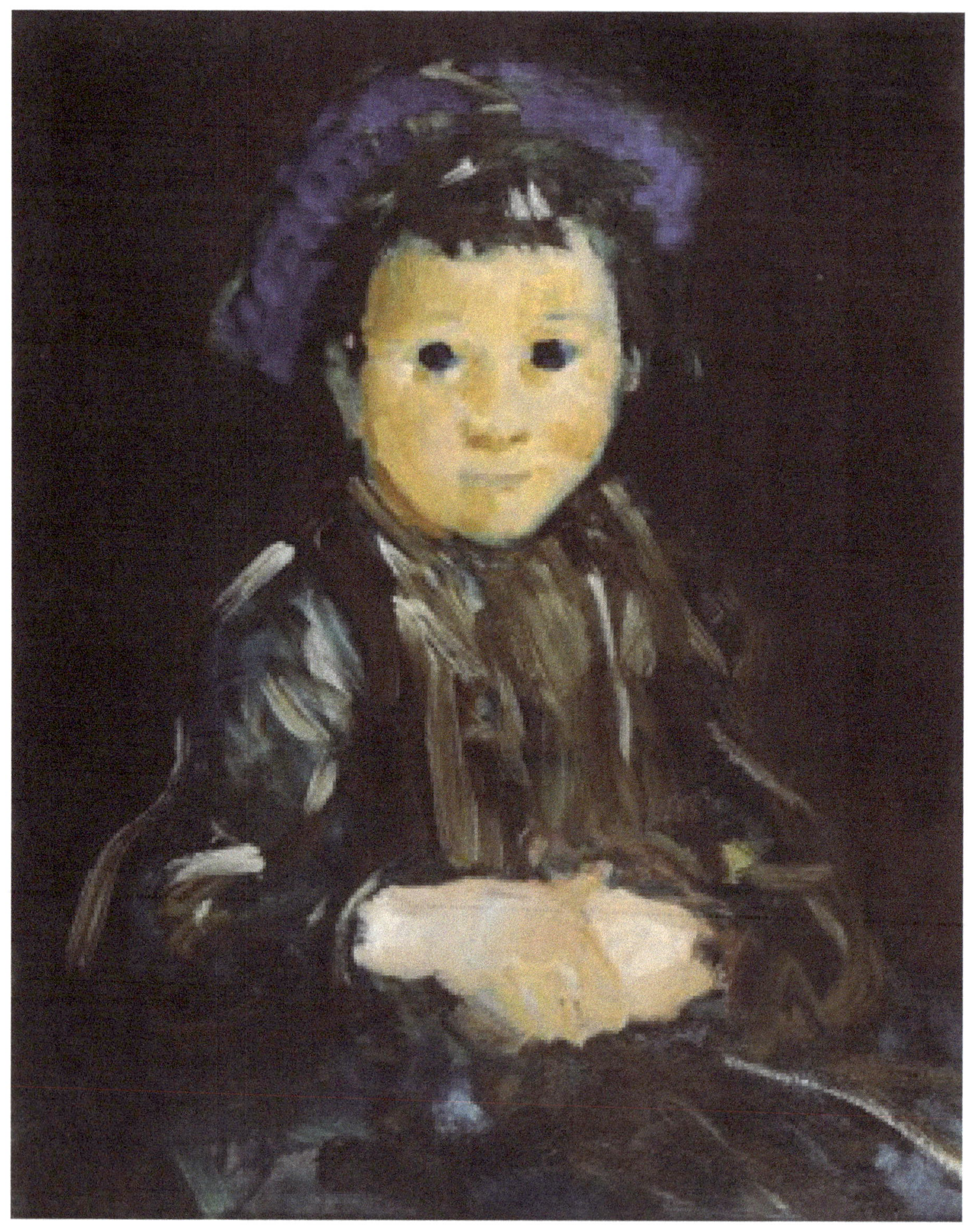

Illustration 24: George Luks, *Boy with Blue Cap*, 1924. Oil on canvas, 20 × 16 inches. Photo by Collisart. Julius and Ann Kaplan Collection.

Beaux Arts in Paris, under the tutelage of Alexander Cabanel. He later traveled extensively throughout Europe. He exhibited at the Salon, the Galeries Georges Petit in Paris and the Goupil Gallery in London, and finally settled in Gerberoy.

Le Sidaner is mentioned in Proust's *Remembrance of Things Past*, where Proust notes that "an eminent barrister from Paris had devoted his income to collecting the paintings of the 'highly distinguished' (but not great) Le Sidaner." The great author obviously could not distinguish between good and great art. The painting of Lake Maggiore is, indeed, a great painting.

Frequently after dinner, I would pour myself a small Calvados, go into the living room, turn off the lights, and merely sit across from the painting, illuminated only by its museum light. I would reflect on its depth and beauty. Sometimes hours would pass. Paradise!

1.6 | GEORGE LUKS (1867-1933)

As noted earlier, when I sold Bellows' Zion painting, I acquired from the buyer (as part of the consideration) not only money, but the Bellows *Black House*. I also acquired a somewhat smaller but delightful painting by George Luks called *Boy with Blue Cap* (Illustration 24). I hung the painting in the ante-room of my home office. I would always smile when looking at the little boy with big darkened eyes.

Luks began his working life in vaudeville. He left the theater when he decided to pursue a career in art. He studied briefly at the Pennsylvania Academy of Fine Arts before he traveled to Europe to study the great masters. He, not surprisingly, liked the work of Velasquez and Frans Hals. In 1983, he returned to Philadelphia where he eventually found work as an illustrator for the Philadelphia Press. Working at the newspaper, he met John Sloan, William Glackens, Everett Shinn, and, of course, Robert Henri. He recognized Henri as a persuasive advocate for the vigorous depiction of ordinary life.

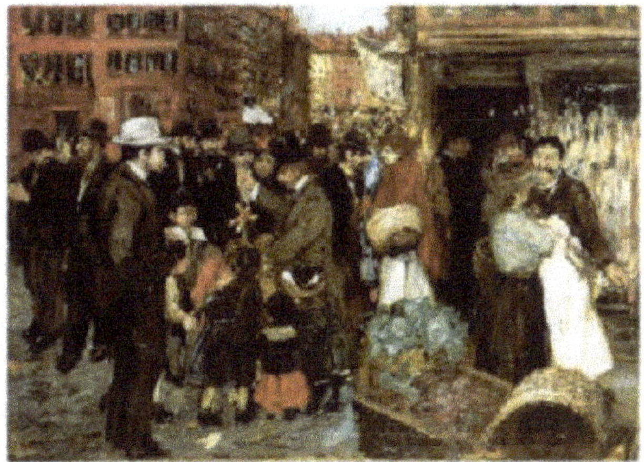

Illustration 25: George Luks, *Street Scene (Hester Street)*, 1905. Oil on canvas, 25 13/16 x 35 7/8 inches. Brooklyn Museum, Dick S. Ramsay Fund, 40.339.

In 1896, Luks moved to New York City, took up painting, and became a early member of the Henri group called the Eight, and was, of course, a full member of the Ashcan School. His paintings are now very much sought after. Luks, in keeping with the teaching of Henri, painted working class subjects and scenes of urban life. I have always appreciated his *Hester Street* (1917) in the collection of the Brooklyn Museum. It captures the life of my parents, and other immigrant relatives, struggling to make it in their newly adopted country. I was impressed by how well "Hester Street" depicts the gritty background details of a lower East Side street in 1917. Henri must have liked the painting too, since it was the very essence of an Ashcan painting (Illustration 25).

Luks is well represented in the permanent collections of numerous major museums, including the Chicago Art Institute; the Addison Gallery of American Art; the Metropolitan Museum of Art; the Brooklyn Museum; the Butler Institute of American Art; the Detroit Institute of Arts; the Phillips Collection, et al.

1.7 | EMIL NOLDE (1861-1956)

I used to go regularly to the European Fine Arts Fair ("TEFAF") in Maastricht, Netherlands. It is an incredibly large fair and attracts collectors and dealers from all over the world. During the season, hotel rooms were scarce, and, (I was told), a place to park your airplane was virtually impossible to find. On every visit, I would always gravitate to the booth of Galerie Thomas, from Munich. What particularly attracted me there was the inevitable collection of beautiful water colors by Emil Nolde, a German/Danish expressionist. He has always had a hypnotic effect on me. Whenever and wherever I spot one of his works, I am compelled to stop and examine it. To me, virtually all of his works in color are stunningly beautiful, particularly his gardens and seascapes.

Nolde was one of the early German expressionists. He was a member of Die Brucke (The Bridge), a small and short-lived group of German expressionists that was formed in 1906. Ann and I happened to be in Berlin in 2006 and were fortunate enough to see the hundredth anniversary show of the group. Die Brucke did not last long, and Nolde ended up in a group started by Franz Marke, called "Der Blaue Reiter." (The Blue Rider.)

Until the 1930's, Nolde had been held in the highest esteem in Germany, but he soon ran up against Adolf Hitler's policy to reject all forms of modernism as "degenerate" art (German: *Entartete Kunst*). This was a term adopted by the Nazi Party as work that "insulted" German feelings or that was not realistic enough to satisfy the authorities, and most contemporary art fell in that category. The Nazi regime officially condemned Nolde's work, and removed a total of 1052 of his works from museums, more than that of any other artist. It is not surprising that Nolde's *oeuvre* was included in the now famous Degenerate Art exhibition of 1937.

Nolde was prohibited from painting - even in private - after 1941. He retired to his home in Seebul, which is in a remote part of Germany, on the border of Denmark. Why Seebul? The artist was so concerned that, if he painted with oils on canvas in a large city in Germany, the smell of the oils would attract the German goons. From that time on, he worked primarily in watercolors and woodcuts, neither of which gave off any odor. He called them his "Unpainted Pictures."

After World War II, Nolde was once again honored, receiving the *Orden pour le Merite*, the highest award given by the post war German government. Today Nolde's work is exhibited in the permanent collections of many of the most prestigious museums in the world, including the Hermitage, the Museum of Modern Art, the Metropolitan Museum of New York, etc. His oil paintings bring millions of dollars at auction.

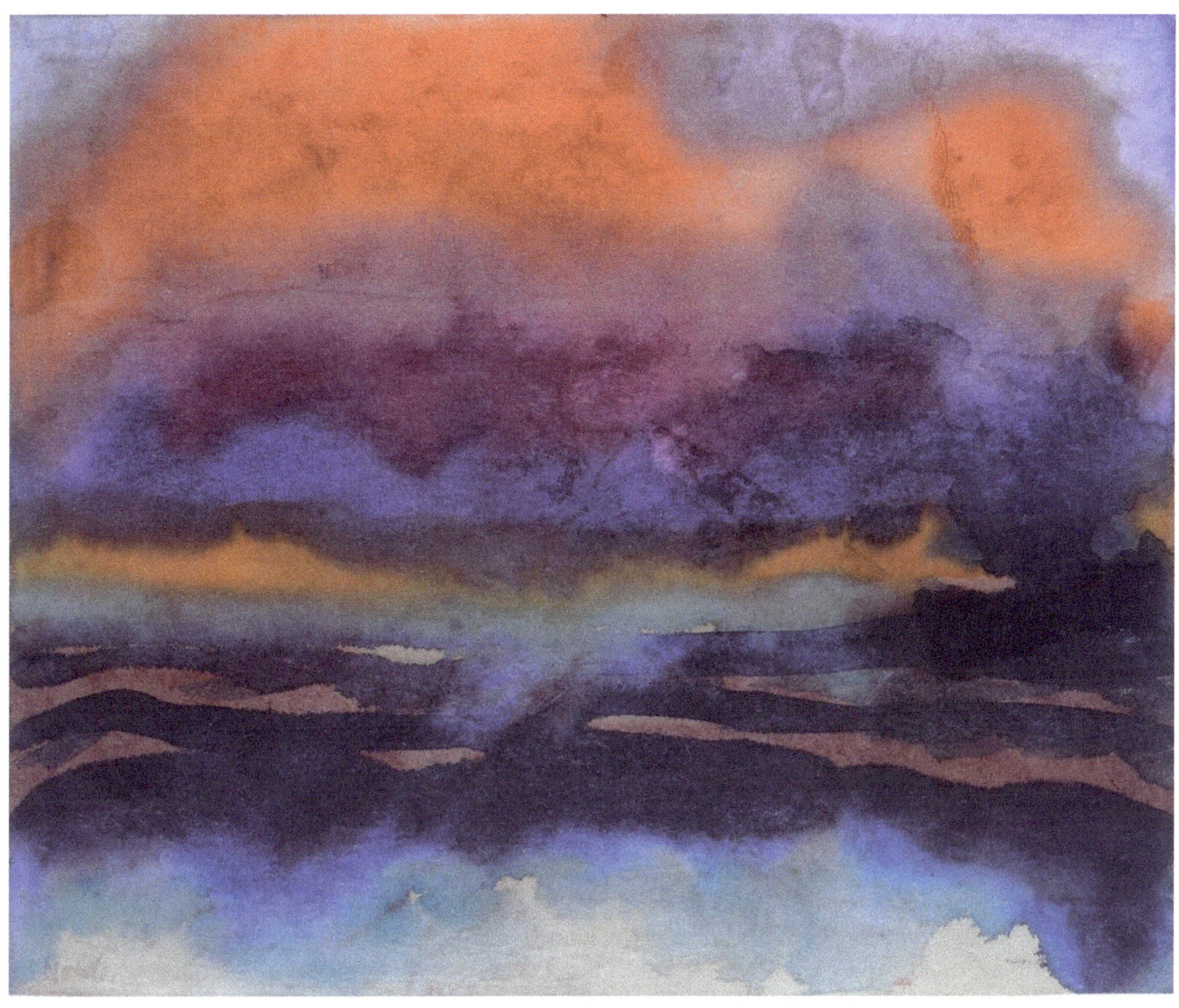

Illustration 26: Emil Nolde, *Rough Sea With Steamboat*, 1941. Photo by Gregory R. Staley. Julius and Ann Kaplan Collection.

After one of my annual trips to Maastricht for TEFAF, I decided to go to Seebull to pay my respects to the memory of this great artist, and to see the large collection of his works on display there. It was a long trip, first to Hamburg, and then another long trip from Hamburg to Seebull. When I arrived at Nolde's Seebull residence, I was struck by the colors of his gardens. They were filled with exactly the same flowers that he often painted in his beautiful floral watercolors. Inside the house there were many paintings by the artist, as well as many watercolors and other works on paper. The number of flower paintings reflects his intense interest in his garden. There were also many seascapes.

Upon arriving, I realized that there was way too much to see in one day, so I decided to spend the night in a small inn affiliated with the Nolde's home/museum, and enjoy a second day in Nolde's home/museum. At dinner time, I walked to a restaurant in a nearby village. I arrived late and was the only client. The friendly owner came over to chat with me, in German, of course. Miraculously, with my several years of German in college, and a heritage of hearing Yiddish as a youth on a daily basis at home, I was able to spend the evening "communicating" with the proprietor. I remember asking him how far we were from Denmark, and he pointed to a house about five feet from the restaurant. There were absolutely no barriers between the two countries.

After seeing the great beauty of the Nolde watercolors, particularly the sea scenes at Seebull, I decided that I must own a Nolde. Walking to the Seebull railway station, I was preoccupied with figuring out what I had to sell, or beg, or borrow, to buy a Nolde watercolor.

At the next TEFAF, I spent most of my time in Galerie Thomas and other German dealers examining all of the available Nolde. I ended up by buying a watercolor entitled *Rough Sea with Steamboat* (Illustration 26) from Galerie Thomas.

I hung the Nolde watercolor in my office where I could gaze upon it whenever I wished. But in staring at it frequently, my eyes started to focus on what I feared to be a defect in the painting; namely, some light blue/grey and dark blue water color marks, in the middle of the lower third of the painting, under the orange under belly of the clouds. It began to disturb me so I called it to the attention of two Nolde experts. The first thought that it was simply a subtle breeze blowing across the water. The second thought it was indeed a defect. I tended to agree with the second expert and decided to return the painting to Galerie Thomas, which accepted it without question, and refunded my money fully, notwithstanding the fact that Mr. Thomas personally agreed with the first expert.

I just learned that there is new, compelling evidence that Emil Nolde was a Nazi. I guess it best that I returned the painting to Mr. Green.

1.8 | JOHN GRAHAM (1881?-1961)

Ann's mother, Lavinia Wade Lanyon, was born in Baltimore, Maryland. She once had an occasion to visit the Cone Sisters of Baltimore; namely, Claribel Cone (1864-1929) and Etta Cone (1870-1949). The Cone sisters had put together one of the finest collections of modern French art in the United States during the first decades of the 20th century. This collection was eventually donated to the Baltimore Museum where it is on permanent display.

On one of my visits to the Baltimore Museum, I bought a catalogue of the collection as a gift for my mother -in-law. I gave it to her one evening when she was our guest for dinner. She immediately opened the book to a page showing Etta Cone's dining room with its walls filled with pictures by Matisse. Mrs. Lanyon pointed to the chairs around the dining table and identified those persons who, when she had been there, sat in each of them. They, of course, included Etta and Claribel, plus her friend Elinor Gibson Graham, and Elinor's husband, John Graham, an artist who my mother-in-law said she had lost track of many years past. Elinor was his third wife.

I told Mrs. Lanyon that there was a very prominent artist named John Graham, (born Ivan Gratianovich Dombrowski), who worked in Baltimore at that time, and later in New York, and who became famous as a painter, and as a mentor figure to Jackson Pollack, Willem de Kooning, and Arshile Gorky. He was also a teacher at the Arts Student League. I said to my mother-in-law "It sounds like your friend John Graham of Baltimore became the famous painter and teacher, John Graham of New York."

That evening after dinner, Ann drove her mother to her home in Alexandria, Virginia, as usual. Ann returned with a painting by John Graham of his then wife, Elinor, which Mrs. Lanyon owned for almost 60 years (Illustration 27). I surmised that she was not a fan of John Graham, who, according to her, was not particularly "refined."

When Ann and I were next in New York, we visited the Andre Emmerich Gallery, which handled the estate of Graham, to seek information about him, and if possible, about the painting we now owned. They suggested that we consult with Eleanor Green, whom lived in Washington, D.C., and who had recently written the catalogue of a show on Graham, that was scheduled to open shortly at the Phillips Collection in Washington.

We consulted at length with Eleanor who had already written the catalogue. She, however, loved our painting and wanted it added to the show. It was added, and a picture of Ann's mother standing in front of the painting was a source of sheer joy for her.

When we read Eleanor Green's catalogue, we noted that a 1919 issue of the *Baltimore Sun* had reproduced a "slightly cubist head of a woman (Elinor?) with Russian domes in the background." Ann researched the archives of the *Sun* and found a picture of "our painting." And the woman depicted was definitely Elinor Gibson Graham.

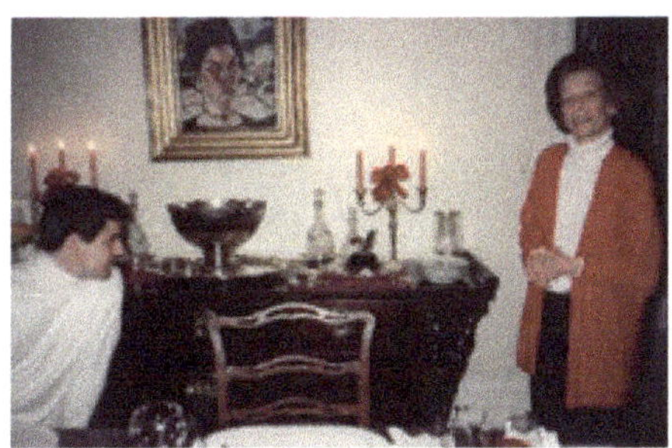

Illustration 28: Ann and Lael with Elinor Gibson Graham portrait.

After the painting was returned from the Phillips, we took it to be professionally cleaned, and then had it framed by Goldleaf Studios in Washington, D.C. They are a recognized authority of frame fabrication, conservation, and gilding. Its owner, Bill Adair, personally designed the compelling frame on the painting. It is a strong painting and with its large Gold Leaf Studios frame, it miraculously holds its own alone on a fairly large wall in our dining room, as can be seen from the photograph of the painting, with Ann standing to the right and Lael seated (Illustration 28).

A somewhat similar John Graham depiction of Elinor Gibson Graham is in the collection of the Whitney Museum, New York. Elinor gave a number of Graham's works to the Museum of Modern Art, New York.

Graham's paintings are in many other major museums, including the Smithsonian American Art Museum, the Yale University Art Gallery, the Hirshhorn Museum and Sculpture Garden, the Metropolitan Museum of Art, et al.

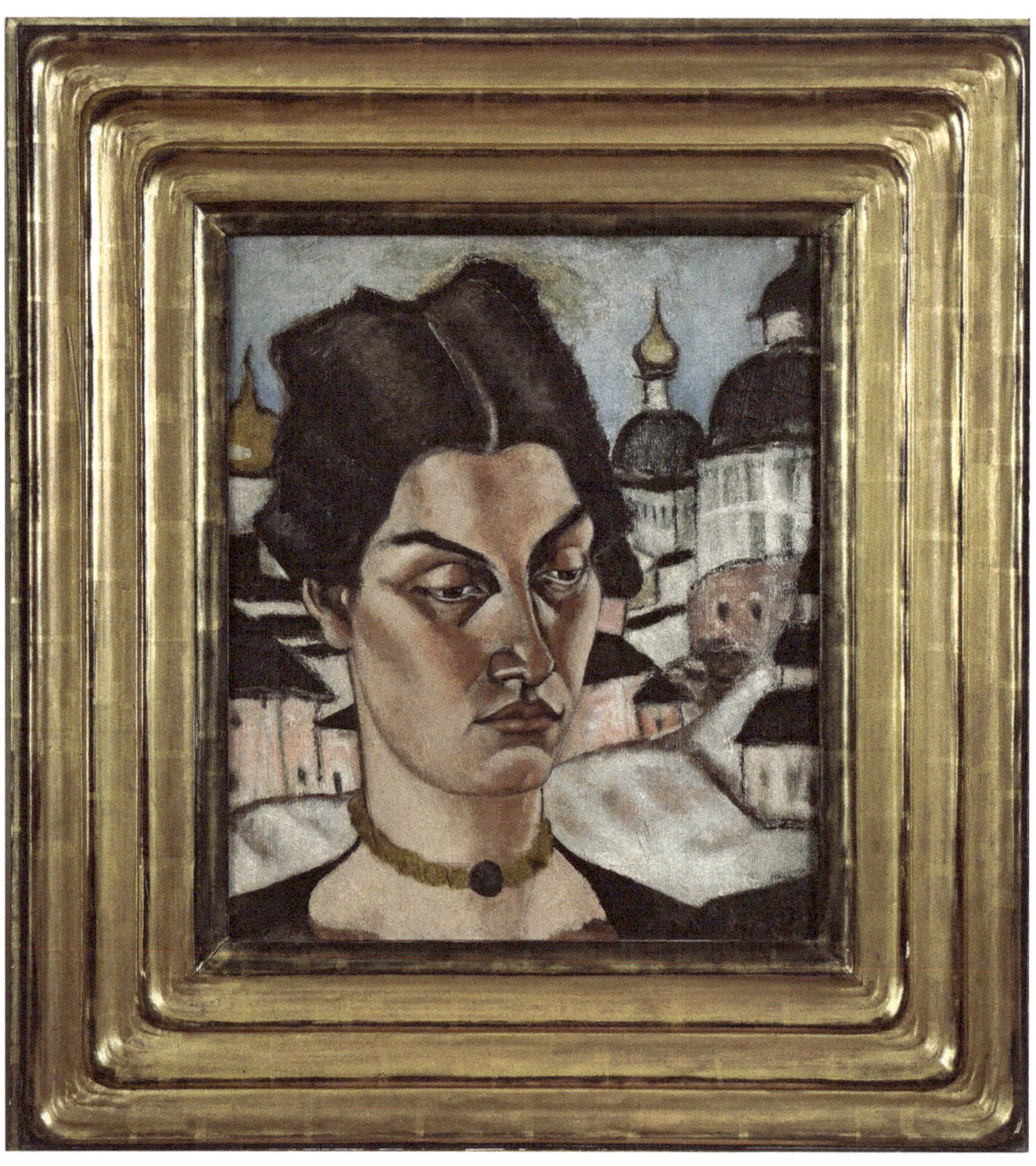

Illustration 27: John Graham, *Elinor Gibson Graham*, circa 1929. Photo by Gregory R. Staley. Julius and Ann Kaplan Collection.

1.9 | NICOLAS ALEXANDROVICH TARKOFF (1871-1930)

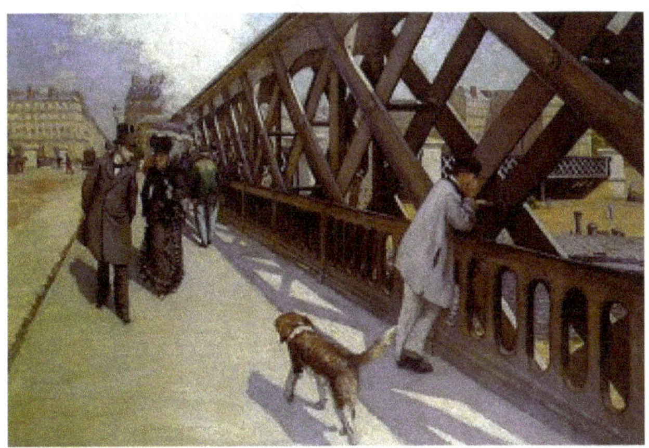

Illustration 29: Gustave Caillebotte, *Le Pont de l'Europe*, 1876. Oil on canvas, 49 × 71 inches.

I used to travel with some frequency to Geneva to see clients, one of whom was Bruce Rappaport (see Chapters 1, 9, and 18 of *Secrets and Suspense: International Law Stories*). On each trip to Geneva I would visit Le Petit Palais Museum. I did this both to view the impressive collection of paintings and to visit with its owner and manager, Baron Oscar Ghez. Oscar became a dear friend of mine. The museum's most important painting was the world renowned *Le Pont de l'Europe* by Gustave Caillebotte (Illustration 29).

Baron Ghez would frequently take me to lunch at his favorite Chinese restaurant or to dinner at his beautiful home. The home was generously decorated with some of his favorite paintings, including enormous landscapes by Henri Martin from his vast collection. And Oscar had an enormous collection. On a couple occasions, he took me to the giant vaults underground, where upwards of 20,000 of his paintings were stored. He, like Joseph Hirshhorn, when seeing a collection of paintings he admired, would buy the entire collection.

One day Oscar mentioned that he would be interested in selling some of his paintings by the Russian artist Nicolas Tarkhoff. Years before, he had found a major collection of Tarkhoff in France, and bought all 71 paintings in the collection.

I told Oscar that I had a close friendship with Fred Hill of the Berry-Hill Gallery in New York, and would be pleased to see if they would be willing to have a Tarkhoff Show. They agreed and a show was arranged which took place from December 13, 1989 to January 27, 1990. The gallery retained Eleanor Green, who did the Graham catalogue noted above, to write the essay for the Tarkhoff catalogue. Oscar was so appreciative of my having arranged an important New York show that he gave me, as a token of his appreciation, one of the best paintings in the show, *Le Défilé Militaire*, c. 1900 (Illustration 30).

There was another Tarkhoff painting in the show which I particularly admired, entitled *Boulevard en movement a la Mi-Carême*, 1901 (Illustration 31).

Le Défilé Militaire maintained a proud place in our home until early 2000 when we decided to sell it at auction. After consulting with some art experts, we estimated that the painting had a modest commercial value. Christie's auctioneers sent an expert on Russian art to our home to examine the painting, who after commenting on its beauty, said that she would estimate (conservatively) its value at almost 10 times our estimated value! Although this was far more than we anticipated, I am pleased and rather proud to say that neither Ann nor I showed any emotion whatsoever when she gave us the sales estimate. Neither of us uttered the "WOW" (or anything else) so often heard on *Antiques Roadshow*.

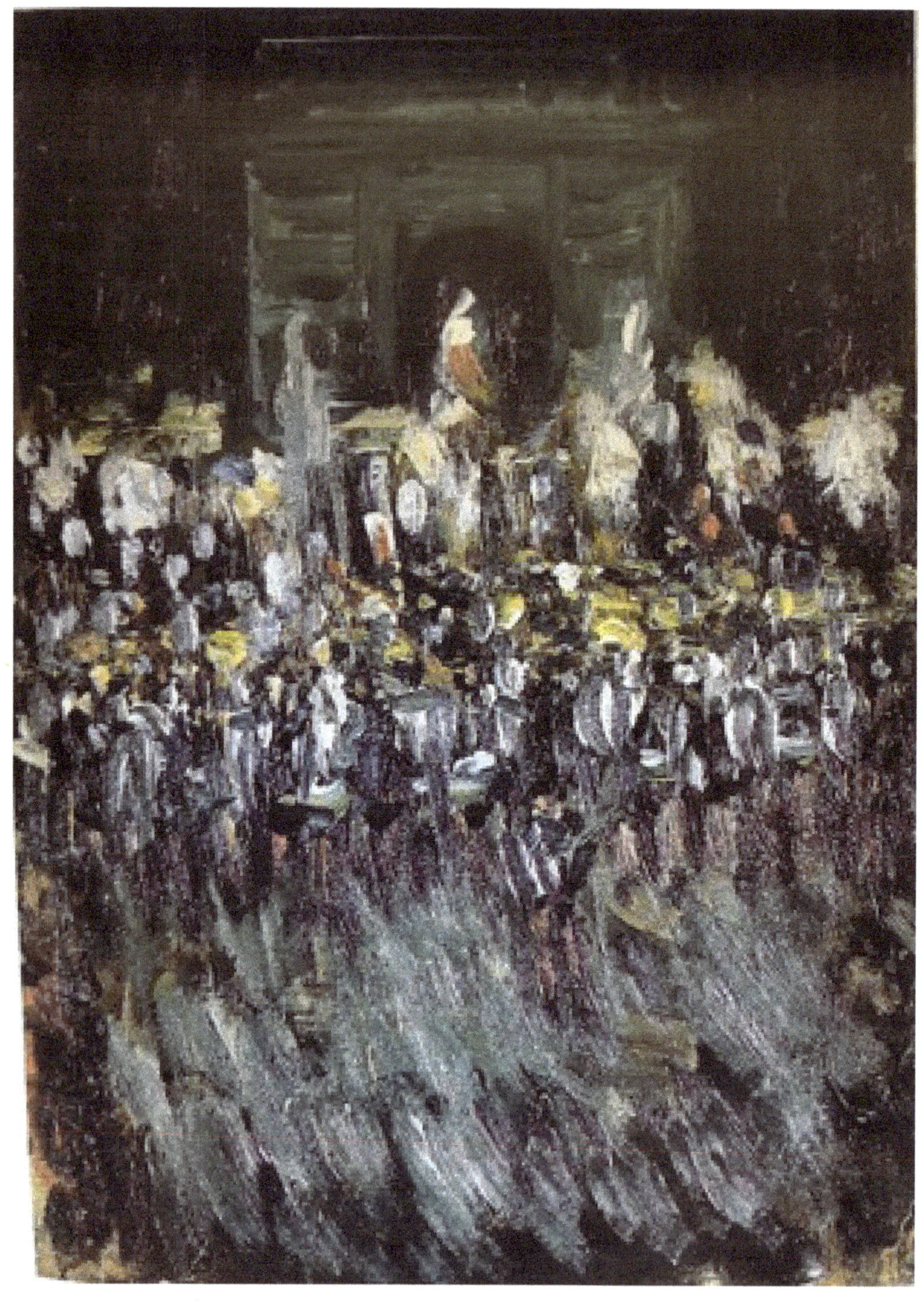

Illustration 30: Tarkhoff, *Le Défilé Militaire*, 1900, Julius and Ann Kaplan Collection (Photo by Le Petit Musée Museum)

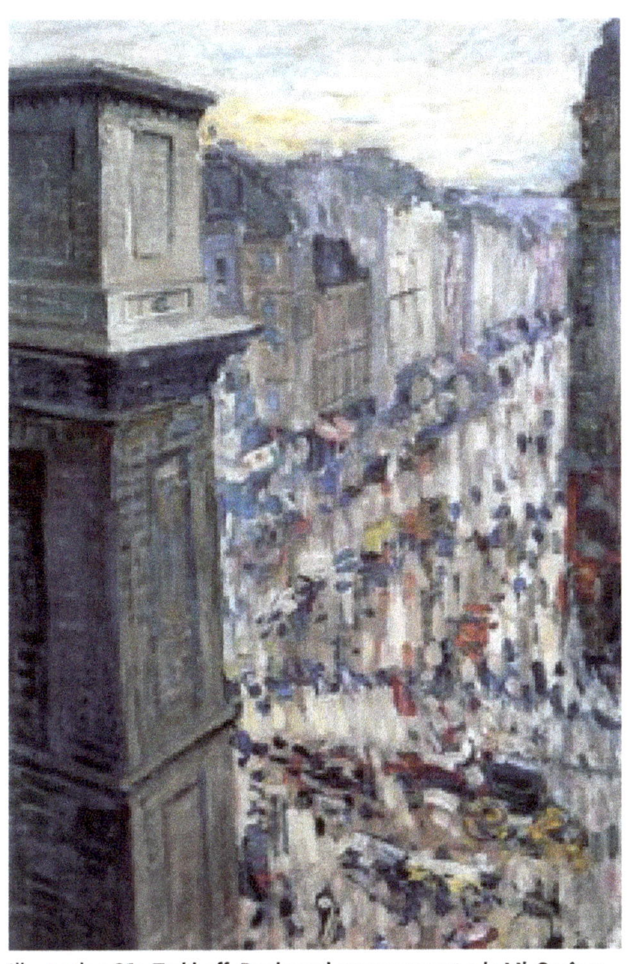

Illustration 31: Tarkhoff, *Boulevard en movement a la Mi-Carême*, 1901 (Photo by Le Petit Musée Moderne)

Somehow, a Russian oligarch client of mine (see chapter 7 of *Secrets and Suspense*) heard that I might be selling the painting, and called me to make an offer on it. His offer was very generous, indeed, and I accepted it. (I, of course, first sought and received permission to withdraw the painting from the auction house.) Some few times in the life of a collector these pleasant surprises occur.

In 1910, an important Russian art critic, Sergei Makovsky, wrote, "Tarkhoff is a great and original talent. The art world has only recently started to wake up to this appraisal of Tarkhoff." It is a great pity that when Fred Hill and I organized the Tarkoff show in New York in 1989, Americans were then unaware of Tarkoff's greatness. We did not sell a single painting!

1.10 | GRIGORY EFIMOVICH GLUCKMAN (1898-1973)

Some 20 years ago, I was in the New York art gallery of a friend, Samuel Rosenfeld, and happened to notice a painting that reminded me of the Russian paintings I had recently seen in the State Tretyakov Museum in Moscow. I asked Sam if the artist were Russian. He said that his name was Grigory Gluckman, and he was indeed Russian, born in Vitebsk, Belarus, which was then part of Russia. He was a contemporary of that town's most famous son, Marc Chagal. At age 19, Gluckman left Vitebsk to study art at the Art Academy in Moscow for several years before he fled to Berlin to escape the Russian Revolution.

He soon made his way to Paris, where he began to exhibit at several of Paris' well-known galleries: Galerie Druet, Galerie Charpentier, and Salon d'Automne. While in Paris his career soared. His paintings were praised by the critics and his sales were strong. He painted Paris street scenes and was accepted in artistic circles. Indeed, he befriended Jasha Heifitz, who became an important collector of his. During this time in Paris, he sold well in London and New York. But alas, in 1941, being Jewish, he had to flee again, this time to New York to escape the Nazis. In New York he had several one-man shows. He eventually settled permanently in Los Angeles in 1945.

Shortly after his arrival in Los Angeles, he showed his paintings at the noted Dalzell Gallery which was located in the Ambassador Hotel on Wilshire Boulevard. He had as collectors several major movie stars. He stayed with Dazell for two decades.

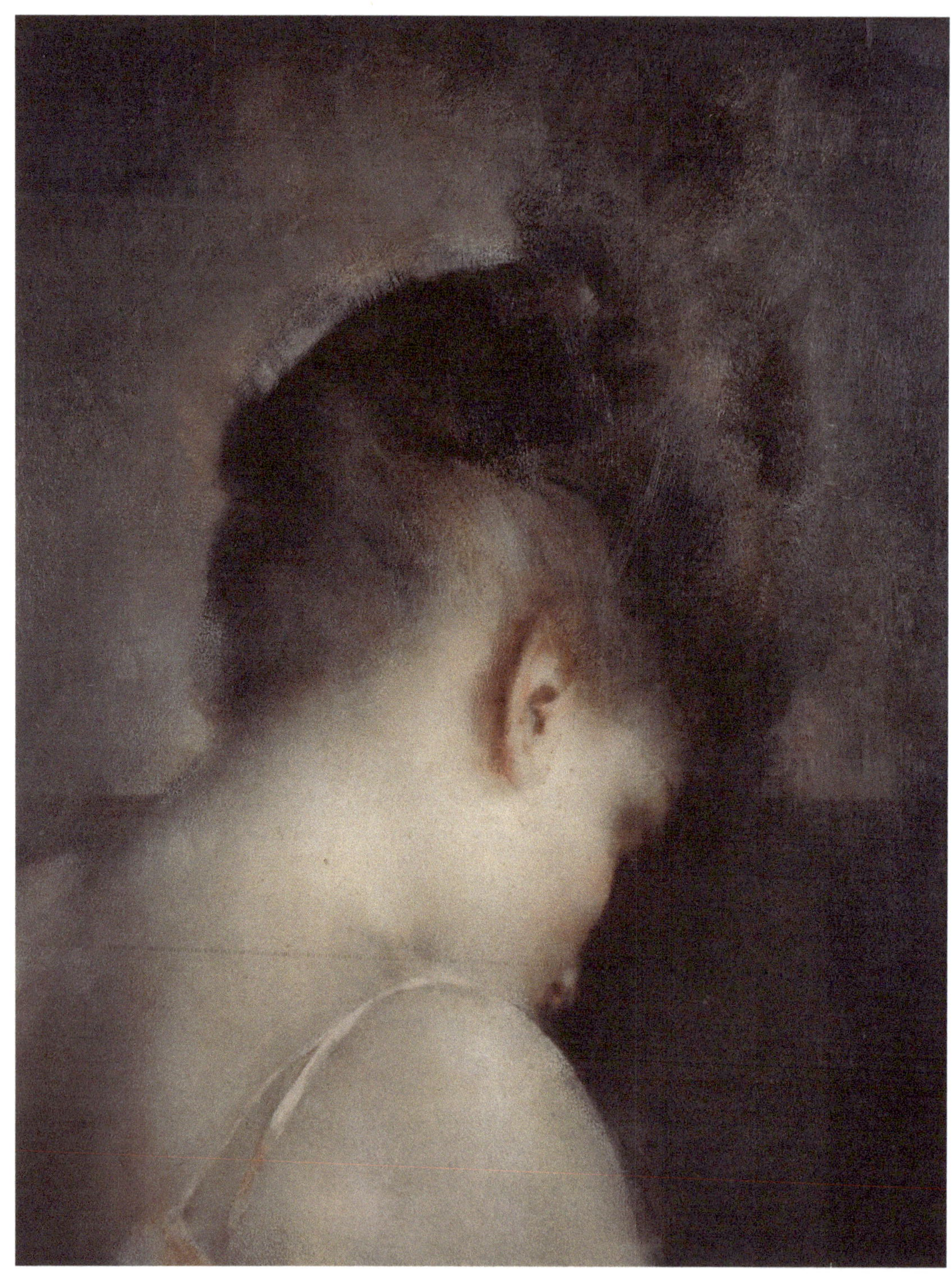

Illustration 32: Grigory Gluckmann, *It's About Time*, 1945. Photo by Gregory R. Staley. Julius and Ann Kaplan Collection.

Gluckman painted a wide variety of subjects, but he was at his best when painting women, particularly seated women viewed from the back and side, a la Mary Cassatt. This pose was also common in the Japanese woodcuts that became popular in Paris in the 1860's, after the arrival of the first Japanese woodcuts in Europe. Ruth Dalzell Hatfield described the artist's bravura for capturing feminine beauty "as a dance of multitudinous shades, tones, and nuances" that enabled him to produce "evocative poetic tones beyond the reality of the figure itself."

Gluckman employed a laborious technique learned at the Moscow Art Academy: he used numerous layers of paint, allowing each layer to dry completely before the application of the next. This had the effect of rendering his paintings with great subtlety of color. The success of this technique is evident in the painting I was considering at Sam's gallery, where the various textures of fabrics were clearly delineated. I decided to buy the Gluckman for which Sam charged me a miniscule price. It is entitled *It's About Time* (Illustration 32).

I bought the painting about 30 years ago. Gluckman was then virtually unknown. Since then Gluckman's reputation has grown substantially. Also, museums have started adding his paintings to their collections.

His works can now be found in the Georgia Museum of Art, the Georgia O'Keeffe Museum, the Austin Museum of Art, and the Carnegie Art Museum.

1.11 | VACLAV VYTLACIL (1892-1984)

My dear friend, the late Graham Williams, was married to the late Anne Vytlacil Williams, the daughter of the artist Vasclav Vytlacil (Illustration 33). Whenever I visited them, I would admire the many beautiful paintings throughout their large home in Georgetown, all painted by Anne's father.

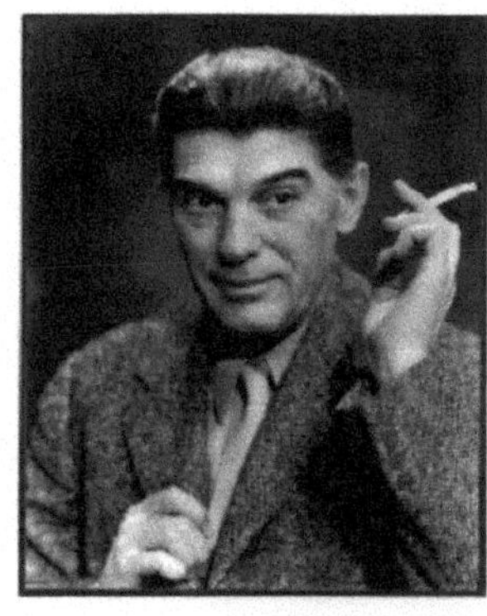

Vaclav Vytlacil

Illustration 33: Vaclav Vytlacil, 1892-1984 (Photo by Graham Williams)

In the fall of 2004, I mentioned to Graham that it would be lovely to add a painting by his father-in-law to our collection. He said that they were going to leave all of his paintings to the Art Student's League in New York, where "Vyt" had worked for several decades as an art teacher. He suggested that we go to Vyt's old studio/converted barn on his 15-acre property in Sparkill, N.Y., and he added, "There are still a lot of his paintings there. Go to Sparkill and select one before it is too late."

Graham added that we should alert a Mr. Marty Diamond, who would let us into the old studio. Shortly, thereafter, we indeed notified Mr. Diamond, and he kindly met us at the nearby railroad station, and took us to see the paintings. It was hard to make a choice, so I left it up to Ann, since she has such an excellent eye. She selected a beautiful still life, *No. 109* (Illustration 34).

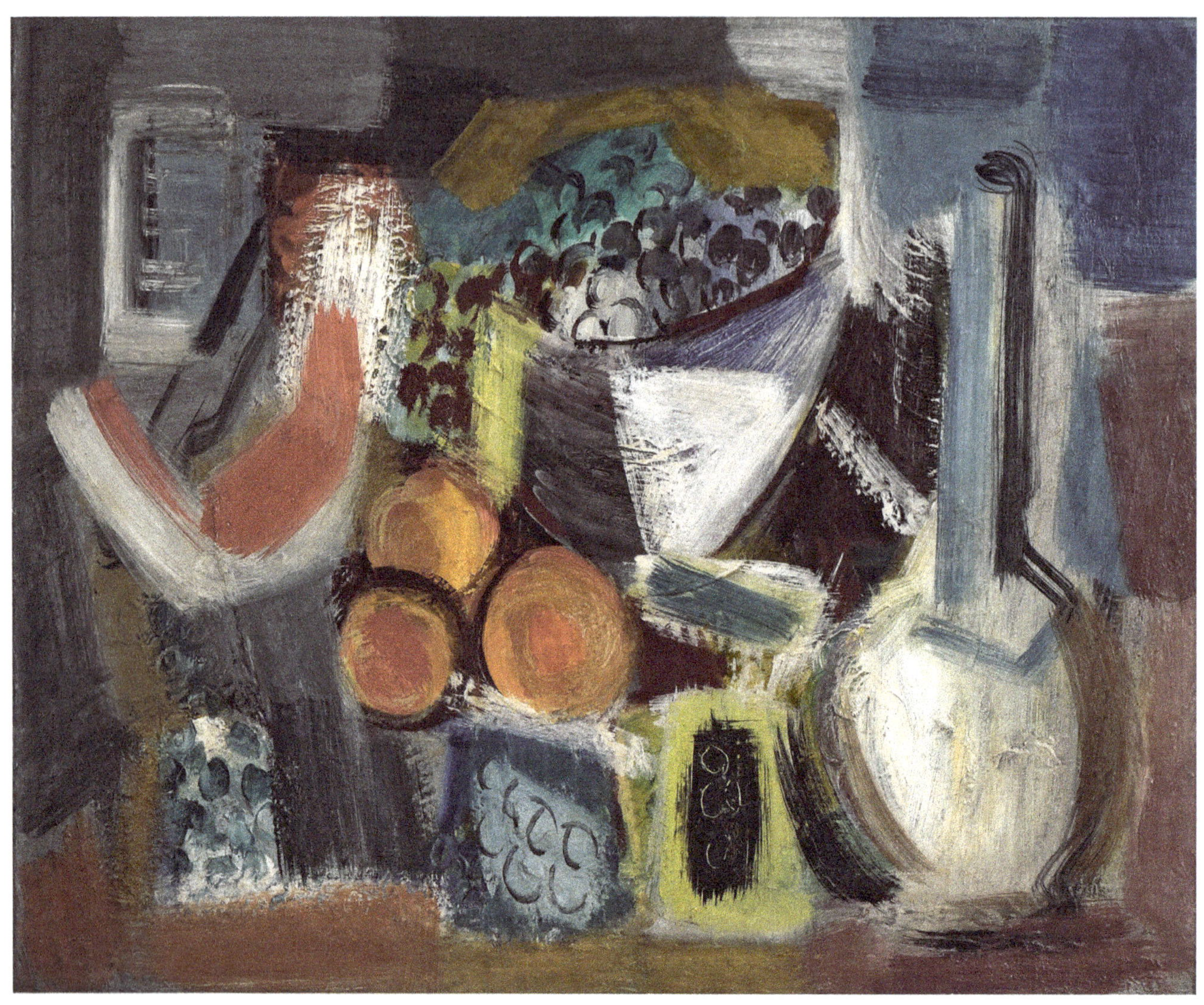

Illustration 34: Vaclav Vitlacil, *No. 109*. Photo by Gregory R. Staley. Julius and Ann Kaplan Collection.

After selecting the painting, we came back to D.C. to have Ann M. Creeger, a painting conservation expert, clean it, and then we took it to Goldleaf Studios to frame. Bill Adaire selected a partially white frame to accentuate the white in the painting. It was a perfect frame for the painting.

Vytlacil was born in New York City on November 1, 1892. He started his art studies at the Art Institute of Chicago. In 1913, he returned to New York on a scholarship given by the Art Students League. While there, he studied under the portraitist John C. Johansen. Vytlacil left the League to take a teaching position at the Minneapolis School of Art. He also spent time in Europe working as an assistant to Hans Hofmann for whom he had great admiration and friendship. I see the influence of Hofmann in many of Vytlcil's paintings, including ours.

During the late 1930's, and very early 1940's, Vytlacil taught at a number of art schools all over the United States. In 1946 he joined the faculty of the Art Students League and remained there until his retirement in 1978. Among his students were Louise Bourgeois, William de Kooning, Knox Martin, Robert Rauschenberg, James Rosenquist, and Cy Twombly, along with many others who became household names.

He was, during this period, also known as one of the founders of the American Abstract Artists. AAA, as it was known, was dedicated to the goal of getting Americans to accept abstract art. This was then not an easy task, given the very long tradition of realistic paintings in America. It is said that in large part through AAA's persistent efforts, Americans began to accept artists such as Vytlacil, along with many other American abstract artists.

Many museum curators and art critics ranked Vytlacil alongside top modernist painters. One big exponent of his work was Howard Devree, an art critic of the *New York Times*. He, as well as many other critics, saw Vytlacil as a major American painter of the first rank. I do not believe that this is the view today.

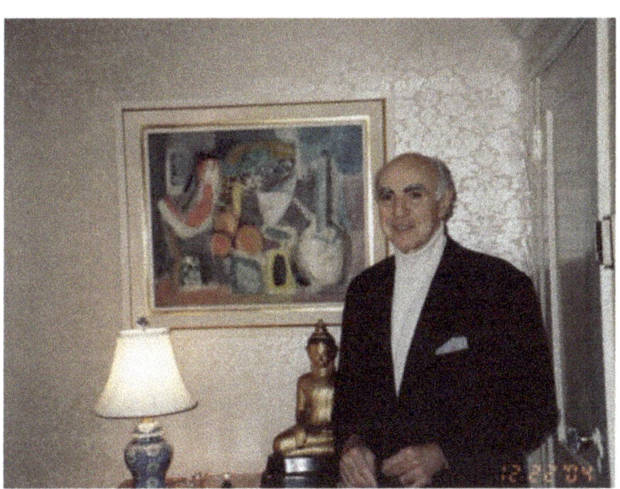

Illustration 35: The author in front of Vytlacil's *No. 109. Julius and Ann Kaplan Collection*

Vytlacil's paintings are represented in the permanent collections of The Museum of Modern Art, The Whitney Museum of American Art, the Smithsonian American Art Museum, The Metropolitan Museum of Art, et al.

Here is a picture of me next to the painting with the Gold Leaf Studios frame well in view (Illustration 35). I believe that the white in the frame does, indeed, pick up the white in the canvas.

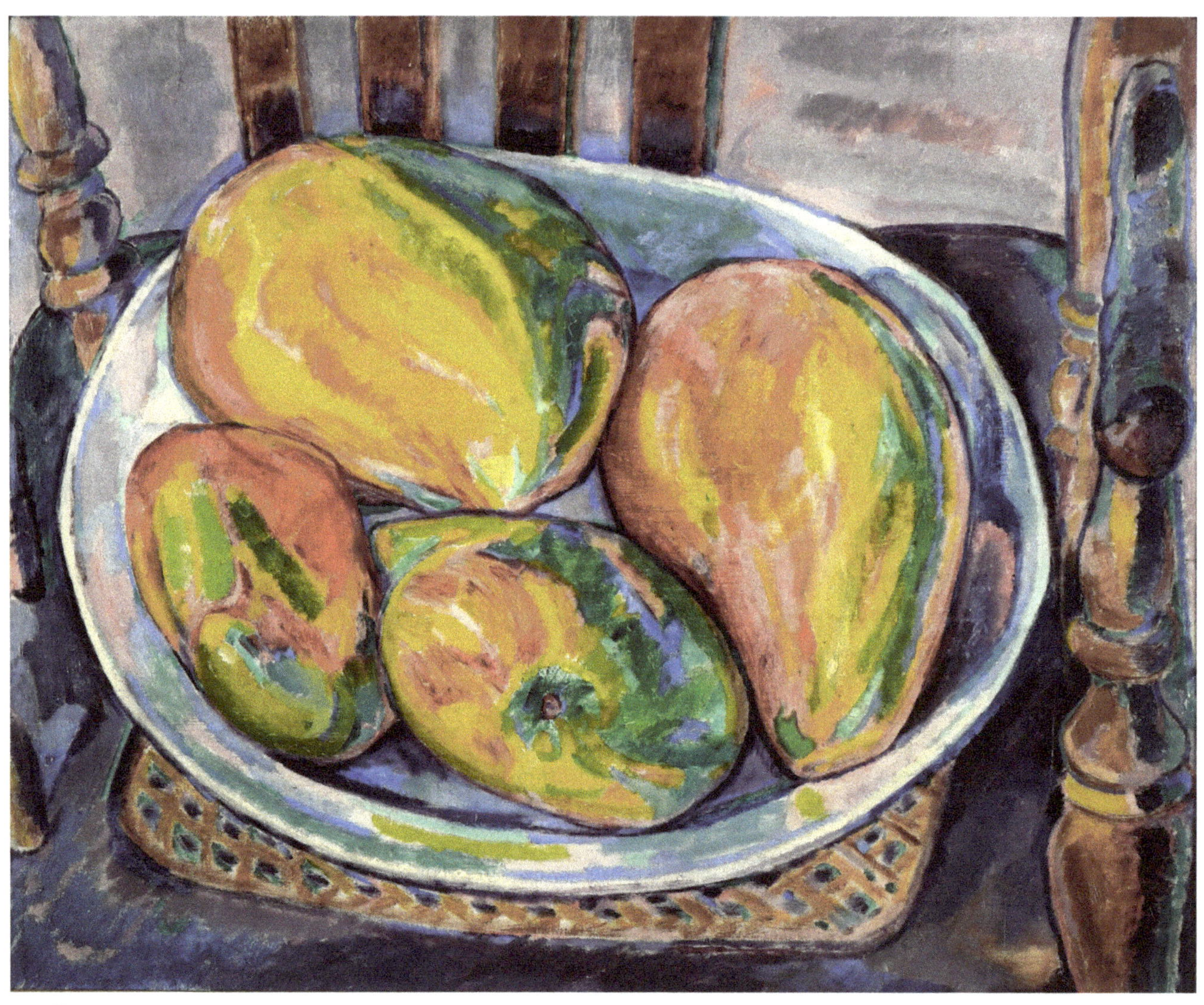

Illustration 36: Jerome Blum, *Still Life with Pomegranates*, 1911. Photo by Gregory R. Staley.

1.12 | JEROME BLUM (1884-1956)

After we sold *Jersey Woods* by George Bellows, we had to find a replacement to assume its role as the keeper of the mantle in our living room. We searched many of the major galleries in New York. Among these was Hollis Taggert. The Gallery started its life in Washington, D.C. I had bought a small painting from them by Frank Briggs of *The Quai du Notre Dame*, which we still have in our dining room, diagonally across from our Frank Meyers Boggs.

At their New York gallery we were shown *Still Life with Pomegranates* by fauvist Jerome Blum (Illustration 36). Being an old lover of European fauvist art by Andre Derain and Henri Matisse, this painting immediately captured my attention. It was a rare example of American fauvist painting. We still have it over our mantel and enjoy its vitality and bold colors very much.

Blum studied at the Francis J. Smith Art Academy and the Art Institute of Chicago. He then went to Paris where he studied painting at the *École des Beaux Arts*. The French Fauve movement was then at its height, and Blum caught the Fauvist fervor.

Fauvism goes back to around 1904 and continued beyond 1910. Artists employing this style were referred to as *les fauves* (French for "the wild beasts"). These twentieth-century artists emphasized painterly qualities and strong color over the representational or realistic values retained by impressionism.

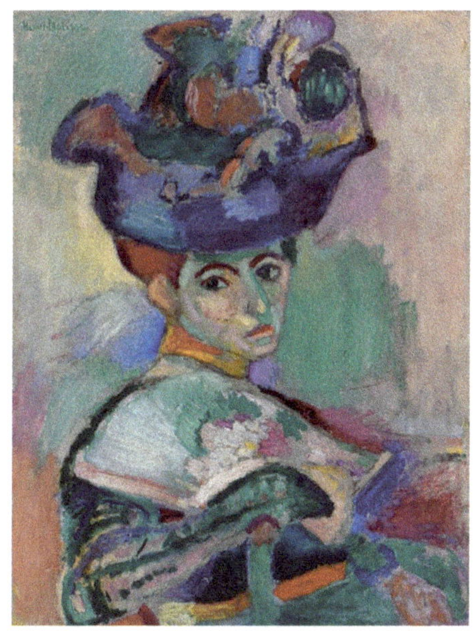

Illustration 37: Henri Matisse, *Femme au chapeau (Woman with a Hat)*, 1905. Oil on canvas, 31 3/4 x 23 1/2 inches. © 2019 Succession H. Matisse / Artists Rights Society (ARS), New York. Collection SFMOMA, 91.161.

Perhaps my favorite French Fauvist painting is *Woman with a Hat*, 1905, which is in the San Francisco Museum of Modern Art. When I visit that museum, I always go first to gaze with delight upon this beautiful painting. (Illustration 37).

While in Paris, Blum wrote: "You go to Paris - you have been in Paris for a few years - you have become modern - you take on color - you leave off brown of the golden ages - you shed your coat of brown for colors of the rainbow - you become another phase of yourself."

After Paris, Blum became a world traveler for almost a year. He visited countries where color abounds such as in the South Seas and Tahiti. He also visited Japan and China in the Far East. During this period, he concentrated on painting seascapes and landscapes.

He then returned to Chicago and introduced his fauvist style of painting to much acclaim in the Windy City. He is now well recognized as an exponent of American fauvism.

Works by Jerome Blum can be found in the permanent collections of the Metropolitan Museum of Art, the Whitney Museum of American Art, the Smithsonian Museum of American Art, et al.

1.13 | J & J FINE ARTS

I made the decision to retire from the practice of law as of 11:59 PM on December 31, 1999. To do so, I had two concerns to resolve. First, I had to find something worthwhile to fill the day. Second, I had to finance my retirement.

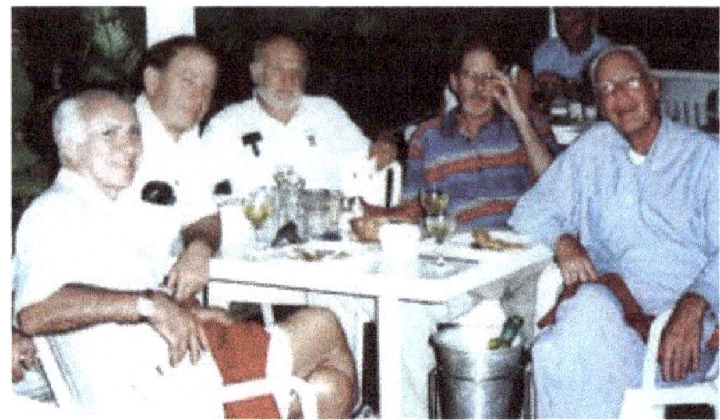

Illustration 38: The 4 Jays (From the left, Jay Kaplan, Jay Goldenberg, Jay Tolson, and Jay Smith, plus Nick Sullivan), February, 2000, at the Great Barrier Reef, Australia

As to the first, I became an explorer. My explorer friends Jay Goldenberg, Jay Tolson, and Jay Smith (the "Three Jays") invited me to join them on expeditions, which I did. We thereby became "The Four Jays." Two or more of us made many expeditions to exotic venues from January, 2000 until October, 2012, when I developed back problems (stenosis) that forced me to retire as an explorer. The most memorable of our expeditions were the following: climbing live volcanoes in Kamchatka, Siberia; climbing the tallest sand dunes in the Gobi Desert, Mongolia; mountain climbing in the Himalayas north of Darjeeling for almost 3,000 meters to reach a village on the border of Nepal named Sandakphu, where at 5:15 AM one had a spectacular view of four of the five highest peaks in the world: Everest, Kangchenjunga, Lhotse and Makalu; climbing the mountains encasing the 900-year-old churches in Lalibela, Ethiopia; and watching the orangutans in Borneo while searching for black orchids. I was elected a member of The Explorers Club ("TEC") and later became Chair (i.e., president) of the Explorer's Club Washington Group (which covers Washington, D.C., Virginia, West Virginia, and Maryland). For a more complete description of my life as an explorer, see the Conclusion of *Secrets and Suspense*. Set forth above is a picture of the Four Jays together with Nick Sullivan (the gentleman in an all blue short on the right, who was then the past President of TEC, and a renowned diver) at a bar in the Great Barrier Reef, Australia in the year 2000 (Illustration 38).

As to financing my retirement, I reluctantly sold some of our paintings, plus our collection of 18th century English glass. It was not a happy occasion, except financially. It was also satisfying to appreciate that the risk I assumed in "investing" in works of art in lieu of stocks and bonds worked out well. I frankly do not know what I would have otherwise done.

Secondly, I decided to create an art company (J & J Fine Arts) and collaborate on some purchases of art for resale, with my art dealer friend, Fred Hill. During the life of J and J, Fred and I looked at many possible joint purchases, but J and J only consummated three. One was the purchase and sale of *Phoebe at Onteora* (1908) by James Carroll Beckwith; a second was the purchase and sale of a 1925 painting entitled *Curtain Call* by Everett Shinn (where I learned that the most sought-after Shinn theater paintings were those done around 1895, not 1925.); a third was a painting by George Luks.

It was a lot of fun going up to New York to participate with the Hills at auctions of American art *chez* Sotheby's and Christie's, and deciding whether I could take the risk of buying a part of some of the paintings they bid on. Fred's firm owned an elegant flat in the same building as their beautiful gallery, whose walls were covered with fine paintings. The flat was kindly made available to me whenever I came to New York. Although it never grew to be as extensive a business as I would have preferred, I learned a lot, and never regretted establishing J & J Fine Arts. However, I lost more money than I could afford, so I had to close the company.

1.14 | AN AMERICAN MUSEUM IN TOKYO

I frankly do not remember how it occurred, but Ann and I became quite friendly in the 1990's with Mimi Kuriyama, the wife of the Japanese Ambassador, Takakazu Kuriyama. There were difficulties then in the foreign relations between Japan and the United States. I suggested to Madame Kuryama that we should cause an American Museum to be built in Japan to help bridge relations between the United States and Japan. Mimi thought it to be a wonderful idea, and she asked me to put a small group of people together to develop the plan, and she would persuade her husband to support it. I put together a group of people I knew who I believed would be helpful in realizing this idea. Among those on the committee were Judith Terra, the wife of Dan Terra (the art collector), William H. Gerdts (the author of numerous important books on American art) and Fred Hill, who is also an American art expert. I thought that Judith could be particularly helpful since her husband, Dan Terra, was a patron of the arts with their Terra Museum in Chicago and Le Musée d'Art Américain in Giverny, France. I had recently visited the museum in France, near the home of Claude Monet, and thought it was a perfect model for the proposed American art museum in Japan.

We hoped that one of the large Japanese companies could be persuaded to finance the museum. Unfortunately, Japan was then going through a severe recession, and the large companies we targeted respectfully refused. I then turned to Dan Terra, who we knew personally, and, of course, we had the benefit of his wife being on our committee. Dan kept saying "No thank you," but I kept trying. One day Dan called me, and invited Ann and me to his home in Georgetown for a dinner party. The dinner was set for a day in the last week of June 1996. He said that Ann and I would be seated at the head table with him. I could not imagine why he should so honor us. After dinner, Dan gave a toast along the following lines. "My friends, this gentleman next to me, Jay Kaplan, has been badgering me for months and months to finance an American Museum in Japan similar to my museum in Giverny. I turned him down constantly. But he persevered. This past week I finally gave in! Congratulations, Jay!" Unfortunately, Dan Terra died 4 days later on July 1, 1996, before any financial arrangements could be made by him for the museum project.

1.15 | CONTEMPORARY AMERICAN ARTISTS AND AN ART DEALER (WHO ARE ALL DEAR FRIENDS)

We were never serious collectors of contemporary art, except for studio glass. We, however, made a few exceptions when dear friends of ours happened to be very talented artists. We generally wanted to have at least a representative piece of their work. The artist-friends were (1) Joan Danziger. She is a fellow member of the Cosmos Club, and a regular at our holiday dinners; (2) Betsy Stewart, a neighbor and fellow member of both the Cosmos Club and the Explorers Club, whose colorful paintings pleased us; and (3) Annette Poland, another member of the Cosmos Club who is a renown portraitist, and who did photographic portraits of me for "Secrets and Suspense."

In addition, although not an artist, I have added the art dealer Fred Hill of Collisart. I discuss each below.

JOAN DANZIGER

Joan is a creative, and celebrated sculptor who was born in the same year as I. The Danzigers and the Kaplans have been friends for many decades. After Joan's husband, Marty, died, Joan would come to our house for all major holidays. She thus became a virtual member of our family during the holiday season. I also bought a number of pieces of Joan's sculptures starting in 1980.

One time about 35 years ago, I commissioned Joan to create a small sculpture of a vase with flowers for a table in one of my law firm's conference rooms. She advised, from month to month, that the sculpture was "growing" in size. Then one day, she announced that I could see my sculpture at a special "opening" in her then new studio. When we arrived, it was covered with a big white sheet. When she pulled it off, I could immediately see that it had indeed grown to be 7 feet tall, but it was a beautiful work of art. It was named *Flores Animales*.

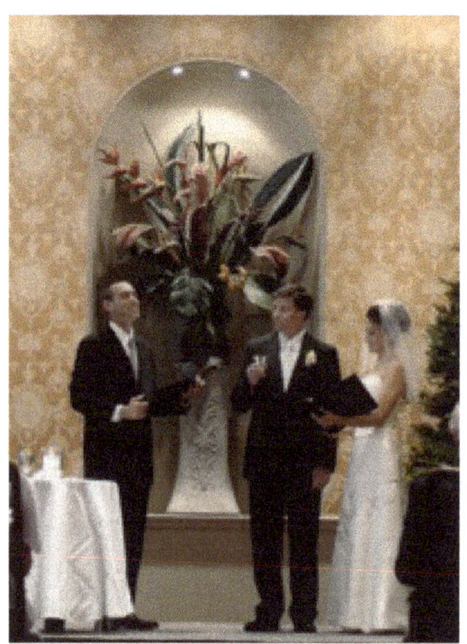

Illustration 39: The marriage of our daughter Samantha to Dirk Mason in front of Danziger's *Flores Animales* in the Cosmos Club.

When we first saw it unveiled, Ann said, "Where in the world could we place it in our home?" Another guest, Jack Coward, curator of the Corcoran Gallery of Art, exclaimed, "I know exactly where it should go. In our museum!" We there and then lent the sculpture to the Corcoran Gallery leaving our-selves the right to withdraw it at our convenience. For several years the museum placed it in its most prime spots.

Then one day the museum put it in storage. This made me unhappy. Shortly thereafter, I noted that the Cosmos Club was redoing its Powell Room. Among other changes in the room, they added a large niche behind the stage. I said to myself, "What a wonderful place for Joan's large sculpture." Upon seeing that it would fit, I took the sculpture back from the Corcoran, and lent it to the Club. They accepted it and it fits perfectly in that niche. It is still there on display, some decades later.

Here is a picture of the sculpture in its niche at the Cosmos Club. The couple getting married in front of it is our daughter Samantha, and her husband, Dirk Mason, with a wine glass in his hand. The other gentleman is the rabbi (Illustration 39).

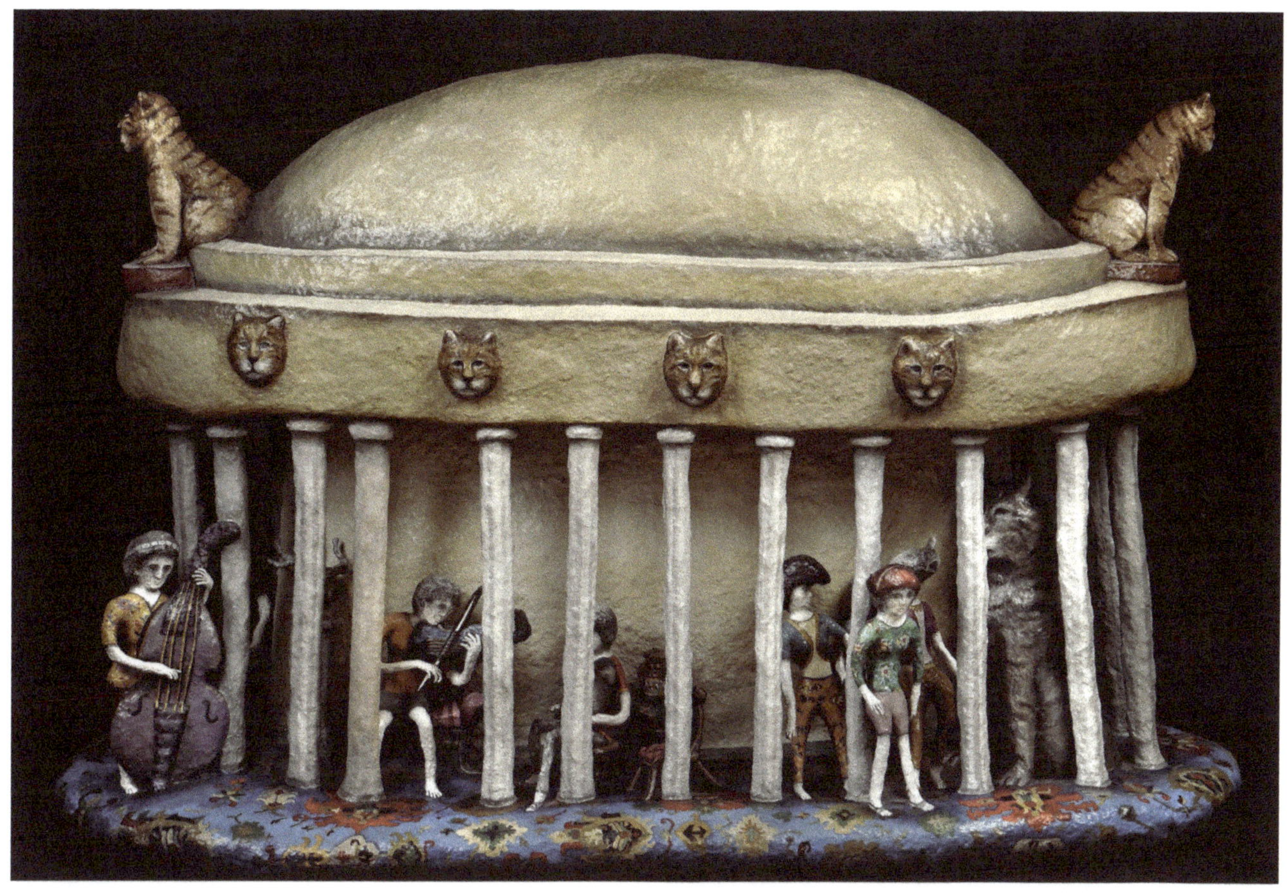

Illustration 40: Joan Danziger, *The Dome of Cats*, 1982. Photo by Gregory R. Staley. Julius and Ann Kaplan Collection.

I bought another large piece of sculpture from Joan which had been on display in the Textile Museum in Washington, D.C. (Illustration 40). It is now housed in my home office. Joan thereafter stopped making large sculptures and turned to beautiful smaller ones.

Joan's most recent sculptures feature trees, flowers and horses. A sculpture from this series, "*Into the Magic*," is now in the collection of the Smithsonian American Art Museum (Illustration 41).

Her next series of sculptures, large beautiful beetles, was shown in a dramatic fashion, with beetles all over the high walls of the Katzen Art Center of American University (Illustration 42)

In Joan's artist's statement, she writes that the world of the beetle gives her great inspiration. It was a big hit and Joan sold many, many beetles thereafter. Her newest sculptures are a series of running horses made up of glass, wire and metal. In Joan's words, "They are running through space." Her running horses are indeed lovely (Illustration 43).

The museums that have Danziger sculptures in their permanent collections are the Smithsonian American Art Museum; the National Museum of Women in The Arts; The Kreeger Museum; American University's Katzen Art Center; Reading Public Museum, Reading, Pennsylvania; the New Jersey State Museum; the Children's Museum of Pittsburgh, Pennsylvania; and the Jacksonville Museum of Science and Art.

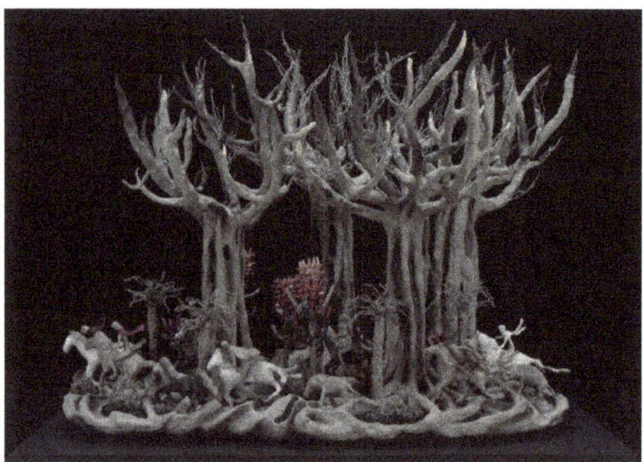

Illustration 41: Joan Danziger, *Into the Magic*, 2007. Mixed media, 4 × 45 1/4 × 32 1/2 inches. Smithsonian American Art Museum, Gift of the artist, 2015.57.

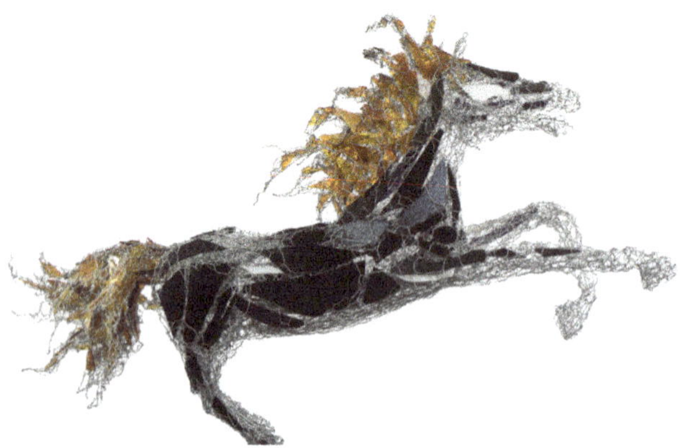

Illustration 43: Joan Danziger, *Black Star*, 2018. Photo by Rebecca Lasky. Courtesy of the artist.

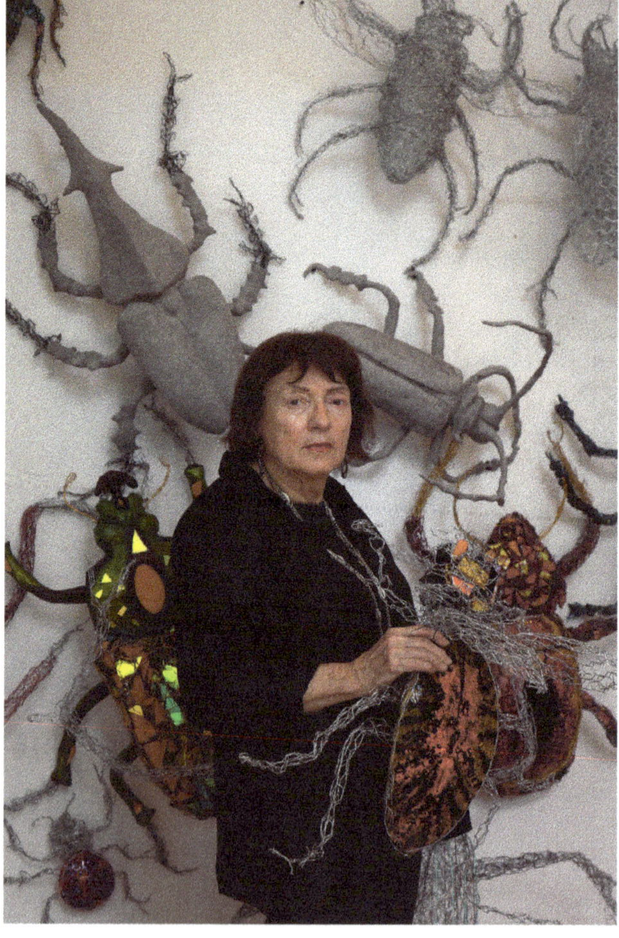

Illustration 42: Danziger with her wire beetle sculptures. Photo by Annette Polan. Courtesy of the artist.

BETSY STEWART

I first met Betsy at the Cosmos Club about 17 years ago. She identified herself to me as an artist and, at my request, showed me a number of pictures of her paintings on her iPhone. They were painted representations of what one would see if one looked at a drop of pond water under a microscope. The shapes and colors of the pictures were stunning. I asked if Ann and I could see any of her "originals." She replied that, by happy coincidence, she was having a show which was to open the following week. Ann and I went to the show and we were both impressed with the beautiful shapes and colors in her work, to say nothing of their vitality. We ended up by buying what the artist calls a *Pond Totem*. In these works, Betsy paints on all four sides of a vertical free-standing piece of wood. It thereby takes the form of a piece of sculpture (Illustration 44 + 45).

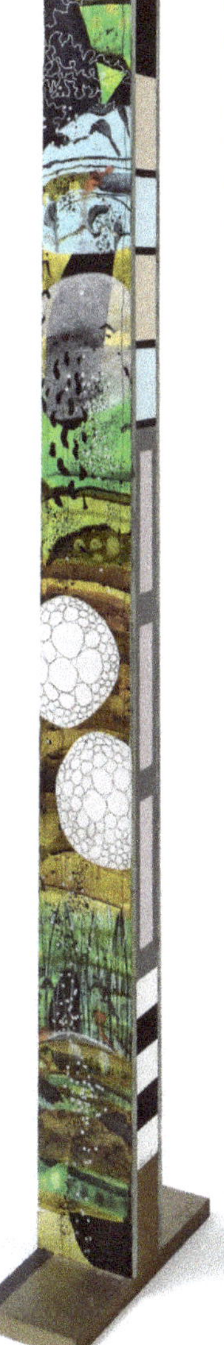

Illustration 44: Betsy Stewart, *Pond Totem* (Side One), 2002. Acrylic and sumi ink on canvas. Photo by Gregory R. Staley. Julius and Ann Kaplan Collection. Courtesy of the artist.

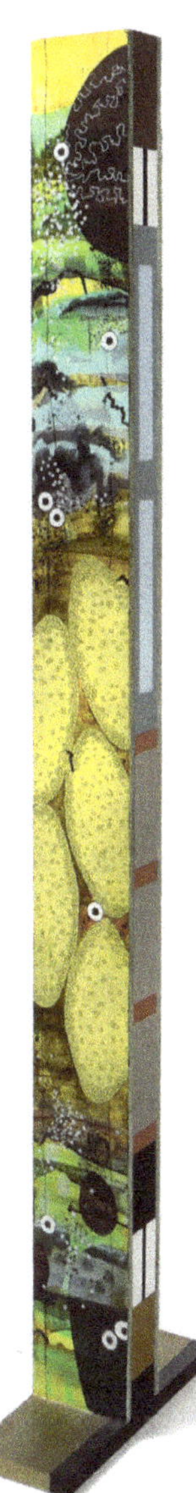

Illustration 45: Betsy Stewart, *Pond Totem* (Side Two) 2002. Acrylic and sumi ink on canvas. Photo by Gregory R. Staley. Julius and Ann Kaplan Collection. Courtesy of the artist.

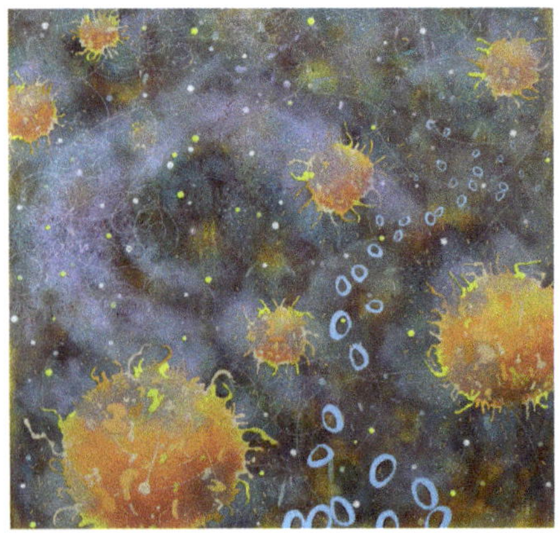

Illustration 46: Betsy Stewart, *Biocriticals No. 3*, 2014. Acrylic and sumi ink on canvas, 48 × 48 inches. Photo by Gregory R. Staley. Courtesy of the artist.

Since painting these totems, she has ventured into the world of space, where she finds many shapes and forms similar to those which she found under a drop of pond water (Illustration 46).

Once, while chatting with Betsy at the Cosmos Club, I learned that she was not only a painter, but also an explorer – a mountain climber who had also done extensive explorations in the Rub' al Khali (The "Empty Quarter" desert of Saudi Arabia). I was then (as I remain today) on the Board of Directors of The Explorers Club's Washington Group. When I learned of her extensive experience as an explorer, I nominated Betsy for membership in The Explorers Club. She has become not only an active member, but was elected to become a member of the Board of Directors of our chapter of the Explorers Club.

I have kept up with her remarkable career as an artist by going to a number of her local shows. Her work has become all the more subtle, elegant, and beautiful. The favorable reviews of her work are ubiquitous and well justified.

Stewart's paintings are represented in numerous private, corporate and museum collections such as the The Kreeger Museum; The Ogden Museum of Southern Art; The American University Katzen Art Center; The Adirondack Museum; The Bellagio Hotel; The Embassy of Finland; The Washington Convention Center; The D.C. Commission on the Arts; and The World Bank Headquarters in Washington, D.C.

Of paintings that I have seen recently, my favorites are Illustrations 46, 47, and 48:

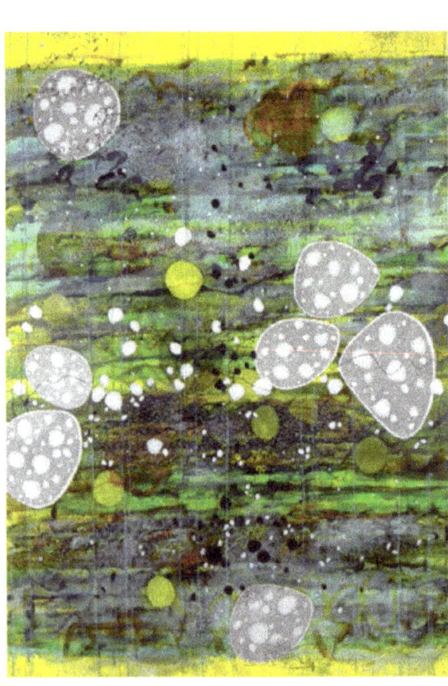

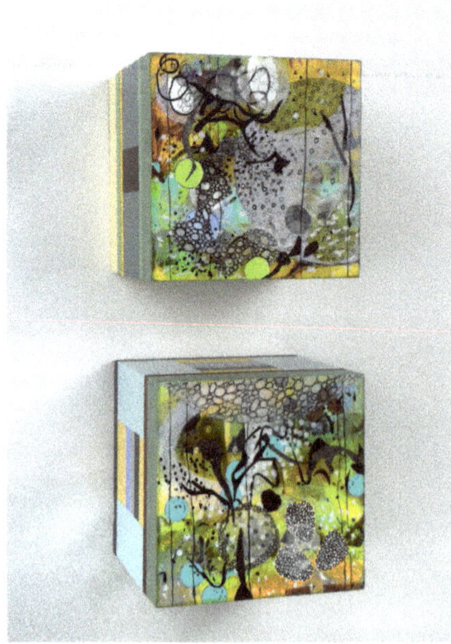

Illustration 47 (left): Betsy Stewart, *Metasculs No. 1*, 2008. Acrylic and sumi ink on canvas, 67 × 47 inches. Photo by Gregory R. Staley. Courtesy of the artist.

Illustration 48 (right): Betsy Stewart, *Fontis, No. 118*, 121, 2014. Acrylic, sumi ink and mylar on wood, 5 × 5 × 5 inches. Photo by Gregory R. Staley. Courtesy of the artist.

ANNETTE POLAN

Annette Polan is well known, both domestically and internationally, as a portrait artist. She has photographed and painted the official portraits of leaders of industry and government, including Justice Sandra Day O'Connor, (former) West Virginia Governor Gaston Caperton, Peter Tarnoff for the Council on Foreign Relations, Judge Rya Zobel for the Federal Judicial Center, Edward Villella of the Miami City Ballet, Lord Baltimore for Kiplin Hall in Great Britain, and me. Her picture of me appeared twice in my first book, *"Secrets and Suspense: International Law Stories"*. Ms. Polan has taught and lectured on her work and contemporary American portraiture in Europe, Asia, and Australia, and has had numerous solo and group exhibitions in the United States and abroad.

Annette was a participant in the U.S. Department of State's Art in Embassy Program, with pieces showing in Denmark and Fiji. Her interest in the narrative extends into video and site-specific installations. I offer photographs of my favorite of her portraits (Illustrations 49 + 50).

She organized *Faces of the Fallen*, an exhibition of 1323 portraits by 230 American artists to honor the servicemen and women who died in Afghanistan and Iraq between October 10, 2001 and November 11, 2004. The exhibition opened on March 23, 2005 at Women in Military Service of America Memorial in Arlington Cemetery. For recognition of her support of the men and women of the Armed forces and their families, Ms. Polan was awarded the Chairman of the Joint Chiefs of Staff Outstanding Public Service Award, the highest civilian award from the Joint Chiefs.

Annette is the former Chairman of the Painting Department at the Corcoran, and she has served on the board of the Washington Project for the Arts. She is on the board of Smith Center for Healing and the Arts. She is a member of Art Table, the Cosmos Club, the International Women's Forum, and the Women's Forum of Washington. She is listed in *Who's Who in America, Who's Who in the East, Who's Who of American Women, Who's Who of American Artists, The Dictionary of International Biography,* and *The World's Who's Who of Women.*

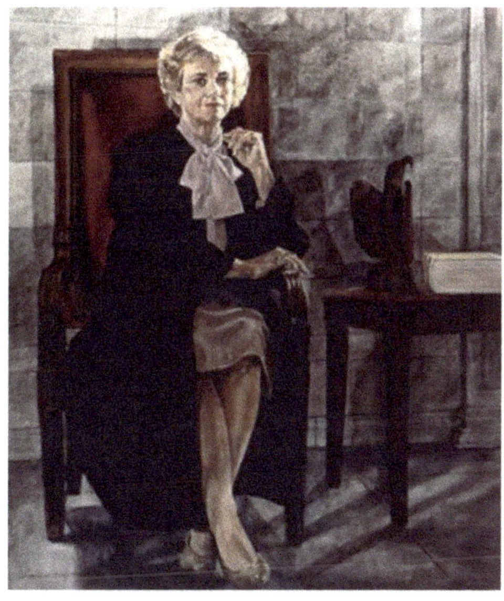

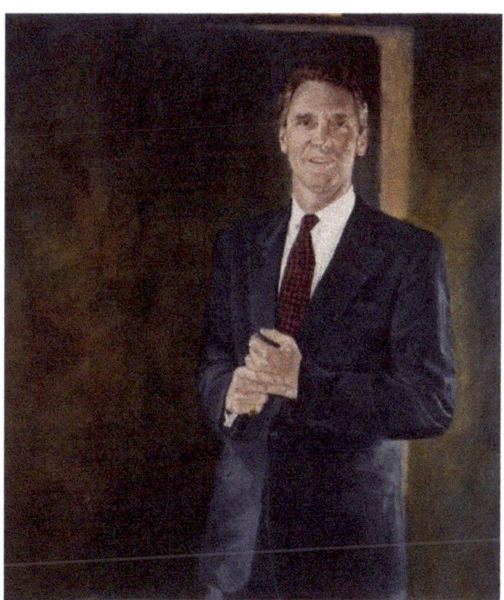

Illustration 49 (left): Annette Polan, *Justice Sandra Day O'Connor*. Photo courtesy of the artist.

Illustration 50 (right): Annette Polan, *Gaston Caperton*, Governor, West Virginia. Photo courtesy of the artist.

FREDERICK D. HILL

For decades, Fred Hill was my art consigliere, my "professor" of art, my partner, my dealer, and my friend. I liked him notwithstanding the fact that he went to Amherst College, which together with Williams College, was the arch rival of my undergraduate school, Wesleyan University. Together they were the "Little Three," and, underneath it all, we admired the academic prowess of each.

I had a special warmth for Amherst since the head of their art department at the time was Leonard Baskin, a wonderful artist. I helped hang one of his first one man shows at the Davison Art Center at Wesleyan in the 1950's. Baskin was the first artist I ever collected. I have one of his works over my bed.

Fred is a partner, together with his daughter Daisy, in an art company called Collisart. The company has a show room in the east side of New York. It is the place to go if you are in the market for a fine American painting of the early 20th Century. Fred and Daisy know American art like few other dealers. They have shown at some on the most important art shows in the world, such as TEFAF (the European Fine Arts Fair in Maastricht) and Masterpiece London Art Show.

Fred has a delightful sense of humor. When they found a new home for one of the first paintings I ever sold, a small inconsequential work by the French artist Maximilien Luce, I called Fred and asked how much did he got for it. He replied, "Some loose change." (Luce is pronounced "loose.")

When I had my J and J Art Company, Fred became my collaborator. I would go to the Sotheby's and Christi's auctions in New York, where I sat up front with Fred. Before he cast a bid on a painting, he asked if I wanted a "piece of the action." As noted above, I very occasionally bought a miniscule percentage of several paintings, which Fred would later sell for both of us.

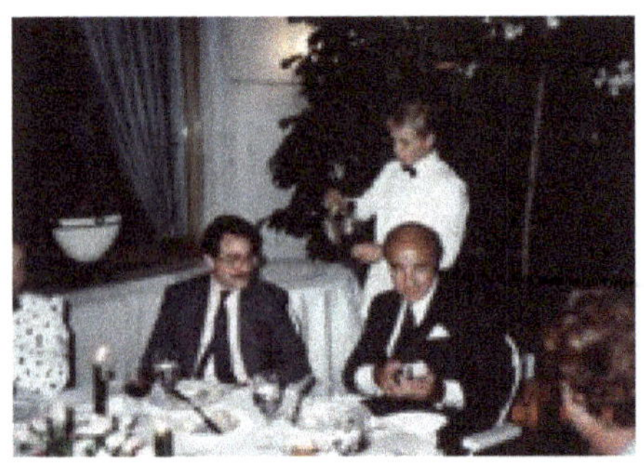

Illustration 51: Fred Hill and Jay Kaplan on the Terrace of the Hotel Beau-Rivage, Geneva.

Fred and I traveled to many art shows, here and abroad. Here we are on the Terrace of the Beau Rivage Hotel in Geneva examining pictures of paintings by Tarkoff for a planned New York Tarkoff Show (Illustration 51).

We worked together on several shows in New York. One was the show of the works of Nicholas Tarkoff. A second was paintings by Armand Guillaumin from the estate of Baron Oscar Ghez.

When it came time to sell some of my paintings to finance my retirement, Fred was my sole agent. He secured a serious price for our Marsden Hartley at a truly elegant "*Hartley Flower Painting Show*" at Berry Hill Gallery, Fred's former gallery, and later for our Bellows, *Jersey Woods*. He also acted on our behalf in the sale of a few other paintings.

It is a delight to visit Fred's current gallery. They carry an array of beautiful American paintings from the first half of the 20th century. If I were a buyer today, I would immediately buy a Bellows painting he currently has for sale where the sky seems inspired by Emile Nolde. It is entitled *Red Sun* (Illustration 52).

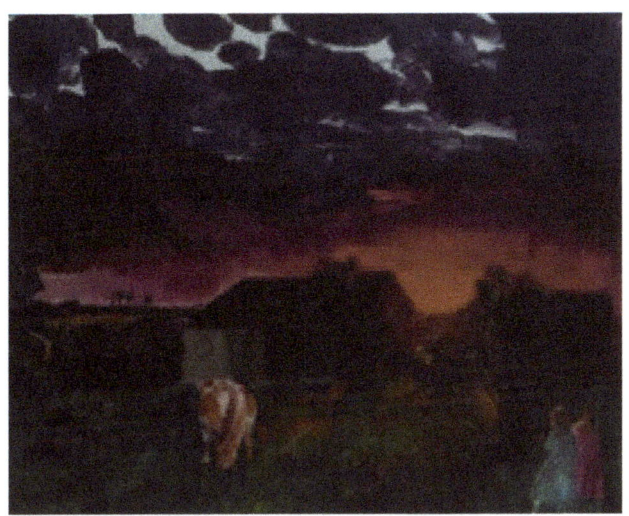

Illustration 52: George W. Bellows, *Red Sun*, 1919. Oil on canvas, 18 × 24 inches. Photo by Collisart.

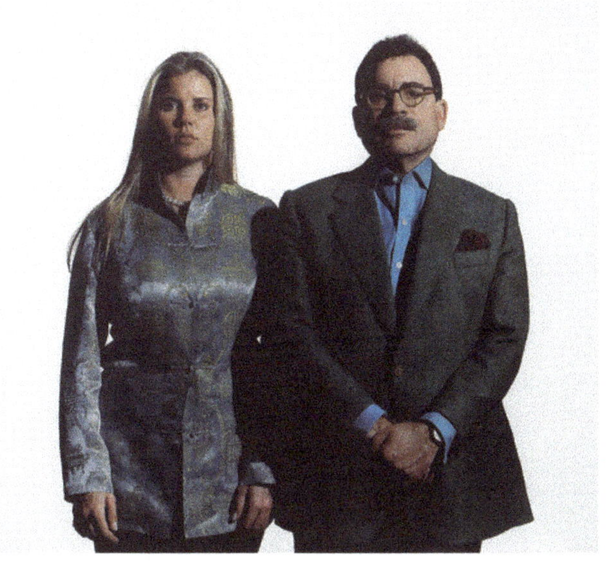

Illustration 53: Robert McCurdy, *Daisy & Fred*, 2001. Oil on panel, 73 × 68 inches. Photo courtesy of Collisart.

Fred had a portrait made of himself and his daughter/partner Daisy, which I think is wonderful, and I share it with you (Illustration 53).

1.16 | CONCLUSION

The collecting of American paintings was a source of much pleasure. The fortuitous acquisition of Bellows' *Jersey Woods* introduced us to the greatness of Bellows as an artist. I then discovered the incredible strength of Marsden Hartley. Our next exposure to truly great art came with our purchase of the Henri le Sidaner painting of *L'ile des Pescheurs*. But what was perhaps an equal contribution from our collection is that it brought to life my 1956 thesis on Robert Henri. I more than ever realized the major role Henri played in the American art world of the early 20th Century. It was an exciting period in American art, not only with the teaching of Henri, but with the impact of the Armory Show in 1913.

CHAPTER 2

English and Dutch 18th-Century Glass

2.1 | INTRODUCTION AND SUMMARY[2]

I had never before paid much attention to glass beyond wanting to drink my martini out of an appropriate one. But then I met Derek Davis at Asprey. He introduced me to the refinement and beauty of Georgian glass. The more he exposed me to 18th-Century English spiral twist glasses, the more their beauty became too much to resist. I was smitten. My tastes broadened to other Georgian glass, as well as 18th-Century stipple engraved Dutch glass. My love affair with glass prevailed for almost 41 years, during which time our collection become well known in the relatively small circle of glass curators, dealers, and collectors.

2.2 | FIRST STEPS INTO THE WORLD OF GLASS

One day in the spring of 1983, I was in London having lunch with an English friend and his wife. While sipping a lovely glass of Meursault, I complained that the Chinese art which I had been collecting had become too expensive for me to continue in that field.

I told my friends, "I am now in search of a new source of beauty to collect, where I can afford to buy the very best."

My friend's wife, Elizabeth, asked, "Have you ever considered collecting antique English glass in lieu of Chinese art?"

I replied in the negative.

She responded that her sister, Meredith, worked in the iconic British luxury shop on Old Bond Street called Asprey, and she constantly talked about the beautiful antique English glass they carried.

2 The photographs in this chapter were by Bonham's, London

Prior to turning to glass, I was devoting most of my time to collecting Chinese ceramics. But the prices for the better objects shot up in price as mainland collectors emerged to join wealthy Japanese collectors. I was in effect driven out of the Chinese market. I still bought paintings on occasion.

I was, indeed, familiar with Asprey & Garrard Limited. I had always loved the store. I had even bought my wife's wedding band there, as well as having them make a suede case for a small gold card case I had bought for her. For those not familiar with this establishment, it is one of the premier luxury goods stores in the entire world.

Elizabeth added that the antique glass department was run by a gentleman named Derek Davis. I later learned that Mr. Davis and his father were known throughout the world as a source for serious glass collectors and museums.

That afternoon, Elizabeth and I went to Asprey. I was delighted to be back in this venerable old store. We met Elizabeth's sister, Meredith, who introduced me to Derek Davis. He looked just as I expected an antiquarian expert to look: distinguished mien, pince-nez glasses, and a dark grey three-piece suit.

After being introduced to him I said, "Mr. Davis, it is a great honor to meet you. I have heard such wonderful things about you and your expertise in antique glass. I know virtually nothing about glass, but from what I see in your display cases, I can understand why Meredith's sister brought me here. I have been a collector of Chinese ceramics for a long time. However, I am now ready to collect something new and beautiful. I would like to examine the possibility of becoming a collector of fine antique English glass."

"Mr. Kaplan, I suspect that you may have come to the right place," Mr. Davis said. "Unlike Chinese art, which has a world market, antique English glass has, for the most part, primarily an English market. Occasionally, your Corning Museum comes to me to add something special to their collection, and we do have a few American and Dutch customers. Also, unlike Chinese art, which has been produced for millennia, the English glass which I will show you will be almost entirely from the Georgian period, which is from 1714 to the end of the century."

He continued. "Now, please allow me to show you our collection, and if you admire what you see, I recommend that you visit the Victoria and Albert Museum ("V&A") and examine the fine Georgian glass in their collection. If you are then still attracted to Georgian glass, please come back to see me. I am confident that we would be able to assist you in assembling an important collection."

Mr. Davis showed me several beautiful 18th-century English glasses from Asprey's collection. I very much liked what I saw, and I decided to take his advice and go to the V&A the next day.

The Museum is located on Cromwell Road, a few blocks from Harrods. It is the largest museum of decorative arts and design, housing a permanent collection of over 2.27 million objects. Founded in 1852 and named after Queen Victoria and Prince Albert, it is a public museum dedicated to human history, and its glass collection is one of the largest and most comprehensive in the world. I sought out the 18th-century English glass, and that collection was also substantial. After almost three hours of careful study, I decided to collect 18th-century English wine glasses.

I was attracted to many of the Georgian wine glasses that I saw in the museum, particularly those from the last half of the century. I found the simplicity of the design compelling. I could easily envision an English gentleman of the period carefully holding, and admiring, one of those glasses, half filled with wine, and savoring the wine and as well as the glass itself.

The next day, after I had finished the legal work that brought me to London, I returned to Asprey and ascended the staircase to the antique glass department. I immediately saw Mr. Davis, and said, "Good afternoon, Mr. Davis. I am now ready to begin collecting Georgian wine glasses."

He said, "I am most pleased that you came to that conclusion. I had hoped from the beginning that we would be able to work together. May I ask how much you are prepared to invest in glass on an annual basis? I gave him an amount which I feared would be too modest to proceed.

But Mr. Davis smiled, and said, "I believe that your budget will allow you to build up an important collection, but you would have to limit your purchases to one or two glasses per year. We must always buy only the rarest and most beautiful glasses. But you are young, and in 40 years you will have a collection that even the V&A would be proud to display." I replied, "Mr. Davis, count me in."

2.3 | COLOR-TWIST GLASS

On the same visit, Mr. Davis went to one of the display cases and fetched several glasses. I was stunned by their beauty. He first showed me a glass that had a stem with intertwined, twisted rods of multicolored glass.

While handing me the glass, he said, "Please note that this glass has a round funnel bowl with a delicately engraved fruiting vine. But the *piece de résistance* is its stem. It is set with a 'corkscrew' made of individual threads of white, canary yellow and translucent blue. It was previously in the renowned Alexander Collection. Glasses with notable provenance tend to support value. This glass was made around 1765."

He explained that "English glass was much heavier in the early part of the century than it was when this glass was made. This results from the imposition of an excise tax in 1745. The amount of the tax on glass was based on weight, and glassmakers thus began to make lighter glasses. Glassmakers molded grooves in the sides of colorless glass rods. They then covered the grooves with more colorless glass thereby creating hollow tubes. The glassmakers then twisted the hollow tubes into spirals. This is what collectors call "air twists." You sometimes hear them colloquially called "worm holes." Starting in the early 1760's, glassmakers began inserting rods of colored glass into the stems, and twisting them. This is what collectors call "color twists." Sometimes "color twists" are combined with "air twists." These are called "mixed twists." The yellow tubes were the most difficult and costly to make. As a consequence, glass stems containing yellow tubes were the most costly.

I found the glass to be most attractive. I, of course, looked at other glasses, but my mind was made up after seeing the one formerly in the Alexander Collection. I started my collection of Georgian glass with this beautiful color-twist (Illustration 1).

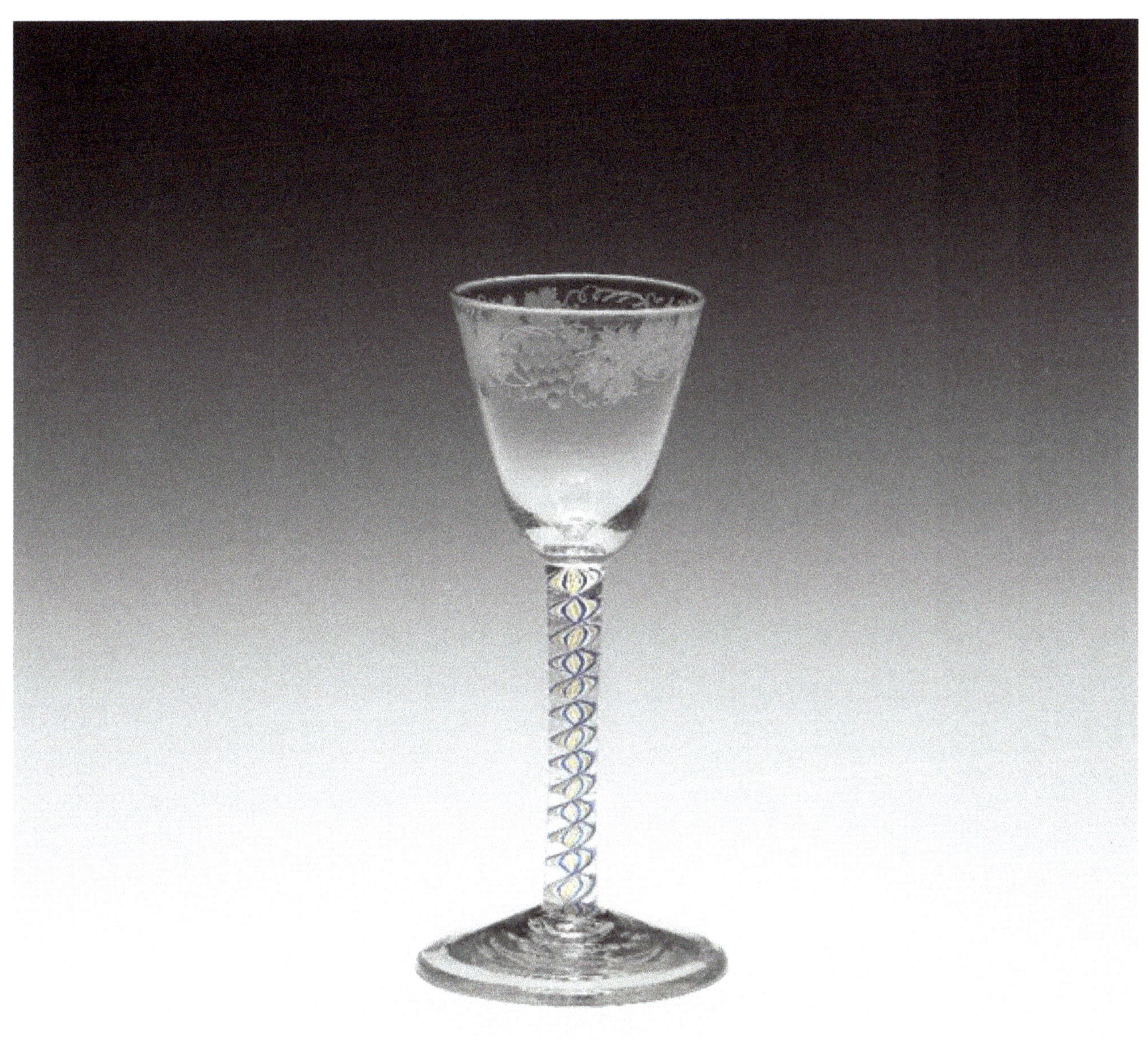

Illustration 1: Engraved Color-Twist Wine Glass with Blue and Canary Threads, circa 1765. Photo courtesy of Bonham's London. Julius and Ann Kaplan Collection.

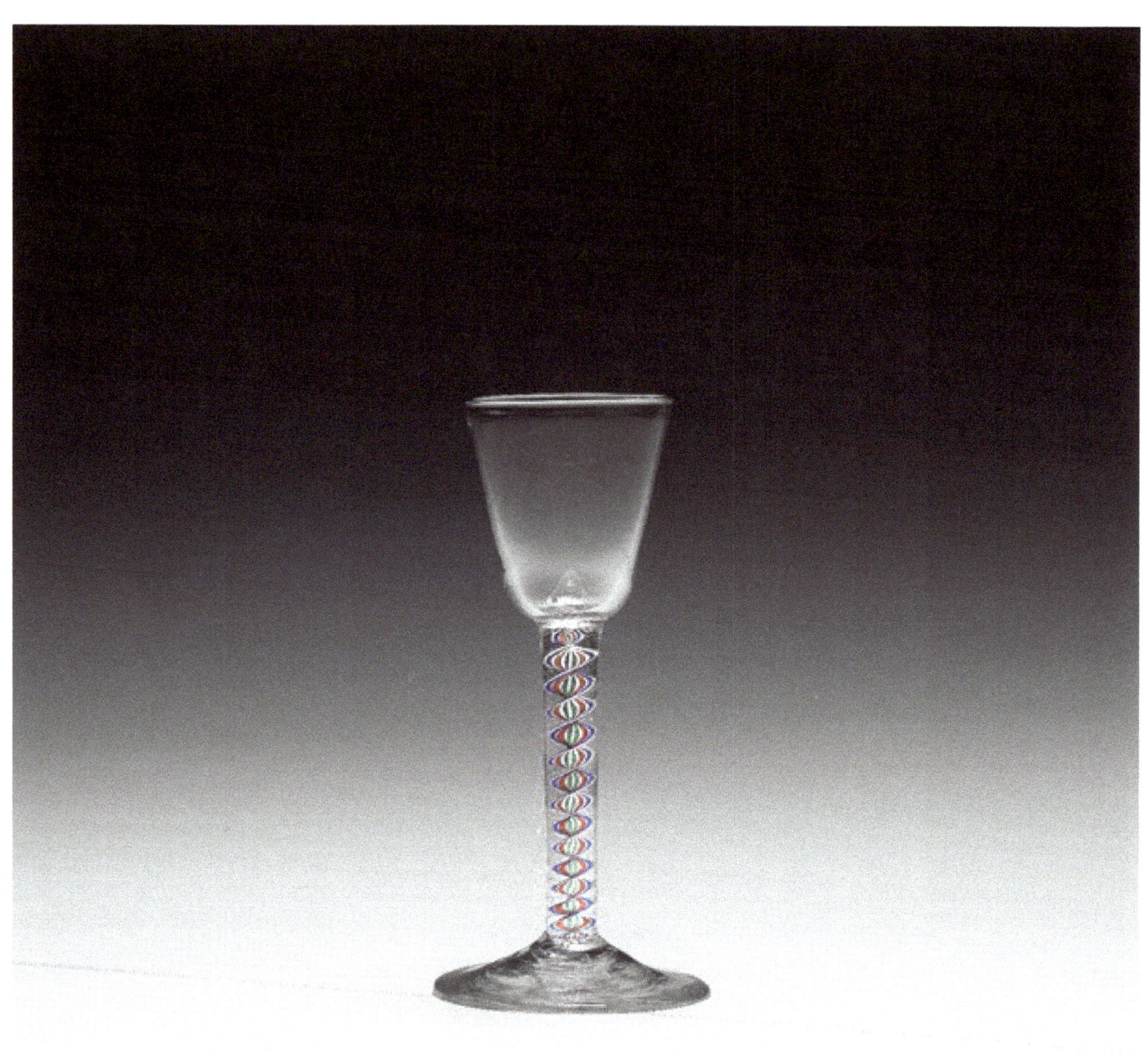

Illustration 2: Rare Color-Twist Wine Glass, circa 1770. Photo courtesy of Bonham's London. Julius and Ann Kaplan Collection.

When I returned to Washington, I put my new color-twist in a display cabinet with a light shining directly on it. It was beauty itself. But I decided that the glass must be lonely, and I should find her some worthy company.

On my next trip to London, about eight months later, I returned to Asprey and bought another color-twist. This one, circa 1770, was an exceptionally rare wine glass with a rounded bowl. The bowl was set on a stem comprised of a multi-colored corkscrew of ruby, green and blue threads edged in opaque white all around a central white thread (Illustration 2).

After I bought the second glass, Mr. Davis invited me for some afternoon tea. During our tea, I mentioned that it would be interesting to find fellow glass collectors in the United States.

Mr. Davis said, "By coincidence, Asprey has another antique glass client in the Washington, D.C. area!"

I asked Mr. Davis if he would be so kind as to introduce this other collector to me?

He responded, "Jolly good idea! I will write to him and get his permission for me to give you his contact information."

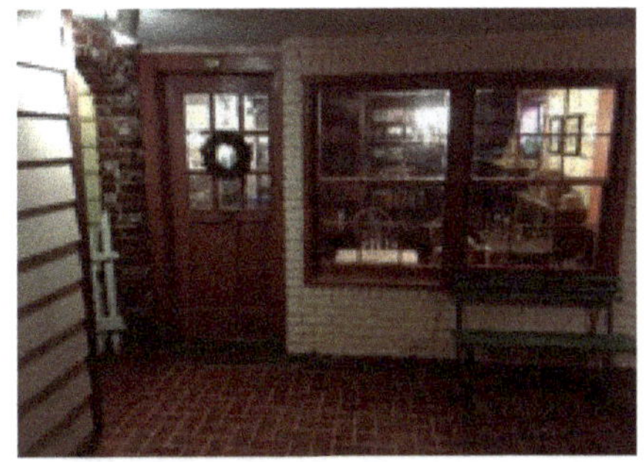

Illustration 3: A "pretend" shoppe chez the Leubas

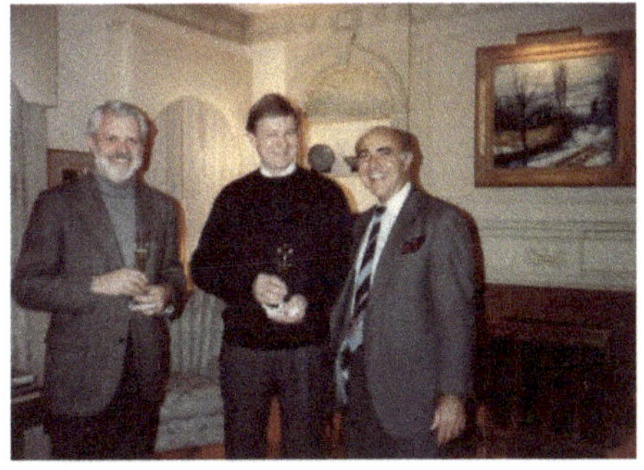

Illustration 4: Harald Leuba, standing between Dwight Lanmon (with a glass of champagne) and the author.

I must confess that I was rather amused at how much more formal the English were in such matters than we. I suspect that the average American would have said, "Sure, here is his phone number!"

Two weeks later, Mr. Davis wrote to me and said that he received a reply from Harald Leuba who would be delighted to meet me, and he provided his contact information.

It turned out that Harald was a delightful gentleman with a serious interest in 18th century English glass. He had an outstanding collection of color twist glasses, as well as other types of English glass of the period. He and his wife, Nancy Kingsbury, were also keenly intelligent. During the Kennedy Administration, the Secretary of Defense, Robert McNamara, caused the Department to go out and locate young people with genius level IQ's to work in the department. These young geniuses were called "the Whiz Kids," and Harald was one of them.

Every year, Harald and Nancy hosted extraordinary two-day Christmas parties in their spacious home, where they shared their collection of glass with many friends. Being enamored with things English, Harald, a handy man *extraordinaire*, built an entire miniature English village in his basement. It included, among numerous other "shoppes," an English glass dealer's store with a sample of 18th-century English glass "for (pretend) sale" (Illustration 3).

Here is a picture of Harald Leuba in our home. Harald is to my right. The other gentleman to Harald's right is Dwight Lanmon, then Director of The Corning Museum of Glass (Illustration 4).

On my next visit to Asprey the following year, I met John Smith, Derek Davis' new, young, and seriously able assistant. John advised me to bid on a very special color-twist that was soon to be auctioned at Sotheby's. The glass had a round funnel bowl set on a stem with a multiple-spiral air twist cable, which was entwined by a bright canary yellow spiral thread and an opaque-white spiral thread.

I examined the picture in the Sotheby catalogue. The glass was indeed stunning, and it carried estimated prices that were quite high. John informed me that when it first came on the market, it brought the highest price ever paid for a color-twist. He added that this time it might bring an even higher price.

I thought to myself, "It surely is more beautiful than any AT&T or other stock certificate."

I had John bid on it, and we secured this yellow-twist masterpiece (Illustration 5).

The next color-twist I acquired from Asprey was one with ruby and yellow threads, circa 1765. Of impressive size, with what people in antique glass trade call a "bucket bowl," the stem was set with a corkscrew in yellow and white encircled by a pair of heavy spiral threads in translucent red (Illustration 6).

In 1985, at a meeting of The Glass Circle of England and Wales, a society of scholars, dealers and collectors of glass that meets periodically, I met Martine Newby. She was a glass expert who worked for Cooper and Shepherd, a firm of glass dealers. She was also curator of the impressive glass collection of the Ashmolean Museum, Oxford. She and I immediately became friends, and in 1998 she helped me write a catalogue of our glass collection (see Annex 3). Martine advised me that a glass similar to the one illustrated above as No. 6, perhaps from the same set, was in the George H. Lorimer Collection in the Philadelphia Museum of Art. I shortly thereafter visited the Philadelphia Museum to see their similar glass, as well as the rest of their small, but excellent, collection of English and American glass. The glass like mine was indeed beautiful, but there was one difference—its inner twist was pure white—not yellow, like mine.

2.4 | BEILBY

By 1985, Derek Davis had also introduced me to the work of the Beilby family. This family, led by William Beilby, enameled glass in Newcastle upon Tyne, in the north of England, between 1762 and 1782. Thanks to John Smith, and another dealer, Christopher Sheppard, I ultimately built up a major collection of Beilby glass, extending well beyond the drinking glasses usually seen in museums. By the time I retired from glass collecting, I had 21 Beilby's, the most in any collection (to my knowledge and that of Bonham's experts) except for the Lang Museum in Newcastle upon Tyne.

Towards the end of 1989, John Smith left Asprey and joined Mallett & Son Antiques on Bond Street, where he founded a specialist glass department. Mallett's was most famous for the beautiful (and costly) antique furniture they sold. I bought several important glasses from their inaugural

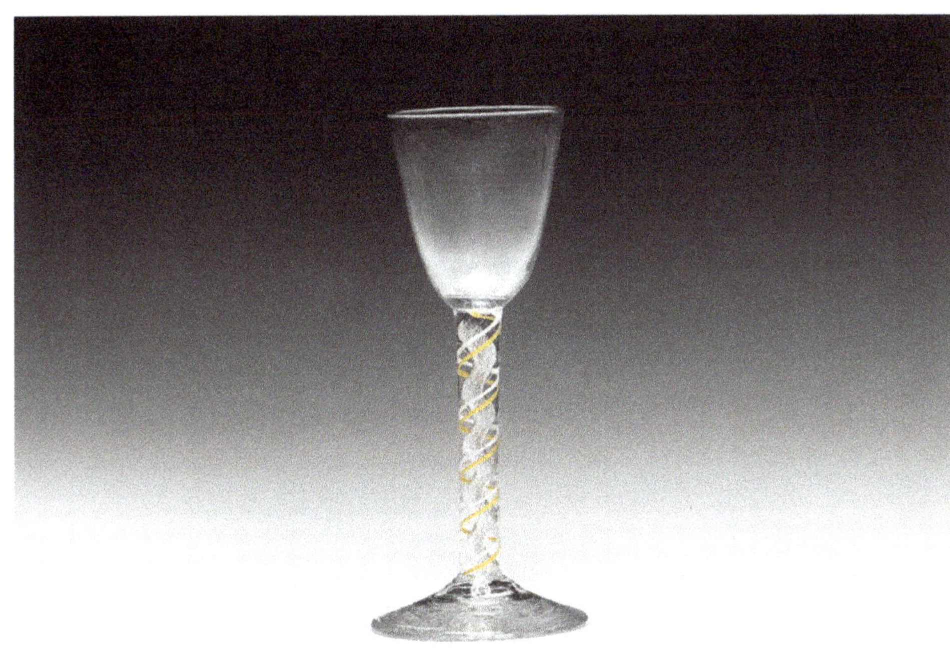

Illustration 5: Rare Mixed Canary Yellow Color-Twist Glass, circa 1765. Photo courtesy of Bonham's London. Julius and Ann Kaplan Collection.

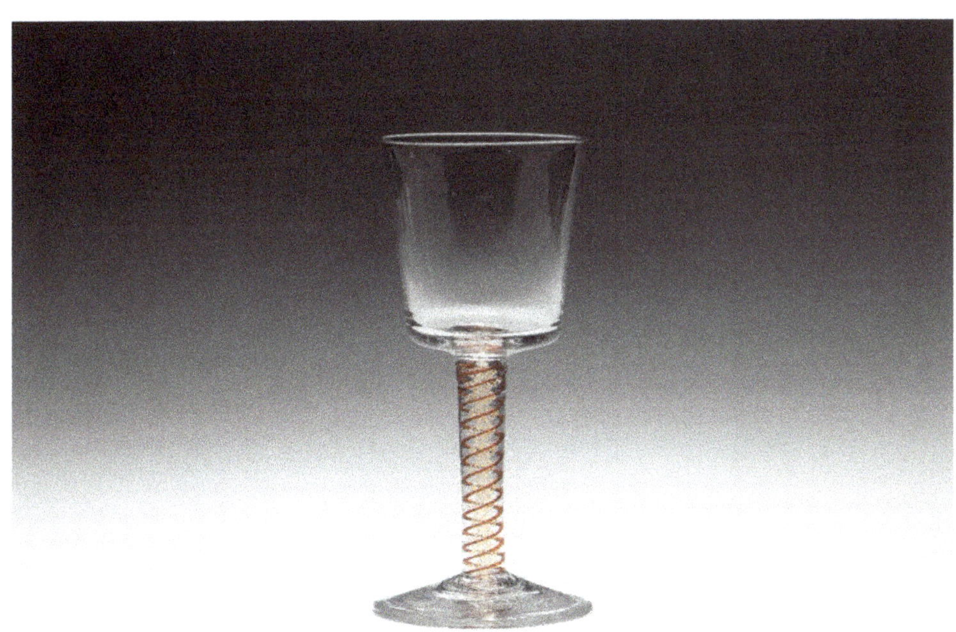

Illustration 6: Color-Twist Goblet with Ruby and Yellow Threads, circa 1765. Photo courtesy of Bonham's London. Julius and Ann Kaplan Collection.

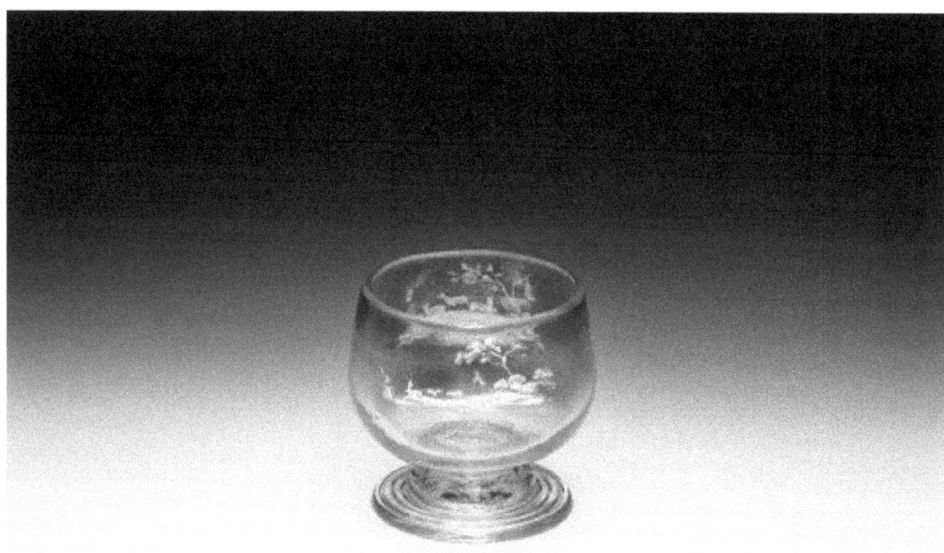

Illustration 7A: Beilby, Enameled Sugar Bowl, circa 1765. Photo courtesy of Bonham's London. Julius and Ann Kaplan Collection.

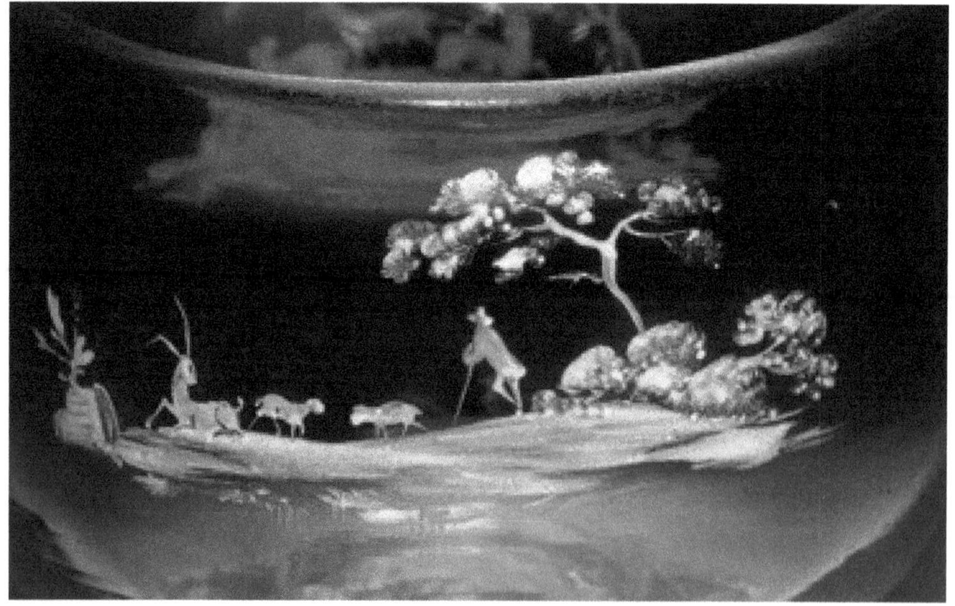

Illustration 7B: Beilby, Detail of Beilby Enameled Sugar Bowl. Photo courtesy of Bonham's London. Julius and Ann Kaplan Collection.

exhibition in May 1990 entitled "From Restoration to Regency." It was held in conjunction with Christopher Sheppard. Christopher went on to become a dear friend, as well as a major dealer of mine (See Annex 1).

John Smith thought that one of the stars of our Beilby collection was a sugar bowl decorated on both sides with rustic landscape vignettes (Illustrations 7 (A) and (B)).

There was only one other Beilby sugar bowl known, and it was in the Strauss Collection in The Corning Museum of Glass. Our bowl was decorated in white enamel with two pastoral scenes. The first was a shepherd leaning on his crook, under the shelter of a tree, while watching over a ram with very long horns and two ewes. On the far side, there were four sheep, three seated and one standing partly sheltered under a tree. They were all masterfully painted.

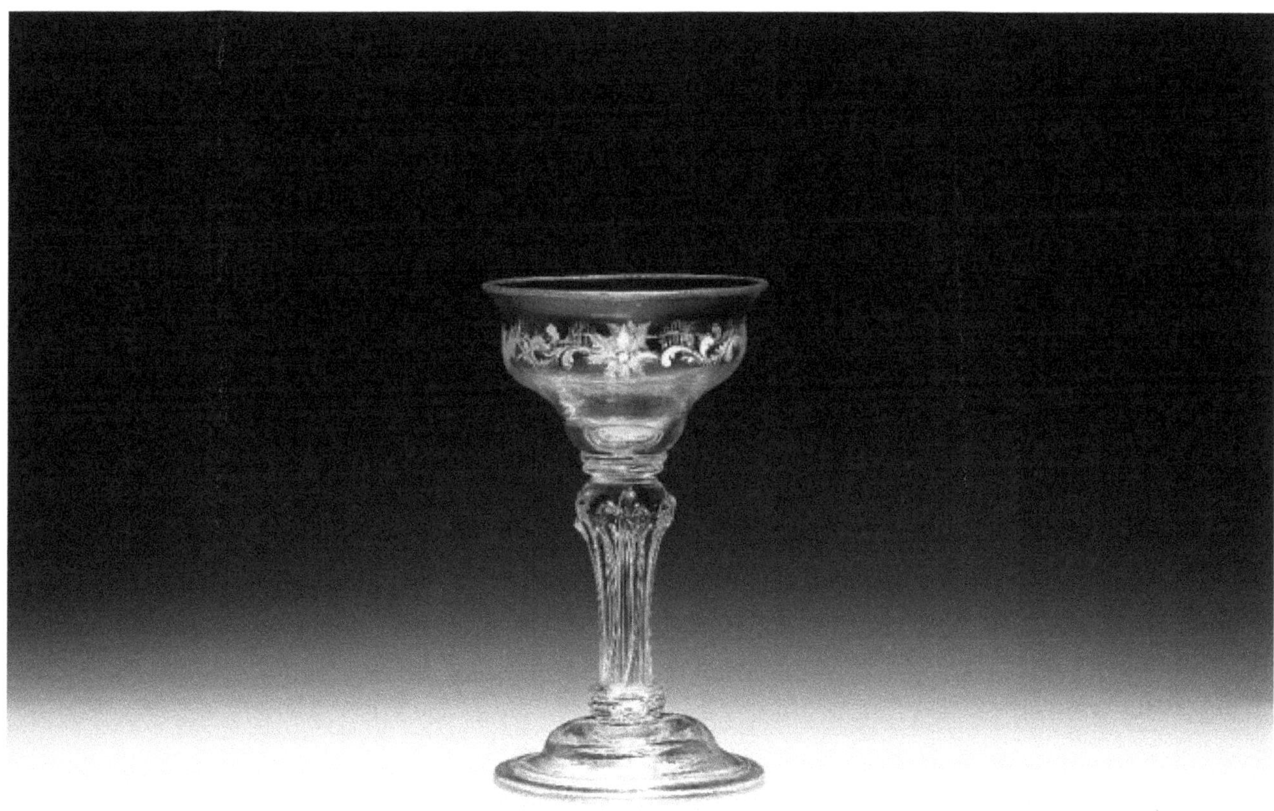

Illustration 8: Beilby, Rare Enameled Molded-Stem Sweetmeat Glass, circa 1765-70. Photo courtesy of Bonham's London. Julius and Ann Kaplan Collection.

Another work by Beilby in our collection was believed by John and other experts to be the only sweetmeat glass so far recorded with Beilby enameled decoration (Illustration 8). It was once in the famous Sir Hugh Dawson collection. The bowl was gilded at its rim and decorated with acanthus scrolls and sunbursts, and it had a molded eight-sided pedestal stem with diamond studs at the shoulder.

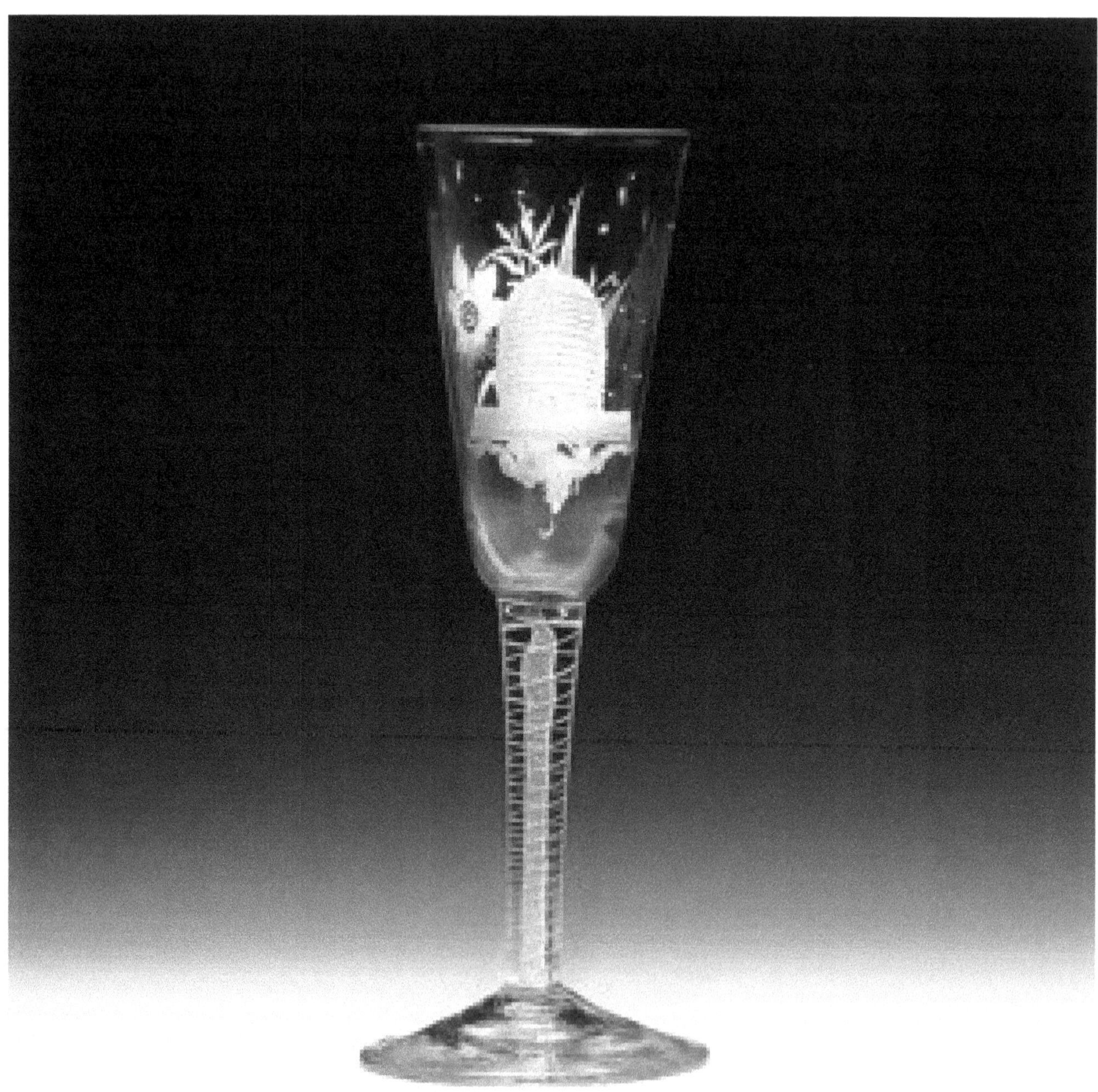

Illustration 9: Beilby, Enameled Ale or Mead Glass Decorated with A Bee Skep, circa 1765. Photo courtesy of Bonham's London. Julius and Ann Kaplan Collection.

One of my favorite Beilby glasses is an enameled ale (or Mead) glass decorated with a bee hive surrounded by flying bees, circa 1765 (Illustration 9). The stem is a complex tapering opaque twist stem. This was sold to me by Christopher Sheppard. I told him that it looked like an 18th-century champagne flute to me. So, we ordered a bottle of champagne and celebrated my acquisition of the glass by drinking an entire bottle from it.

Let us now examine a Beilby wineglass with a shooting scene done in 1765 (Illustration 10) and compare it with a flask with a very similar shooting scene presumably made by Beilby 10 years earlier (Illustration 11). The latter belongs to a small group of opaque white glass items probably made in a single workshop in South Staffordshire in the late 1750's. At that time, William Beilby was

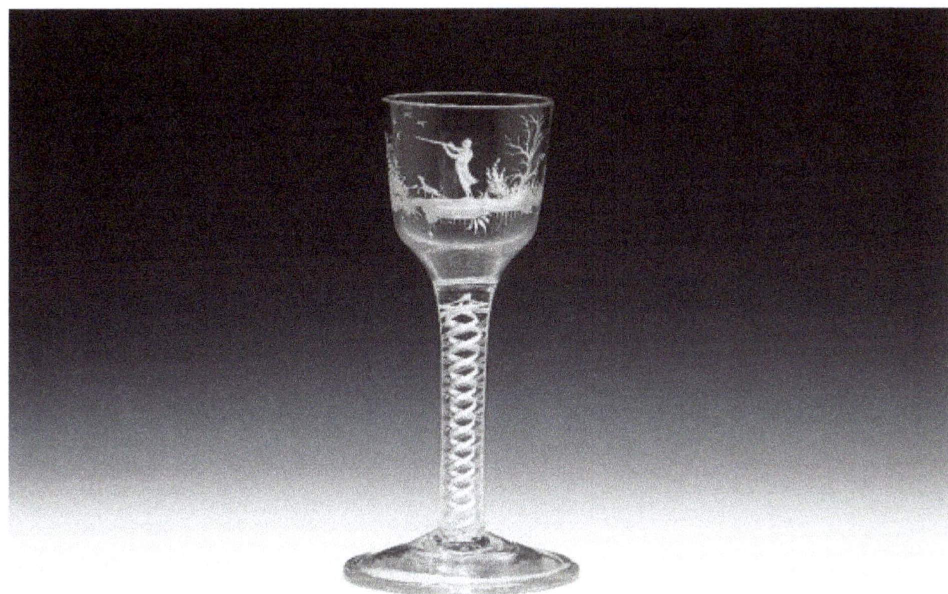

Illustration 10: Beilby, Shooting Scene, circa 1765. Photo courtesy of Bonham's London. Julius and Ann Kaplan Collection.

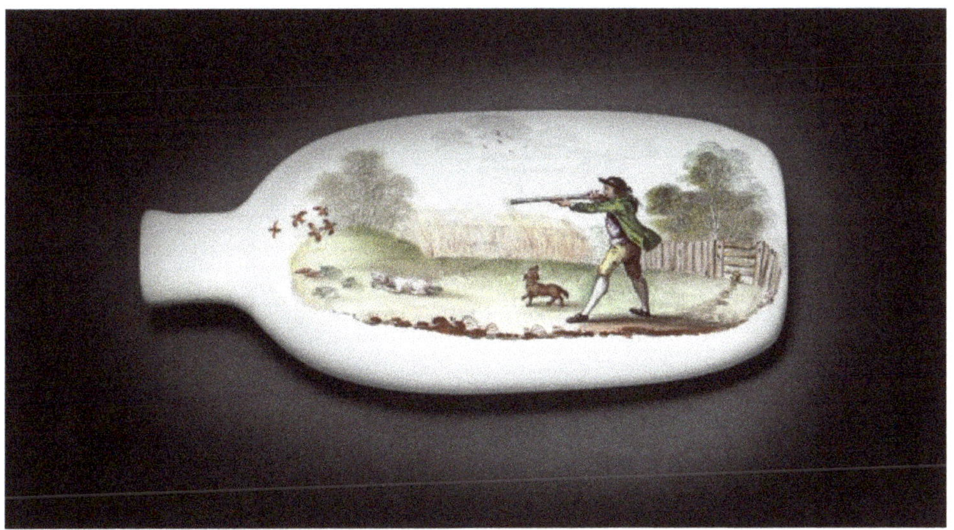

Illustration 11: Shooting Scene on White Glass Flask (attributed to Beilby), circa 1755-60. Photo courtesy of Bonham's London. Julius and Ann Kaplan Collection.

apprenticed to John Hazeltine, a copper box enameller from Birmingham. Christopher Sheppard believed that the painting on the flask was by the young William Beilby. He opined that it was painted before Beilby moved to Newcastle and started painting on clear glass. I bought the flask and displayed it next to the Beilby shooting scene done in 1765.

2.5 | BEILBY ARMORIAL GLASSES

Our collection also had two rare colored armorial glasses by Beilby. I, however, had to be content to buy restored examples of these two remarkable colored glasses. Fortunately, the repairs were not made on the front of the glasses, so the scenes depicted remain unobstructed. Most buyers shied away from these repaired examples, and as a consequence, they generally sold at a fraction of those in perfect condition. These two glasses had interesting stories attached to them.

Let us look first at the Beilby wineglass with a royal polychrome armorial (Illustration 12). The bowl was decorated with the coat of arms of William V, Prince of Orange (Holland) and of Princess Frederika Sophia Wilhelmina (the daughter of Prince Louis Charles of Prussia). The Prince and Princess were married in 1767, and this glass celebrated that marriage. There was a crown over the coats of arms, which showed that it was a "royal Beilby".

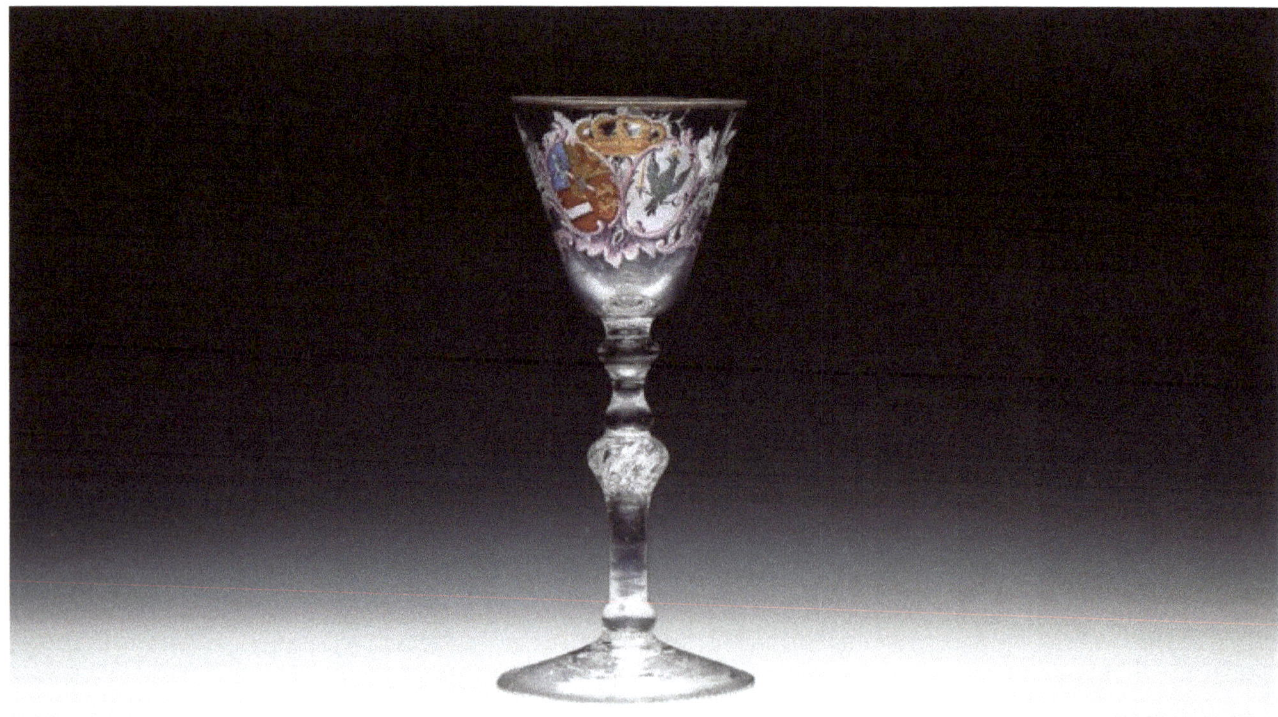

Illustration 12: Beilby, Enameled Dutch Royal Armorial Wine Glass, circa 1767. Photo courtesy of Bonham's London. Julius and Ann Kaplan Collection.

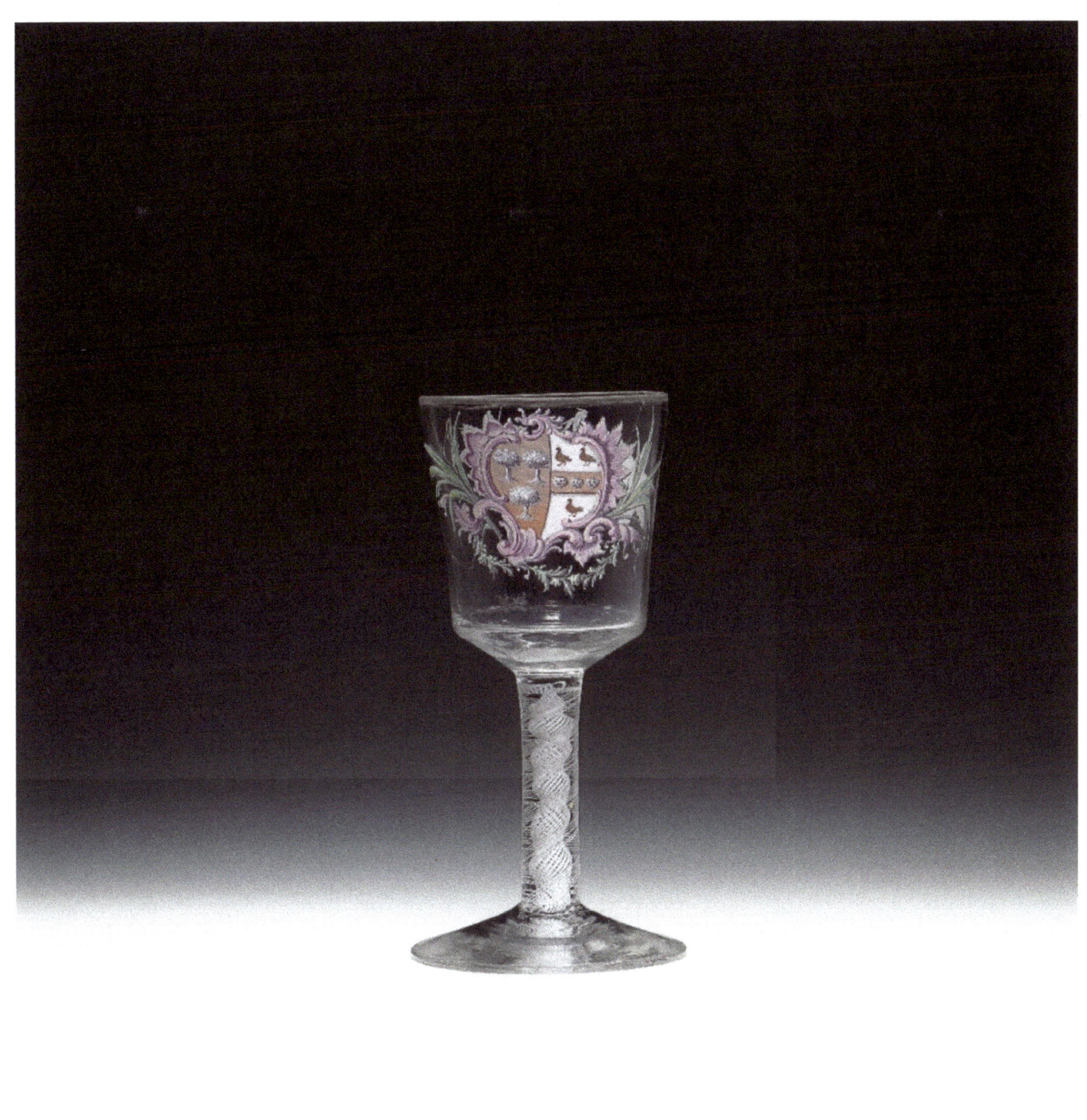

Illustration 13: Beilby, Enameled Polychrome Armorial Goblet, circa 1765. Photo courtesy of Bonham's London. Julius and Ann Kaplan Collection.

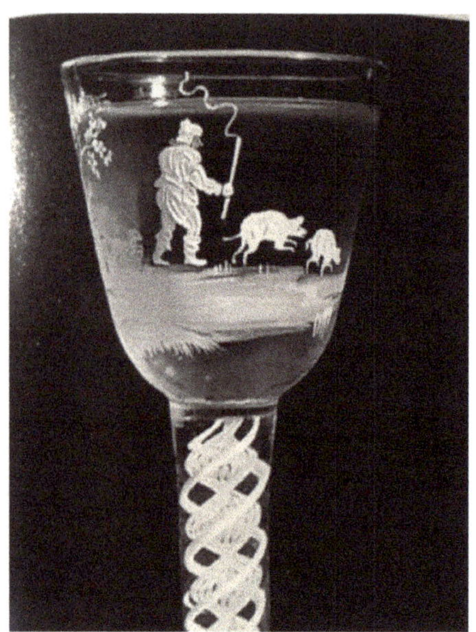

Illustration 14: Fake Beilby Glass, circa 20th century. Julius and Ann Kaplan Collection.

The second was a goblet with the arms of the Anderson and Consett families, which was made to celebrate the marriage of a member of each family (Illustration 13). Martine Newby observed that the Anderson arms were impaling those of Consett, which may have been an indication that Anna Anderson was an heiress, and her husband Mathew Consett took her name.

2.6 | A FAKE BEILBY GLASS

After Derek Davis and John Smith left Asprey, the company hired a gentleman I did not know to head the glass department. I bought one Beilby glass from him (Illustration 14), and paid 4000 pounds sterling for it. About ten years later, Simon Cottle of Bonham's, who is THE expert on Beilby, visited me in Washington. He asked me if I would take one glass out of the display case so he could look at it more carefully. After close examination, he asked me to bring the glass to London on my next trip, as he felt that it may not be right. I asked why. He noted that Beilby frequently gilded the rim of his work, but first, he slightly roughened the rim so the gilt would hold. He showed me that the rim of the glass in question was very smooth. The next time I went to London, I took the glass with me. Over a lunch at the Athenaeum Club, Simon, John Smith, Jeanette Hayhurst, and Christopher Sheppard passed the glass back and forth, each expert examining it with a magnifying glass. It was concluded that it was a fake!

Simon advised that, if it were not a fake, it would easily be worth 15,000 pounds sterling. I, of course, took the glass immediately to Asprey and explained the situation. The manager assured me that I would get a full refund, but he first had to clear it with his legal department. When I returned to D.C., I found a letter from the Asprey's legal department, advising me that in their legal opinion, I was only entitled to 4000 pounds sterling, the price I paid. I was about to respond in a polite fashion, when a lawyer friend of mine, Tom Mansbach, paid me a visit. He looked at my draft letter and said, "No, that is not the approach to take."

He then picked up a pen and paper and drafted an email "To the Director of Asprey Ltd. Mr. Julius Kaplan bought a glass from you ten years ago for 4000 pounds sterling, which today would be worth 15,000 pounds sterling, except for the fact that your company sold him a fake. As you are aware, Mr. Kaplan is a serious collector of English glass and is well known to the community of English collectors, many of whom are your customers as well. Now, do you really want the story of his losing 11,000 pounds sterling of appreciation because Asprey sold him a fake glass to become common knowledge to that circle of collectors - to the detriment of the reputation of Asprey? The full 15,000 pounds sterling please." A check for the full 15,000 pounds came in the next mail! Perhaps that explains why Tom is so much wealthier than I.

For those desiring to know more about the incredible Beilbys, I refer you to Annex 3, an essay entitled "Beilby Glass Recollected," written by Simon Cottle for the sale of our glass collection by Bonham's on November 15, 2017. Simon Cottle was previously the Director of the Lang Museum in Newcastle on Tyne. Simon was the glass expert and auctioneer both at Sotheby's London and at Bonham's London. He is now a senior Vice-President of Bonham's. I do not know of anyone with greater knowledge of Beilby painted glass than Simon.

2.7 | COLORED GLASS

Our collection of colored glass was limited, but only in number, not in quality. With the expert advice and strong encouragement of Christopher Sheppard, I fortuitously acquired two of the most desirable 18th-century English colored glasses that existed. One had a stunning blue bowl, with a blue foot and a clear twist stem. The other was a similar glass, but in green, with a green foot. The blue glass was the bigger star, due to its extreme rarity. It was made in 1760-1770. Only a few other examples with this color combination have been recorded. One is a slightly smaller wineglass, now in the Beves collection in the Fitzwilliam Museum, Cambridge. Another was sold at Sotheby's in 2002 (at over three times the price I paid for mine) and is now in the Durrington Collection. When we sold our glass collection, the price reached over six times the amount that I thought I had overpaid.

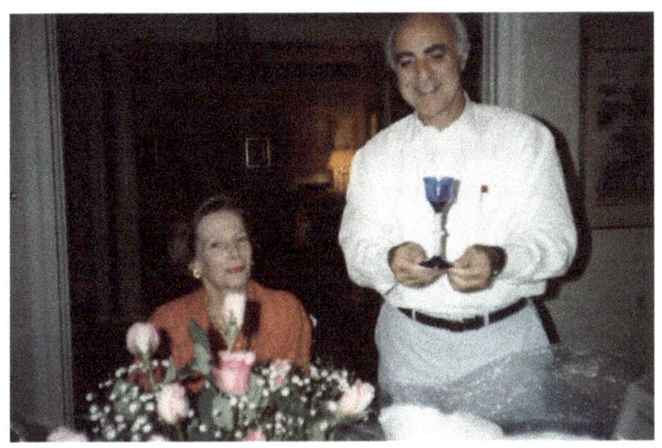

Illustration 15: The author unwrapping the newly arrived blue glass.

When Christopher first approached me with the blue glass, I told him that I simply could not afford it. He responded, "You cannot afford not to buy it."

He then added, "The glass world has always marveled over the beauty and rarity of this glass, and you should not pass up the opportunity to own it. Jay, I promise you that this is a glass you will deem to be a star of your collection."

I bought it (in lieu of yet another stock certificate), and I never regretted it. It was indeed one of the prize glasses in our glass collection. Here is a picture of me admiring my new acquisition, having just unwrapped the package that Christopher sent to me (Illustration 15). The blue glass itself is shown as Illustration 16.

Some years ago, this color combination became even more rare when an American customs agent accidently dropped one of the few remaining glasses and it smashed into too many pieces to reassemble.

The companion green glass also had a similar twist with a green bowl and foot (Illustration 17).

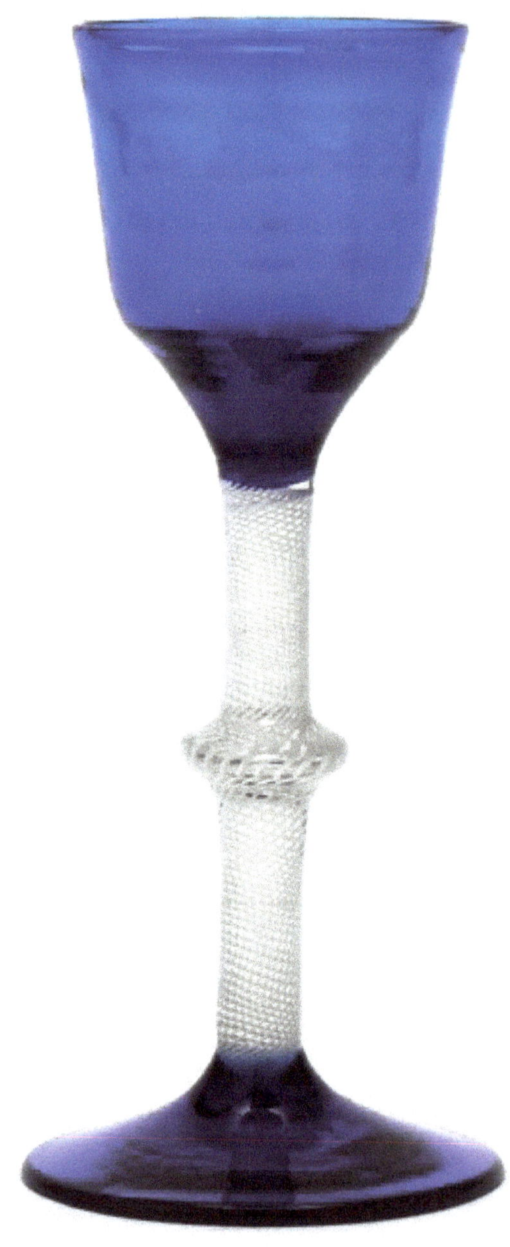

Illustration 16: Rare Opaque-Twist Wine Glass with Blue Bowl and Foot, circa 1765. Photo by Gregory R. Staley. Julius and Ann Kaplan Collection.

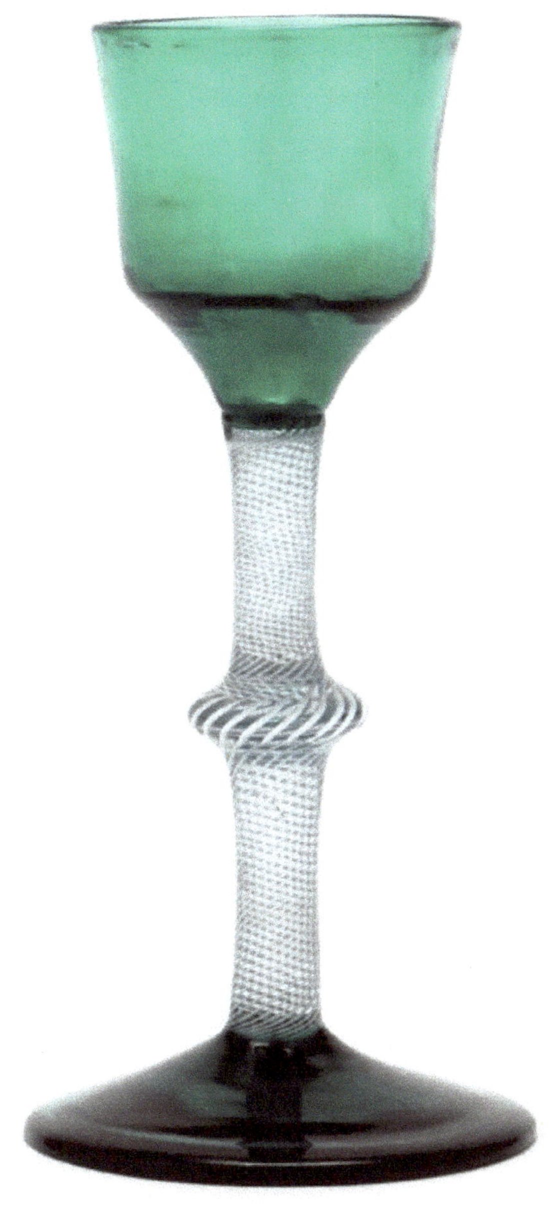

Illustration 17: Rare Opaque-Twist Wine Glass with Green-Tinted Bowl and Foot, circa 1765. Photo by Gregory R. Staley. Julius and Ann Kaplan Collection.

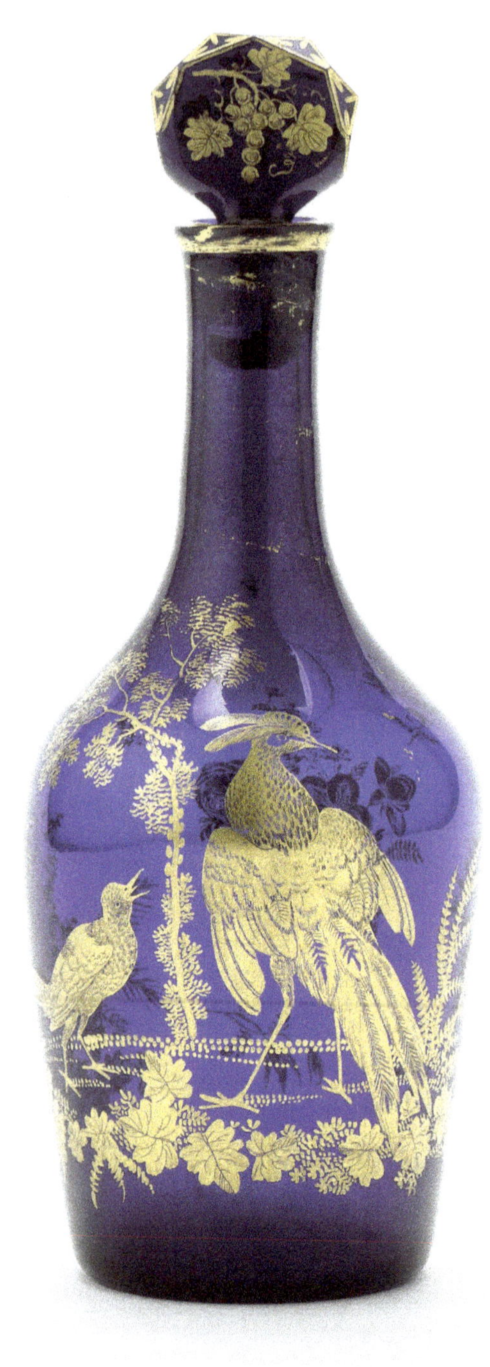

Illustration 18: Giles, Blue Glass Decanter and Stopper, circa 1760-1770. Photo by Gregory R. Staley. Julius and Ann Kaplan Collection.

At least six examples of the glass with a green bowl are known. They were probably made in the same glasshouse as the glass with a blue bowl. Martine Newby believes that the green glass is possibly more even in color, which is indicative of a better prepared and mixed batch. There are examples of the green glass in the Fitzwilliam Museum (formerly in the important Beves Collection), in the Cinzano Collection, two in the Durrington Collection, and one was in the collection of my friend, A.C. Hubbard in Baltimore.

Our collection also had a blue glass decanter and stopper with gilt decoration made by James Giles. It was circa 1760-1770 (Illustration 18).

Giles was a decorator of glass vessels who created gilt and enameled glass objects, such as decanters and drinking vessels. Ours was a club-shaped decanter with sloping shoulders in Bristol blue glass. The gilt Giles decanters often tend to show the effects of use through rubbing and even scratching against the gilt. This one, by contrast, was remarkable, almost as if it had just emerged from the atelier of James Giles in London in the 1760's. I bought it at Mallett's on the strong recommendation of John Smith.

2.8 | DUTCH STIPPLE-ENGRAVED GLASS

In the 1990's, I occasionally turned my attention to glass produced during the mid-18th century in Holland. Glass could be decorated on the surface by enameling or gilding, but the most lasting decoration method was to engrave the surface. This was often done with small rotating copper wheels, which continuously fed with wet abrasive powder. The other form of engraved decoration on glass in Holland was diamond point engraving. This, in turn, developed into a form of pointillism called stipple engraving.

For this technique, the surface of the glass was tapped with a diamond pointed instrument, leaving a stipple effect. This required great craftsmanship, allied with infinite patience. Only a few practitioners, such as David Wolff and the elusive *Alius*, obtained really superior results. John Smith opined that our glasses illustrated with the *Allegory of Amsterdam*, circa 1780 (Illustration 19) and *A Dutch Stipple-Engraved Topographical Goblet*, circa 1780-1790 (also referred to as *Country House*) (Illustration 20) were "as good as they come."[3]

There is an interesting story related to my acquisition of the great *Allegory of Amsterdam*. One day when I was in London, Christopher Sheppard called and asked what I was planning to do the next day. I said that I had no specific plans.

He replied,"You are now going to Amsterdam with me to see the single most beautiful Dutch stipple-engraved glass ever *chez* Frides Lameris, and we are leaving on BA flight 34 from Heathrow Terminal 5 tomorrow morning at 8:30."

---

3 The description of diamond stipple engraving was based on John Smith's *Introduction* to the *Catalogue of the Collection of Julius and Ann Kaplan*. Annex 3.

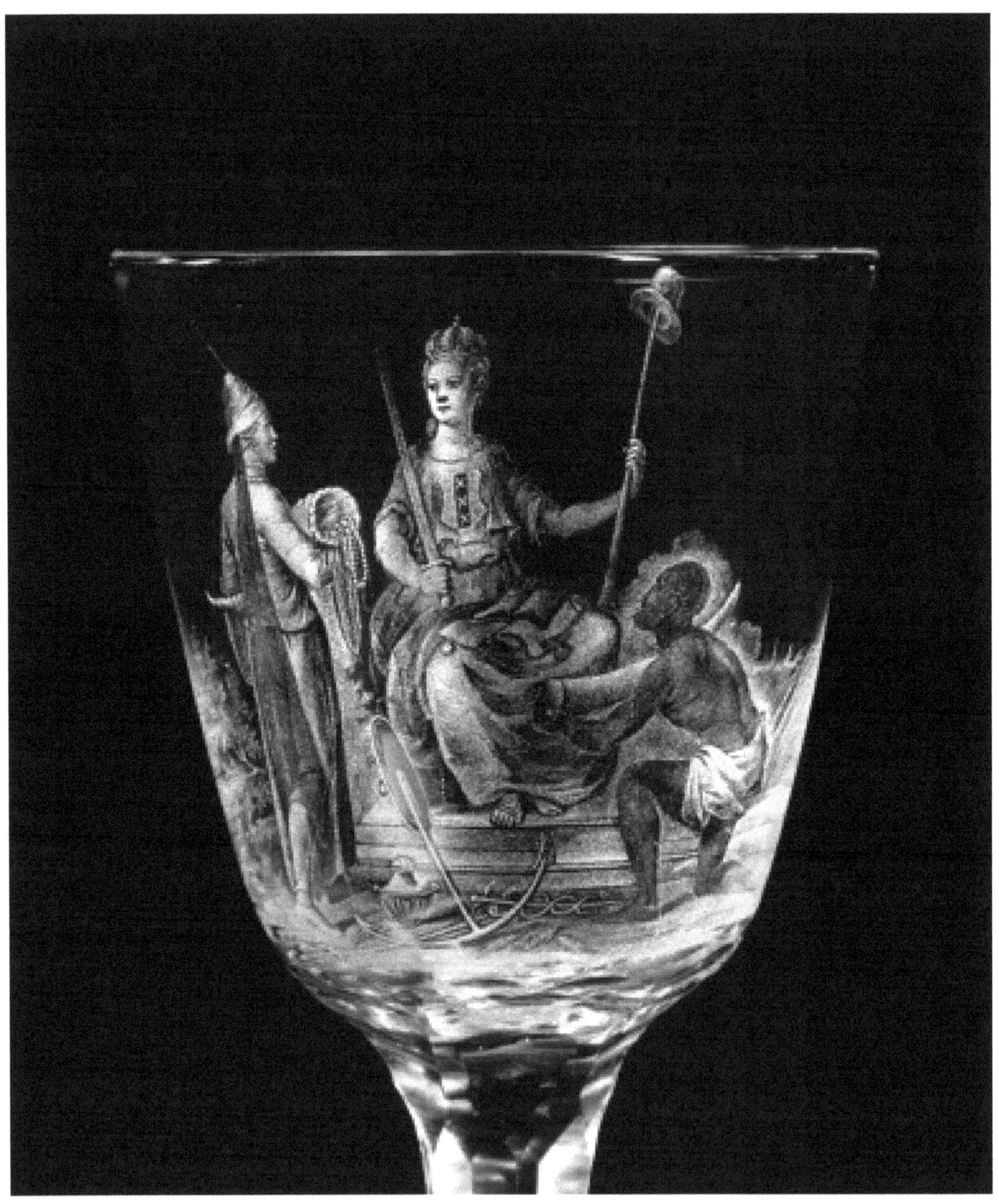

Illustration 19: David Wolff, *Allegory of Amsterdam*, 1780. Photo courtesy of Bonham's London. Julius and Ann Kaplan Collection.

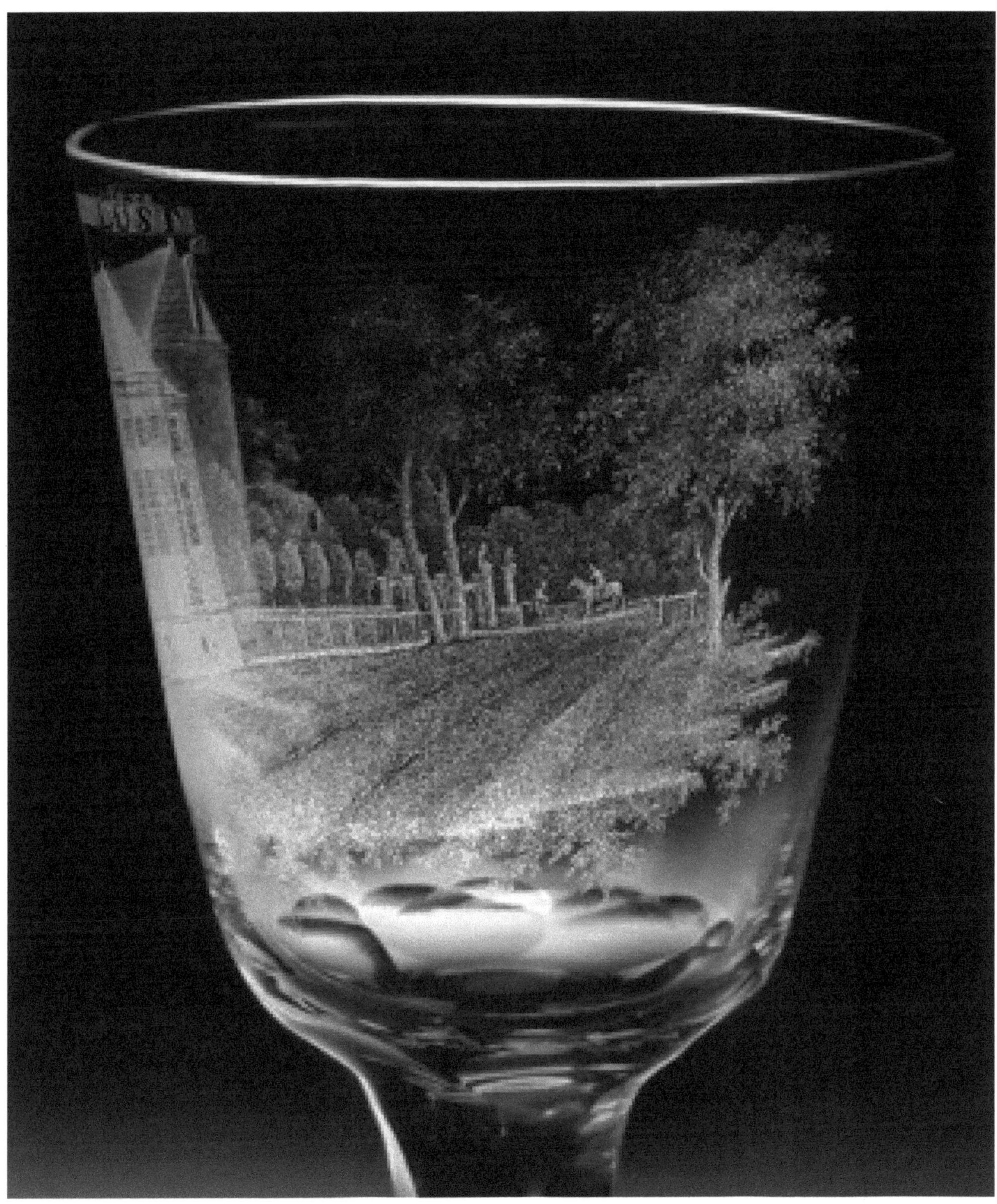

Illustration 20: David Wolff, Country House (side view), circa 1780-1790. Photo courtesy of Bonham's London. Julius and Ann Kaplan Collection.

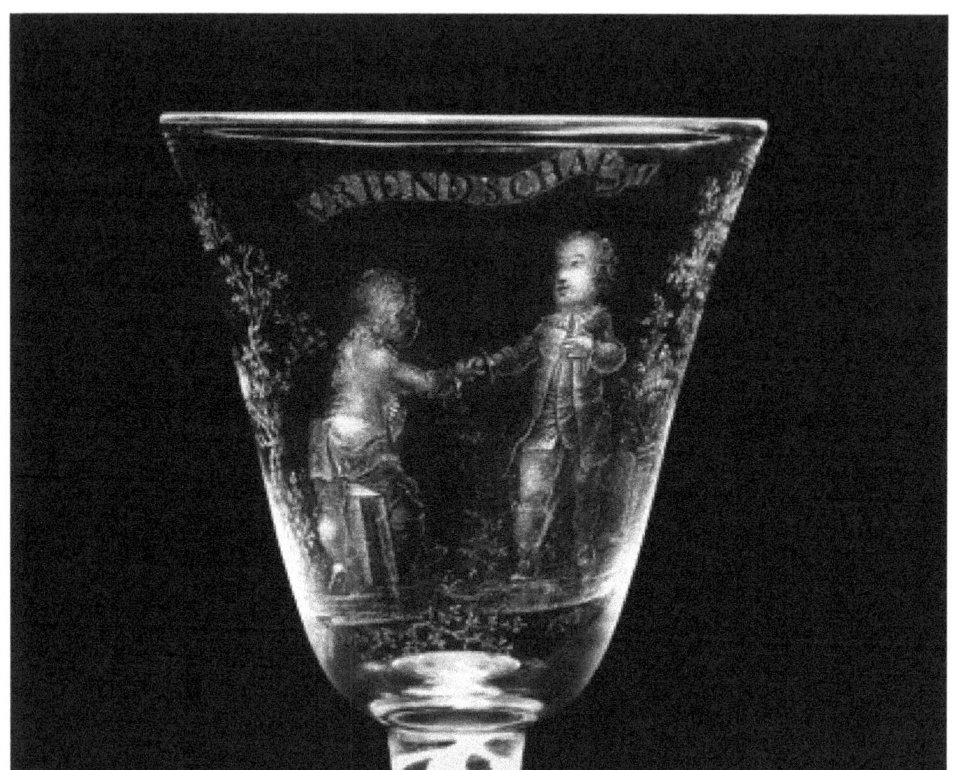

Illustration 21: Alius, Dutch Stipple Engraved Wine Glass Representing Friendship, circa 1770-1780. Photo courtesy of Bonham's London. Julius and Ann Kaplan Collection.

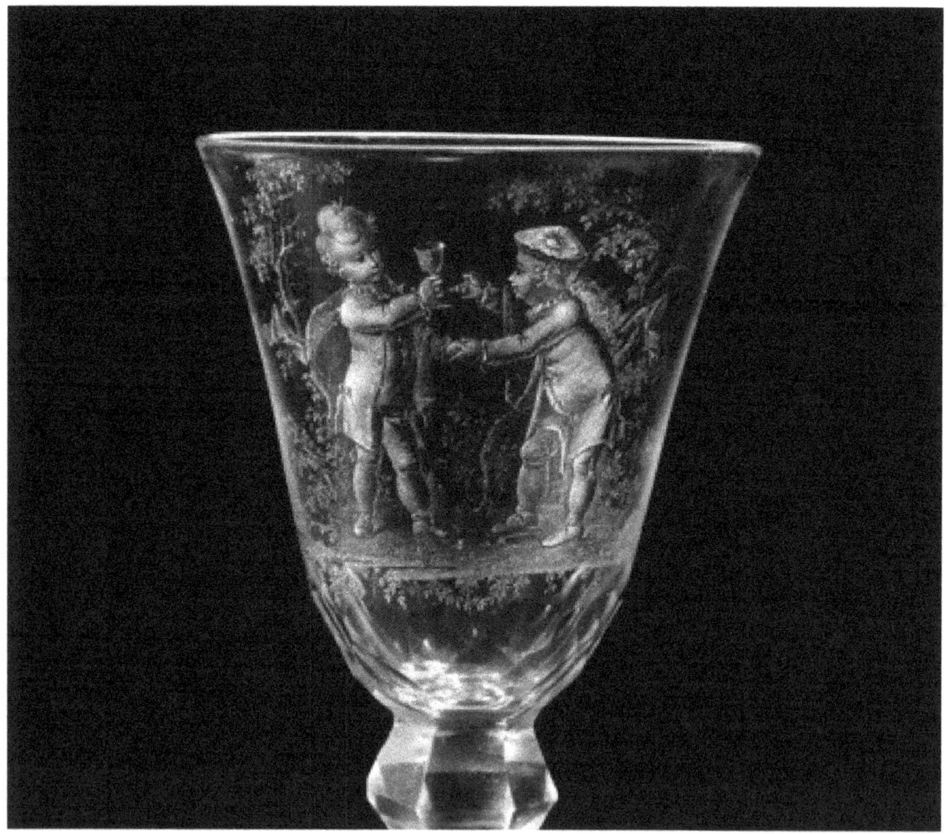

Illustration 22: Alius, Dutch Stipple Engraved Wine Glass, circa 1780. Photo courtesy of Bonham's London. Julius and Ann Kaplan Collection.

When we arrived, Christopher hailed a taxi and instructed the driver to take us to the Rijkesmuseum. I said, "But Christopher, I thought that we were going to the Lameris shop." He responded, "Don't worry. There is method in my madness." When we arrived at the Rijksmuseum, we were met by the Curator of Glass. Christopher told him, "Here is Jay Kaplan, the collector I told you about on the phone. He must be educated about Dutch stipple-engraved glass by seeing your collection, which is, of course, one of the best in the world. Please describe to him what to look for in truly fine stippled glass, so he can recognize the best."

We spent the next 2 hours studying the Rijksmuseum's collection. Christopher then came to fetch me and said that we were now going to the Lameris shop.

When we arrived Frides Lameris was busy unpacking a crate of wrapped glasses, which were from the estate of a bankrupt Dutch collector. Lameris had been hired by the court to do a catalogue for the sale of the glass, the proceeds of which were to be used to pay the collector's debtors.

As he unwrapped a large glass, the "Allegory of Amsterdam," he said, "This remarkable glass is attributed to the renowned David Wolff, but I do not think that even David Wolff was good enough to make this glass" (Illustration 19).

I took one look and could immediately see how finely the seated lady on a stepped dais was stipple-engraved. To her right, there was a black slave representing Africa, and to her left, there was a man with a conical hat representing Asia. Both were bringing offerings to the Princess. They were exceptionally well engraved.

Martine Newby wrote about this glass in the catalogue of our collection as follows: "This remarkable goblet is a tour de force attributed to David Wolff, especially in the treatment of the black slave." She noted that it is the only known example decorated with the personification of Amsterdam.

When Christopher and I left Amsterdam with the Princess carefully rewrapped, he said, "Jay, you may now own the most important Dutch stipple-engraved glass in existence."

Let us next look at a remarkable Dutch stipple-engraved topographical goblet by David Wolff, circa 1780-90 (Illustration 20).

John Smith thought the "Country House" that I acquired from Frides Lameris in 1996, and attributed to David Wolff, was in the same league as the "Allegory of Amsterdam." He was fascinated by the finesse of the engraving of the man in the background, perhaps the owner, conversing with a gentleman on a horse. We always displayed the glass so that this scene was most prominent. The front of the glass pictures a country house with the words "VRYHEIDS" (the name of the house) above it.

Our collection also contained two lovely "friendship" Dutch stipple-engraved glasses by 'Alius.' (The maker is unknown and has simply been referred to as "Alius" for many years.) One of the "Alius" glasses was an Opaque-twist representing "friendship." (Illustration 21).

This glass had two chubby boys in contemporary dress shaking hands while holding their other hands to their breasts. The banderole above is inscribed VRIENDSCHAP (Friendship). This glass was formerly in the collection of Richard, Earl of Bradford, Weston Park. Richard was a school mate and dear friend of Christopher Sheppard and a friend of mine.[4]

The second friendship glass by "Alius" was a facetted wineglass with two boys in contemporary dress transferring a wine glass from one to the other. c. 1770-1780 (Illustration 22). My friend Richard Bradford also once owned this glass.

Finally, the collection had a lovely wine glass with a galloping horse stipple-engraved by David Wolff, circa 1780. It had a banderol above inscribed "AUREA LIBERTAS." Wolff's treatment of the mane and tail of the horse was similar to the only two other glasses he engraved with a horse, both of which are in the Riksmuseum, Amsterdam.[5]

Our glass had a replacement faceted stem and circular foot. I had bought the glass with a wooden stem, and Martine Newby offered to design a stem and foot to resemble what was originally on the glass. I agreed. Ann felt that it should have had a gold band where the reproduced stem fitted on to the original bowl to demonstrate that the stem and foot were added. She was correct.

2.9 | CONCLUSION

In the Forward to this book, I stated that one of the great benefits of collecting is the other collectors and museum people you meet. Two of them were my main dealers, the late John Smith and Christopher Sheppard. In Annex 1, I have written a Moratorium honoring these two dear friends. In Annex 2, there is a short description of some of our fellow collectors and friends. Other material related to our glass collection are found in Annex 3-4.

Collecting 18th-century English and Dutch glass was a most meaningful experience. We displayed our collection in the second-floor landing and the dining room. I could not walk into the dining room without stopping to admire some of the glasses. This would inevitably lead me to recall the circumstances surrounding their purchase. It enriched our lives. It was a most successful search for beauty.

---

4 A year after the death of Christopher, Richard and I celebrated Christopher's birthday in his favorite Italian restaurant and we sat at Christopher's favorite table. We were joined by Richard's wife, Penny, who is a physician. Richard wrote a delightful book on the trials and tribulations of owning a stately home and being an English aristocrat entitled "Stately Secrets, Behind-the-scenes stories from the stately Homes of Britain."

5 The glass is pictured in Sheppard and Smith, *Engraved Glass Masterpieces from Holland* (1990), p.83, No. 44

CHAPTER 3

Chinese Art

3.1 | INTRODUCTION AND SUMMARY

I attribute my early interest in Chinese culture to my sister Jean, who exposed me to Chinese culture and cuisine at an early age. Indeed, she took me to Ruby Foos Chinese Restaurant every Saturday from the age of 6 for a good number of years., and often then to the Freer Gallery of Art. She and her late husband, Manny Sulkes, later collected Chinese jade works of art. I would occasionally go to New York with them to visit Chinese art dealers.

My collecting began with Chinese art soon after my securing a position with the Kennedy Administration in 1961. My government salary did not then permit me to collect works that would be of interest to serious collectors or museums. I was, nevertheless, driven to buy the best I could afford and learn as much about Chinese art as I could fit into a busy lawyer's schedule. My interest in things Chinese also extended to Chinese cuisine. For 23 years, I was a part owner of a Chinese restaurant called The Empress. I always believed that great Chinese cuisine was another side of Chinese art.

I began my collecting of Chinese art with blue-and-white porcelain. We next purchased some pieces of Chinese furniture inexpensively from a friend of Ann's mother who was moving to a retirement home. My partner, Rob Parker, who managed our firm's office in Taipei, and who was also a collector of Blue-and-white, introduced me to Song dynasty (960-1279) wares and in particular, Jun ware, also called Jun Yao. A Hong Kong dealer, Susan Chen, who became a friend, introduced me to Tang (618-907) wares. A Chinese Minister of Foreign Affairs introduced me to the Han dynasty (206 BC - 220 AD).

I must underscore that my collection of Chinese art is hardly Chinese art at its finest (except for a couple of pieces which have been promised to the Freer-Sackler Gallery), and I do not offer it as such. This reflects the fact that my collecting occurred early in my career. When I started to earn enough money to make more serious purchases, very wealthy Japanese and some mainland Chinese were getting into the market. As a result, prices of fine examples of Chinese art became too expensive for me.

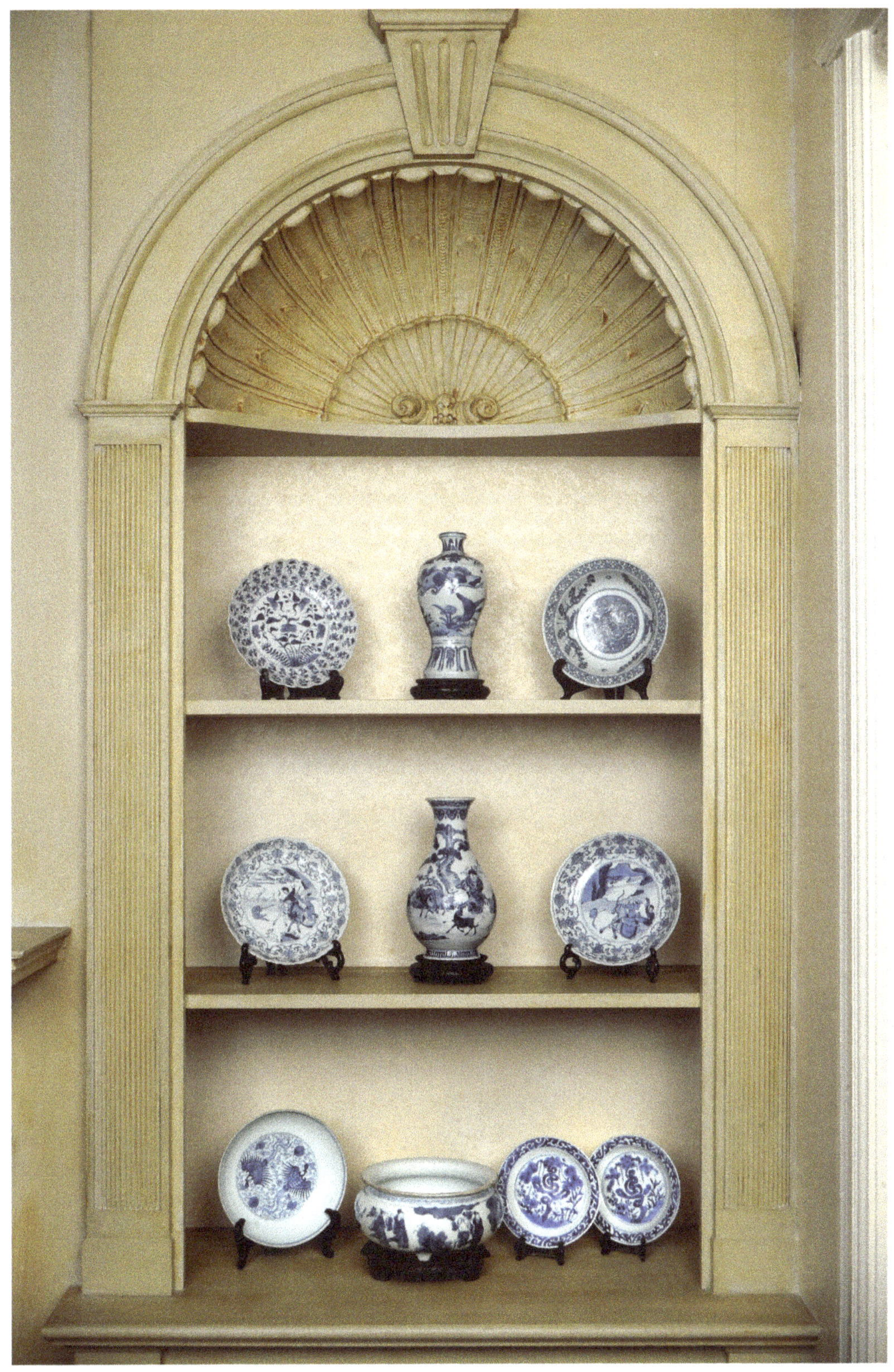

Illustration 1: Collection of Chinese Blue-and-white porcelain in the author's home. Photo by Gregory R. Staley.

3.2 | BLUE-AND-WHITE

When I became an international lawyer in the Kennedy Administration in 1961/2, my foreign legal assignments required frequent trips abroad, and many were to or through London. Just a few steps from my London hotel, there was a highly regarded dealer in Asian art named Sidney Moss. I visited this haven for fine Chinese ceramics on virtually every visit to London. I soon became particularly attracted to their Chinese porcelain painted with cobalt oxide under a colorless glaze, which is known as blue-and-white ware. This stunning type of porcelain was of Chinese origin.

Cobalt is one of the pigments that can withstand the very high firing temperatures that are necessary for porcelain. Blue-and-white porcelain reached great sophistication in China starting in the later years of the Yuan dynasty (1279 to 1368) and, I believe, reached its pinnacle, qualitatively speaking, in the first half of the 15th Century, in the Ming dynasty (1368-1644). It is still made today in China and in other countries.

After a number of visits to Sidney Moss, I decided to start a collection of Chinese Blue-and-white porcelain. My plan was to buy one piece on each trip to London. By doing this I would be able to build up a small collection slowly over time, which I did after about nine visits. Having relatively limited financial means as a young government lawyer, and, almost non-existent knowledge, I relied upon the expert advice of the salesmen at Sidney Moss. The Blue-and-white I bought was late Ming dynasty and Qing dynasty (1644 – 1911). Now, decades and decades later, I realize that these salesmen did not lead me astray. Although I could only afford to buy the least costly objects, they turned out to be of enduring interest. The Blue-and-white porcelain I purchased from Sidney Moss are in a cabinet in our living room (Illustration 1).

During one of my trips to London, an occasion arose that encouraged me to examine the different types and qualities of Blue-and-white porcelain more closely. *Par hazard*, I discovered the incredible Percival David Foundation of Chinese Art. It was then housed in a building which was a part of the University of London. (It is now in Room 95 of the British Museum.) The Foundation's main purpose was to promote the study and teaching of Chinese art and culture. The collection consists of some 1,700 pieces of mostly Song, Yuan, Ming and Qing dynasties porcelain from the 10th to 18th century. Its collection of Blue-and-white (and virtually every other type of Chinese porcelain) is substantial and of top quality.

A catalogue of the collection was then available for students and visitors. As I was admiring the beauty of a certain piece of Blue-and-white, I opened the catalogue and, much to my surprise, it described the item (let us call it Number 1437) as being inferior to other examples, such as Number 1533. The catalogue pointed out that the latter piece was painted with a rich cobalt blue imported from Persia, while item 1437 was less expertly painted with an inferior domestic cobalt. Likewise, item 1256 was vastly superior to 1330 because of the quality of the brush strokes. I looked at each of the superior pieces and compared them with the inferior ones, but simply could not perceive any significant difference! I told myself that since this was a university collection and the catalogue was written to instruct students, it had to be taken seriously. I was determined to study the Blue-and-whites in the collection until I could discern at least some differences between the lesser examples and the superior ones. I had intended to spend an hour in the museum, but I ended up spending the rest of the day, as well as a good part of the following day. After this effort, I realized the catalogue was not jesting, and I started to detect qualitative differences between and among the Blue-and-white porcelain on display.

Once I returned to Washington, I became a frequent visitor to the Freer Gallery of Art (which is now the Freer Gallery of Art and the Arthur M. Sackler Gallery, and together these form the Smithsonian Institution's national museums of Asian art) to examine their collection of Chinese art, including important examples of Blue-and-white porcelain. Their collection is justifiably renowned.

Blue-and-white remained my favorite Chinese *objets d'art* for some years. I also read about its history. The place of origin of this color-scheme was probably Iraq. Craftsmen in Basra attempted to imitate imported white Chinese stoneware with their own tin-glazed, white pottery and added decorative motifs in blue glazes that had been developed by preexisting Mesopotamian cultures. Such Abbasid-era "Blue-and-white" pieces have been found in present-day Iraq dating to the 9th century A.D.

Blue-and-white decoration first became widely used in Chinese porcelain in the 14th century, after the cobalt pigment for the blue began to be imported from Persia. Chinese Blue-and-white porcelain was widely exported, and it inspired imitative wares in Islamic and Japanese ceramics, and later European tin-glazed earthenware such as Delftware. After the techniques for making porcelain were discovered in Dresden in the 18th century, European porcelain was born. Blue-and-white pottery in all of these traditions continues to be produced, most of it copying, or re-interpreting earlier styles.

I am often asked what period of Blue-and-white I prefer. I lean towards the Blue-and-white of the first half of the 15th century, particularly those made during the Yong-le (1409-1424) and Xuande (1426-1435) periods. During these were periods imported cobalt blue was employed, resulting in very deep and rich tones. Moreover, during these periods the painting was exceedingly well executed. However, one of the greatest authorities on Blue-and-white, John A. Pope, formerly director of the Freer Gallery of Art and author of *Chinese Porcelain from the Ardebil Shrine*, wrote, "...for sheer perfection in every detail, the best Blue-and-white wares of Ch'eng-hua [1456-1487] stand in a class by themselves." I will certainly not take issue.

3.3 | CHINESE FURNITURE

In the mid-1980's, we learned that Annette Wattles, a dear friend and neighbor of Ann's mother, was moving to a retirement home which would require her to sell, among other things, her dining room set. It consisted entirely of Chinese furniture which she and her Navy Admiral husband had carefully selected in China many years before. (She also had a lovely collection of Amari plates, but they were not for sale.) Ann and I immediately agreed to buy some of the furniture which would be appropriate for our dining room, plus a couple of benches formerly used for sitting at Mrs. Wattles large dining room table, with large Ming dynasty chairs at each end. A visitor from Sotheby's thought that the furniture was of the Qing dynasty. Illustrations (2) (A)(B) and (C)

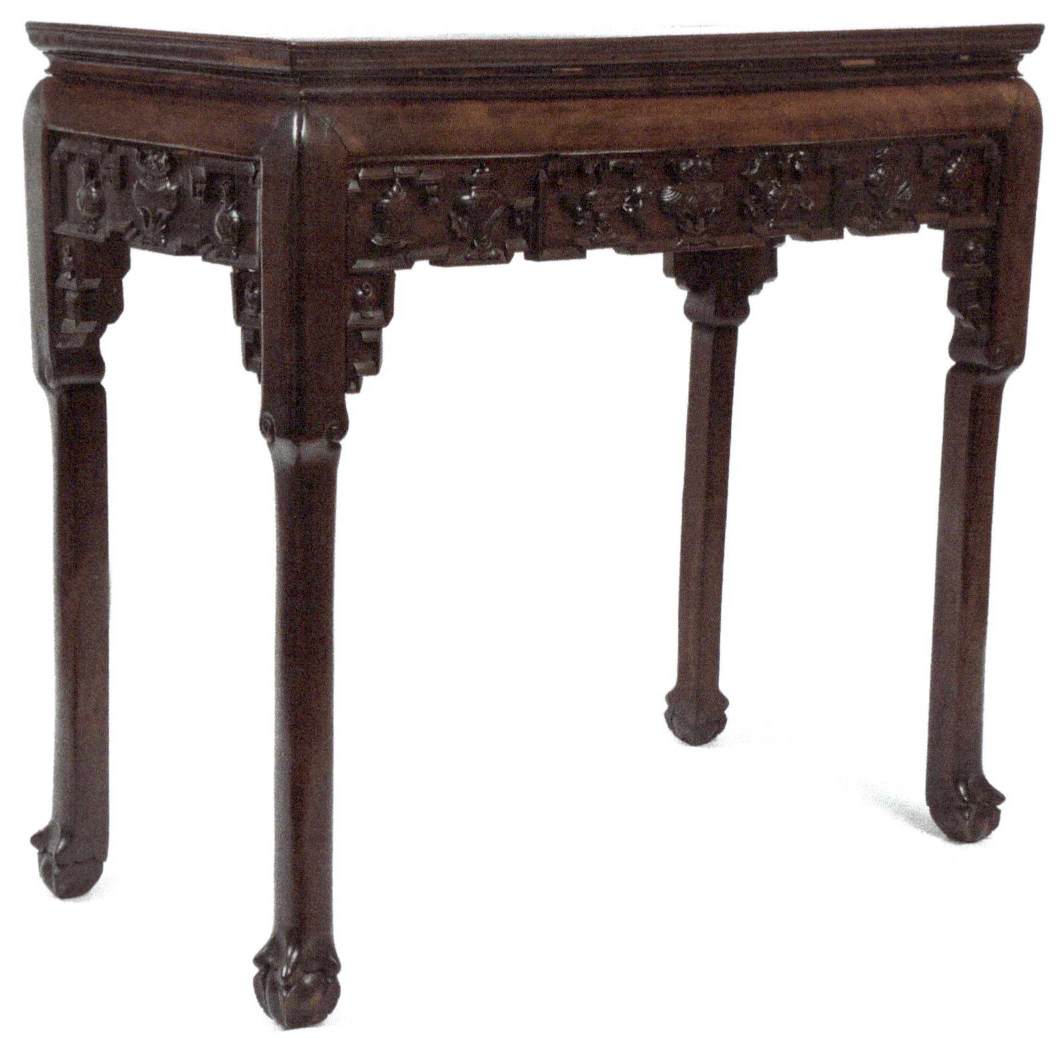

Illustration 2A: Table, Qing Dynasty. Photo by Gregory R. Staley. Julius and Ann Kaplan Collection.

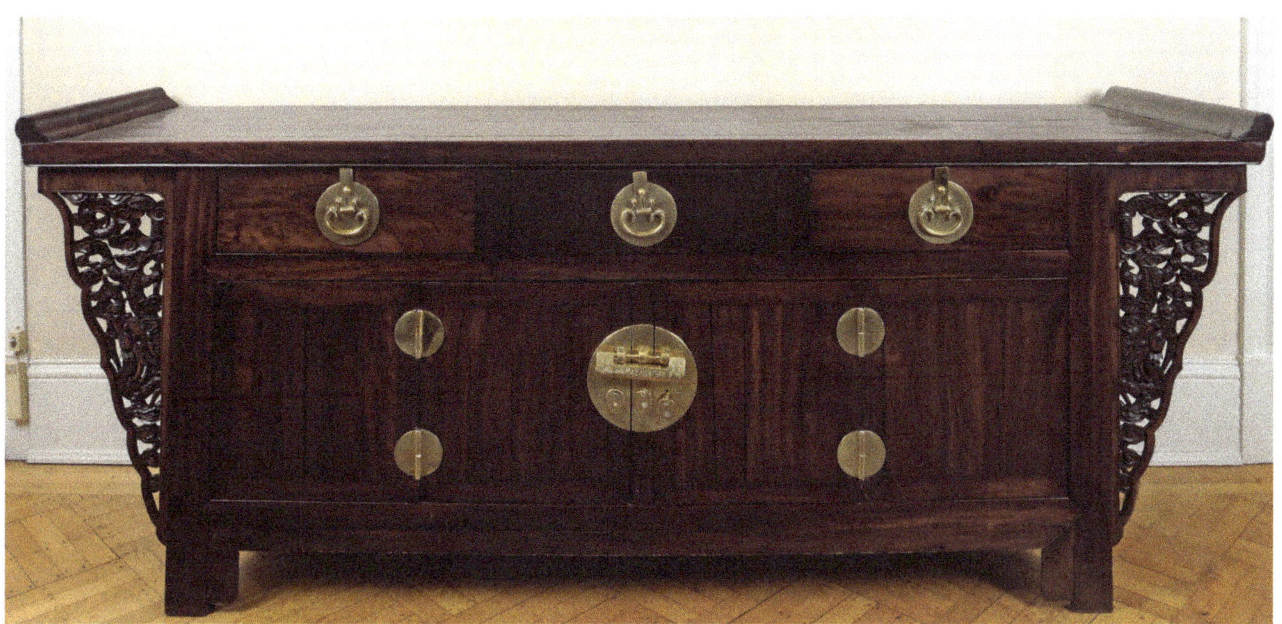

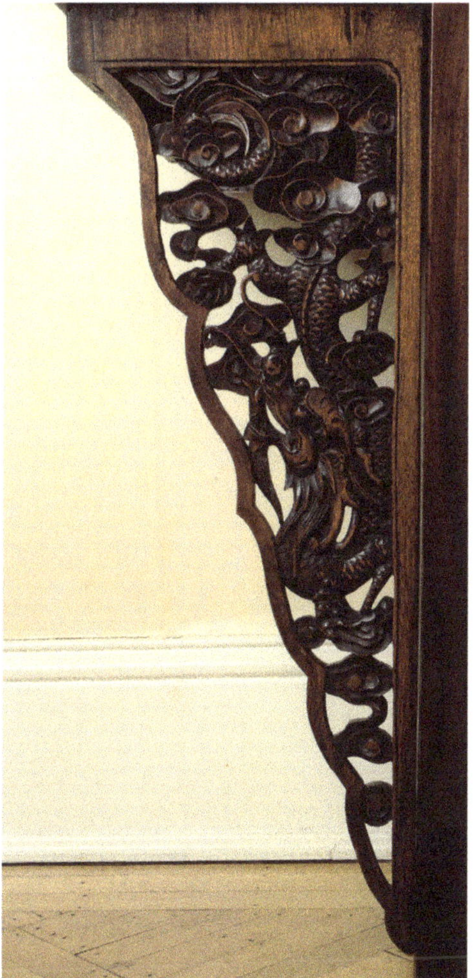

Illustration 2B:Coffer table, Qing Dynasty. Photo by Gregory R. Staley. Julius and Ann Kaplan Collection.

llustration 2C: Detail of Coffer table (2B), Qing Dynasty. Photo by Gregory R. Staley. Julius and Ann Kaplan Collection.

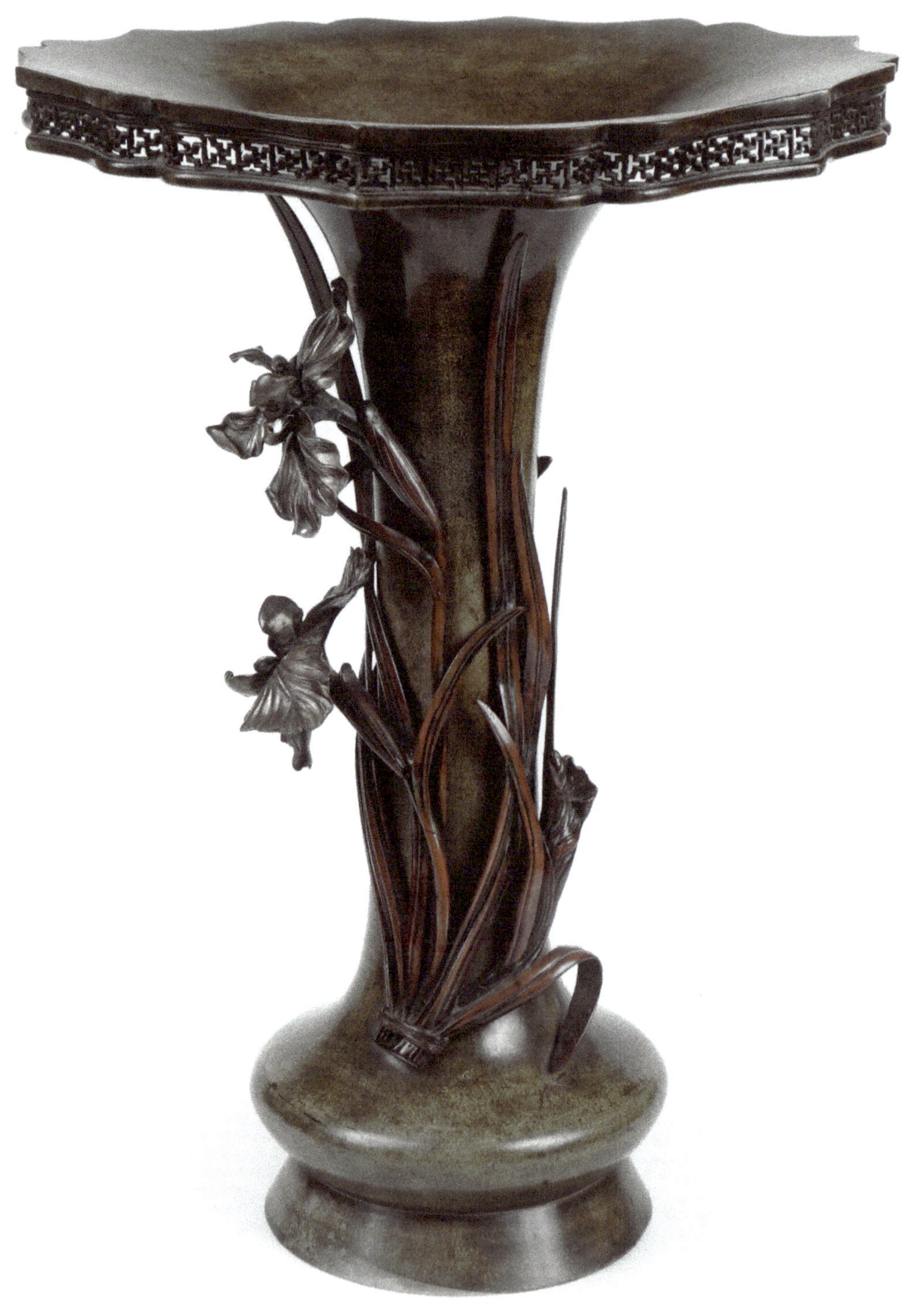

Illustration 3: Japanese Vase, circa 1905. Photo by Gregory R. Staley. Julius and Ann Kaplan Collection.

I appreciate that this is a chapter on China; however, I could not resist digressing a bit and reproducing what I believe is a beautiful Japanese bronze vase that resides amidst the Chinese furniture in our home. Some decades ago, I went to a show of Asian antiques to look at Chinese art. My eye, however, caught what I thought to be an art nouveau Japanese bronze vase. The salesman said that it was made in 1905. (Illustration 4) It has been standing on a Chinese table for so long that it now may be said to have dual nationality. Indeed, it may even be Chinese! I asked a Japanese friend to translate the signature on the base of the vase. She (and her Japanese friends) concluded that it was a Chinese character! To complicate the issue, Jan Stuart, a Curator of the Chinese Art at the Freer-Sackler Museum, advised me that Japanese artists sometimes signed their work with a Chinese character. Notwithstanding the Chinese character, Jan Stewart advises that it is indisputably Japanese. (Illustration 3)

With our purchases of furniture from Mrs. Wattles, my curiosity about Chinese furniture grew. This led me to discover the comprehensive collection of Chinese furniture in the Nelson-Atkins Museum of Art in Kansas City, Missouri. The Museum was a pioneer among American museums in the collecting of Chinese furniture, and is famed for its Ming and early Qing hardwood furniture. It also has important collections of other genres, such as paintings, of Chinese art.

At the Nelson-Atkins I discovered that huanghuali, a highly regarded member of what is often translated as the rosewood family, was a beautiful wood. The finest huanghuali has a translucent shimmering surface with abstract figured patterns that the Chinese have found for centuries to be pleasing to the eye. When I am in a museum which has Chinese furniture, I always look for this beautiful wood. I eventually learned to recognize it almost at a glance. But I could only look. Furniture made of this wood was always beyond my means.[6]

In addition to the furniture discussed above, I also had a cabinet made in Hong Kong. I caused the doors to be inlaid with antique Chinese wood carvings I had previously bought. The cabinet was designed to "hide" our television set in the living room. Such cabinets were then most popular in France where they were called "cache téléviseurs" (literally television hiders.)

3.4 | SONG WARE

In 1979 and the 1980's, I frequently visited our law firm's office in Taipei. The office was opened in late 1978 by my partner and friend, Rob Parker, who managed it for years. To prepare Rob for running that office, we hired a teacher of Mandarin to come to our offices in D.C. and introduce Rob to the fundamentals of the language. By happy coincidence, Rob also had an interest in collecting Chinese art. He, like me, had begun his foray into the field with Blue-and-white. Rob, however, had also discovered the beauty of Song dynasty ceramics, and was starting to buy Jun Yao—a ware which usually was pale blue, and often with a purple splashes. Rob encouraged me to examine the beautiful ceramics of the Song.

---

6 My ability at a private brunch to recognize the host's Ming dynasty table made of huanghuali wood happily opened the door for me to a happy lawyer/client/friend relationship with Dr. Arthur Sackler (as in the Freer-Sackler Museum). This relationship is described in Chapter 5 of *Secrets and Suspense*.

To teach me more about the breadth and depth of both Chinese arts and the Song dynasty's ceramics, when in Taipei, I visited, and often revisited, the National Palace Museum, located in Shilin, near Taipei. It has a permanent collection of nearly 700,000 pieces of ancient Chinese imperial artifacts and artworks, making it one of the largest of its kind in the world. The collection encompasses 8,000 years of Chinese art, from the Neolithic age to the modern. Much of the collection consists of treasures collected by China's emperors.

The National Palace Museum shares its roots with the Palace Museum in the Forbidden City, whose extensive collection of artwork was built upon the imperial collections of the Ming, Qing and earlier dynasties. When Generalissimo Chang Kai-shek retreated from the mainland to Taiwan, he brought with him much of the imperial collection. It contained so many important works of art that he had a mountain hollowed out to store them, and parts of the collection not displayed in the museum are stored there to this day; as well as displayed in the southern branch of the National Palace Museum. Art in storage is rotated for items in the museum on a quarterly basis. To see the entire collection, one must visit the museum once every quarter for 17 years! I visited the museum frequently, but certainly not enough to see the entire collection!

My visits to the National Palace Museum were certainly educational as well as aesthetic. But the most memorable learning experience in Taiwan was when Rob arranged for me to visit the home of, according to him, "the most important private collector of Chinese art in Taiwan, if not, in all the world." Let us call him Mr. Lin. Also invited were Rob's friend, Wang Xieu ying, who was a curator at the National Palace Museum, and Li Xiu ying, who was a major dealer in Chinese art in Taiwan. Of course, Rob was there too.

I expected, upon entering Mr. Lin's home, to see cabinets of Chinese art everywhere, and walls hung with Chinese paintings. But there was absolutely nothing on display. We were instructed to sit at a round table that had a lazy Susan on it. When all of us were assembled, Mr. Lin rang a little bell. One of his staff then brought out a work of Chinese art from Mr. Lin's vast collection. The game plan was for Mr. Lin to describe the art brought out, and then the guests were to examine the work closely, and make such observations about the work of art as each saw fit.

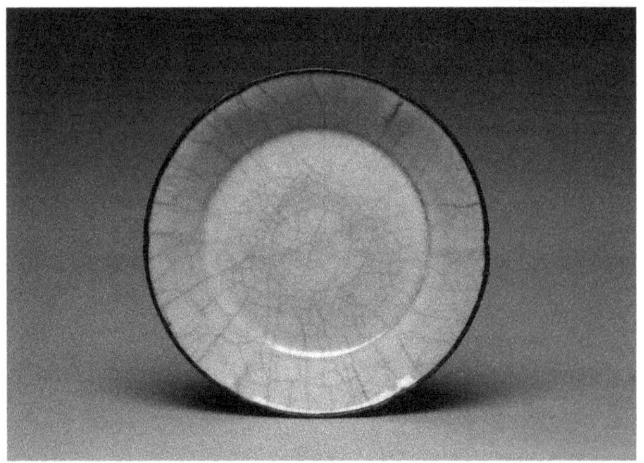

Illustration 4: Ru Ware Dish, late 12th–13th century. The Metropolitan Museum of Art, New York, Fletcher Fund, 1924.

The first was a simple shallow bowl which Mr. Lin identified as Ru ware. Ru ware, or Ju ware, is an extremely rare type of Chinese pottery from a brief period of the Song dynasty around 1100. It was produced for the imperial court exclusively, and, according to Mr. Lin, fewer than 100 complete pieces survive. He noted that most, like his, have a distinctive pale "duck-egg" blue glaze, "like the blue of the sky in a clearing amongst the clouds after rain." (Illustration 4)

Mr. Lin said, "Ru ware is perhaps the first "official ware" specifically commissioned by the imperial court. Production ended when, or shortly before, the kilns were occupied by invaders who overthrew the Northern Song dynasty in the 1120's. The wares have remained famous and highly sought after."

Rob asked if Ru ware ever came up at auction. The answer was "with great rarity." (I recently learned that a Ru ware bowl had been sold recently at auction for $28 million.)

Mr. Lin next caused his assistant to bring out another rare example of Song ware. It was a Jun Yao bowl. He explained that "Jun Yao" was made in one of the Five Great Kilns of Song dynasty ceramics. Some of the wares were popular, especially the drinking vessels, but others seem to have been made for the imperial court, and are known as "official Jun wares". The one before us was an official Jun Yao.

Before the session ended, Mr. Lin turned to me, and asked if I had any comment! I replied that I had seen some Ru ware in Mr. Wang's National Palace Museum, but also in the Percival David Collection in London, the Victoria and Albert in London, and the Philadelphia Museum of Art. Mr. Lin smiled, and said, "Mr. Kaplan, you have a good memory of the fine Chinese art you have seen. You will be a very good collector of Chinese ceramics."

I later learned that Mr. Lin included a Jun Yao in the evening's study group for my sake since I had been admiring Rob's small collection, and I told Rob that I was then ready to start collecting this ware. Rob told me that some beautiful Jun Yao was available in Hong Kong.

I was then visiting Hong Kong with some frequency. An important Hong Kong client of mine, Sir Lee Ka-shing, had a deputy chairman, George Magnus, who was a collector of Chinese art. He introduced me to his favorite Chinese art dealer in Hong Kong, Susan Chen. She was perhaps one of Hong Kong's most serious art dealers. I visited her shop frequently over the course of years. Indeed, she and I became good friends.

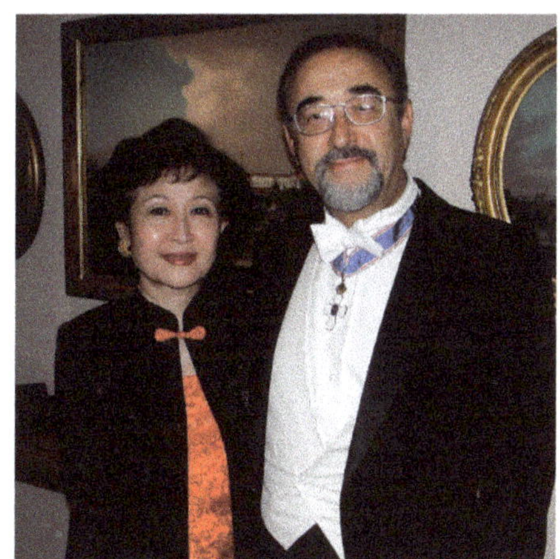

Illustration 5: Susan Chen and Anthony Hardy. Photo courtesy of Hong Kong Maritime Museum.

Susan, herself, was a major collector of ancient Chinese bronzes. Her collection, together with that of her husband, Anthony Hardy, was at one time on display at the Hong Kong Museum of Art. Susan's sister lived near Washington, D.C. and Susan would visit me whenever she came to see her sister. Here is a picture of Susan and Anthony on the occasion of the opening of Anthony's Hong Kong Maritime Museum. (Illustration 5)

During one of many visits, I bought a small Jun Yao bowl from Susan. It was pure blue without any purple splashes. (Illustration 6) This beautiful bowl was the first Jun Yao bowl I ever purchased. It was circa 1981.

I later learned that an identical bowl is in the collection of the Art Institute of Chicago. On my next trip to Hong Kong the following year, I had the good fortune of finding chez Susan a larger Jun Yao bowl which was also pure blue. (Illustration 7)

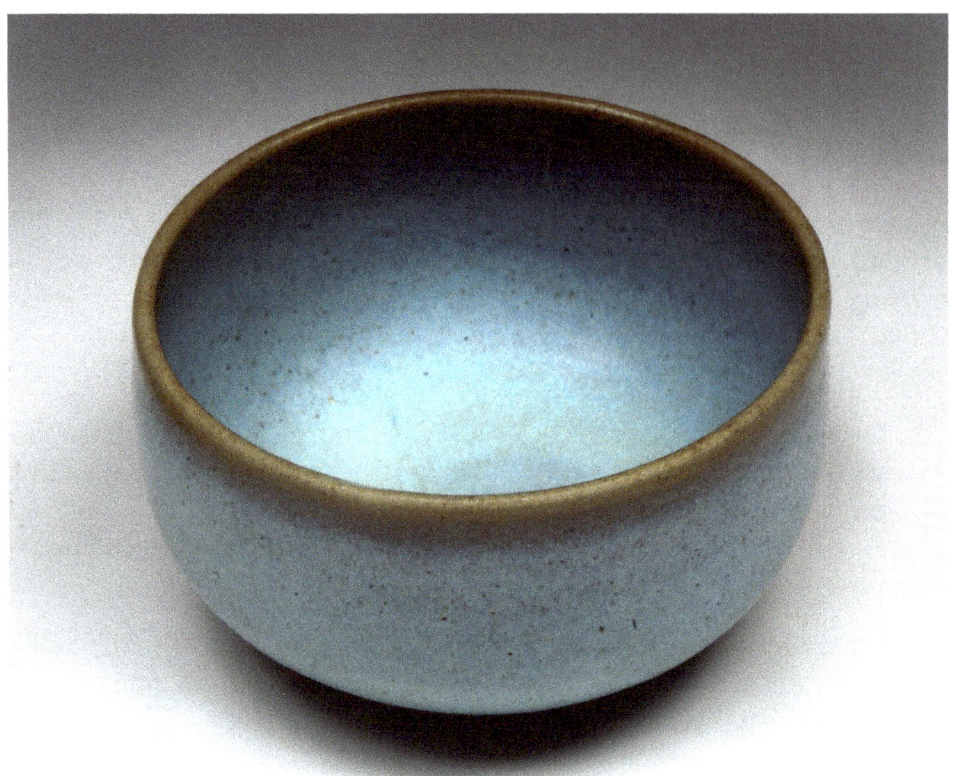

Illustration 6: Jun Yao, Northern Song dynasty. Photo by Gregory R. Staley. Julius and Ann Kaplan Collection.

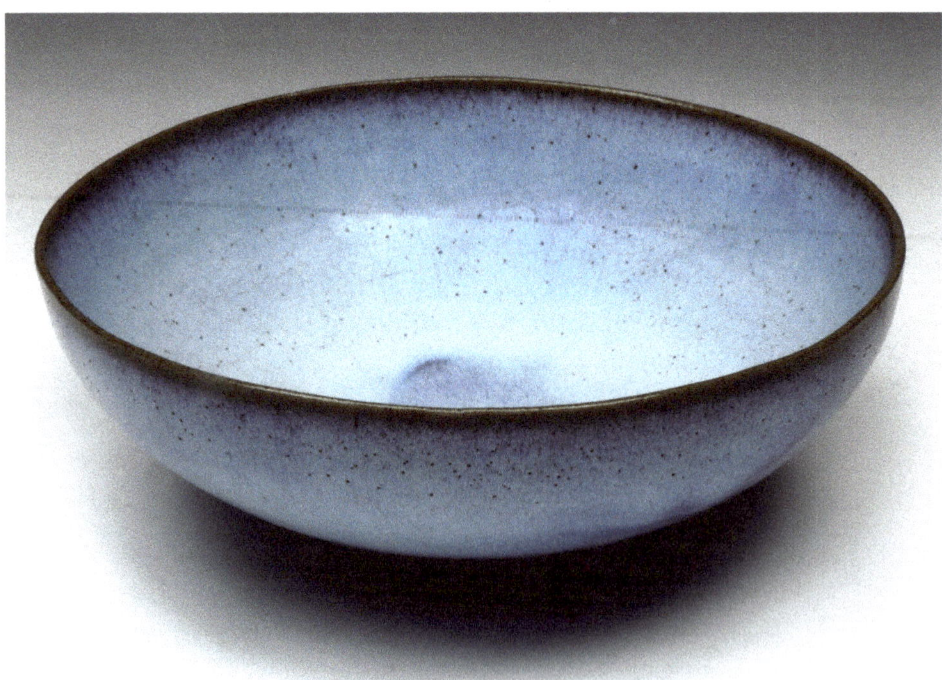

llustration 7: Jun Yao, Song dynasty. Photo by Gregory R. Staley. Julius and Ann Kaplan Collection.

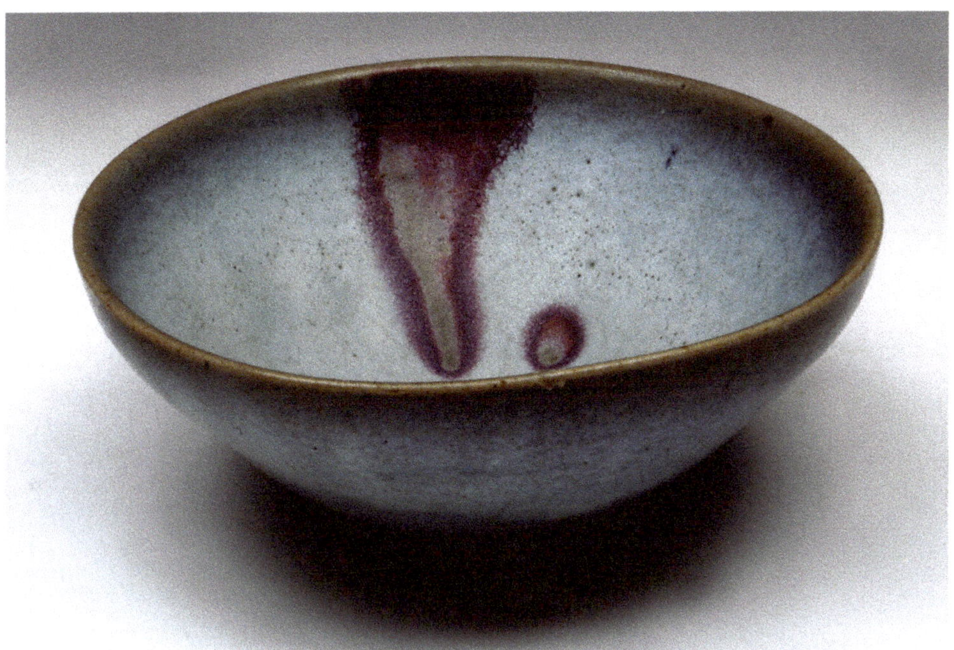

llustration 8: Jun Yao, Northern Song dynasty. Photo by Gregory R. Staley. Julius and Ann Kaplan Collection.

After these purchases, I was determined to buy a Jun Yao bowl with purple splashes. The one I found was perhaps not as fine as the earlier ones I had purchased, but it was quite a nice one with a purple splash (Illustration 8).

Over the years, I bought other Jun Yao wares, some Song and some Ming. These later Ming purchases are not as prized as the Northern Song and Yuan wares, but they are still lovely, and reasonably priced. Allow me to show you my small collection of Jun Yao (Illustration 9).

I also acquired many pieces of carved malachite, mostly animals, in Hong Kong! This arose in a curious fashion. In Hong Kong there were no fixed prices for Chinese art, so one always had to negotiate a final price. With several dealers, when I believed that their offer was the lowest I could negotiate, I would tell the dealers that I would accept their offer only if they threw in a malachite animal sculpture. I soon had a malachite menagerie.

I had a curious, and most memorable, experience with one Hong Kong art dealer. I received a call one day in the mid-1980's from Rob Parker who told me that he heard from a reliable source in Taipei that a certain dealer in Hong Kong, from whom I had bought two Jun bowls, was having dire financial problems. This had allegedly motivated him to try to maximize his return by selling works of art that were "not right," but at the price of the proper ware. For example, he would say that a Ming dynasty Jun Yao was of the Northern Song dynasty. (Ming Jun Yao are less desirable than those of the Northern Song, and meaningfully less costly.)

Rob said, "I just remembered that you bought two small Jun Yao bowls from that dealer. Jay, bring them to Taipei on your next visit so we can have them examined by my friend Mr. Wang, who, as

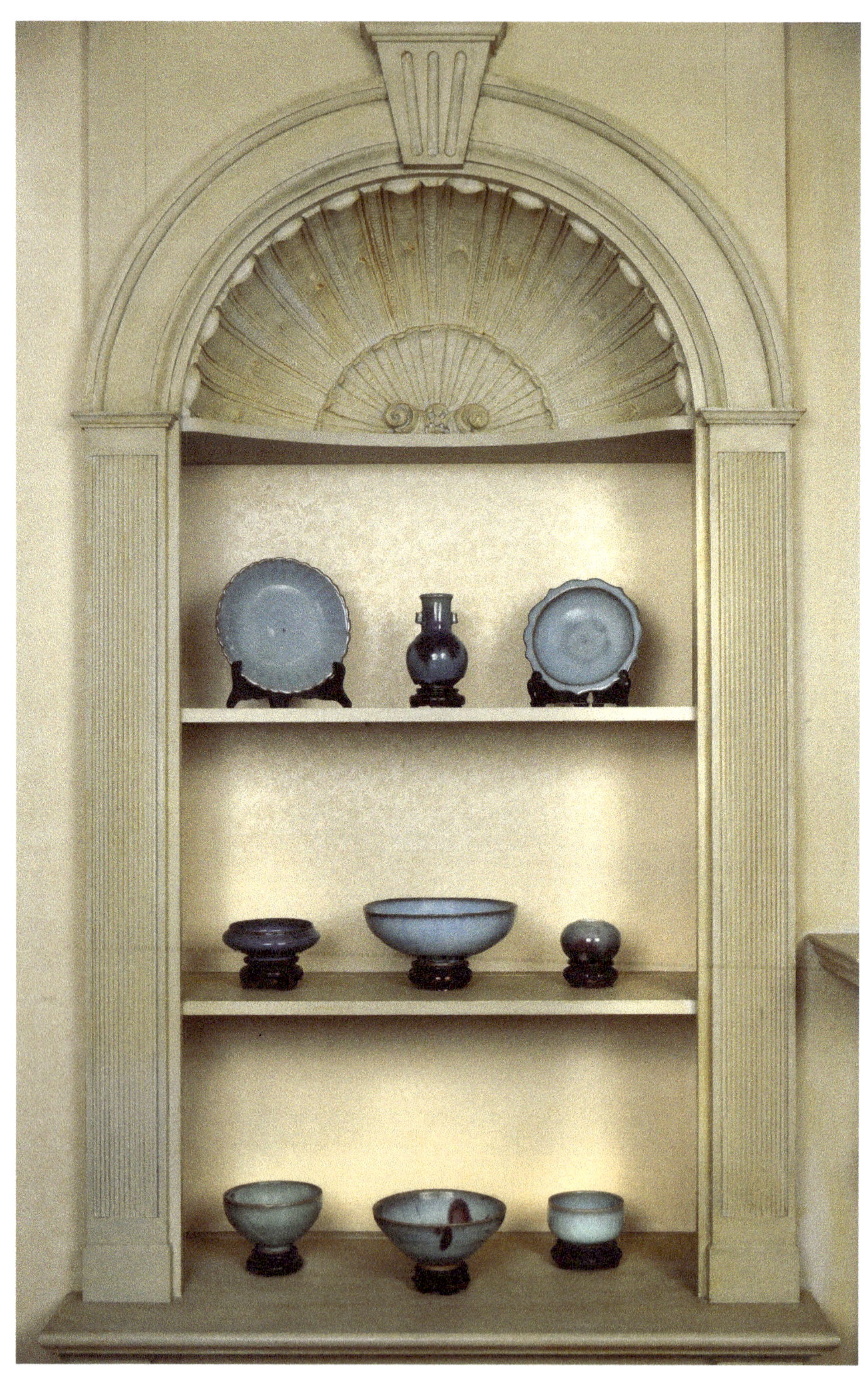

Illustration 9: Collection of Jun Yao Song ware in the author's home. Photo by Gregory R. Staley. Julius and Ann Kaplan Collection.

you may recall, is a curator at the National Palace Museum. If they are not right, you can hop over to Hong Kong and demand a refund." I replied to Rob that I would do just that in a couple of weeks.

When I arrived in Taipei, Rob and I met with Mr. Wang. He confirmed that these bowls were not of the Song dynasty, but were of the Ming dynasty. I immediately went to Hong Kong to visit the dealer. On my way, I decided that in confronting the dealer, I should have a "story" as to why I wanted my money back that would not cause him to "lose face." I decided to tell him that he must have had an unreliable clerk who sold me these pieces while he was on vacation. I told him just that and he replied, "Mr. Kaplan, I do not take vacations. Moreover, I personally buy all of the merchandise sold here, and I personally sell every item." I must have had a crest-fallen face, since he then said, "You are obviously unhappy with these pieces that I sold you, so I will be pleased to refund your purchase price."

I was gleeful until I saw him pull out his HK dollar check book. I certainly did not want the risk of a bad check. I said, "I appreciate your willingness to refund my money, but I need U.S. dollars to pay a dollar debt I incurred with another dealer." He looked at his watch and said, "In that case, we must rush to the bank so I can get U.S. dollars for you." We went to the bank and 10 minutes later I had a pile of one hundred U.S. dollar bills in my hand! I was so relieved that I decided to celebrate by going into the elegant French DuPont boutique right next door to the bank, where I bought a beautiful, and very expensive, pen and pencil set. I still have the set, but I do not use it. I merely touch it for good luck.

3.5 | TANG WARE

After visiting Susan Chen's shop many times, my interests started to expand beyond Song ware. Susan also carried Tang dynasty (618-907) objects in her studio. During that dynasty, emperors and other royalty had sculptures made for their tombs, to protect or entertain them in their after-life's. Such objects frequently included horses, grooms, soldiers, musicians, dancers and camels, et al. I always admired a Tang horse that Susan had in her shop. It was, however, too expensive for me. Every time I went to her shop, Susan would invite me to say hello to "my" almost three foot tall Tang horse. One day when I visited her, she told me that she was retiring, and selling everything in the shop at "bargain" prices for her friends and regular customers. I asked her the price of the horse. She said, "Anything you feel you can easily afford to pay!" Before I knew it, I was the owner of a good-sized unglazed Tang horse (Illustration 10).

Susan said that she would cover the cost of packing, crating and shipment to my home in Washington, D.C. When the box arrived, there was not only the horse, BUT also a Tang dynasty groom, AND a Tang camel (Illustration 11), AND a piece of scholars' rock I had always admired (Illustration 12). The scholars' rock (*Gonshi* in Chinese) is now on my desk encouraging me to write another chapter before going to bed![7]

---

7 Scholars' rocks or Gonshi are naturally occurring or shaped rocks. The National Arboretum in Washington D.C. has a large collection of them.

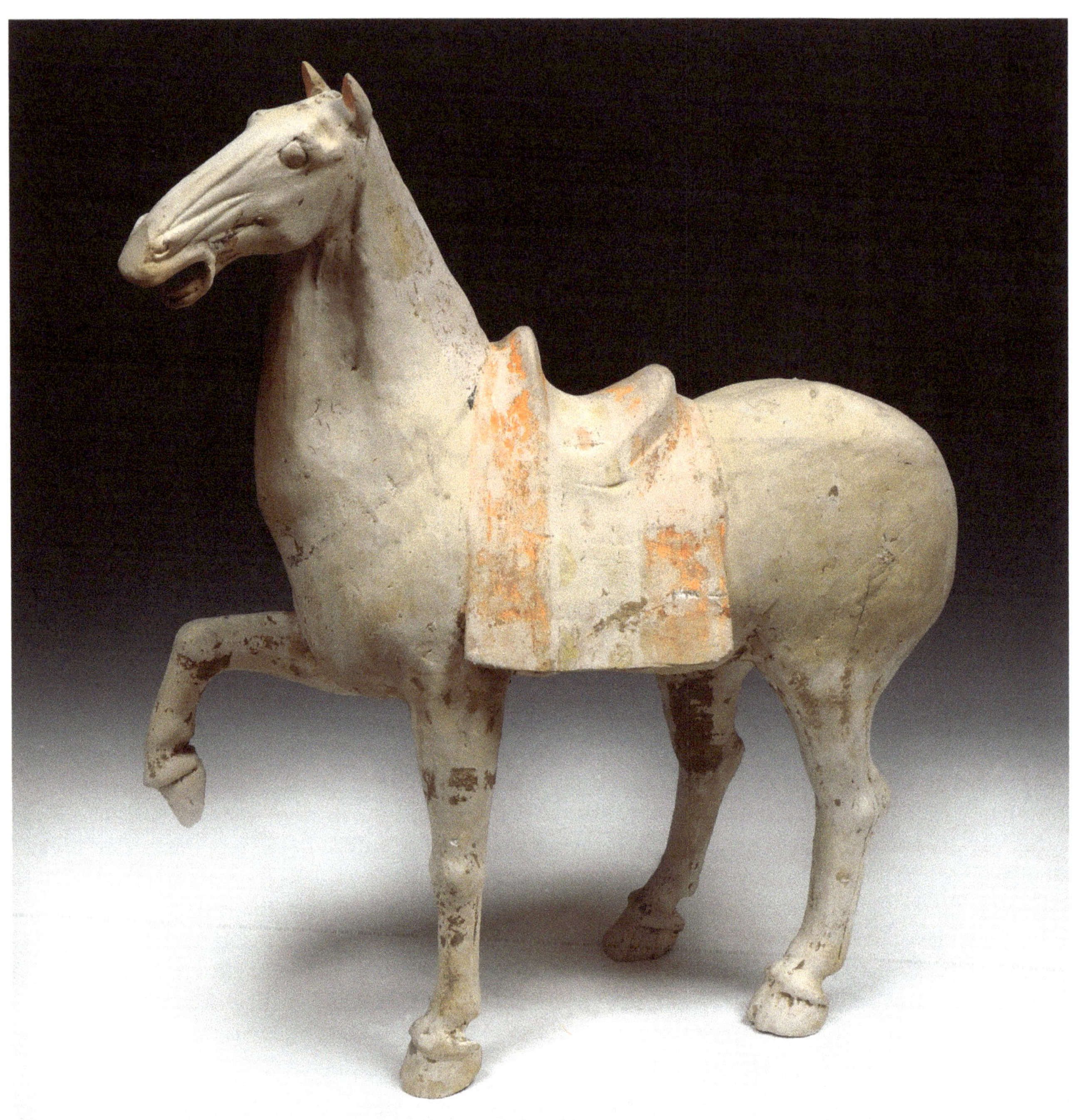

Illustration 10: Horse, Tang dynasty. Photo by Gregory R. Staley. Julius and Ann Kaplan Collection.

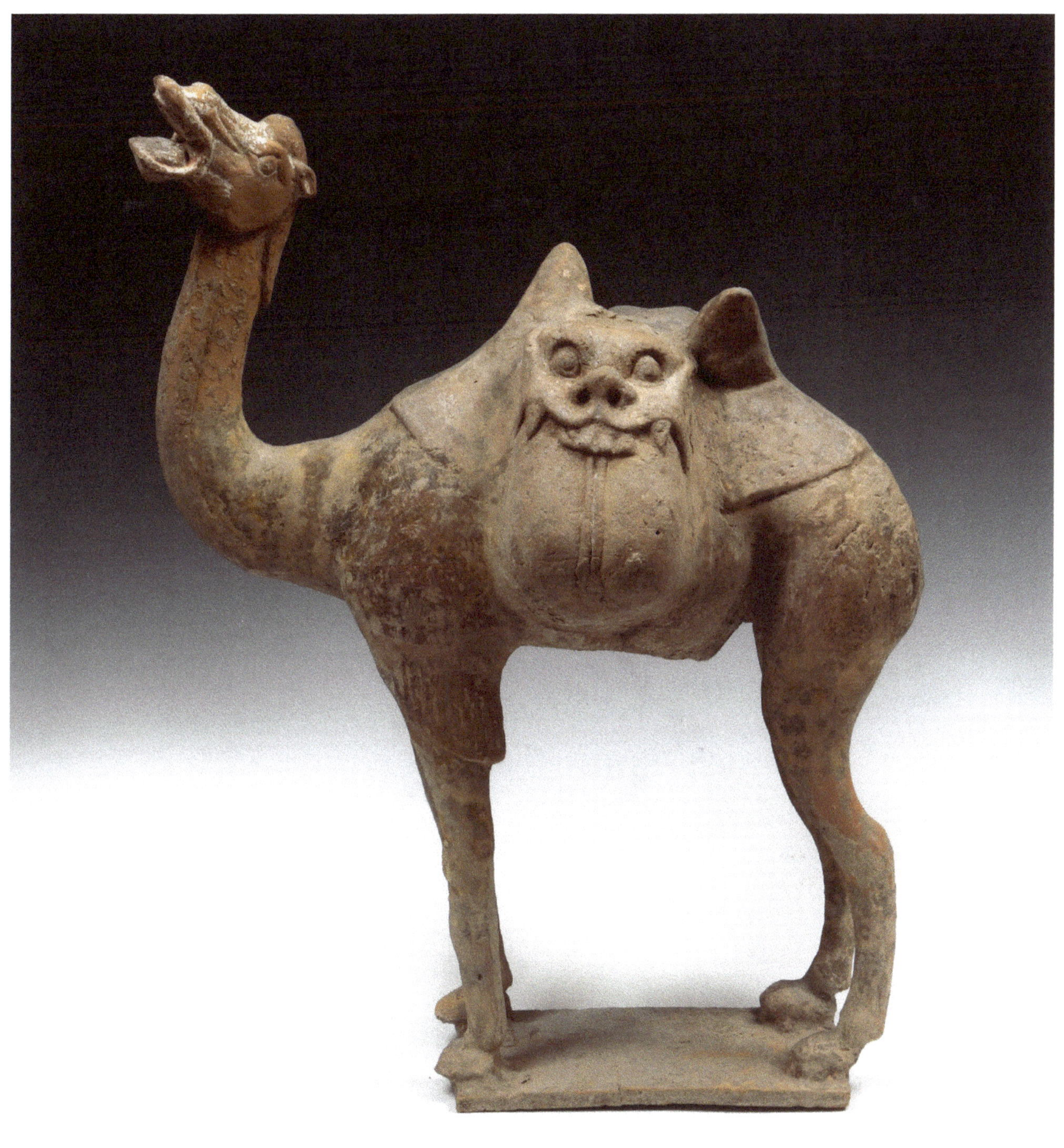

Illustration 11: Camel, Tang dynasty. Photo by Gregory R. Staley. Julius and Ann Kaplan Collection.

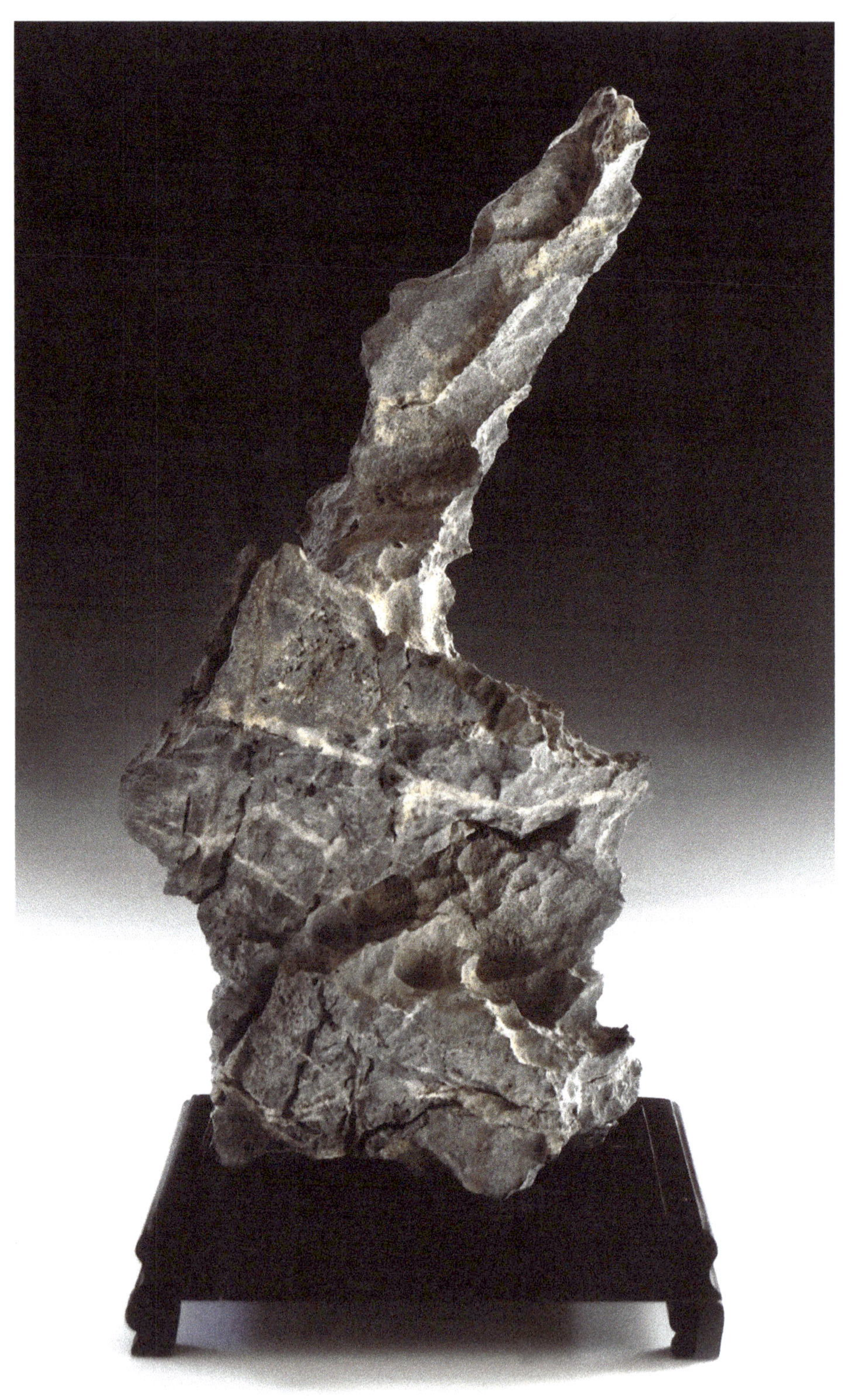

Illustration 12: Gonshi, Scholar's Stone (11 inches tall). Photo by Gregory R. Staley. Julius and Ann Kaplan Collection.

Although the prices of fine Chinese art are currently on the rise, this is not the case with unglazed Tang ware prices which have generally declined. The reason for this, I am told, is that Chinese buyers are often predisposed against anything associated with death, and most Tang ware was made for funerary purposes. This Chinese sensitivity once almost caused me extreme embarrassment. I had a friend in Taiwan, whose father was an elderly, and distinguished lawyer named Joseph Twanmoh. He became Of Counsel to the Taipei office of our law firm when we first opened in Taiwan. I was invited to his 80th birthday dinner, and I bought a beautiful (and expensive) Cartier table clock as a present. When I arrived at the home of Mr. Twanmoh, carrying my gift, I was met at the entrance to the house by a Chinese business woman, who was then a client of the firm. She asked me what I brought as a present. When I told her, her eyes glowed in horror, and she virtually screamed at me to leave at once with the clock, and buy an appropriate birthday present. I asked her what was wrong with the clock? She explained that the Mandarin word for clock resembled the word for death, and one simply did not give a gift of a clock to an elderly person. I asked her what could I buy on such short notice. She said, "Buy him half a kilo of Da Yu Ling tea." I responded with surprise, "Tea?!" I exclaimed. However, I learned the majesty of the tea she was referring to when I ran to a nearby tea shop and requested Da Yu Ling. The shop keeper raised an eyebrow, and then went to his private back room for my tea. A half kilo cost me as much as four Cartier clocks.

3.6 | HAN WARE

After many trips to Taiwan and Hong Kong, I finally made a trip to the People's Republic of China. I went with a client for a meeting with the Minister of Foreign Affairs, who invited us to lunch afterwards. I imagined we would be served some special Chinese delicacies, since we were going to eat in the Minister's private dining room. The dining room was decorated with some beautiful examples of antique Chinese art from the Minister's own collection. During the lunch, the Minister and I discussed Chinese art. The other diners simply smiled. As we sat around the dining room table, the Minister announced that he had a special treat for us, genuine Kentucky Fried Chicken! The franchise had just opened its first outlet in China, which was the "talk of the town."

During our conversation, I mentioned to the Minister that this was my very first trip to the Peoples Republic of China. He said, "Mr. Kaplan, I cannot believe that this is your first trip, since you are so knowledgeable about our art and culture." I replied, "Mr. Minister, I have not come earlier since I did not think your government would issue me a visa." He exclaimed,"Why would we do that?" I replied, " My law firm has an office in Taiwan, and I represent the Board of Trade of the Republic of China." The Minister floored me with his response: "Mr. Kaplan, Taiwan is part of China. *If you represent Taiwan, you are our lawyer.* You are always welcome in China."

That evening, when I returned to my hotel, I found a package containing a pair of horse heads from the Han dynasty. (206 B.C. - 220 A.D.) (Illustration 13) There was a card with it that read, "Welcome BACK to China." It was signed "Compliments of the Minister of Foreign Affairs of the Peoples Republic of China."

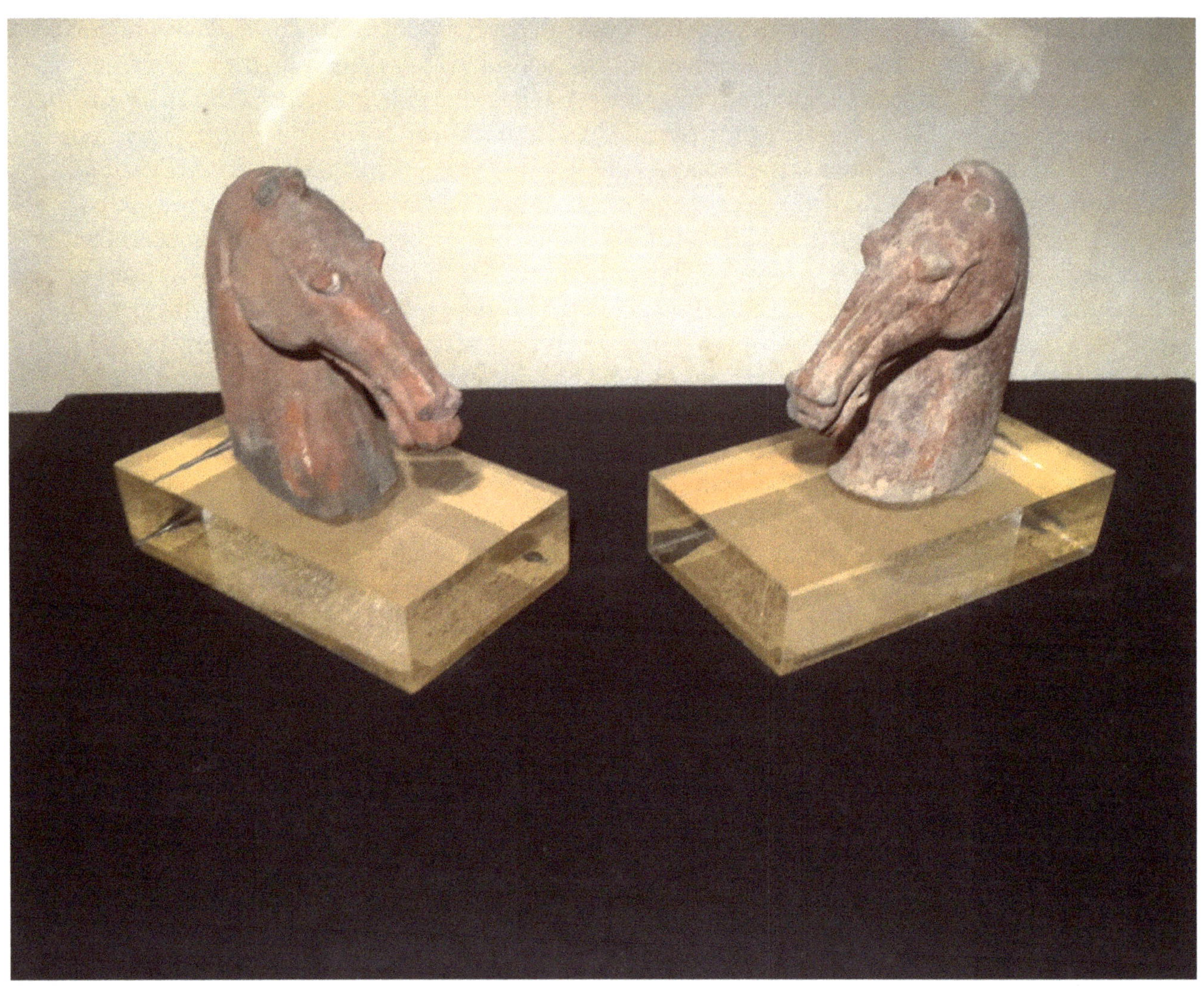

Illustration 13: Pair of Han Dynasty Horse Heads. Photo by the author. Julius and Ann Kaplan Collection.

3.7 | CONCLUSION

I stopped buying Chinese art after I started collecting English and Dutch glass. I, however, never stopped loving Chinese art, but I wanted to buy the very best, which I could do with glass, but could not do with Chinese art. Fortunately, only 15 minutes from my home is the Freer-Sackler Museum, with its outstanding collection. It may not be my own collection, but nothing is stopping me from appreciating their collection as if it were my own. We are now Friends of the Freer-Sackler. Here are some other major museums which have very important Chinese art collections.

1. In the East of the United States, there is the Metropolitan Museum of Art in New York, the Museum of Fine Arts in Boston, and the Sackler Museum in Cambridge.
2. In the Mid-West, my favorites are the Cleveland Museum, the Nelson-Atkins Museum of Art in Kansas City, and the Art Institute of Chicago in Chicago.
3. In the west of the United States, there is the Asian Art Museum in San Francisco.
4. In Paris, there is the Musée Nationale du Guimet and the Musée du quai Branly.
5. In London, there are the British Museum and the Victoria and Albert. The latter museum will play a role in the last chapter.
6. In Beijing there are two important museums: The Palace Museum and The National Museum of China.
7. In Shanghai, there is the Shanghai Museum.
8. In Seoul, there is The National Museum of Korea.
9. In Tokyo, how can one not visit its National Museum?
10. In Istanbul, there is the remarkable Topkapi Palace Museum. I have only been there once, but who can forget its stunning collection of Chinese art, the largest outside of China and Taiwan.
11. And finally, in Taipei, there is the memorable National Palace Museum in nearby Shilin. It has one of the largest collections of Chinese Art in the world.

In conclusion, suffice it to say that my collecting Chinese art, and my visits to great museum collections of this art, certainly enhanced my search for beauty.

CHAPTER 4

Studio Glass

4.1 | INTRODUCTION AND SUMMARY

Before the early 1960s, glass art was generally made by teams of factory workers, using large furnaces. This form of glass art, which was used by Tiffany and Steuben (among many others), grew out of a system in which all glass objects were hand-or mold-blown by teams of workers in factories.

The studio glass movement, by contrast, is based on the principle that glass artists could originate their own creations with small furnaces in their own studios, thus bypassing the factory system. The movement was propelled by Harvey Littleton's now-famous experimental workshops at the Toledo Museum of Art in 1962. He there demonstrated how to melt glass in a small furnace, so individual artists could use glass as an art medium in a non-industrial setting, such as their own studios. And thus the name "studio glass." These workshops were a major catalyst to the studio glass movement. They properly earned Littleton the honorific title of "Father of Studio Glass."

Following Littleton's workshops, educational centers opened throughout the United States to teach studio glass. Eventually, universities got into the act. The University of Wisconsin in Madison, where Harvey Littleton taught, being the first. New private schools emerged where the making of studio glass was taught. These notably included the Pilchuck Glass School, founded by Dale Chihuly and others, the Toledo Museum, and, The Studio of the Corning Museum of Glass.

For the consumer, galleries opened in many centers. One of the largest, and most important ones was Habatat Galleries in Royal Oak, Michigan. Its close proximity to the home of my sister and brother-in-law in Bloomfield, Michigan, had the effect of introducing them to studio glass, and they, in turn, got me *addicted*. I started collecting studio glass when such glass was in its early years. I bought most of my glass from Habatat, and the Littleton Gallery in Georgetown, D.C. (owned and run by Maurine Littleton, the daughter of Harvey Littleton.)

For purposes of this book, I have selected works by artists in our collection who have made a major impact on the growth of the studio glass movement. They are, for the most part, among the "old masters" of studio glass.

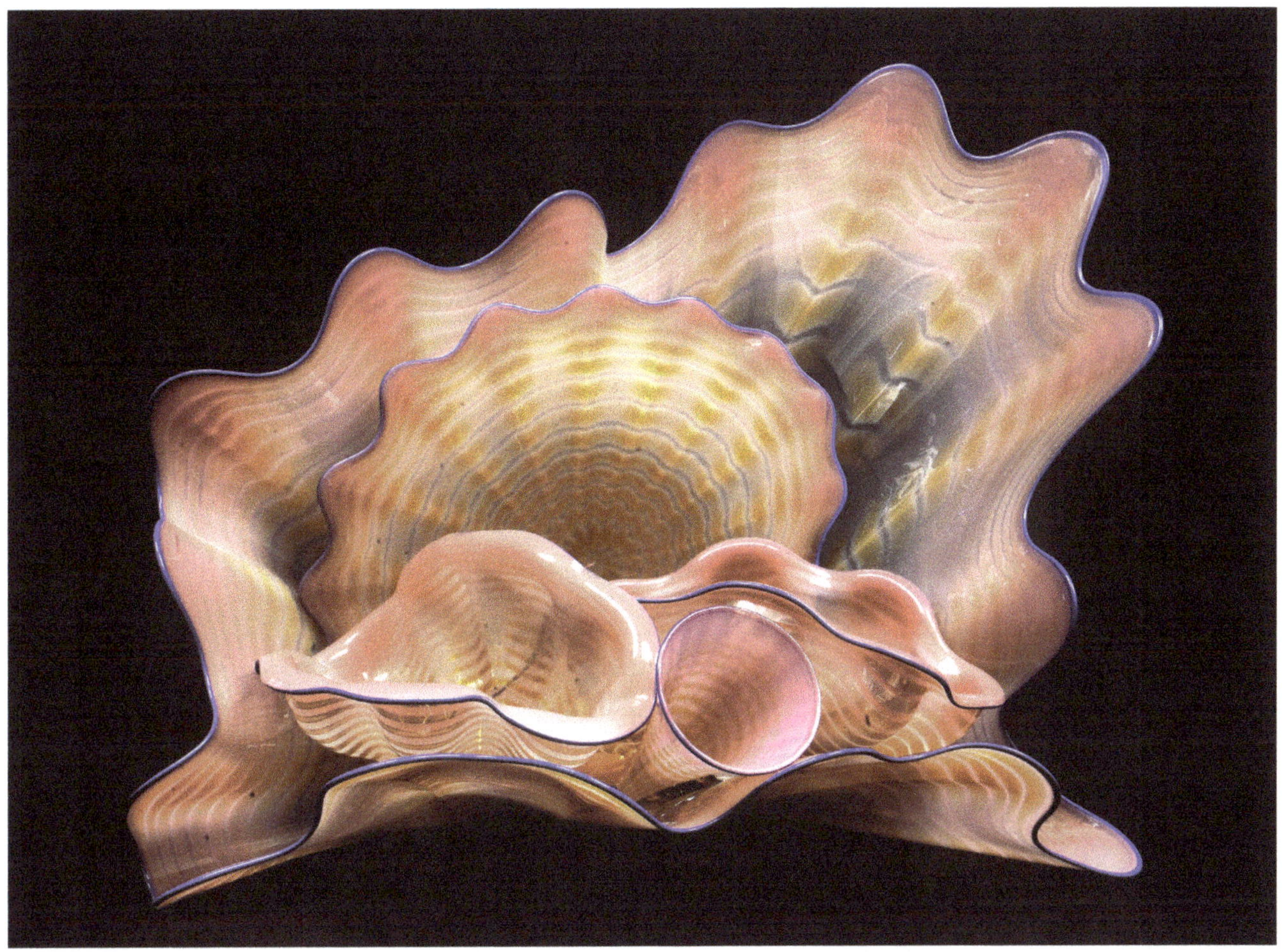

Illustration 1: Dale Chihuly, *Seaform Set*, Julius and Ann Kaplan Collection. Photo by Gregory R. Staley.

4.2 | DALE CHIHULY

The first piece of studio glass I ever purchased was an early Dale Chihuly *Seaform*. It comprises five elements ranging from deep rose pink to light pink in color, with each piece rimmed in dark blue. It is a restrained piece by comparison to the bright colors and designs Chihuly turned to in his later works (Illustration 1).

At the time I purchased the *Seaform*, our daughter, Samantha, was doing graduate work at the University of Wisconsin, Madison, where Chihuly had studied glass blowing under Harvey Littleton. Chihuly donated a large cache of his work to the university, which he wished to have displayed in, of all places, the sports stadium!

After his studies in Madison, Chihuly went to the Rhode Island School of Design where he earned an MFA. He then worked and studied in a renowned glassblowing workshop in Murano, Venice, named Venini, which was founded in 1921. After returning to the States, Chihuly became a co-founder of Pilchuck Glass School, which quickly became a mecca for young artists wanting to learn studio glass-making. At Pilchuck, he stunned all with a dramatic group of bulbs floating on Pilchuck Pond.

Chihuly liked to stun his audiences, and he did this often in forthcoming years.

Although the technical difficulties in creating simple studio glass are formidable, indeed, virtually impossible for many, Chihuly was nevertheless able to create multiple forms, sizes, and colors that dazzle the eye and imagination. He is unafraid of going where other glass artists would fear to tread.

Unfortunately, in 1976, Chihuly lost sight in his left eye in an automobile accident. But that did not stop him. He went ahead designing, and caused his glassblowers to realize his creative designs, while he watched and gave instructions.

In 1996, he created *Chihuly Over Venice*, a spectacular undertaking involving the installation of *Chandeliers* around the city.

Chihuly also loved dramatic ceiling installations. I saw my first one in Las Vegas in the ceiling of the lobby of the Bellagio Resort. I tried to read, but that was impossible. I was mesmerized for most of the evening, virtually hypnotized by the array of colors and lights above me on the ceiling. Its beauty also kept me away from the "tables."

I was likewise impressed by his famous *Light of Jerusalem* project in 1999, located in the courtyard of the Tower of David Museum, where he placed multiple glass installations together with the rough textured stone of the ancient site. It resulted in an exciting juxtaposition of glass and stone. It received high praise. The exhibit was an unparalleled success and received extensive press coverage. A world record 1, 300,000 visitors visited the exhibit during the year it ran—an unprecedented number of visits to an exhibition both in Israel and around the world.

In 2001, Ann and I were in London for one of our annual 18th-century English glass visits. We had occasion to come to the Victoria and Albert just as the museum was setting up its now famous Chihuly show. Many of our 18th-century glass friends came to the show. They were all singularly impressed. The show became the talk of the town.

Almost every year there is a major Chihuly show somewhere in the world, many of which were in botanical settings. One of these shows, *Chihuly Garden and Glass*, in Seattle, was greatly celebrated. It encouraged the artist to do many more shows in gardens.

Chihuly's art appears in permanent museum collections all over the world, including the United States, Canada, England, Singapore, the United Arab Emirates, and Kuwait. There is also a Chihuly Collection housed in the Morean Arts Center on Central Avenue in St. Petersburg, Florida. One of the largest collections of Chihuly artwork can be found at the Oklahoma City Museum of Modern Art.

4.3 | HARVEY LITTLETON

Soon after my purchase of Chihuly, I became aware of the major role that Harvey Littleton played in the emergence of studio glass. Moreover, I greatly admired his glass sculptures. I thus decided that, if we were going to build a serious collection of studio glass, I had to have a significant example of Littleton's work in our collection. It seemed that the logical way to accomplish this was to go visit Maurine

Littleton's Gallery in Georgetown, D.C. Maurine is Harvey Littleton's daughter, but she carrries many other artists. She is most knowledgeable and her gallery is a mecca for many local collectors.

I looked over Maurine's collection of her father's work, but there was nothing that struck me as being the "knock-out" piece I sought. I asked Maurine if she would kindly call her father and ask him if he had a major glass sculpture available for sale "at home." She called, and he replied that, indeed, he had a major glass arc embedded with lines of red, blue, and white. Moreover, there was also a separate end piece cut from the arc that would be "thrown in," which the artist called his "dividend" for the buyer. I bought it on the basis of Littleton's telephonic description. I never regretted the purchase. Quite to the contrary. It has become one of the stars of our collection (Illustration 2).

Harvey Littleton was born in 1922 in Corning, New York. He grew up "in the shadow" of Corning Glass, where his father, Dr. Jesse T. Littleton, worked. After he received his BA in industrial design from Michigan University in 1947, and a Masters of Fine Arts degree in ceramics from the Cranbrook Academy of Art in 1951, Littleton joined the faculty of the University of Wisconsin-Madison in the latter year. At Wisconsin, he started a hot glass program, the first of its kind at any university. He went on to promote similar courses at numerous other universities. Most importantly, he gave workshops at the Toledo Museum of Art in 1962, which had the effect of initiating the studio glass movement. He there demonstrated how to melt glass in a small furnace in the artists' studio, thereby permitting glass artists, for the first time, to create glass outside of a factory setting. That earned Littleton the honorific title of "Father of Studio Glass."

Chihuly acknowledged the role Litttleton played in the careers of all glass artists as follows: "He had a major influence on my career and the careers of all the artists who chose glass as their medium. He will forever be remembered for moving the material from its decorative, industrial and craft roots to a fine art which allows all artists access to techniques, tools and concepts—thereby transforming the use of glass for all time."

Museum acclaim for Littleton's groundbreaking work followed shortly. He was invited to have solo shows at both the Art Institute of Chicago in 1963 and the Museum of Contemporary Craft in 1964. One of his glass sculptures was then added to the permanent collection of the Museum of Modern Art, New York.

Littleton retired from teaching in 1977, in order to become a studio glass artist himself. For this, he moved to Spruce Pine, North Carolina, where he opened a glass studio and produced the most technically advanced and demanding work of his career. His glass was often rendered transparent and embedded with thin lines of color. He continued producing studio glass for the next 13 years, until he was forced to give it up due to the onset of intense back pains. Our Littleton *Arc en Ciel* is of this period, and is likewise transparent, with embedded thin lines of red, blue and white.

Today, Littleton's work is in the collections of many museums, including the Metropolitan Museum of Art; the Museum of Modern Art; The Corning Museum of Glass; the Smithsonian Museum of American Art; and the Victoria and Albert Museum, London; as well as many other museums worldwide.

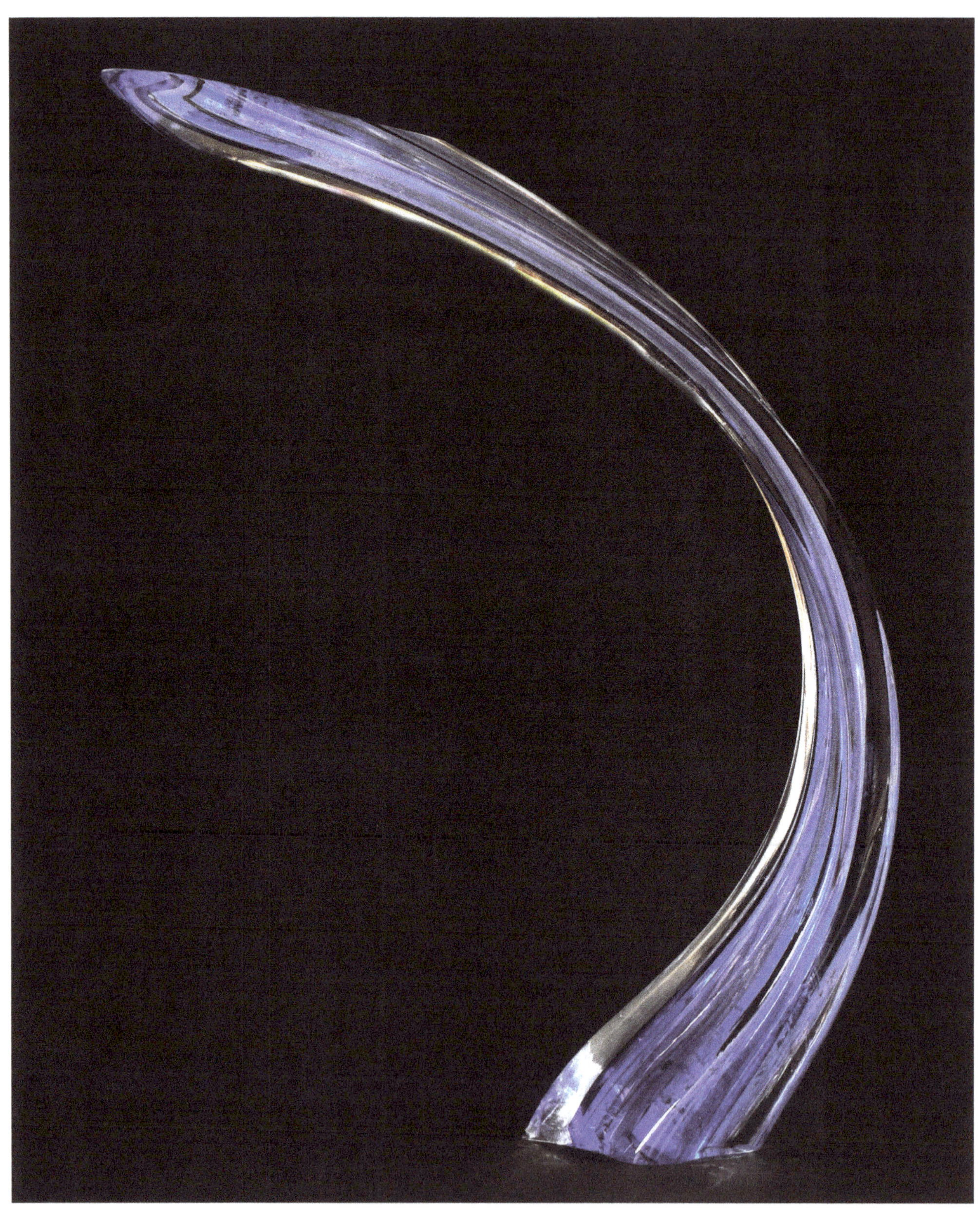

Illustration 2: Harvey Littleton, *Arc en Ciel,* 1988, Glass. Photo by Gregory R. Staley. Julius and Ann Kaplan Collection.

4.4 | COLIN REID

We have a beautiful Colin Reid pyramid sculpture in our collection, which has a place of honor in our home (Illustration 3). Rather than joining our other studio glass in my office or an adjoining room, it sits by itself on a round table next to a window in our living room. Invariably, visitors gravitate to the pyramid, and stare, and stare further, and inevitably ask, "How did the artist do it?"

Colin Reid was born in England in the town of Poyton, Cheshire. He knew from an early age that his future was to be in art. When he was just 15 years of age, he was accepted in the Guildford School of Art. His college career began at St. Martins School of Art. This was one of the most competitive art schools in England. Before he completed his course of study, Reid became caught up in Indian mysticism and joined an ashram in London. From there he spent his time, from 1973-1975, in Israel. In 1975, Reid returned to London to enroll in a government backed course at Waddon Skillcenter. He there learned glass-blowing. After another short trip to Israel, and a job in a lampworking company,

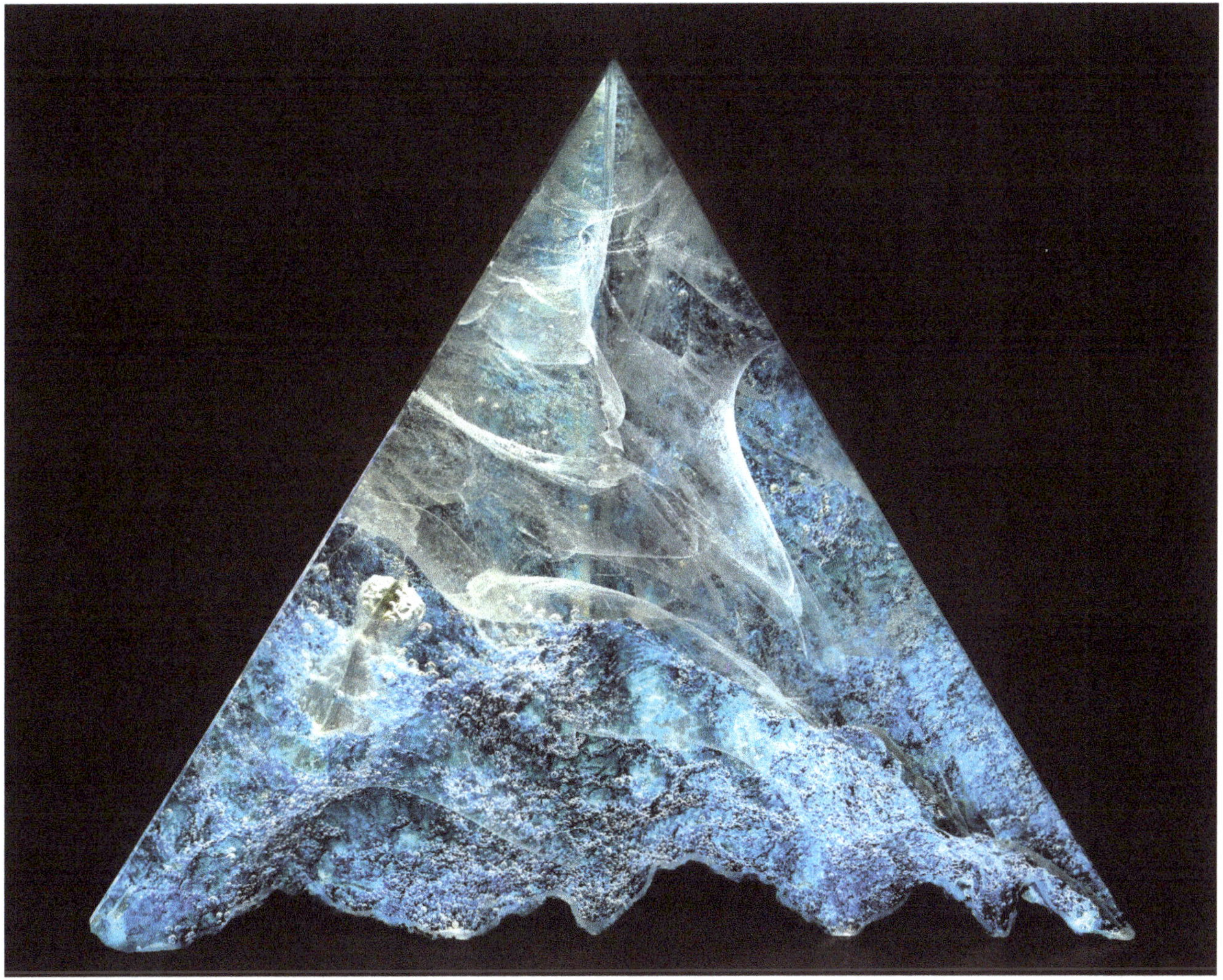

Illustration 3: Colin Reid, *Pyramid*, Cast Optical Glass. Photo by Gregory R. Staley. Julius and Ann Kaplan Collection.

he enrolled in Stourbridge College of Art where he concentrated on casting and kiln-forming. This led him to study further at Aston University in Birmingham with Keith Cummings, the leader in kiln-formed glass. With this expertise, he was ready to take on the world of glass. He converted an old mill into his studio and in 1981 he became a self-employed independent artist.

His career took off quickly. In 1982, the Ivor Kurland Gallery in Los Angeles included him in a major show which drew a great deal of attention to his work. In the same year the Victoria and Albert Museum and The Corning Museum of Glass each acquired a piece of his work. Then Habatat, an important glass gallery in Michigan, included his work in one of its major shows, entitled *Concepts 3*. Reid was invited to show at *Studio Glass Now*, put on by British Artists in Glass at the British Crafts Center, London and Toronto. From this time on, his work was often exhibited virtually everywhere fine studio glass was shown.

According to an essay on Reid by Jennifer Hawkins Opie, "By the mid-1980's, Reid's reputation was securely established as one of the new generation of dynamic, ground-breaking artists...". Reid then started on an almost annual basis to receive important awards. His first major award in 1982 and was given by Corning in the Corning New Glass Review III. His recent awards include the prestigious 2014 Coburg Glass Prize, and the Alexander Tutsek Award for his "*Ring of Fire*" (Illustration 4). In 1912, he was the winner of the London Glass Sellers Prize. Then in 2011, he won the Corning New Glass Award. From 1981 to 2011, he won 16 important awards.

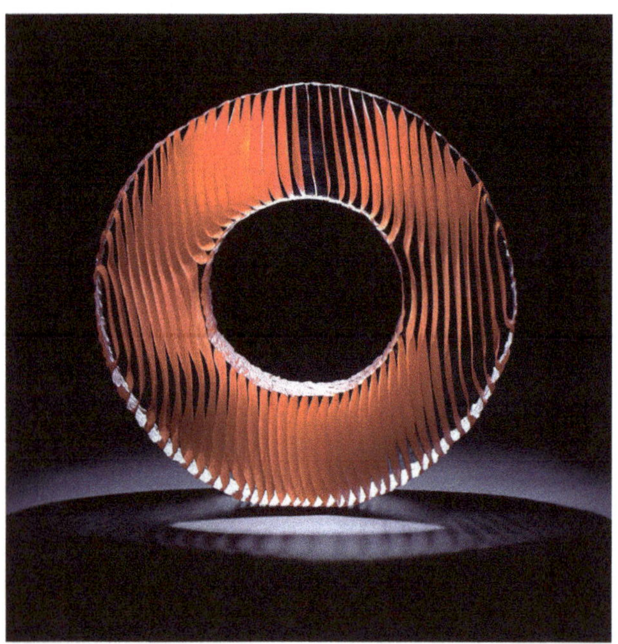

Illustration 4: Colin Reid, *Ring of Fire*, 2013. Kiln-cast glass, 24.4 x 25.2 x 4 inches.

I bought the Colin Reid *Pyramid* in London from Adrian Sasoon's Gallery in the mid-1990's. While completing the transaction, the Director of the Fitzwilliam Museum, Cambridge University, came into the gallery. He immediately came over to me, introduced himself, and said, "Well done. You have just bought a beautiful sculpture. Our museum has one by Colin Reid which is very similar to yours. It is one of the most popular glass sculptures in our museum."

Reid is a member of the Royal Society of British Sculptors and an honorary member of the Contemporary Glass Society.

Colin Reid works principally in kilncast glass, using the lost wax casting to creates sculptures with rough, highly textured areas in the interior, contrasted with immaculately polished and reflective surfaces. "Kilncast glass casting is the process in which glass objects are cast by directing molten glass into a mold where it solidifies. The technique has been used since the Egyptian period. Modern cast glass is formed by a variety of processes such as kiln casting, or casting into sand, graphite or metal molds." Milton Townsend, *Kiln Casting Glass*.

David Sasoon and the Cheltenham Art Gallery & Museum jointly published "Colin Reid Glass Sculpture" in 2013. It has some informative essays on Reid, a large number of wonderful photographs of Colin Reid's sculpture, and a comprehensive biography of the artist. Allow me to quote a small portion of two of the essays.

"Colin Reid is an exception in British glass. No one else has built such a career around exhibitions and gallery successes, awards, major public and private commissions, and popular appeal," Jennifer Hawkins Opie.

Sophia Wilson of the Cheltenham Art Gallery & Museum commented on his first show, which took place at her museum. "Visitors of all ages were fascinated by its optical reflections and spent time trying to figure out how... the form were created inside and why its appearance changed at different angles... His work is always refreshing, surprising and beautifully executed."

Colin Reid's sculptures are in the permanent collections of many museums, including the Victoria and Albert Museum, London; the Fitzwilliam Museum, Cambridge; Musée des Arts Decoratifs, Louvre Museum; Corning Museum of Glass; Los Angeles County Museum of Art; the Toledo Museum of Art; Tokyo National Museum of Modern Art, Tokyo; Hokkaido Museum of Modern Art, Sapporo; Shanghai Museum; and well over 40 other important museums worldwide.

4.5 | ALBERT PALEY

In 2014, there was a major show at the Corcoran Gallery of Art of the works of Albert Paley. I attended and was impressed by the beauty of his creations. Before leaving the museum, I checked to be sure that Maureen Littleton's Gallery was still open since I was determined to add an Albert Paley sculpture to our collection. It was open, and I went directly there from the museum. Maureen showed me "*Red Wrap*" by Paley (Illustration 5). It is a brilliant work by the artist with red metal "legs,", an upper -section of enwrapped red metal strips holding the "legs" together, and a slightly curved tube of glass within the length of the metal structure. I added it to our collection.

Paley was born in Philadelphia, Pennsylvania during World War II. He decided that he was not going to college. He planned to get a job and support his mother. (His father had developed debilitating arthritis.) A girlfriend took him to the Tyler School of Art, a part of Temple University, where his interests in art were but ignited. He there and then decided to study art, and become an artist.

Paley entered the Tyler School and earned his Bachelor of Fine Arts in sculpting, with a minor in metalsmithing, in 1966. He was, thereafter, determined to have a career in art. However, he could not decide between sculpting and metalworking as a subject for a master's degree. He finally decided to do his graduate work in goldsmithing. He earned his MFA from the Tyler School in 1969, and moved to Rochester, New York, to teach at the Rochester Institute of Technology. He now holds an endowed chair there, the Charlotte Frederick Mowris Endowed Chair in RIT's School for American Crafts. He thus went from rejecting higher education to embracing it as a career in a matter of a handful of years.

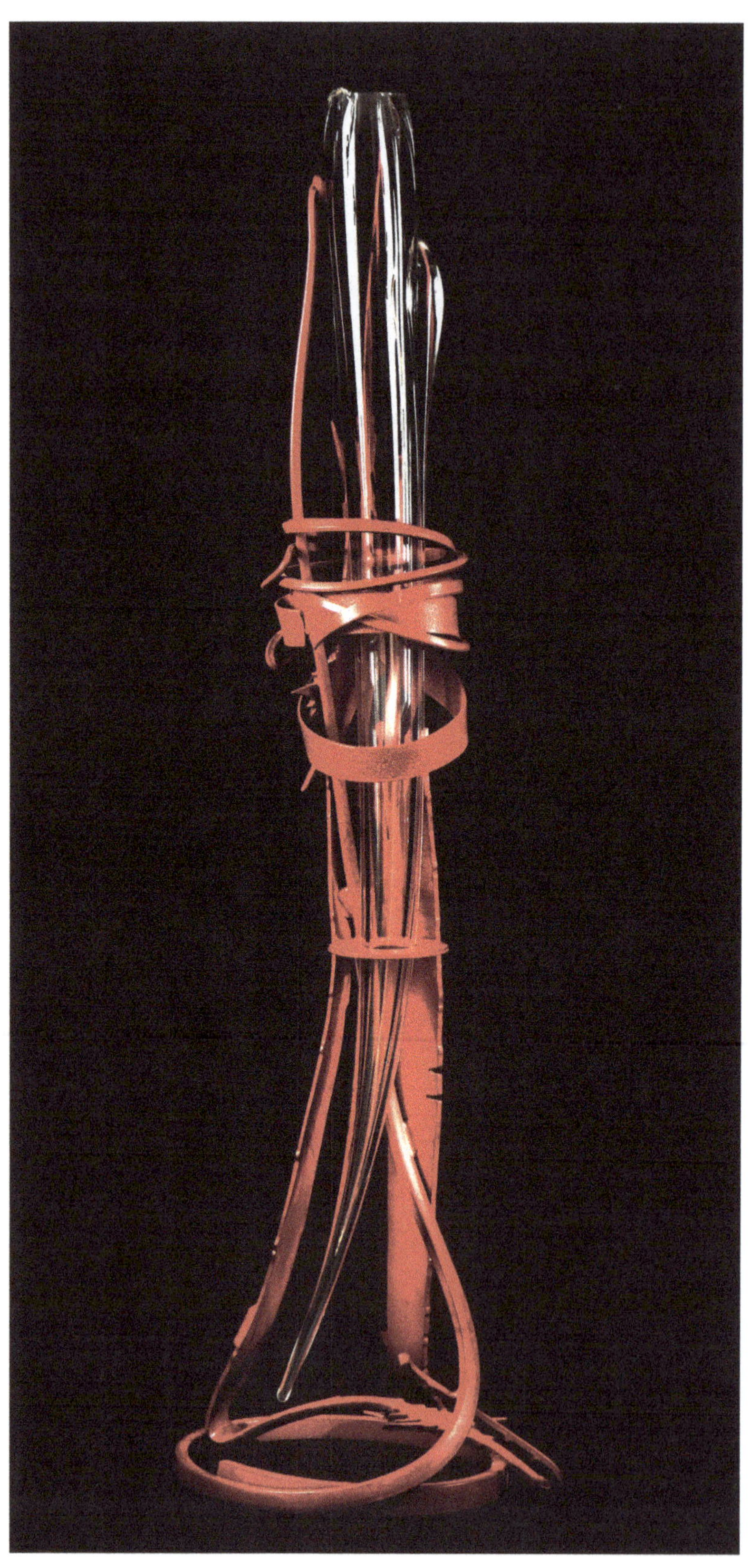

Illustration 5: Albert Paley, *Red Wrap*. Photo by Gregory R. Staley. Julius and Ann Kaplan Collection.

After receiving his MFA, Paley became a jewelry designer. He took delight in making dramatically large-sized jewelry that he described as being ideal "for a strong woman."

In the early 1970s, he decided that his real gift may not be in making jewelry, but rather in metalworking. Notwithstanding, Paley still continued to make jewelry, even while successfully doing metalworking. Since 1965, Paley's jewelry and metal work have been exhibited in over one hundred and fifty national and international shows!

Paley got his big break in metal working when he secured a commission from the Smithsonian Institution to create portal gates for the Renwick Museum. To do the work, he rented a garage to work in, hired an assistant, and bought the required machinery. Paley, with the aid of his assistant, created the now famous Renwick *Portal Gates* (Illustration 6).

This project was an enormous success. Paley's career then "took off." He continued doing gates along with a number of other things; however, gates became his hallmark, and he continued to forge gates for a number of years. In addition to the Renwick *Portal Gates,* he created the *Portal Gates* for the New York State Senate Chamber of the State Capitol (1980), the Victoria and Albert Gates for the Victoria and Albert Museum (1982), and the Animals Always Gateway Sculpture for the St. Louis Zoo (2006), currently the largest sculpture at any zoo in the U.S.

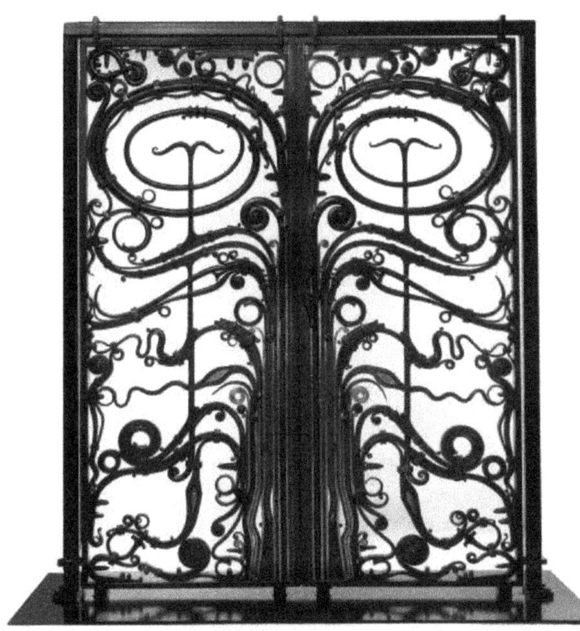

Illustration 6: Albert Paley, *Portal Gates*, 1974. Steel, brass, copper, and bronze, 90 3/4 × 72 × 4 inches. Smithsonian American Art Museum, Commissioned for the Renwick Gallery, 1975.117.1A-B.

In the 1980s, Paley then turned to works of monumental size. His first super-sized piece of sculpture was for the Strong Museum in 1982. It was a huge success and he made several other large-scale sculptures to much acclaim. A number of these were in the show at the Corcoran where I first saw works by this skilled artist. They were, indeed, very large.

During the 1990's Paley began working in glass in addition to his traditional work in metals. He did not blow glass, but like Chihuly after he lost vision in his left eye, he created the designs and worked with gaffers who blew the glass.

His interest in working with glass led him to take a summer residency in 1999 at the Pilchuck School of Glass. He later studied the art of glass more comprehensively at the Corning Museum of Glass. In both schools he was exposed to beautiful works of glass and was inspired to incorporate glass in some of his steel structures. *Red Wrap* is an example of this marriage of glass and steel.

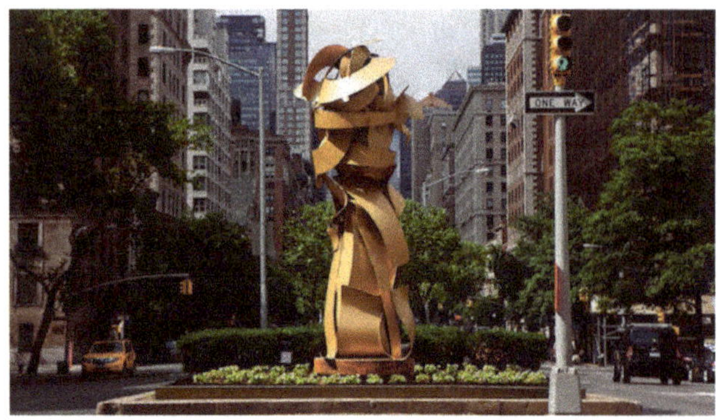

Illustration 7: Albert Paley, *Envious Composure*, 2012, Formed and fabricated steel with a painted finish 18'3" x 7'6" x 7', Paley Studios Archives.

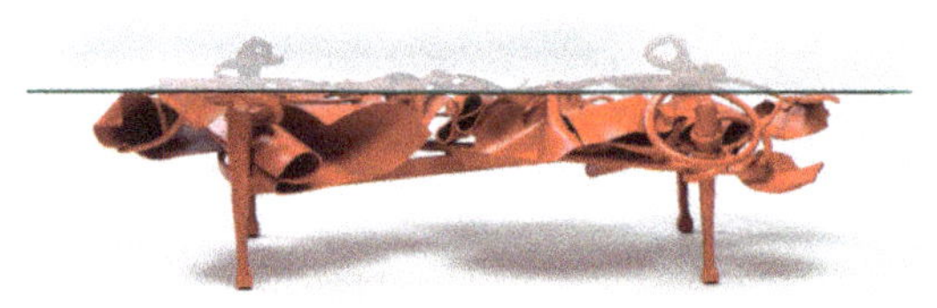

Illustration 8: Albert Paley, New Muse, 2016, Painted steel. Photo by KeneK Photography, courtesy of Wexler Gallery.

In addition to his "indoor" art, Paley undertook a major outdoor exhibition. In the summer of 2013, he created thirteen steel sculptures, which he displayed on Park Avenue in New York City, between 52nd and 67th Streets. This was one of his largest exhibitions (Illustration 7).

Although Paley had included works containing glass in a number of shows, his first show exclusively of glass and steel sculpture took place in 2017/2018 in the Museum of Glass. It was entitled *Complementary Contrasts: The Glass and Steel Sculptures of Albert Paley*. My favorite piece in the show was a steel coffee table (Illustration 8).

Paley's work is in the permanent collections of the Metropolitan Museum of Art; the Museum of Fine Arts, Boston; the Museum of Fine Arts, Houston; the Victoria and Albert Museum, London; the British Museum, London; the Renwick, Smithsonian Museum, et al.

4.6 | STEVEN WEINBERG

When I was in Palm Beach for an art and antique show in the mid-1990's, I bought a glass cube by Steven Weinberg. I was attracted to the cube since it resembled one in the Renwick Gallery in Washington, D.C. that I had admired for years. However, the Renwick version was clear glass, while the one I bought had blue streaks within the cube.

That evening, I received a phone call from the artist, who angrily asserted that the gallery had made a terrible mistake, and the price of the glass cube ought to have been more than triple the price I paid. I was frankly disturbed by his angry, argumentative voice, and the lawyer in me then told Mr. Weinberg that I thought that the price was exclusively a matter between him and the gallery which sold me the cube. That concluded the conversation.

For weeks following this call, I wondered whether I had done the right thing. Was I being insensitive to the needs of a young artist? Should I have found a way to return the glass to the gallery, and secure a refund, leaving the gallery to resell the work at Weinberg's price? But the gallery did not call me to suggest it. By the time I focused on it, this terribly heavy cube had arrived in my home, and besides, I was traveling abroad on business and had little time to focus on the matter.

But then, I began to find fault with the cube. Perhaps I was affected by the artist's phone call. Perhaps I was adversely affected by the color blue that he had spread throughout the otherwise clear cube. Indeed, as time passed, I liked it less and less, and I finally sold the cube at a Habatat auction. I received a price meaningfully less than the price I paid, and enormously less than the artist claimed to be the correct price. But regardless of the loss, I was frankly glad to be rid of the Weinberg cube. I also happily used a portion of the proceeds of the sale to purchase Albert Paley's *Red Wrap* from the Littleton Gallery.

But it would be manifestly unfair and inappropriate for me to leave you with the negative reaction I had to the cube, since Weinberg is a highly regarded glass artist with a large following, and his work is universally praised. With a fine arts degree from the Rhode Island School of Design, and a Bachelors of Fine Arts from Alfred University, Weinberg launched such a successful career in glass sculpture that he became a two-time recipient of grants from the National Endowments for the Arts. He has a large and happy following. My own sister and brother-in-law bought a Weinberg glass sculpture which they praised.

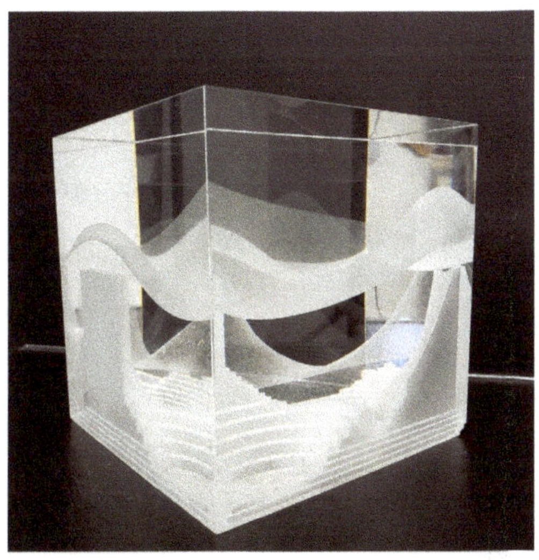

Illustration 9: Steven Weinberg, *Cube*, 1990s. Cast Glass. Photo courtesy of Le Shoppe Too.

I never made a picture of my Weinberg cube, but here is a picture of another cube that is similar to mine (Illustration 9). My cube, as noted above, however, had streaks of blue in it. In retrospect, that, together with the artist's phone call, was perhaps what caused my negative reaction. I find the one pictured below to be much more to my taste. It is unfortunate that I did not buy a clear one like the one pictured below, in which case I likely now would be singing praise for the work of Weinberg.

Museum curators have high regards for Weinberg's work. He is represented in the permanent collections of over 50 art museums around the world, including the Musée des Arts Decoratifs at the Palais du Louvre, Paris; the Metropolitan Museum of Art, New York; the Victoria & Albert Museum, London; and the Smithsonian Institution; inter alia.

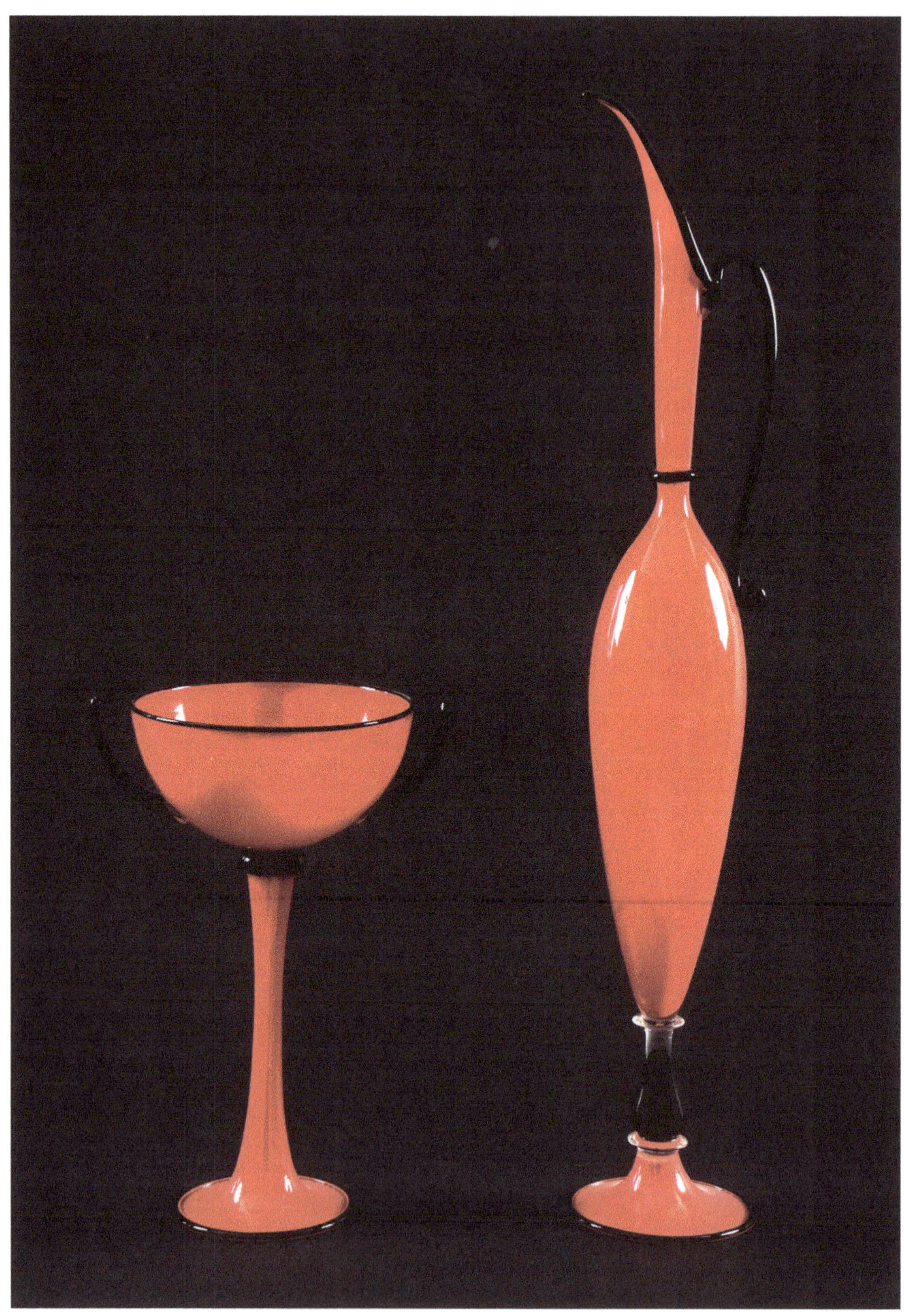

Illustration 10: Dante Marioni, *Pitcher and Cup*. Photo by Gregory R. Staley. Julius and Ann Kaplan Collection.

4.7 | DANTE MARIONI

Dante Marioni grew up in the San Francisco Bay area. While still a teenager he knew that he wanted to be a studio glass artist. This is not surprising given the fact that his father was one, and he was often surrounded by such artists while growing up. When he was still 15, the family moved to Seattle, and he enrolled in a well-known glass school called The Glass Eye. It was there that he learned glassblowing.

Dante's father worked at the Pilchuck Glass School in Stanwood, Washington. As a consequence, Dante spent his summers there. At Pilchuck he met Lino Tagliapietra, a highly acclaimed Italian studio glass artist, and he learned a great deal about the art of glass sculpture from him. Marioni often mentions the influence of Tagliapietra on him. He has been heard to say, "There is not a day in the studio that I do not ask myself, how would Lino do it?"

When he finished his academic studies, Dante began to teach at The Glass Eye, where he also became a serious and skilled glassblower. He loved teaching and later taught in Europe and Asia, as well as in the United States.

I find Marioni's elongated glass vessels to be strikingly beautiful. He often made tall cups, goblets, and pitchers. I was particularly attracted to a pair of Marioni giant cup and a tall pitcher, both in red, and I bought it (Illustration 10). There is a real touch of elegance in their tall, sleek shapes.

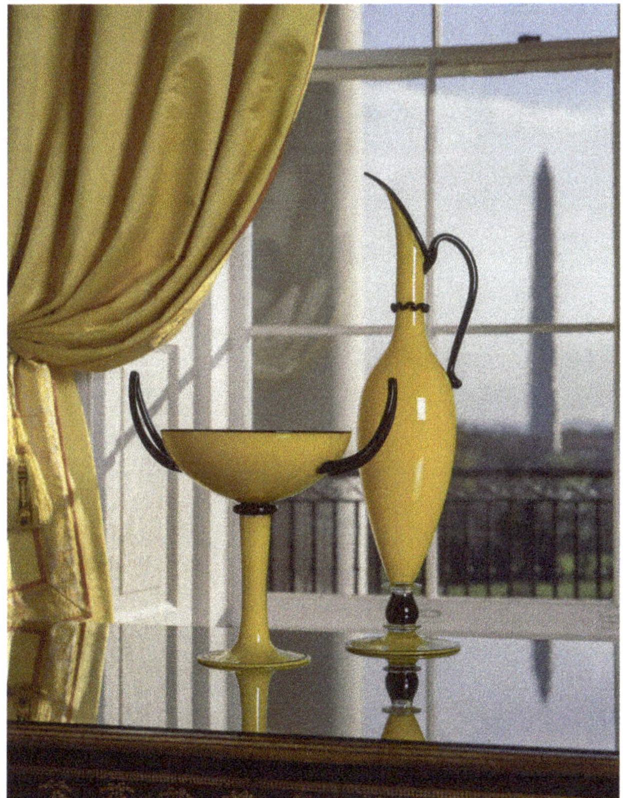

Illustration 11: Marioni's elongated glass vessels as shown on the cover of *The White House Collection of American Crafts*. Photo by John Bigelow Taylor.

But given the influence of Tagliapietra, it is not surprising that he also employed 'reticello' and 'murrini' in his oeuvre. Reticello is a needle lace dating back to the 15th century which was frequently employed in Murano glass of the Renaissance. Murrini are colored patterns made in a glass cane dating back to the Middle East of 4000 years ago, and resuscitated in Italy during the Renaissance.

By coincidence, President and Mrs. Clinton chose an identical pair for the White House. Theirs is, however, in bright yellow. They are pictured on the cover of "*The White House Collection of American Crafts*" by Michael W. Monroe (Illustration 11).

Marioni has received his share of awards, including the "Outstanding Achievement in Glass" award in 1997, given by Urban Glass,

Brooklyn, and the "Young Americans" award in 1988, from the American Craft Museum, New York. In 1987, he received the "Louis Comfort Tiffany Foundation Award." In 1985 he received a The Glass Eye scholarship.

Dante Marioni's works are in the permanent collection of the National Gallery of Art; The Los Angeles County Museum of Art; the Corning Museum of Glass; the White House Collection of Crafts; the Seattle Art Museum; the Carnegie Museum; the Chrysler Museum; the Cincinnati Art Museum; the New Zealand National Museum of Art; the Smithsonian Institution; the National Museum of Craft, Tokyo; the Yokohama Museum of Art, et al.

4.8 | DANNY LANE

Danny Lane was born in 1955 in Urbana, Illinois. As a young adult he traveled widely outside the United States. On his travels he visited, and fell in love with the United Kingdom, and specifically, with London. He moved there in 1975, and remains a resident of London to this day.

Lane took courses in fine art at the Byam Shaw School of Art and the Central School of Art & Design, London. After graduating, he began to construct art furniture. On a visit to Mallett's, John Smith showed me a fascinating chair Lane had made, his *Etruscan Chair*. I was sorely tempted to buy it, but Ann did not think that it would fit in with the décor of our home. She was right.

By 1989, Lane's focus turned to larger-scale works. This required that he move to an extra-large studio and gallery. This led him to convert a 10,000 square-foot factory in Willesden, West London, into his studio.

At this time, he began experimenting with giant curving glass walls that refract light. To construct these sculptures, Lane utilizes the strength of glass under compression, a technique he calls this "shish-kebabing." He places a steel rod through layered glass. Lane thereby constructed monumental structures. They were made of industrial float glass and steel, colored glass sculptures, casts, and design objects.

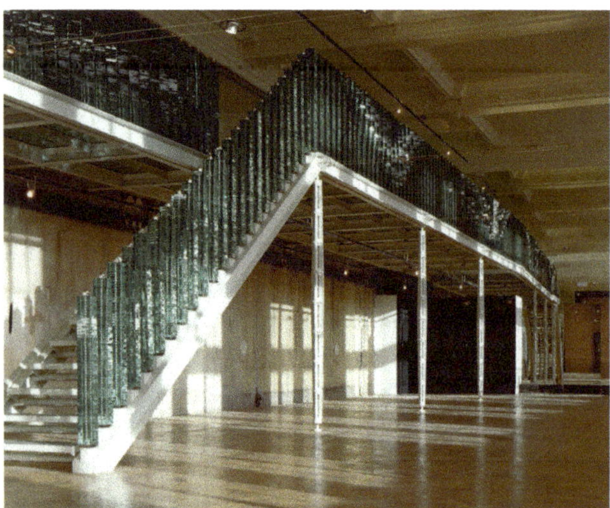

Illustration 12: Danny Lane, Balustrade, 1992. Float glass, cut and drilled, stacked on stainless steel rods. H 114 cm. © Danny Lane / Victoria and Albert Museum, London. C.249:1-1993.

In 1994, Lane was retained by the Victoria & Albert Museum, London, to construct a glass balustrade for the museum's new Glass Gallery (Illustration 12). The balustrade is made up of 140 pillars of cut glass, lining the stairs leading to a glass mezzanine floor. Ann and I have spent many pleasant hours in the Glass Gallery, including on Lane's balustrade. The V&A glass collection is one of the largest and most comprehensive in the world. It showcases 3500 years of glassmaking.

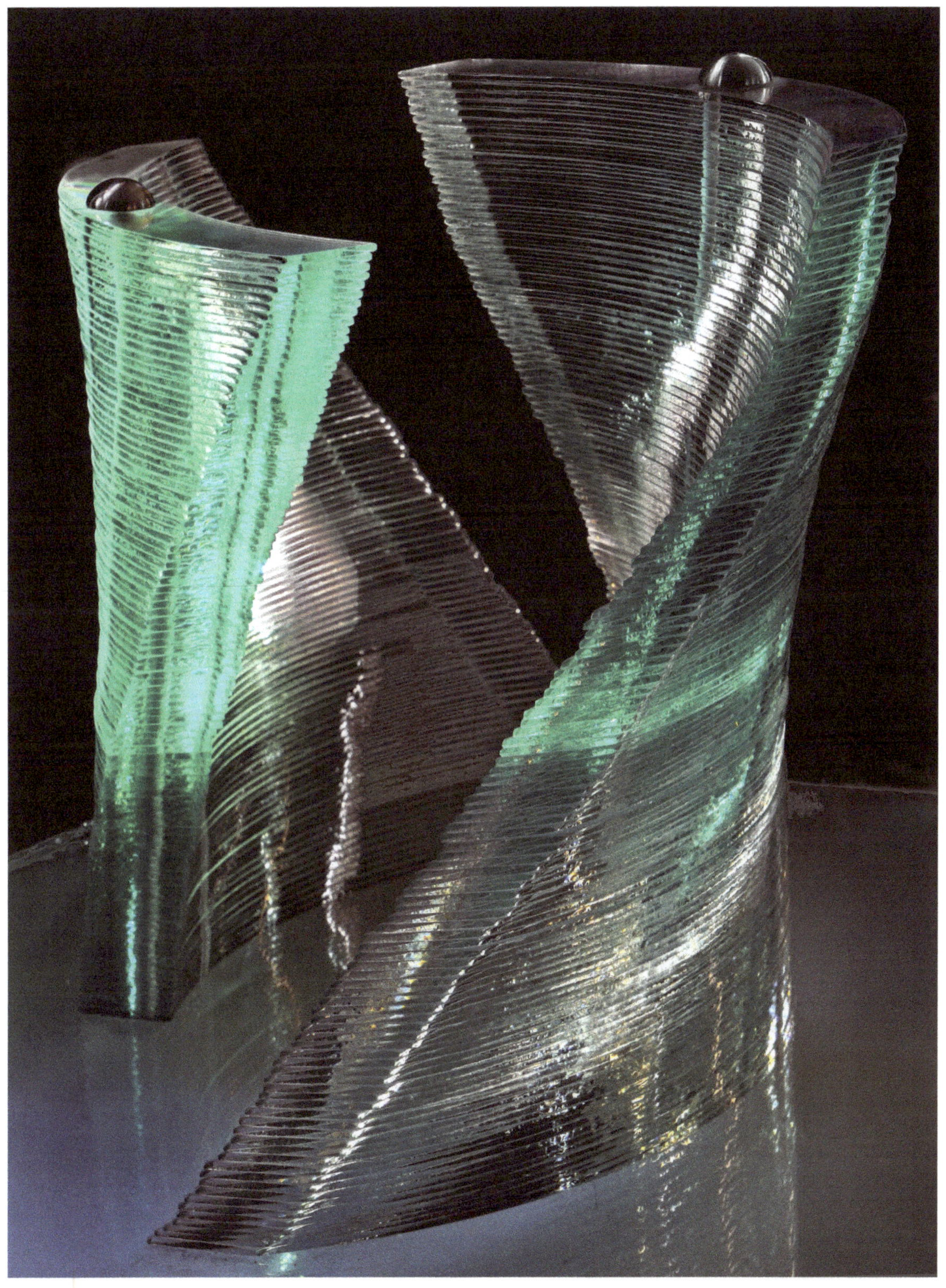

Illustration 13: Danny Lane, Moquette for a Sculpture in Germany. Photo by Gregory R. Staley. Julius and Ann Kaplan.Collection.

There are three displays of glass in the V&A that always capture my utmost attention. First, of course, are the cases containing the English glass of the 18th century. The vitrines holding the glass of this period are comprehensive, with excellent examples of many glasses of that period. Second, I always visit with awe the collection of Egyptian 8th dynasty (1400 BC – 1336 BC) core-formed glass. I do not recall ever having gone to the V&A without visiting these famous glasses. And the third, the vitrine of fake glass on the balustrade. I have always been fascinated with great fakes and fakers. I unfortunately had one fake glass in our Beilby collection (see Chapter 2). Indeed, I like to read books on great forgers. My favorite forger was Han Van Meegeren. I think that I have read most of the books published in English on this famous Dutch forger who painted early Vermeers in the 1930's, and fooled many prominent museums and painting experts. There was even a fake Van Meegeren portrait in the Mellon collection of the National Gallery of Art.

There came a time in the middle of his career when Lane's focus shifted to making large-scale glass and steel sculptures for public and corporate spaces. For many of these giant sculptures, Lane would first construct a moquette. One day, when I wandered into Mallett's to say hello to John Smith, I spotted one of Lane's moquette's. I was intrigued by it, and bought it (Illustration 13). In addition, John Smith kindly gave me a gift of two beautiful champagne flutes designed by Lane.

I have never seen the large sculpture in Sweden based on our moquette, but I did find a picture of it (Illustration 14). The Swedish large sculpture clearly replicates our moquette.

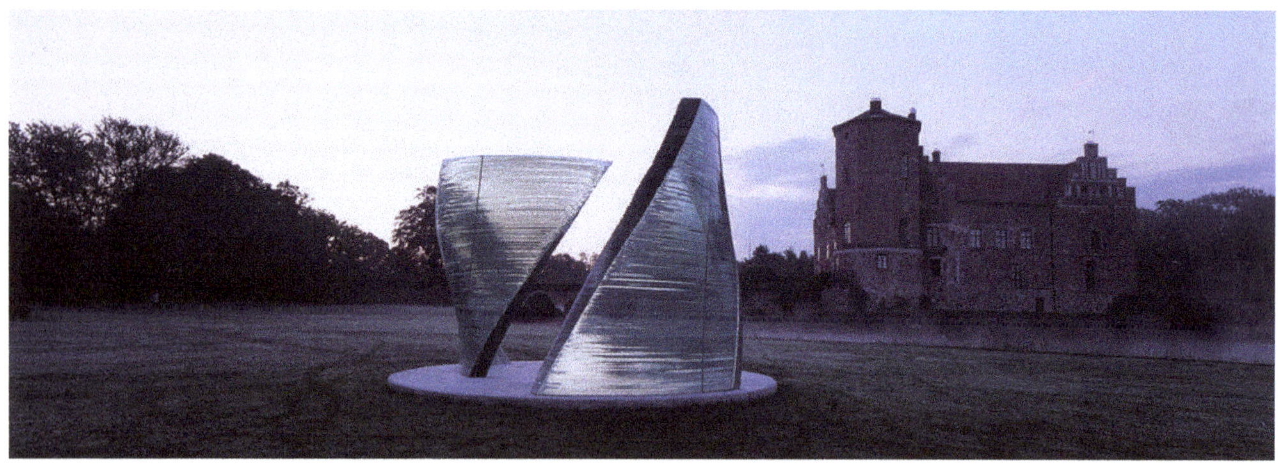

Illustration 14: Danny Lane, Reeling Walls Torup, 2000. Photo by Peter Wood. Courtesy of the artist.

4.9 | LAURA DONEFER

I went to the annual art festival at Habatat regularly. One year, I met an energetic red-headed glass sculptor from Canada named Laura Donefer. She made big, colorful "caldrons", which she called "*Witch Pots.*" I bought two of her colored *Witch Pots* soon after meeting her. Before my next visit to the Annual Exhibition at Habatat, I told myself that even if I were attracted to another Donefer sculpture, I would not buy another *Witch Pot*. But, on my next trip to Habitat the following year, I saw a beautiful white *Witch Pot* by Laura that I simply could not resist (Illustration 15).

The next year, when I saw Laura at the Habatat festival, I told her that I had enough "*Witch Pots*" and was now interested in something totally new, *created just for me*. I asked Laura if she would be prepared to make me a special-order sculpture. She replied, "Any special specifications?" I responded, "No, so long as it is unique among your oeuvre, and you do not deliver it unless you verily believe it to be your masterpiece."

Months later, a large crate was delivered to my office with a simple note, "A Masterpiece, just for my friend Jay" (Illustration 16).

When I looked at the massive piece of sculpture, I was absolutely thrilled. I could envisage otherworldly snakes climbing in a circular manner around the vessel, with their duck-shaped heads occasionally peeking out. I found it to be beautiful. It was indeed a "masterpiece."

Laura later sent me several pictures of the making of the bowl. It required any number of helpers. I have selected two of these photos which show Laura and her crew creating the "Masterpiece" (Illustrations 17 and 18).

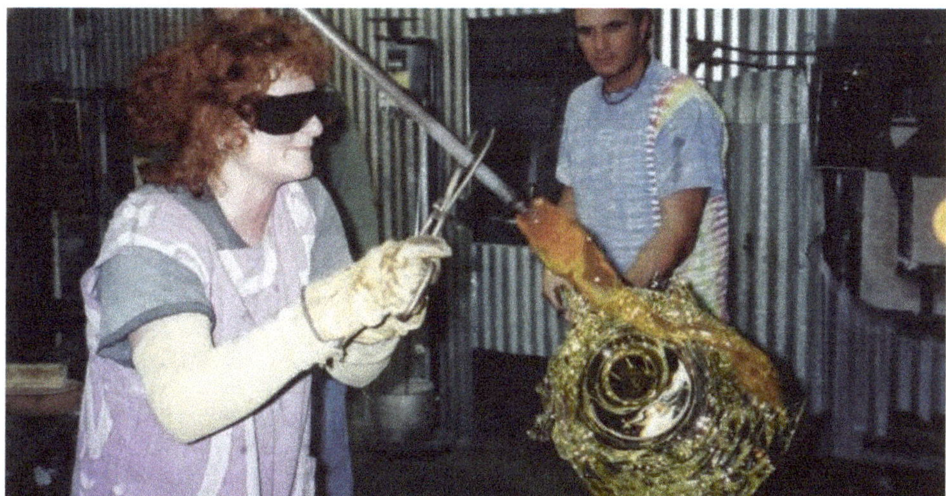

Illustration 17: Laura Donefer "Sculpting the Bit" (left with red hair and dark glasses). Photo courtesy of Laura Donefer's Studio.

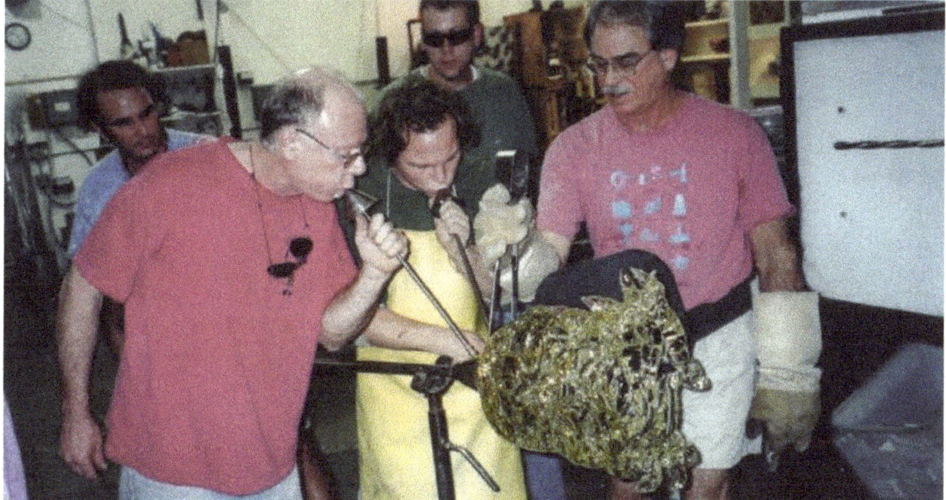

Illustration 18: Cooling before the "take off". Photo courtesy of Laura Donefer's Studio.

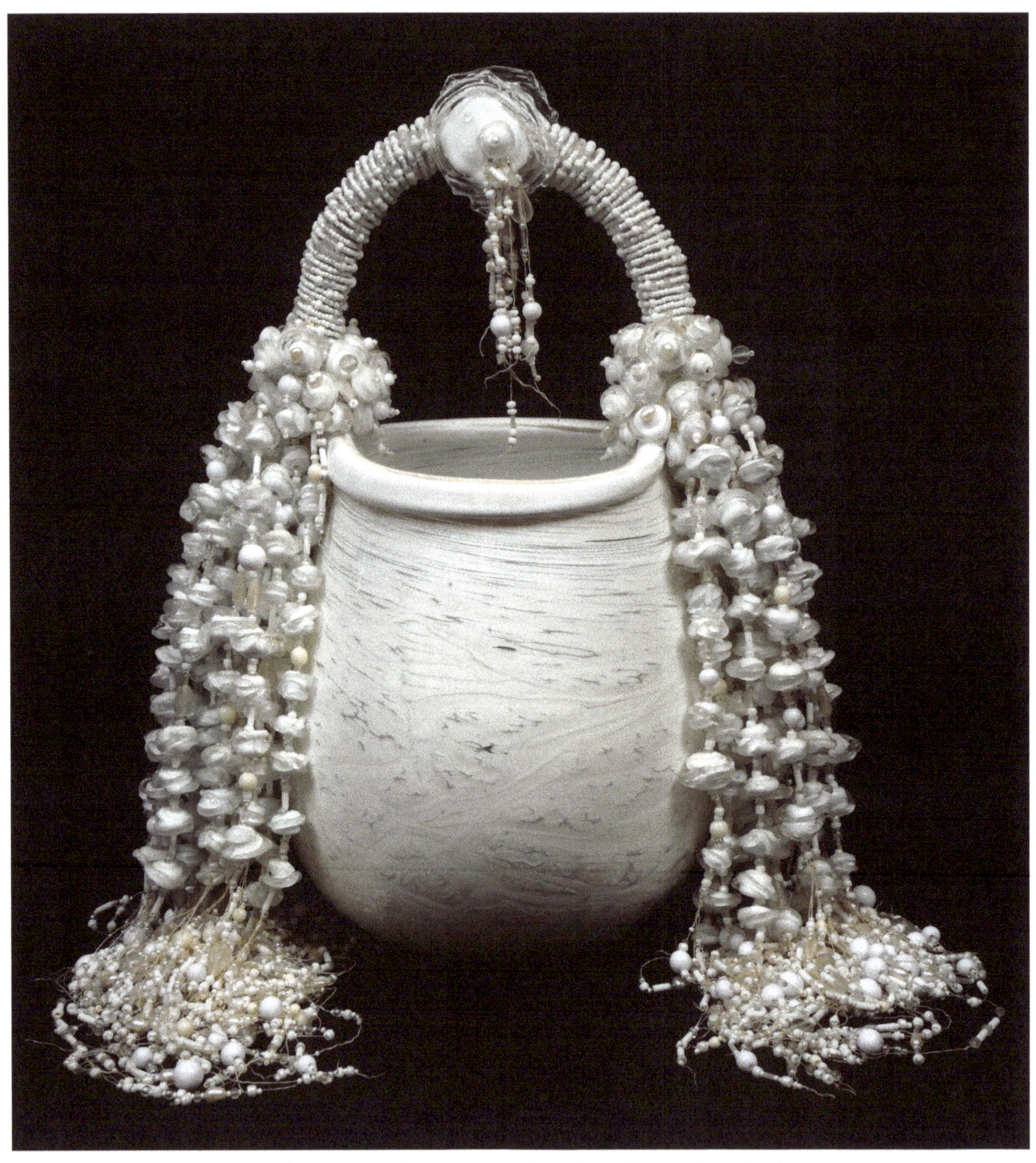

Illustration 15: Laura Donefer, *White Witch Pot*. Photo by Gregory R. Staley. Julius and Ann Kaplan Collection.

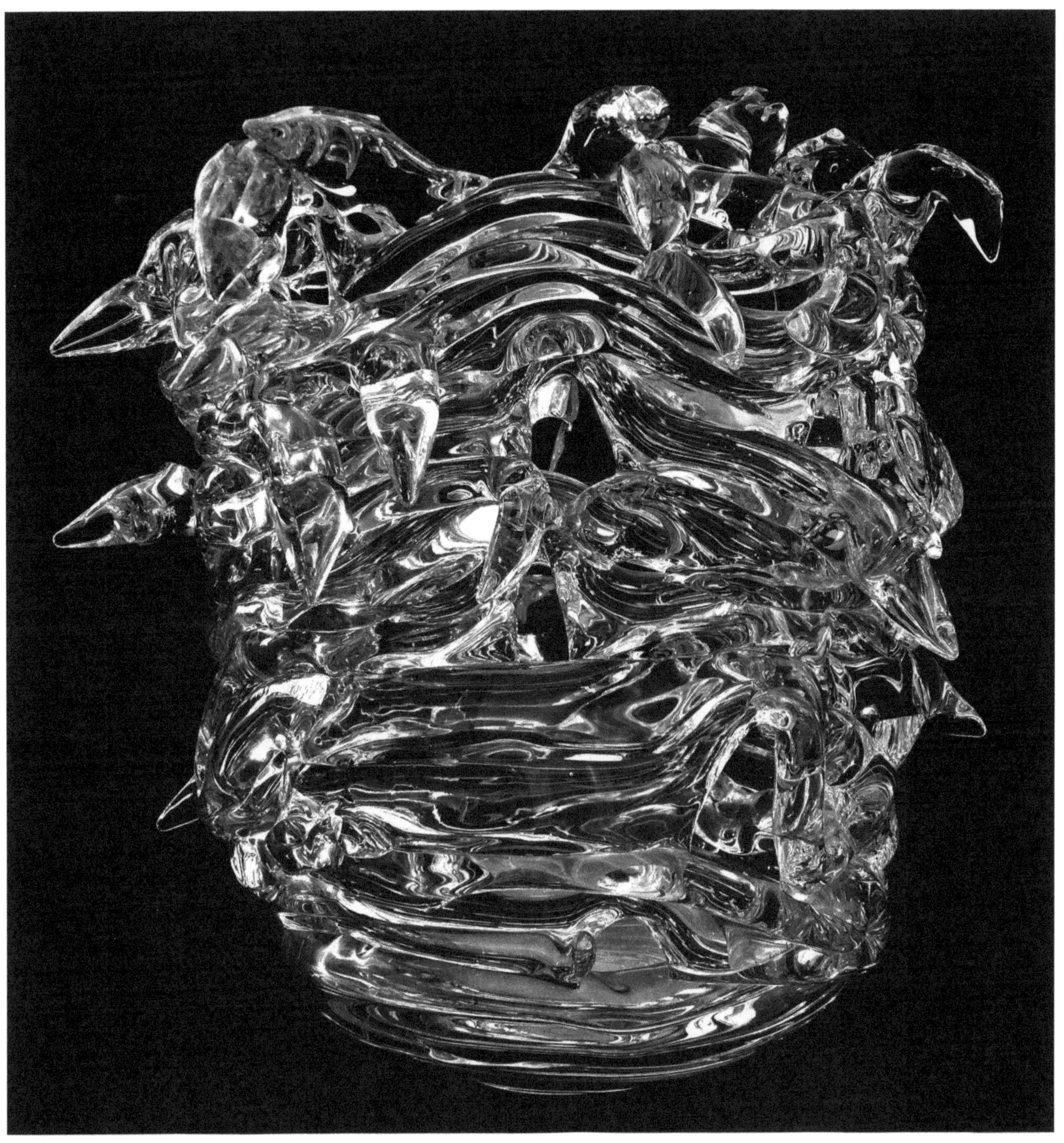

Illustration 16: Laura Donefer, *Masterpiece*. Photo by Gregory R. Staley. Julius and Ann Kaplan Collection.

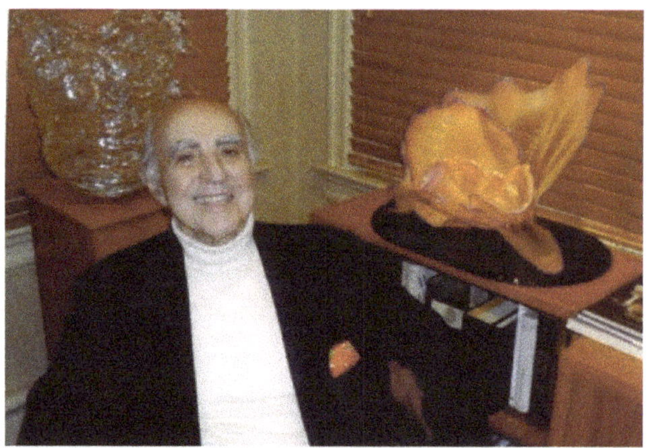

Illustration 19: The author with Donefer's *Masterpiece* (left) and Chihuly's *Seaform* (right)

Here is a picture of me in my home office shortly after *Masterpiece* arrived (Illustration 19).

I later introduced Laura to my friend Fred Hill, a major art dealer in New York (see Chapter 1), who in turn introduced her to the famous chef-restaurateur Daniel Boulud, whose New York restaurant, *Daniel*, was then *le dernier cri* of New York restaurants. Daniel retained Laura to design a small glass candle holder for each table. Her final product was so beautiful that guests decided it would make an ideal souvenir of their memorable dinners chez Daniel. I saw the candle holders only once when I had dinner there with Laura and my daughter, Samantha.

Laura has since become famous, and her work has been exhibited in too many places to list here. I was recently in Sarasota's Ringling Museum's Glass Museum. As I walked in, I could not miss a very large and very colorful Donefer *Witch Pot*. It was quite similar to, but much larger than *Doris Amulet* below. I offer pictures of *Doris Amulet* and another relatively new sculpture by Laura (Illustration 20 and 21).

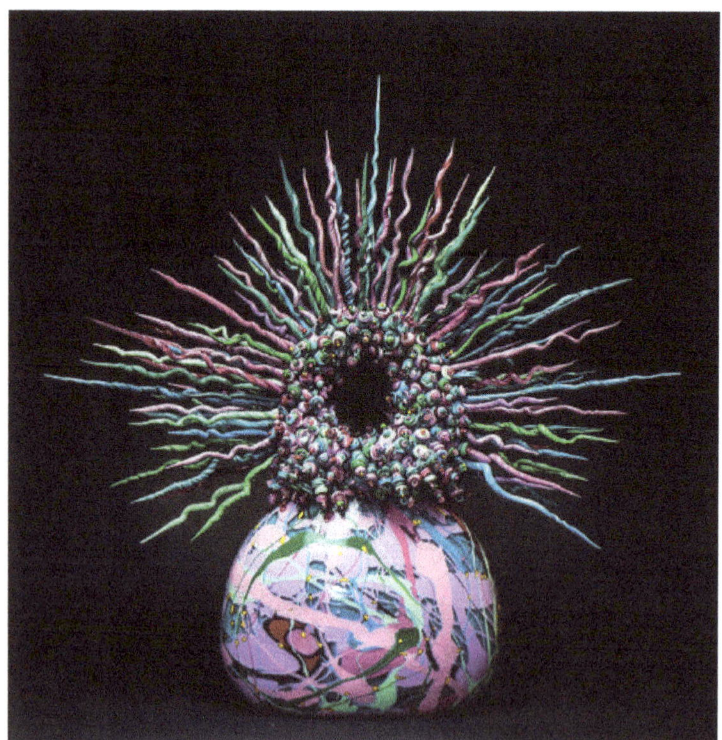

Illustration 20: Laura Donefer, *Primavera Amulet Basket*, 2018.

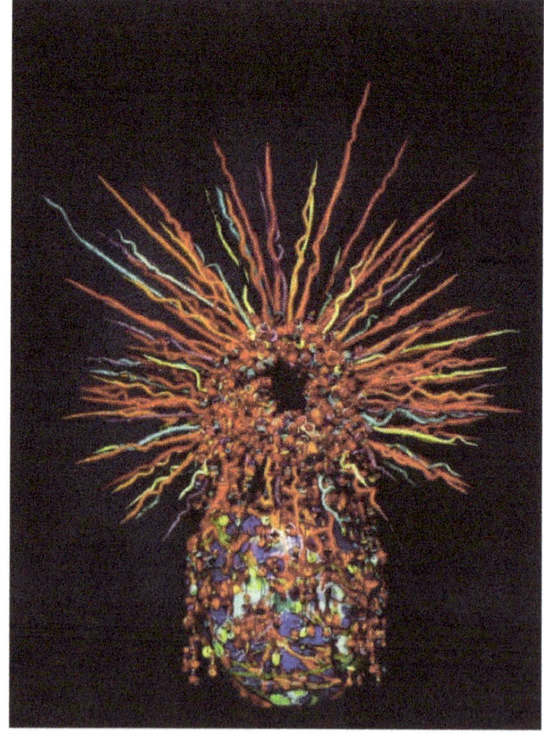

Illustration 21: Laura Donefer, *Doris Amulet*, 2018.

4.10 | JAY MUSLER

On one of my annual trips to the Habatat Gallery in the 1990's, my eyes alighted on a striking piece of sculpture, a round orange bowl with a black outer rim resembling a burnt-out city. It was called *Cityscape* by Jay Musler (Illustration 22).

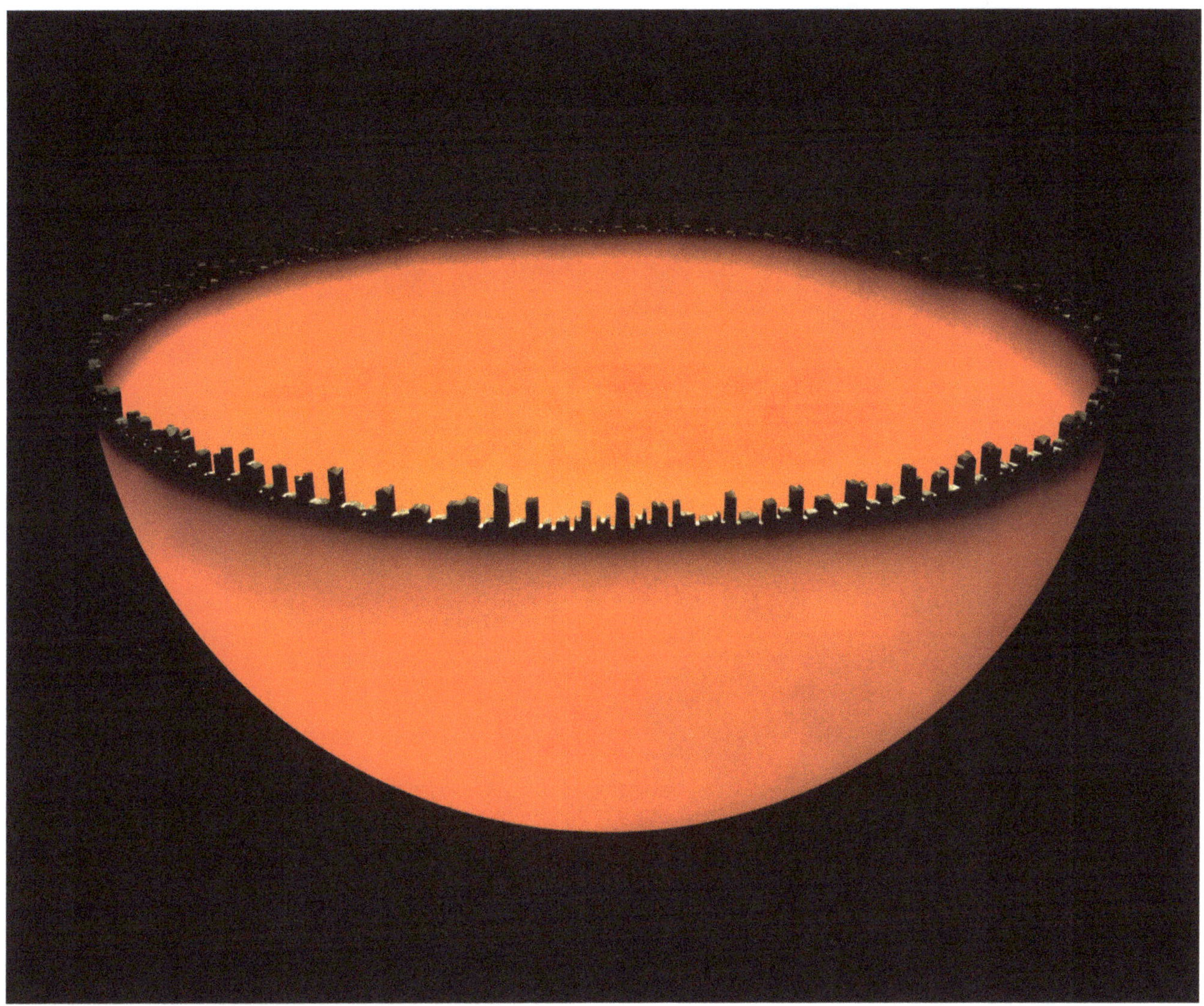

Illustration 22: Jay Musler, *Cityscape*, 1981. Oil paint, borosilicate glass. Photo by Gregory R. Staley. Julius and Ann Kaplan Collection.

I could not resist. I bought it within minutes of first seeing the bowl. That evening, when I viewed my new acquisition, with a dim light illuminating the bowl, I realized that I now possessed one of the single most dramatic glass sculptures that exists. I remain today so taken with this bowl that I have put an image of *Cityscape* on the cover of this book.

It turns out that an illustration of another bowl *Cityscape* by Musler, almost identical to ours, was on the cover of the catalogue of studio glass of The Corning Museum of Glass. It is entitled

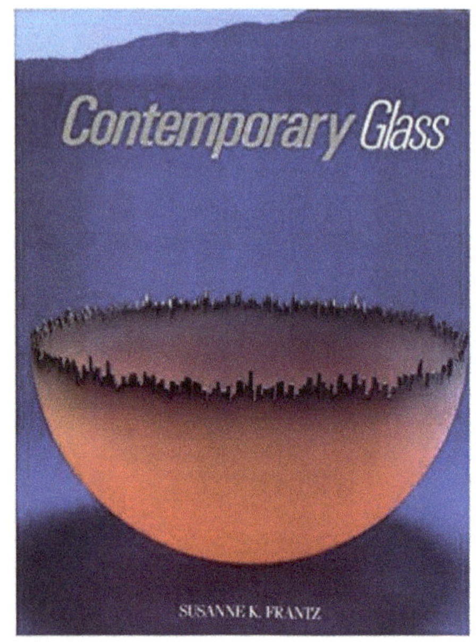

Illustration 23: Musler's Cityscape on the cover of *Contemporary Glass* by Susanne K. Frantz, Abrams Books.

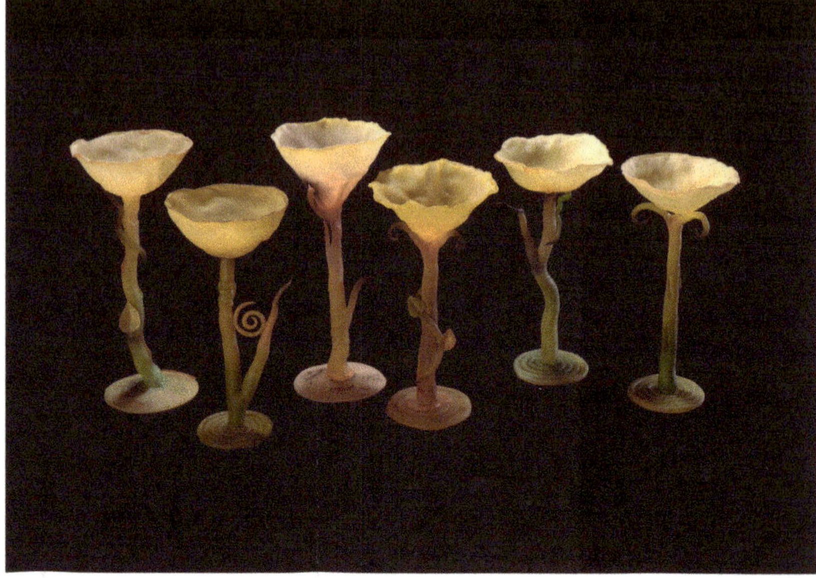

Illustration 24: Jay Musler, wine glasses.

Contemporary Glass by Susanne K. Frantz (Illustration 23). It is his signature piece and often cited as one of the major works of 20th-century American studio crafts.

It is such a beautiful work of art that it deserves two book covers!

Jay Musler was born in Sacramento, California, in 1949. From 1968-1971, he attended the California College of the Arts and Crafts in Oakland, where he took classes from Marvin Lipofsky, who, together with his teacher, Harvey Littleton, was one of the early exponents of studio glass.

Under the influence of Lipofsky, his first creation was a bottle, and later some fanciful wine glasses (Illustration 24). The artist commented about them as follows: "You had to grab the molten glass from the furnace with a long pipe, then wrap it around – like taffy. Once you had it under control, you'd roll it on a marver, a steel table. You could then blow into the pipe, creating a bubble by turning it and blowing into it at the same time. It takes a while, but you soon develop a rhythm and coordination."

He performed so well in college that he received two fellowships: one from the National Endowment for the Arts and another from the California Arts Council. These awards encouraged him to show his work abroad, including Japan. He submitted work at the Hokkaido Museum of Modern Art's exhibition, *World Glass Now*, in Sapporo. He won the top prize.

His early work centered on making lamps. His lamp designs were distinctive and brought him early fame. He individually cut, assembled and then saturated the surfaces of his innovative lamps with rich colors. In 2012, he was the featured artist at the World Lampworking Conference in Salem, New Jersey.

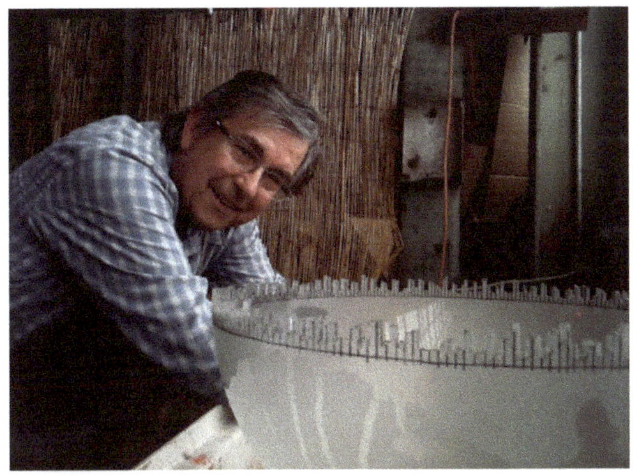

Illustration 25: Jay Musler with a Cityscape before it was painted orange and its rim black.

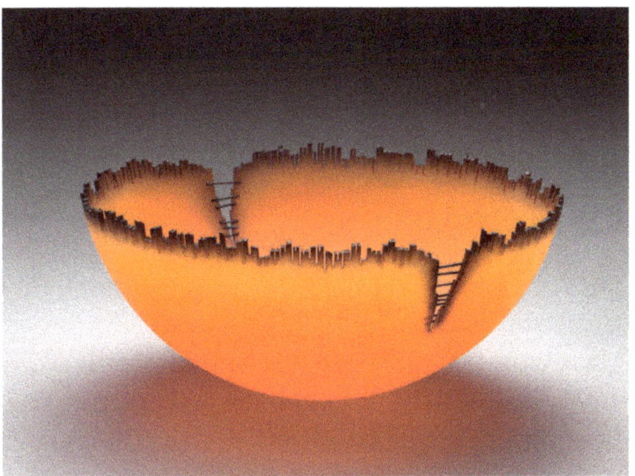

Illustration 26: Jay Musler, *Untitled (Cityscape Bowl)*, 1992. Honolulu Museum of Art, Gift of The Contemporary Museum, Honolulu, 2011, and partial purchase with funds given by Sibyl N. Heide, partial gift of James Jensen in honor of Sibyl N. Heide (TCM.1994.8)

Notwithstanding his success making lamps, Musler wanted to expand into glass sculpture, as others were then starting to do in the Bay area. To quote Musler, "There were some artists at UC Berkley who were doing things with glass that picked up from the industry but went further. You could see a range of "pop art works"—from fetuses to pickles."

Musler then moved into making non-functional objects, such as his *Cityscapes* (Illustration 25). He created big bowls painted orange. He then cut black colored skylines into the rim of the bowl, suggesting cities after an atomic blast. It is claimed that this is symbolic of Musler's strong rejection of war. Notwithstanding, Musler contends that his works are not representational.

These orange bowls became so popular that he made many variations on them, such as the Illustration 26.

On his recent travels to Mexico and Central America, he became fascinated with the ruins he visited of ancient civilizations. Musler was inspired by them to create a series of masks which are to be used as wall pieces. They are heavy and quite fragile.

Musler's oeuvre, created over more than 50 years, is prodigious. The artist now operates the Jay Musler Gallery in San Francisco.[8]

Jay Musler's works are in many museum collections around the world. They include the Renwick Gallery of American Art, the Smithsonian Institution, Washington, DC; The American Craft Museum, New York; The Corning Museum of Glass, Corning, New York; The Metropolitan Museum of Art, New York; Los Angeles County Museum of Art, Los Angeles; M.H. de Young Memorial Museum, San Francisco; The Oakland Museum, Oakland; Detroit Institute of Arts; Honolulu

8 I am indebted to Mathew Rose's Jay Musler, *California Glass Man*, 2018, for the quotes by Jay Musler and for much information on the life and career of the artist.

Academy of Art; Milwaukee Art Museum; The Toledo Museum of Art; Hokkaido Museum of Modern Art, Sapporo, Japan; Kitano Museum, Tokyo, Japan; Musée de Design et d'Arts Appliques Contemporains, Lausanne; and many more.

4.11 | CONCLUSION

Suffice it to say that it is an almost daily delight for me to enter my home office and see most of these above beautiful studio glass sculptures, as well as others not discussed. I have followed studio glass from its infancy to its general popularity around the world today. Indeed, I recently visited a new museum in Sarasota devoted entirely to studio glass. I am sure that there are many more. In addition, major museums, such as the Corning Museum of Glass and the V&A, have extensive collections of studio glass. I attribute much of the great success of studio glass to two of its pioneers: Harvey Littleton and Dale Chihuly. They started an artistic revolution.

CHAPTER 5

Miniature Hanukkah Menorah

We represented the State of Israel as their lawyers on trade matters. As a result, I often had to travel to Jerusalem. I most frequently stayed at the King David Hotel, one of the world's legendary hotels. There were, for me, two important reasons for selecting that hotel. First, they had rooms overlooking the incomparable Old City. And second, Yossi Safed's antique shop was just across the street.

On my first visit to the Yossi's shop, I spotted a tiny silver sailboat with 8 tiny cannons on its port side. I was delighted to find that it was a miniaturized menorah. The eight "cannons" were in reality holders for wicks to be lit during the Hanukkah holiday. I picked it up and studied it closely to find on its hull an inscription reading (in Hebrew), "These lights are sacred." I discovered that when the tiller was turned, the stern section opened up to reveal a storage compartment for wicks. Moreover, the prow section removed to serve as the shamash (servant). The boat is 5.1 inches long by 5.5 inches high. It was made in England in the 19th century (Illustration 1).

Until this visit to Yossi's shop, I did not even suspect that such a thing as a fantasy menorah existed. I was thoroughly delighted by the very idea of miniaturizing a nautical object and turning it into a menorah. I told myself to remain calm or the price would go up with each twinkle of my eyes. But I knew there and then that I was going to become a collector of miniature fantasy menorahs—if they existed beyond this charming boat.

I asked Yossi if he had any other "fantasy" menorahs.

He responded, "No, but there is an elderly gentleman here in Jerusalem who has several. But he hoards them, and will only sell one from his collection when he is short of cash. He needed some cash recently and came in with this sailboat-menorah just last week."

I replied, "Yossi, the boat is fascinating, but as a single item in a display cabinet, it would get lost. I, nevertheless, will buy it if you promise to put aside any additional '"fantasy"' menorahs he decides to sell to you, or any you discover in the market."

Yossi smiled and proffered his hand and said, "It's a deal, Mr. Kaplan; however, I doubt whether I

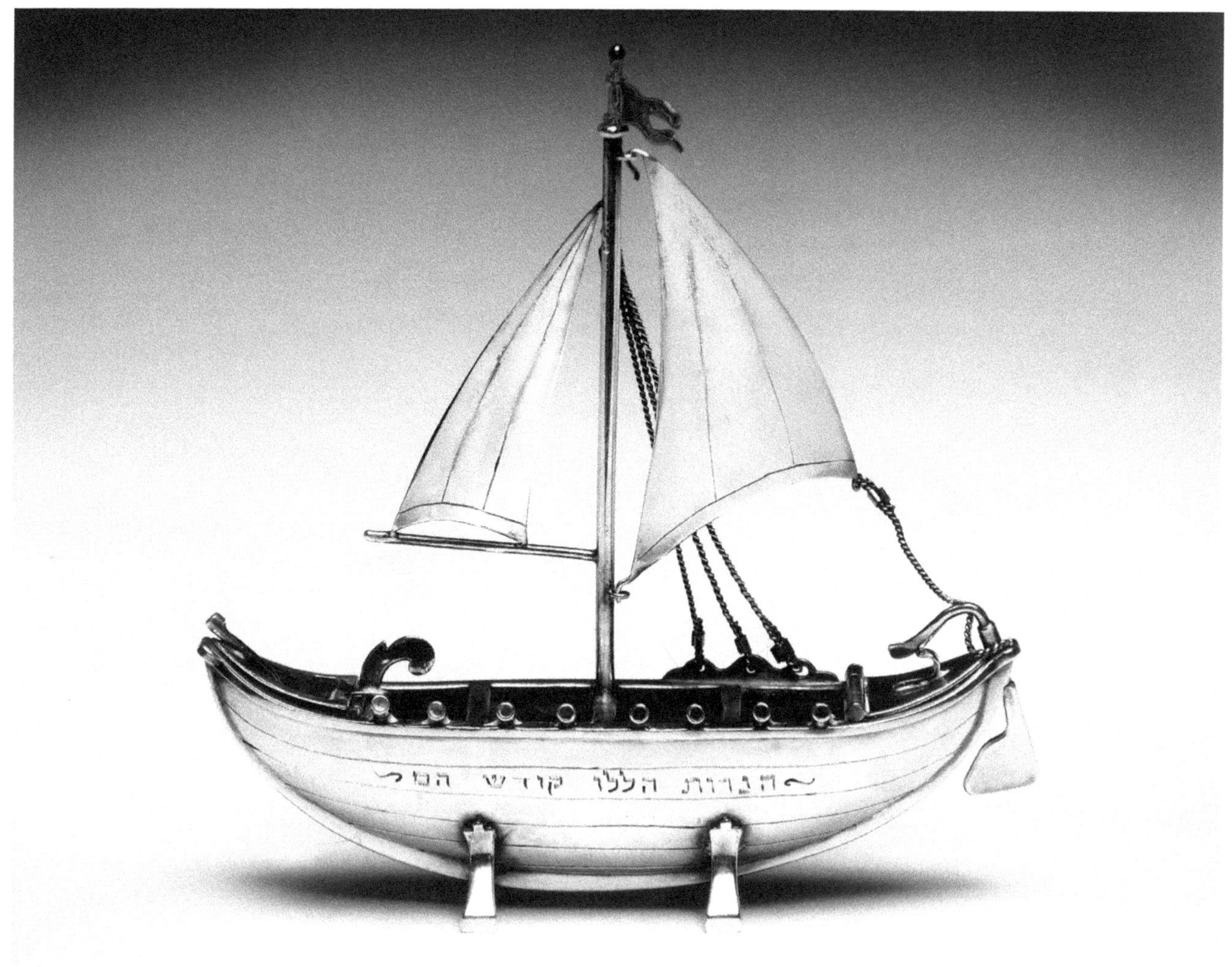

Illustration 1: Fantasy Miniature Hanukkah Menorah in the Shape of a Sailboat. Photo by Gregory R. Staley. Julius and Ann Kaplan Collection.

will find any in the general market. A menorah like this is 'rarissimo.' I will simply have to urge the former owner to sell other gems from his little collection."

As hoped for, over the course of the next eight or nine years, the gentleman in Israel sold Yossi one or sometimes even two menorahs every year. As per our agreement, Yossi alerted me of the new acquisitions, and sent me pictures. Each new miniature menorah was beautiful, rare, and fairly priced. I bought them all.

Over the years, I looked elsewhere for such miniaturized fantasy menorahs, but never found another. On my next trip to Jerusalem, I visited the Judaica Section of the major Israel Jerusalem Museum in search of fantasy miniature menorahs, but found none. (I did find the impressive Feuchtwanger Collection of Judaica, but, alas, no fantasy menorahs.)

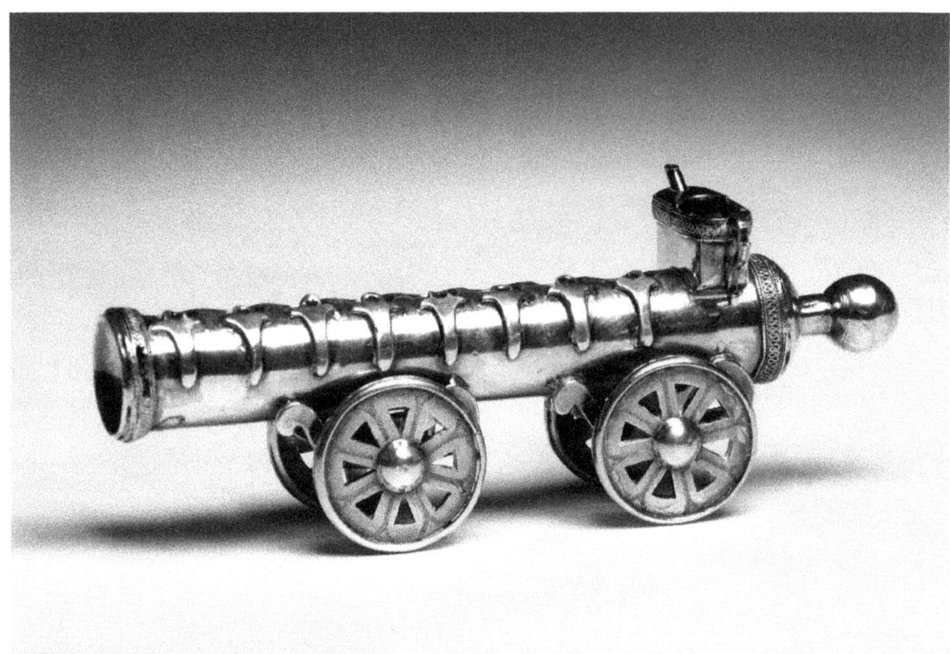

Illustration 2: Miniature Hanukkah Menorah in the Shape of a Cannon. Photo by Gregory R. Staley. Julius and Ann Kaplan Collection.

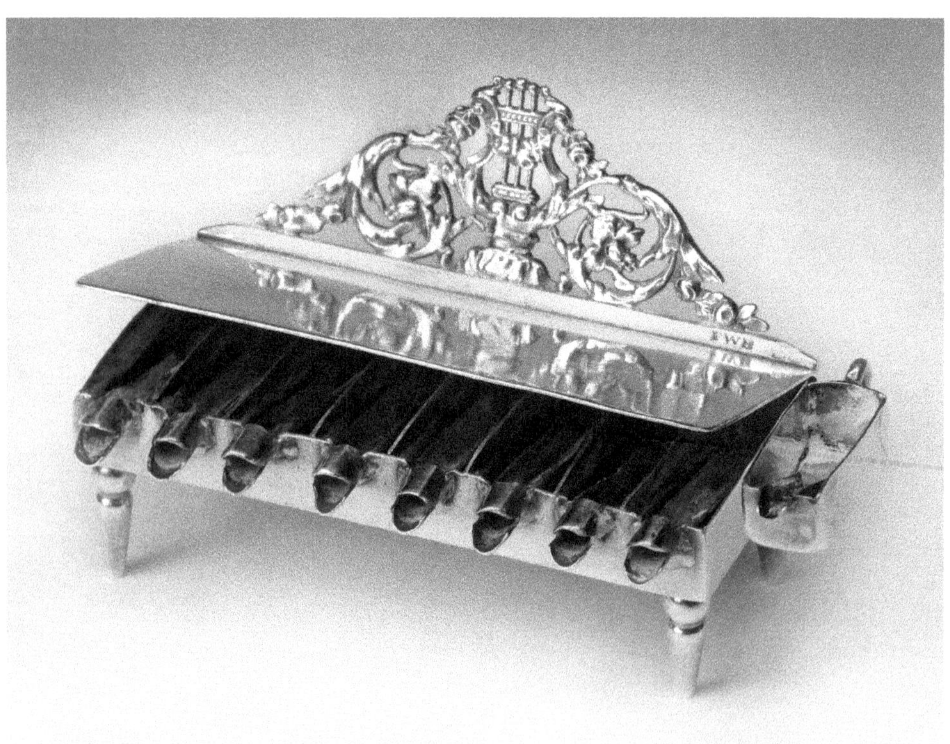

Illustration 3: Miniature Hanukkah Menorah in the Shape of a Piano. Photo by Gregory R. Staley. Julius and Ann Kaplan Collection.

The next "fantasy" menorah Yossi secured from the elusive collector was in the form of a cannon. I bought it after only one glance at the menorah. It too was a delight to the eye and the imagination.

The barrel of the cannon was on wheels, with the words "Feast of Lights" and a Star of David engraved on it. The knob at the base of the cannon rotated an interior cylinder which opened and closed all of the chambers. There was an incised decoration on the barrel, and the wheels revolved, so the cannon could be rolled. It was 6.3 inches long by 1.77 inches high (Illustration 2). It was likely made in England in the late 19th century or early 20th century.

One day I was looking at my two fantasy menorahs, and gave thought to how much I enjoyed them, and wished that I would hear from Yossi that he secured yet another one for me. As if by magic, the very next day Yossi called to advise that he had acquired a miniature menorah if the form of a piano. Before he could finish asking me if I were interested in buying it, I cried out. "Yes, Yes, Yes." (Illustration 3).

The piano was Austro-Hungarian, made in the mid-19th century. It had a maker's mark. It also had an openwork backplate with scrolling foliage supporting a stylized menorah, and the hinged piano lid rose to reveal oil chambers. It was 3.54 inches wide, 2.36 inches high, and 2.1 inches deep.

Yossi also said that he had acquired from the same source a most important traveling Hanukkah menorah. He explained, "Traveling menorahs were usually silver, very small in size, like a woman's compact. They are small enough for travelers to keep in their pockets and pocketbooks. When opened, they reveal a tiny menorah with openings to hold wicks. The body would be filled with oil. Travelers light the wicks as they would candles at home."

Yossi explained further, "This menorah opens to display a shamash (servant) to be connected to an arm which slides into and out of the menorah. There is a compartment on the side to store wicks, and another one to hold a dreidel, a children's toy for a traditional Hanukkah game. There is also a compartment on the side to store wicks (Illustration 4(a) and (b)). This travelling menorah was made in 19th Century Russia by Pavel Ovchinnikov. His mark was on the underside of the lid."

Ovchinnikov was a renowned Russian jeweler, silversmith, goldsmith and enameller, almost as well known in his day as Peter Carl Fabergé. He opened his own workshop with his wife's dowry of a thousand rubles in 1851. By 1865 he was appointed official purveyor to the future Tsar Alexander. Ovchinnikov was awarded the Légion d'honneur in1867 and the Order of the Iron Crown in 1873.

The Ovchinnikov traveling menorah is pictured in Illustration 4(a) assembled and in 4(b) disassembled for use.

Over the years, Yossi sold me several additional rare antique traveling menorahs, which were very lovely, and added them to my Judaica collection. He also made me a very small compact gold square which opens to become a menorah. I also found miniature traditionally shaped menorahs. In all I have 13 miniature hanukkah menorahs.

Our miniature menorah collection has been on public display in a number of museums and other venues, including the St. Petersburg Art Museum, the B'nai B'rith Museum, and the Cosmos Club.

The Director of the St. Petersburg Museum told me that he was most appreciative of the loan of

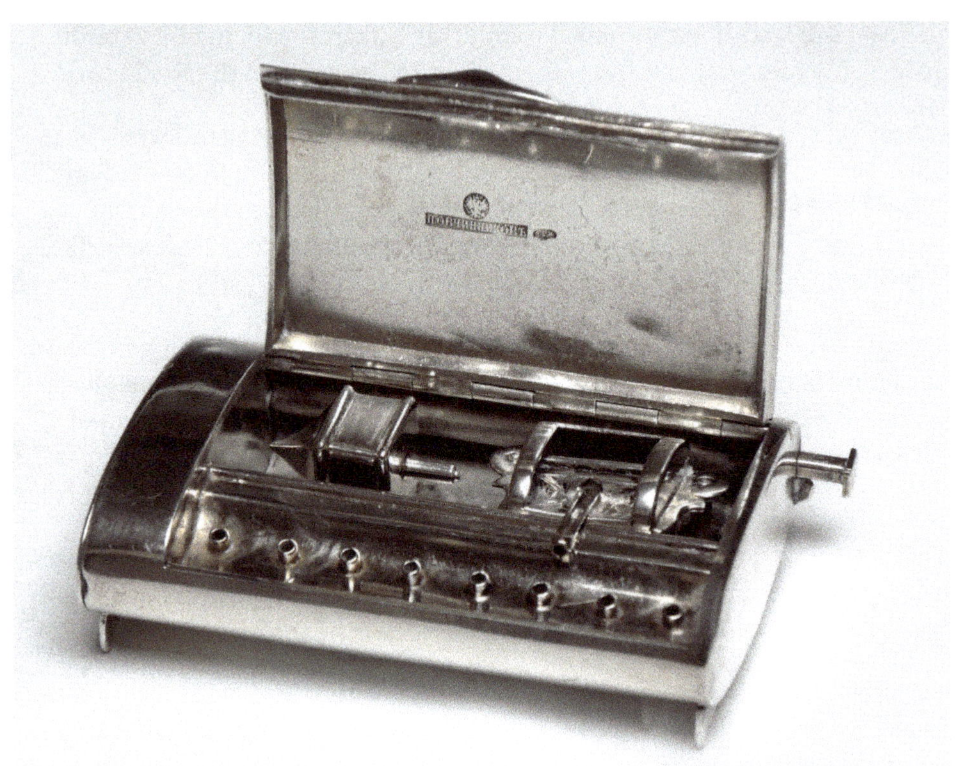

Illustration 4a: 19th Century Russian Traveling Menorah by Pavel Ovchinnikov. Photo by Gregory R. Staley. Julius and Ann Kaplan Collection.

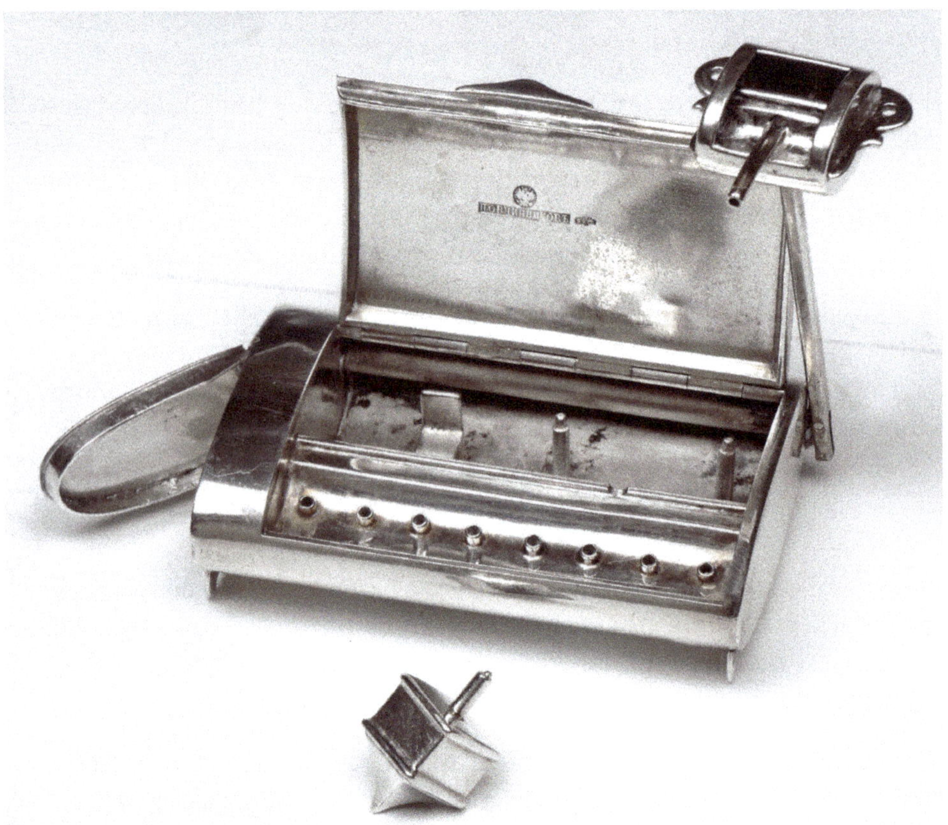

Illustration 4b: Pavel Ovchinnikov's Traveling Menorah as in (4a) but opened for use. Photo by Gregory R. Staley. Julius and Ann Kaplan Collection.

our collection during the Christmas season, since they otherwise had only Christmas decorations. Several members of the museum's board of directors were Jewish and had previously complained that there was nothing in the museum to show that it was also the Hanukkah season. He advised me that our collection seemed to pacify the Jewish directors.!

The Hanukkah menorah and its kindred lights has, from the time of the Maccabees to the present, served as the pre-eminent reminder of the struggle of the Jews against religious oppression. The specific structure of the Hanukkah menorah—eight lights, with a ninth, the shamash, to kindle the others—derives from the story told in Maccabees II. There was only a tiny portion of pure oil, barely enough to rekindle the Temple menorah for a single day. However, after the Maccabean victory, the tiny portion served to last not one day, but eight days. The menorah, in memory of this event, has eight lights, which are lit progressively from one wick per night, up to eight on the eighth night.

In the catalogue of a show of our collection at the B'nai B'rith Museum in Washington, D.C., in 1991-92, the then Director of the Museum, Ori Soltes, wrote, "It is perhaps the joyous symbolism of the Feast of Lights, celebrated at home rather than in a temple, that has led to the high interest in the Hanukkah menorah. The traditional menorah has a stem and eight branches, one for each light, and a ninth "shamash" to light the others. The Kaplans have several traditional types of menorahs in their collection, but instead of being twelve to twenty-four inches in height, as is the norm, theirs are only two or three inches in height. They are thus miniature menorahs, and ones as fine as those in the Kaplan collection are very rare indeed."

Ori Soltes concludes his essay by writing, "The Kaplan Hanukiyyot are a particularly stunning symbol of the triumphant side of the human spirit."

CHAPTER 6

Indian Miniture Paintings

Ann and I made a honeymoon trip to India in 1963. After doing the things tourists do, we visited Sundar Nagar market in New Delhi, where we had been told by friends, who were collectors of Indian art, to meet a Mr. Bharany who was a highly regarded dealer in Indian miniature paintings and Mughal jewelry. We found him in his shop, not surprisingly named "Bharany's". It appeared to be a jewelry shop, but when we said that we were interested in miniature Indian paintings, he ushered us into his back room where he had numerous folios of such paintings. He explained that there were a number of different schools of Indian miniature paintings which he described. He showed us samples of each. Both Ann and I were particularly taken with the Mughal school and selected an 18th-century Mughal painting of a bearded gentleman standing alone on a large green field, with a decorated sword in hand and its case hanging from his waist. He wore a long white robe-like garment, and a ring on his right thumb, and another on his left little finger (Illustration 1).

Mr. Bharany advised that genuine Mughal portraits like the one we were considering had become very rare. We bought the painting, and have enjoyed it for almost 55 years.

On subsequent trips to India, I bought a number of other Indian miniature paintings from Mr. Bharany. They were all from the Pahari hill country and one from Jaipur, in Rajasthan. Our favorites are described below. But before turning to them, let us briefly examine what a Mughal painting is, and secondly, examine a "wee bit" of the history of Mughal paintings over the centuries.

6.1 | MUGHAL ART

Mughal painting was at its height in the 16th-19th centuries during the Mughal Empire. The paintings were most often miniatures, more or less the size of a book page. They were mainly painted in the courts of the Emperors, and were generally in the form of book illustrations. Mughal emperors often caused memoires to be written with lavishly decorated texts. Mughal paintings were influenced by Persian miniature paintings. Moreover, the Persian tradition of decorating the borders of paintings was common. In a recent book by Dr. Mika Natif, entitled *Mughal Occidentalism: Artistic*

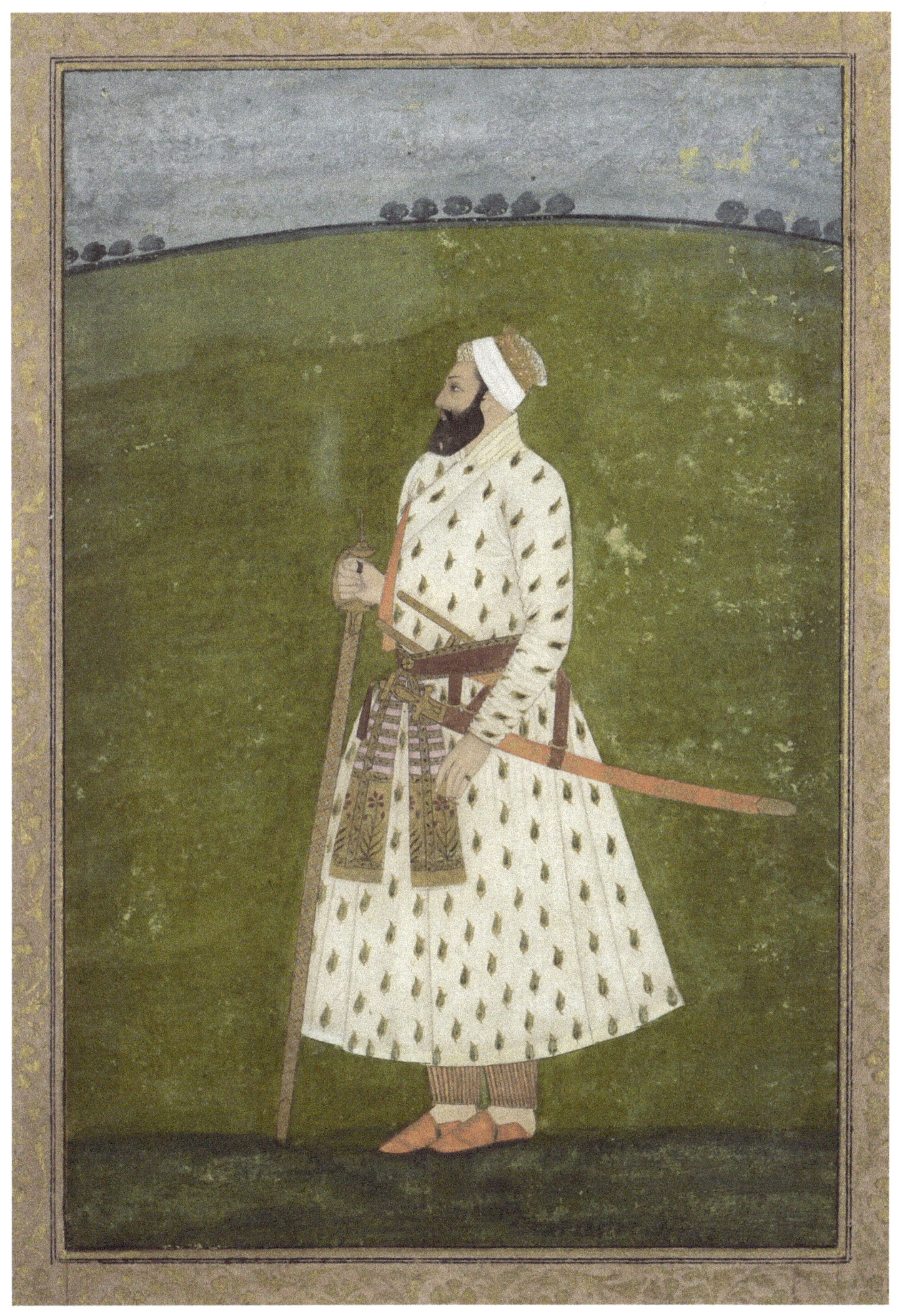

Illustration 1: Mughal Portrait of a Gentleman, 18th century. Photo by Gregory R. Staley. Julius and Ann Kaplan Collection.

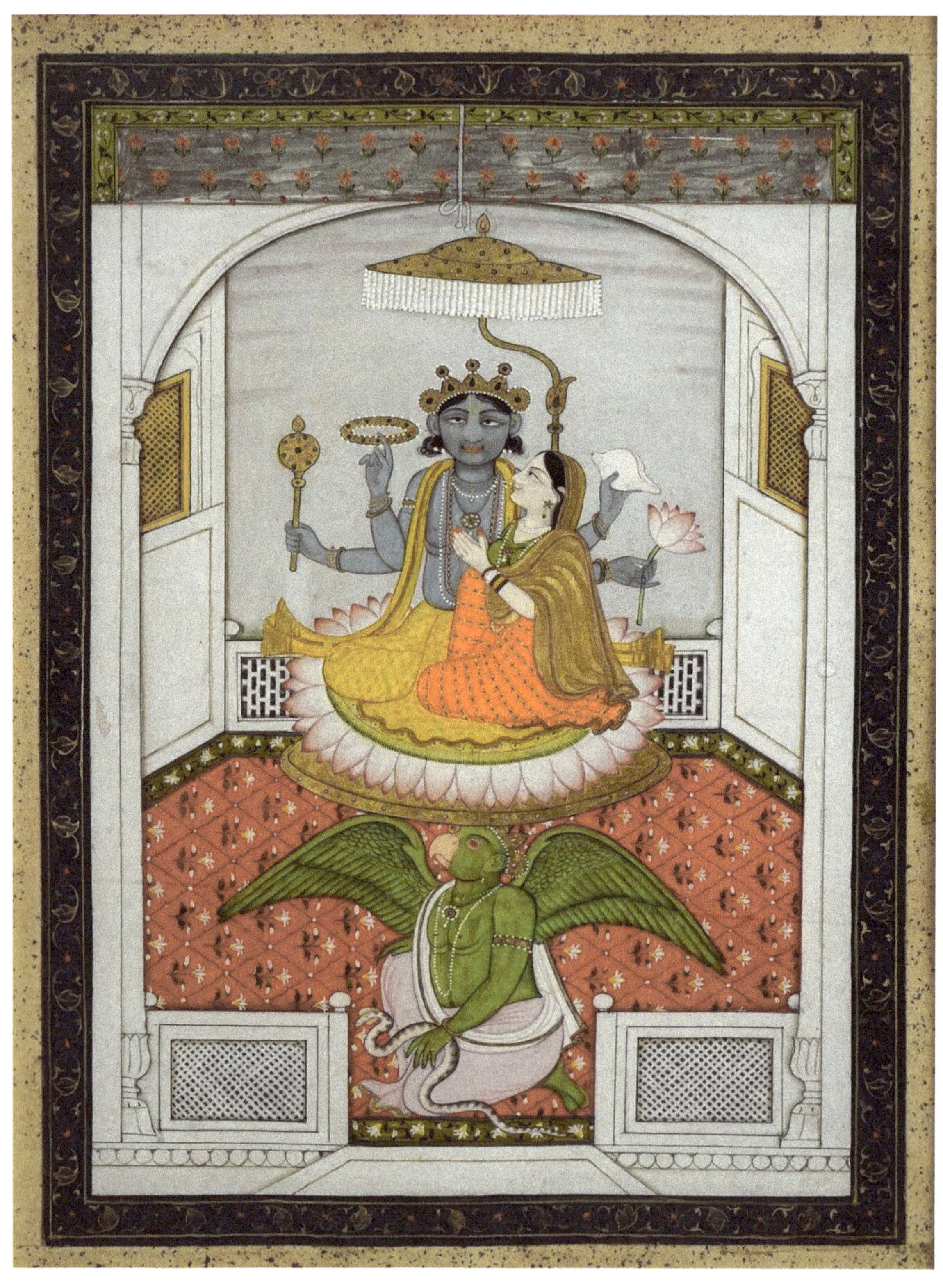

Illustration 2: *Vishnu and Lakshmi Enthroned on a Lotus, Attended by Garuda* (circa 1750). Attributed to the Workshop of Manaku in Guler. Photo by Gregory R. Staley. Julius and Ann Kaplan Collection.

Encounters Between Europe and Asia in the Courts of India, 1580-1620, the author contends that there was also European influence in Mughal paintings.

6.2 | VERY SHORT HISTORY OF MUGHAL ART

Emperor Akbar's reign (1556–1605) ushered in Indian miniature painting using artists from both Persia and India. He was the first monarch to establish his own atelier with more than a hundred painters. A new Mughal School of miniature paintings thus came into being under his direction.

One of the popular subjects of Mughal art was the Hamzanama series, which were stories of Amir Hamza, an uncle of the Prophet. Many were illustrated by a famous artist named Mir Sayyid Ali. The usually large paintings of the Hamzanama were painted on cloth in the Persian Safavid style.

After Akbar, Jahangir became the emperor (1605-1627). He encouraged artists to paint portraits and court scenes. Shah Jahan (1627–1658) followed Akbar and continued the patronage of painting. However, Aurangzeb (1658-1707), who followed Sha Jahan, had no taste for fine arts. As a result, artists migrated to Hyderabad in the Deccan, to the Pahari in the Himalayan regions, and to the Hindu state of Rajasthan in search of new patrons.

The other non-Mughal Indian miniature paintings we bought from Mr. Bharany were painted in several of the areas where the formerly Mughal artists migrated to; namely, the Pahari and Rajasthan.

6.3 | PAHARI PAINTINGS IN THE KAPLAN COLLECTION

One of the Pahari paintings in our collection is Vishnu and Lakshmi Enthroned on a Lotus, Attended by Garuda. It has been attributed to the workshop of Manaku, an influential artist from Guler. The painting dates from circa 1750 (Illustration 2).

Pahari paintings, such as the present one, were executed in the hilly regions of India, in the sub-Himalayan state of Himachal Pradesh.

According to Dr. Debra Diamond, curator of Indian paintings at the Freer-Sackler Gallery, this painting is probably part of a series depicting the avatars of Vishnu. She writes, "This folio depicts Vishnu's supreme form, with four arms holding aloft mace, discuss, conch, and lotus. The goddess Lakshmi, with her hands clasped in the worship gesture of Anjali mudras, looks adoringly at her husband."

Manaku Chitraka was a highly esteemed artist. According to B.N. Grosmamy's "Manaku of Guler," Manaku "was endowed with a soaring imagination and great painterly skills, ... capable of painting the world of impassioned lovers." And that is reflected in this painting by one of his followers.

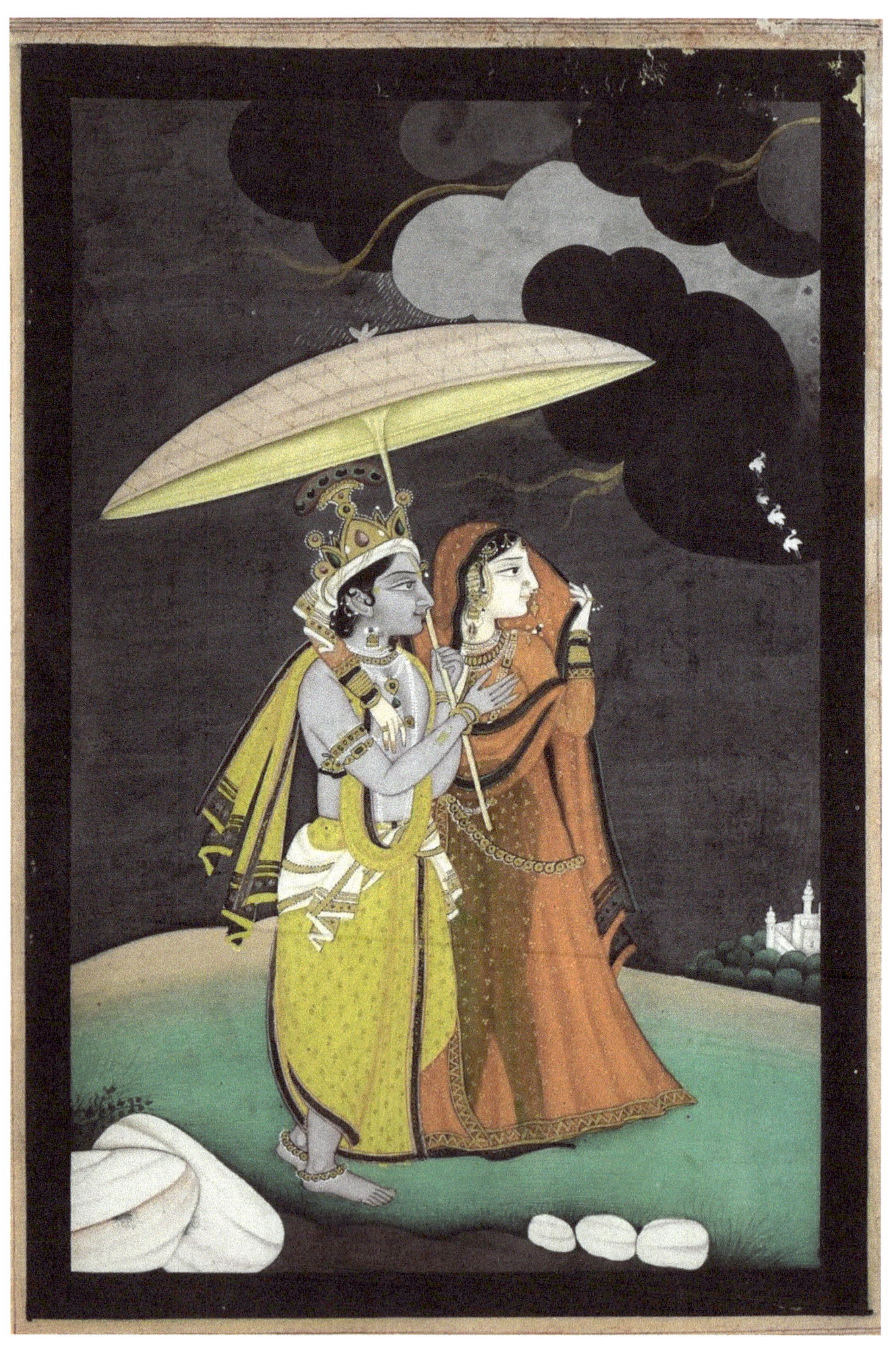

Illustration 3: *Krishna and Radha on a Monsoon Night*, Kangra, circa 1820-1846. Photo by Gregory R. Staley. Julius and Ann Kaplan Collection.

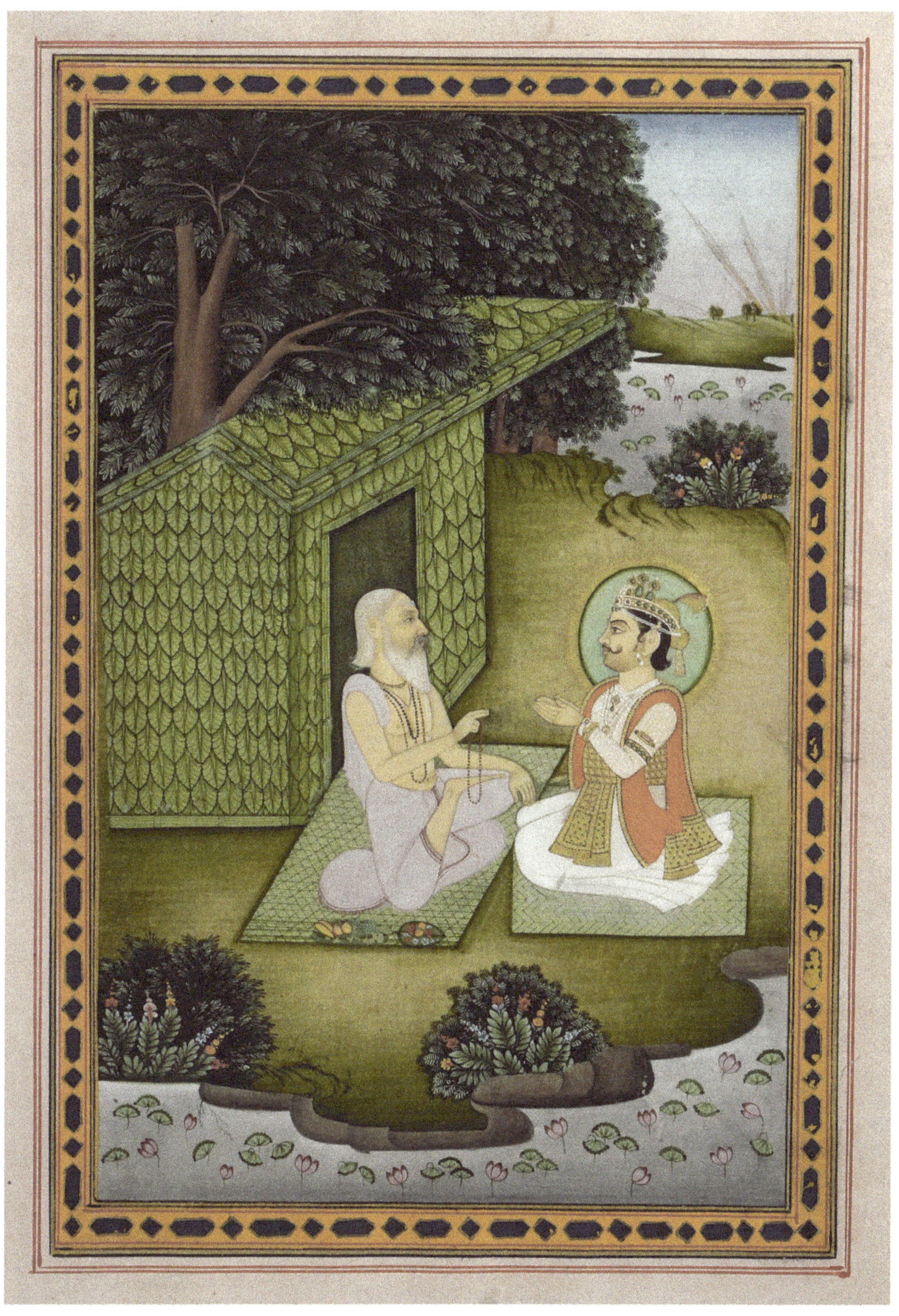

Illustration 4: *Maharaja Sawai Pratap Singh Visits a Sage in a Forest Hermitage*, circa 1800. Photo by Gregory R. Staley. Julius and Ann Kaplan Collection.

6.4 | KRISNA AND RADHA ON A MANSOON NIGHT. KANGRA, CA. 1820-1840

According to Dr. Diamond, the bright colors, particularly the green of the grass, and harder edges, indicate that our painting, Krishna and Radha on a Monsoon Night, was painted in the second quarter of the 19th Century.

In the late seventeenth and eighteenth century, Krishna and Radha became the archetypal lovers of courtly poetry. Quoting Dr. Diamond, "This lovely work represents the two on a monsoon evening. The monsoon was associated with joy, auspiciousness and romance (not least because men stayed home during the monsoon season.) Krishna is characteristically dressed in a peacock-feather topped crown and a yellow dhoti" (Illustration 3).

Kangra paintings of ancient India were done in the Pahari between the 17th and 19th centuries. Kangra was located in the sub-Himalayan state of Himachal Pradesh. The Kangra School, which represents a mature level of Pahari paintings, became the most important center of such art.

These Radha-Krishna love scenes were a popular theme in Kangra paintings. They are usually depicted in nature, such as in this painting, or against an architectural background of walls, balconies and windows. (The latter are referred to as "Sat Sai" depictions.)

6.5 | SCHOOL OF JAIPUR

We have one Rajasthani painting in our collection: Maharaja Sawai Pratap Singh (1764-1803) Visits a Sage in a Forest Hermitage. The painting was made in Jaipur, Rajasthan, circa 1800 (Illustration 4).

Maharaja Saewai Pratap Singh was ruler of Jaipur from 1778 to 1803. He succeeded his father, Madho Singh I. He was a grandson of Maharaja Sawai Singh II, founder of Jaipur.

According to "Jaipur Painting" by Rita Pratap, "The Jaipur School of art was aristocratic and decorative, while its expression was conventional and the theme traditional; the aesthetic sense was hypersensitive and the style was pompous...The paintings from Jaipur are often referred to as Rajasthani paintings, since Jaipur is the capital of the state of Rajasthan in northern India. The art of each reign differed slightly from preceding reigns, although they have many stylistic features in common."

6.6 | CONCLUSION

Although I loved Indian miniature paintings, and I traveled from time to time to India (since I represented the Indian government on certain matters), the Kaplan collection of Indian miniature paintings is small. The major reason for this is that, in or around 1973, the Indian government prohibited the exportation of these paintings. I accordingly discontinued buying Indian miniature paintings from India. I, however, continued seeing Mr. Bharany, who sold me some beautiful Indian Mughal jewelry for Ann.

CHAPTER 7

Gandhara Art

"Gandhara" is the name given to the land and its associated civilization in what are now northern Pakistan (in the area of Peshawar) and eastern Afghanistan. The state of Gandhara lasted from the mid-1st millennium B.C.E. into the 2nd century C.E. Although multiple dynasties ruled over this area, they all had Buddhism as a religion, and Greco-Buddhist art as their cultural identity. Indeed, Gandhara art has been described as the melding of Buddhism with classical Greek culture left over from Alexander the Great, who came to the region in the 4th century B.C.E.

Gandhara became a "jewel" of Buddhist civilization. It included the earliest oil painting in human history, and it gave the world some of the most beautiful depictions of the Buddha in human form.

I was originally exposed to the art of Gandhara in an art course at Wesleyan University, and found it to be intriguing. I hoped someday to own a piece of Gandhara sculpture. Whenever I visited a museum with an important collection of Gandhara, I always tried to set aside enough time to do the collection justice. The best collections of Gandhara art that I have visited are housed in the Metropolitan Museum of Art, the Guimet Museum in Paris, the British Museum in London, and, of course, the Peshawar Gandhara Museum. The latter has the largest collection in the world. Other museums in Pakistan are also rich in Gandara art.

In the mid-1960's, I made my first trip to Karachi, the then capital of Pakistan, on a mission for AID. I saw this as my opportunity to realize my undergraduate hope of someday owning a Gandhara sculpture. I was advised by friends who had bought Gandhara art in Karachi to visit a certain carpet shop in the city. I dutifully searched out and found it. However, as I entered the shop, I saw many carpets, but no Gandhara art, except for a small piece in the doorway. I asked the owner if he had any more Gandhara sculpture. He told me to go to the back room.

Entering the room, I saw before me a veritable museum of Gandhara sculptures. I was most intrigued with a standing Buddha about five feet tall, at least until the owner told me the price. I explained that I was only a government bureaucrat, and could unfortunately not afford to pay anything like the price of the standing Buddha. The owner then showed me a sculpture from the second/third centuries C.E., which he said had come from a stupa. (He explained that a stupa was a commemorative monument, usually housing sacred relics associated with the Buddha.)

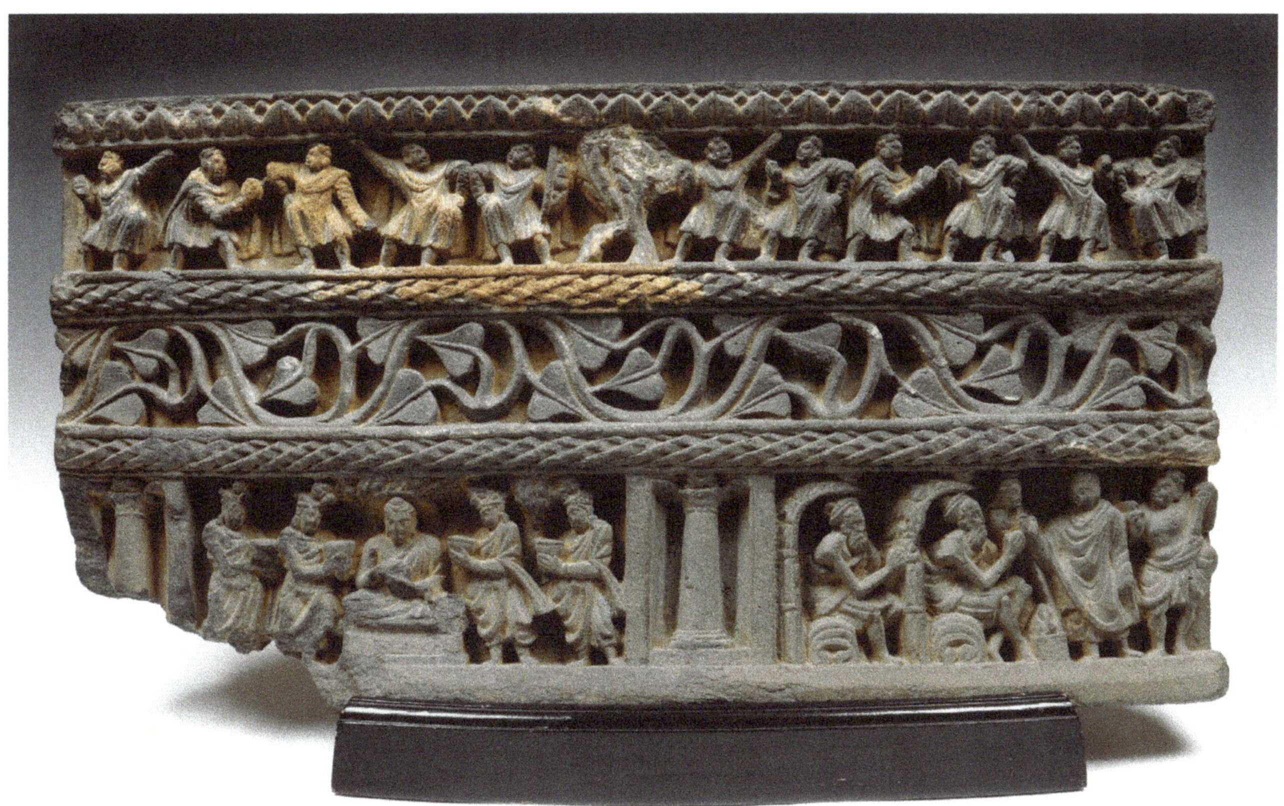

Illustration 1: Gandhara Sculpture from a Stupa, c. 250 C.E. Photo by Gregory R. Staley. Julius and Ann Kaplan Collection.

He extolled both the beauty and the fine condition of it. The shop owner went on to say that it was not easy to find Gandhara sculptures in such good condition, pointing at the other sculptures in his collection. I saw that almost every sculpture was damaged, and some very severely. I asked how this had happened.

He explained, "Although these sculptures are pre-Islamic, in the 7th century C.E., when the Islamists invaded eastern India, including the area where Pakistan is now, they injured and often destroyed virtually all of the sculptures as being the work of infidels. The followers of Islam did not countenance the representation of a human figure, since it goes contrary to the dictates of Islam. The fact that these figures all pre-dated Islam was irrelevant. As a result of this destructiveness, it is rare in the extreme to find a Gandhara sculpture which is in perfect condition."

I later learned that the invaders had actually tolerated the local Greco-Buddhist sculptures for some years, until they were told by visiting strict imams that they violated Islamic law and should be destroyed. They, thereafter, damaged or destroyed most of the sculpture.

At one point, I asked the owner of the shop, how a carpet dealer in Karachi got into the Gandhara sculpture business. He explained, "I originally sold only carpets, although I did have a small piece of Gandhara sculpture to keep the door open. I bought it on a trip to Peshawar. At that time, in

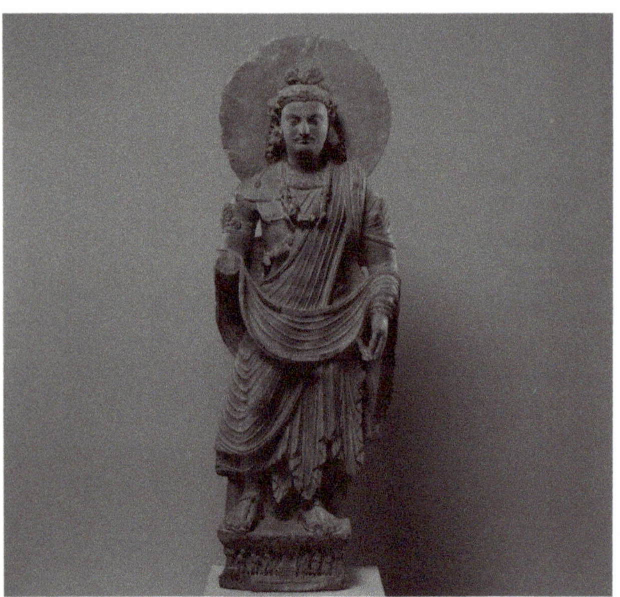

Illustration 2: Standing Bodhisattva Maitreya (Buddha of the Future), circa 3rd century, Metropolitan Museum of Art. Purchase, Lita Annenberg Hazen Charitable Trust Gift, 1991.

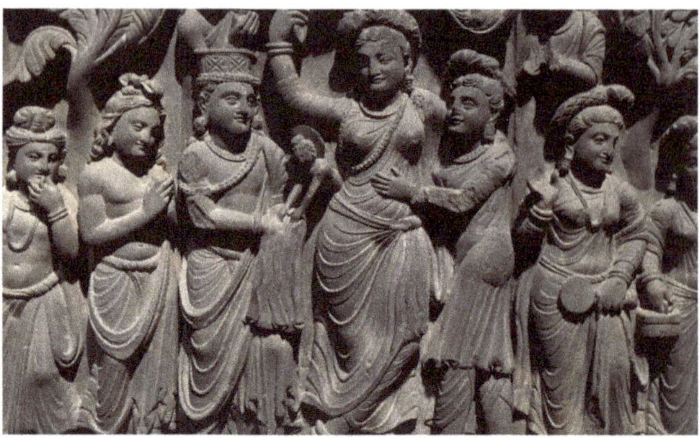

Illustration 3: Four Scenes from the Life of the Buddha - (Detail) The Birth of the Buddha, Kushan dynasty, late 2nd-early 3rd century. Freer Gallery of Art, Smithsonian Institution, Washington, D.C.: Purchase — Charles Lang Freer Endowment, F1949.9a-d

Peshawar, small fragments and loose heads of sculptures were ubiquitous, and children would dig them up and sell them in the streets. One day, a German woman came into my carpet shop, looked carefully at the Gandhara door stop, and asked how much it would cost. I recalled having paid about 10 rupees for it, that is, 90-80 U.S. cents. I looked closely at the woman. She looked wealthy in her black leather outfit, and the leather briefcase she carried was elegant. I decided to make a few extra rupees, and said, '"One thousand,"'—of course, meaning rupees. I assumed that she would make a counter-offer, but to my surprise she immediately said, 'O.K.', and handed me ten one hundred-dollar bills! I thereafter enlarged my shop and added Gandhara sculpture to my business."

After some smiles on my part in appreciation of his story, and after a bit more reflection, I decided to buy the stupa fragment, and asked him the price. It was too high, but I had been forewarned that in Pakistan you had to bargain. I made a counter offer of 50%. He added a few rupees to my counter offer, and I accepted. I thereby became the owner of a lovely Gandhara schist sculpture (Illustration 1).

The sculpture I bought was a slightly curved piece of schist stone dated from around 250 C.E., according to the owner of the shop. It was 11 inches high and 22 inches long, and had three levels. The top-level displayed men dancing; the middle level was a classic Buddhist design; and the lower level displayed two scenes from the life of Buddha.

I have during subsequent visits to Pakistan bought some fragments of Gandhara sculpture, but the purchase described was my only "major" Gandhara purchase.

When my Gandhara sculpture finally arrived in Washington, D.C., we noted that parts of it had particles of sand embedded in it (see upper left portion). Ann and I tried to remove the sand, particle by particle. Before we could remove much of it, we had the occasion to go to Paris and visit the Guimet Museum of Asian Art. As noted above, they have a large collection of Gandhara. When we looked carefully at the objects in the museum's collection, we noted that many of them contained spots where the sand from the burial of the sculpture remained. We immediately decided that if the Guimet did not feel it was necessary to remove the sand, we would not either.

Since my Gandhara is hardly an important example, may I offer two images of more serious Gandara sculptures. I chose these examples from the collection of the Metropolitan Museum of Art with the hope that they will encourage some of my readers to visit them (Illustrations 2), and for the ease getting copyright permissions. I had originally selected several images from Asian museums, but getting copyright permission was just too difficult.

For years, I was legal counsel to the Islamic Republic of Pakistan. During the 1980's, Pakistan's ambassador to the United States was Jamsheed Marker. I worked closely with him on major issues, such as those related to the Russian invasion of Afghanistan. Ann and I became close friends with Jamsheed, who is now deceased, and his widow, Arnaz Marker. They owned a stunning Gandhara emaciated buddha. I found it fascinating and sought it out on visits to their home. I unfortunately do not have an image of Jamsheed's fascinating buddha, but I do offer an image of an excellent one from the Metropolitan Museum of Art and the Freer-Sackler Gallery that I find to be special (Illustration 3).

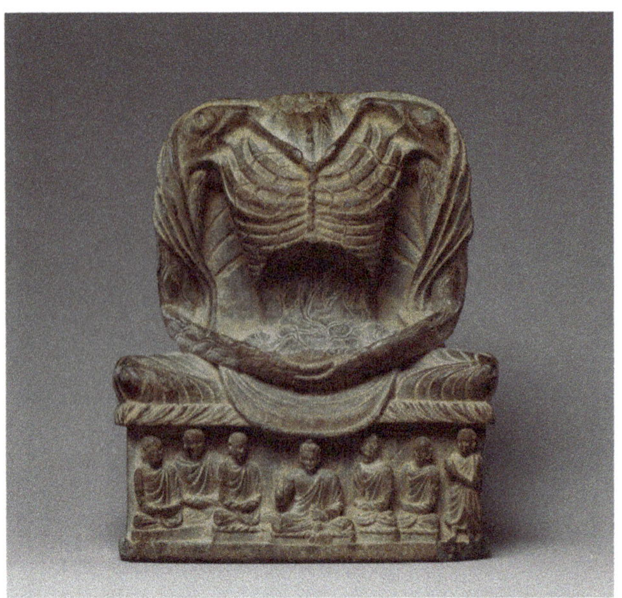

Illustration 4: Fasting Buddha Shakyamuni, 3rd–5th century, Metropolitan Museum of Art, Samuel Eilenberg Collection, Ex Coll.: Columbia University, Purchase, Rogers, Dodge, Harris Brisbane Dick and Fletcher Funds, Joseph Pulitzer Bequest, and Lila Acheson Wallace Gift, 1987.

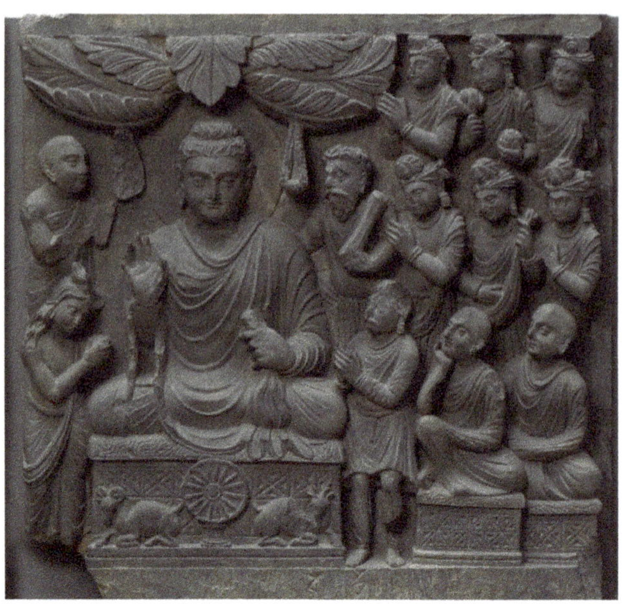

Illustration 5: Four Scenes from the Life of the Buddha - (Detail) The Birth of the Buddha, Kushan dynasty, late 2nd-early 3rd century. Freer Gallery of Art, Smithsonian Institution, Washington, D.C.: Purchase — Charles Lang Freer Endowment, F1949.9a-d

I was always curious as to why emaciated Buddhas were made. The following quote from the writings of Dyung Le is relevant: "A very central Buddhist teaching is 'The Middle Path,' that is, not going to either extreme. It is said that in his quest for Enlightenment, Prince Siddhartha (before he became Gautama Buddha) starved himself to the point of eating just a few sesames seeds a day, and thus he became so skinny he could touch his backbone through the belly! When he was near death, a 13-year-old young girl ("Sujata") offered him a milk type porridge, which he accepted. Six years of self-imposed harsh and extreme asceticism came to an end, and the Buddha declared that going to the ascetic extreme (as was the case with many religious Gurus at the time) was not the way. This was such a shock to his original five disciples that they abandoned him!"

My initial purchase of a Gandhara sculpture in Karachi 57 years ago did indeed motivate me to visit many important collections of Gandhara around the world that I may have otherwise declined. In retrospect, it was a wise decision to buy our Gandhara sculpture.

CHAPTER 8

English Placecard Holders

Ann and I frequented numerous art shows in New York and London. In addition, I went to Maastricht, Holland, for TEFAF (The European Fine Arts Fair) almost every year for about a dozen years. We normally went to these shows as observers, since prices tended to be beyond our means, but rather than return home totally empty handed, we often bought relatively inexpensive English Victorian or Edwardian sterling silver decorated place card holders. (On very rare occasions, we acquired place card holders made from materials other than silver, and from countries other than England.) These place card holders were commonly used at dinner parties during the reigns of Victoria and Edward I. The name of a guest would be placed on a paper card which was inserted in the holder, and the holder was then placed where that guest was to be seated.

Over the decades, we built up a collection of about 85 of these card holders. They are of every subject imaginable. Our first set of card holders was decorated with replicas of Chinese Blue-and-white dishes. (I was attracted to, and bought them, since I was, at that time, collecting antique Chinese Blue-and-white porcelain). (See Chapter 3) We then moved on to English hunting scenes. These were followed by holders representing classic children's shows, such as "Punch and Judy." Animals of all varieties are represented, including dogs, wolves, birds, butterfly's, et al. We have boats and boat lanterns, and two sets of four-leaf clovers. We even have one made by Cartier in France with a perfect replica of the official American Eagle. (I have always hoped that a close American friend would be appointed United States ambassador to an American embassy abroad, and we would donate that set to the embassy.)

Among the designers of these place card holders were Otto Ramsdon, Sampson Morden, Tiffany, Alkyn Carr, William Comyns, Liberty & Co., et al. We keep all of our place card holders in a special cabinet in the dining room that Ann had made specifically for their display. I turn on its interior lights every evening to gaze upon the beauty of these place card holders (Illustration 1).

A game I have played with these place card holders at dinner parties, is to choose a holder for each person on the basis of the similarity of the design on the holder to the interests of the person whose name will be inserted into it. Thus, the proud owner of a yacht would find his name being held by a boat's lantern.

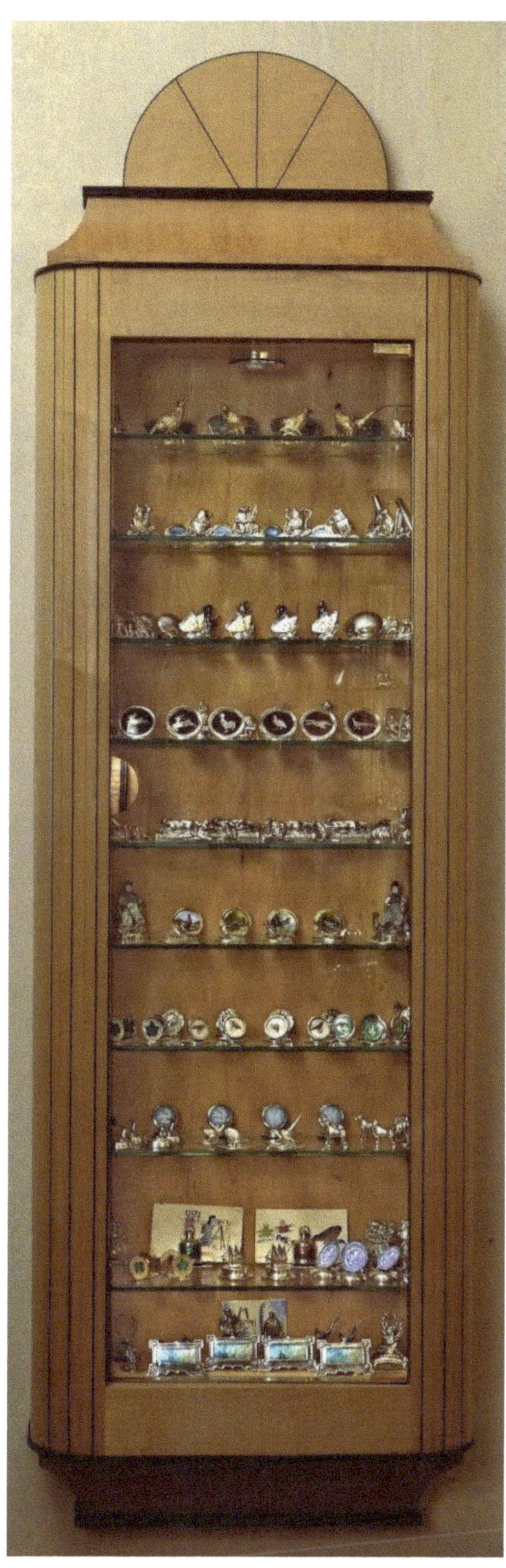

Illustration 1: Collection of Placecard Holders in author's home. Photo by Gregory R. Staley. Julius and Ann Kaplan Collection.

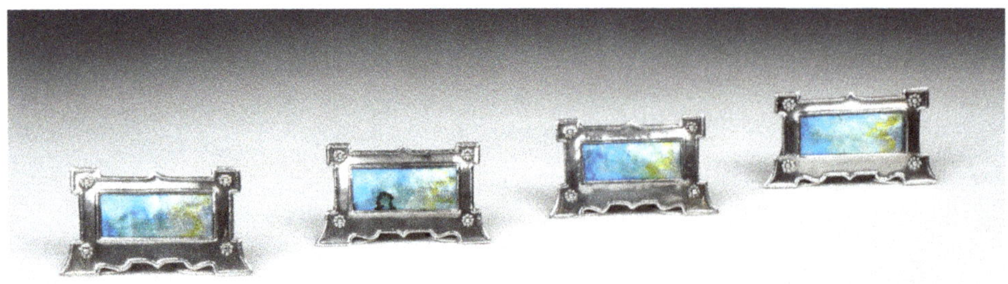

Illustration 2: Otto Ramsden Design. Photo by Gregory R. Staley. Julius and Ann Kaplan Collection.

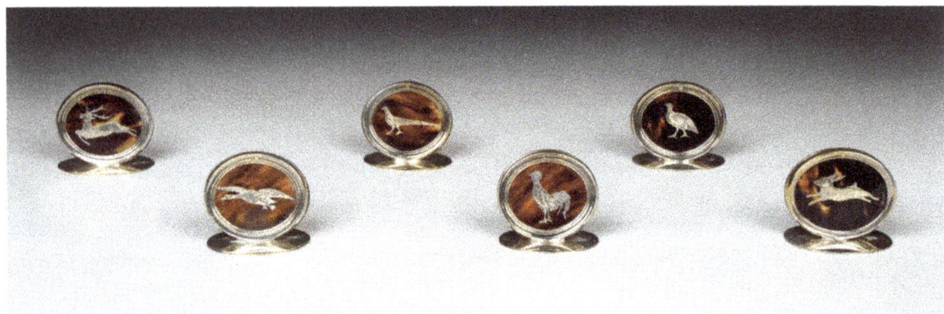

Illustration 3: Animals on Tortoise Shell Background. Photo by Gregory R. Staley. Julius and Ann Kaplan Collection.

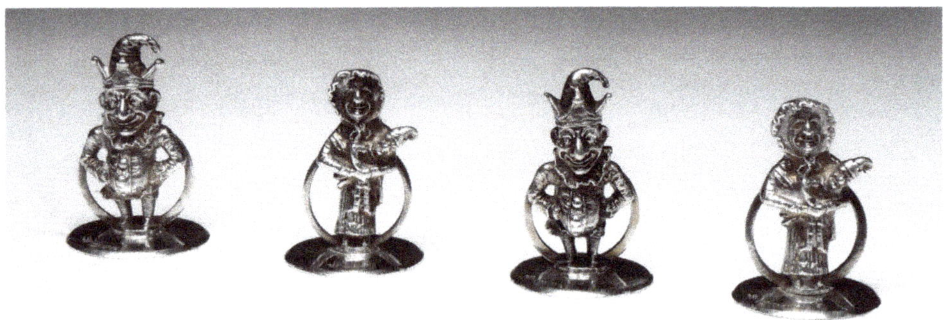

Illustration 4: Punch and Judy. Photo by Gregory R. Staley. Julius and Ann Kaplan Collection.

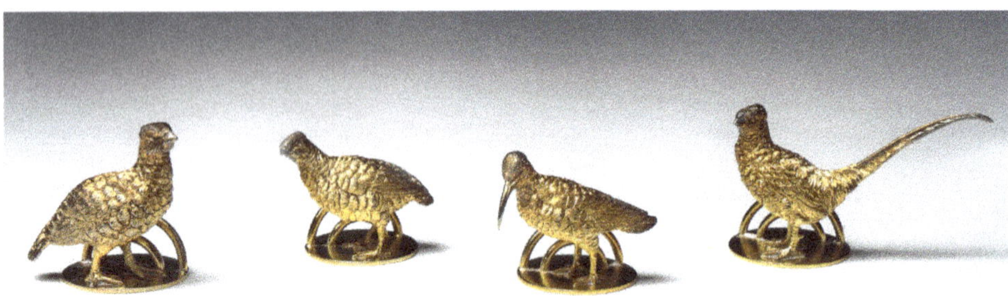

Illustration 5: Game Birds. Photo by Gregory R. Staley. Julius and Ann Kaplan Collection.

Space does not permit the display of each of the place card holders in our collection. Here are some illustrative samples photographed by Gregory R. Staley (Illustrations 2-6) and one made by Ann's mother for herself and Ann's father (7).

For those with an acquisitive instinct for beautiful antiques, but with limited budgets, place card holders are a lovely and fun thing to collect.

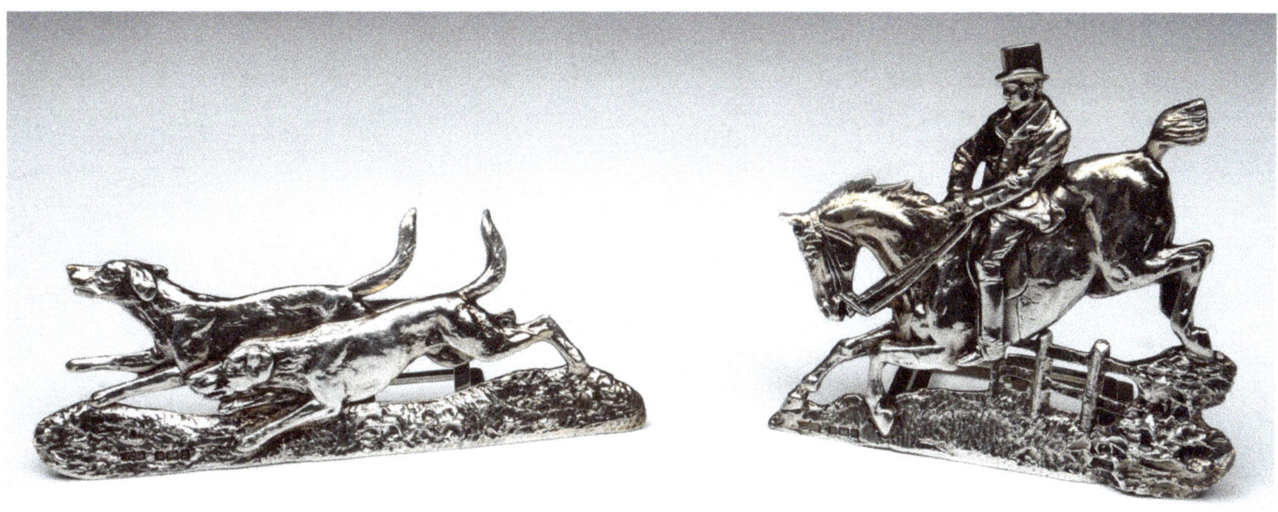

Illustration 6: English Hunting Scene. Photo by Gregory R. Staley. Julius and Ann Kaplan Collection.

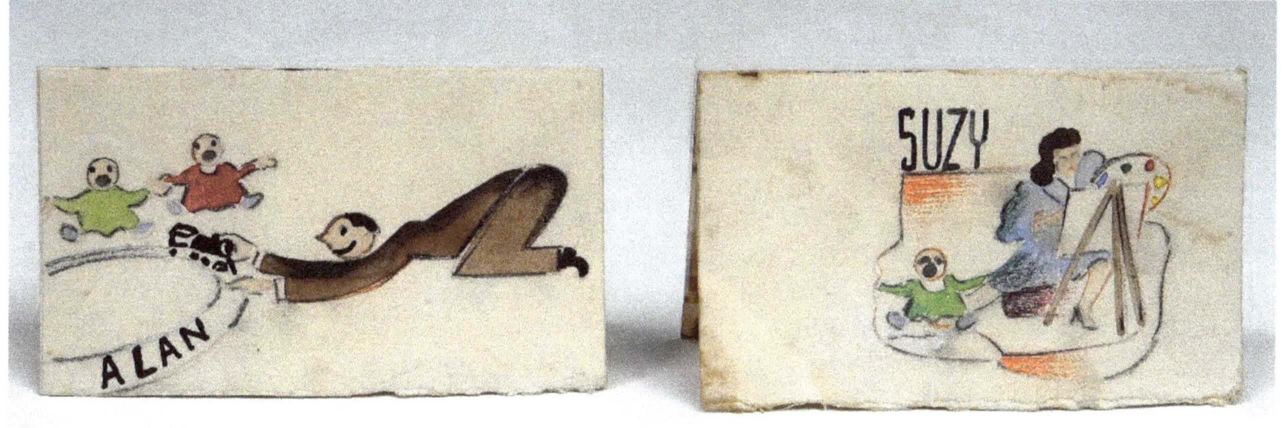

Illustration 7: Hand Made Place Cards by Lavinia Wade Lanyon, circa 1935. Photo by Gregory R. Staley. Julius and Ann Kaplan Collection.

CHAPTER 9

Martini Glasses

9.1 | INTRODUCTION AND SUMMARY

I have always been fascinated by the shape of a martini glass. This led me to search out glass artisans at craft shows to buy their martini glasses. Since I have English 18th-century spiral twist glasses (see Chapter 2), I thought it would be interesting to see if these contemporary glass blowers could emulate those Georgian glasses. I brought pictures of our English color-twists to give them an idea of what I sought. I found several glass blowers who were willing to make a facsimile of those English glasses. I also acquired several of the first glasses ever made in America for the drinking of the martini. These were designed by the great glass designer, Frederick Carder, of Corning. A dealer in London then discovered the first glasses ever made in Europe for the drinking of the American martini, which he sold to me. They were made in Venice by Venini. To top off the collection, I discovered late 16th-/ early 17th-century Venetian glasses that have a bowl closely resembling an American martini glass, as well as a Non-Venetian Europe glass with a similar bowl of even date. And finally, I acquired a copy of an 18th-century Spanish glass which I accepted into the martini family of glasses.

9.2 | MADE TO ORDER COLOR-TWIST AND OTHER MARTINI GLASSES

It all started when we went to craft shows where fine contemporary table glass was often sold. These venues included the wonderful Smithsonian Craft Show in the incomparable Building Museum in Washington, D.C., and the fine Baltimore Craft Show. Having a long-standing interest in English Georgian glass, I would always visit the booths of the glass makers and study their displays. I often brought pictures of English color-twists glasses from our Georgian glass collection (See Chapter 2) and requested them to make us a martini glass with color-twist stems that mimicked the 18th-century ones. Since yellow was an especially sought-after color in Georgian glass, I would often ask them to add that color to the stems of the martini glasses I ordered. On the whole these glass blowers made us lovely martini glasses with yellow twist stems (Illustration 1).

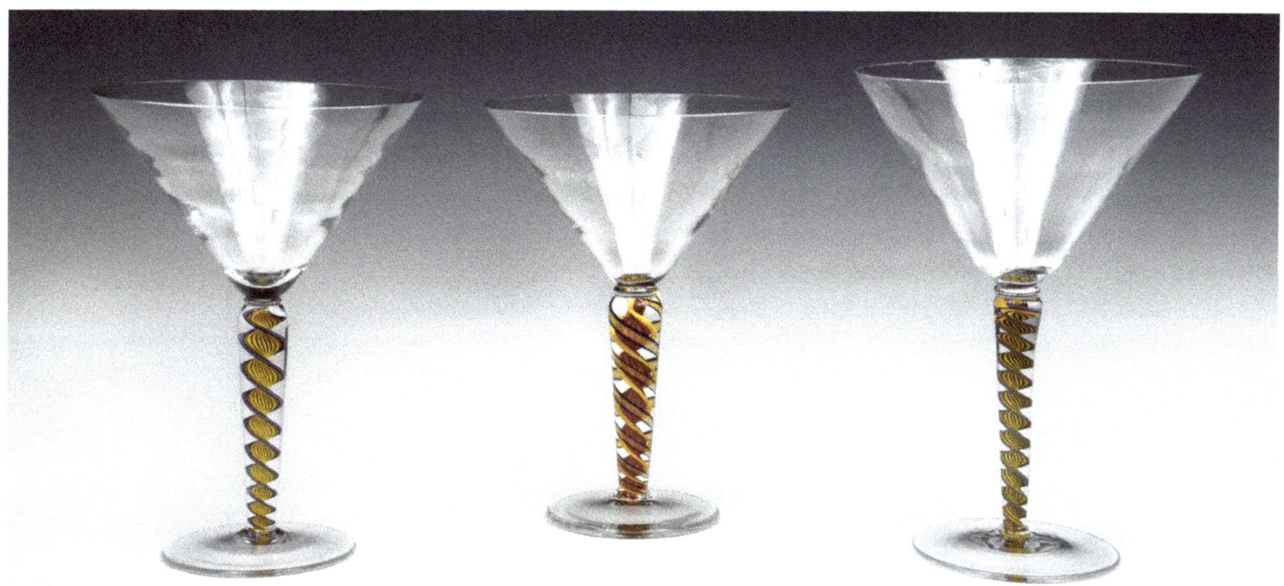

Illustration 1: Yellow Twist Martini Glasses. Photo by Gregory R. Staley. Julius and Ann Kaplan Collection.

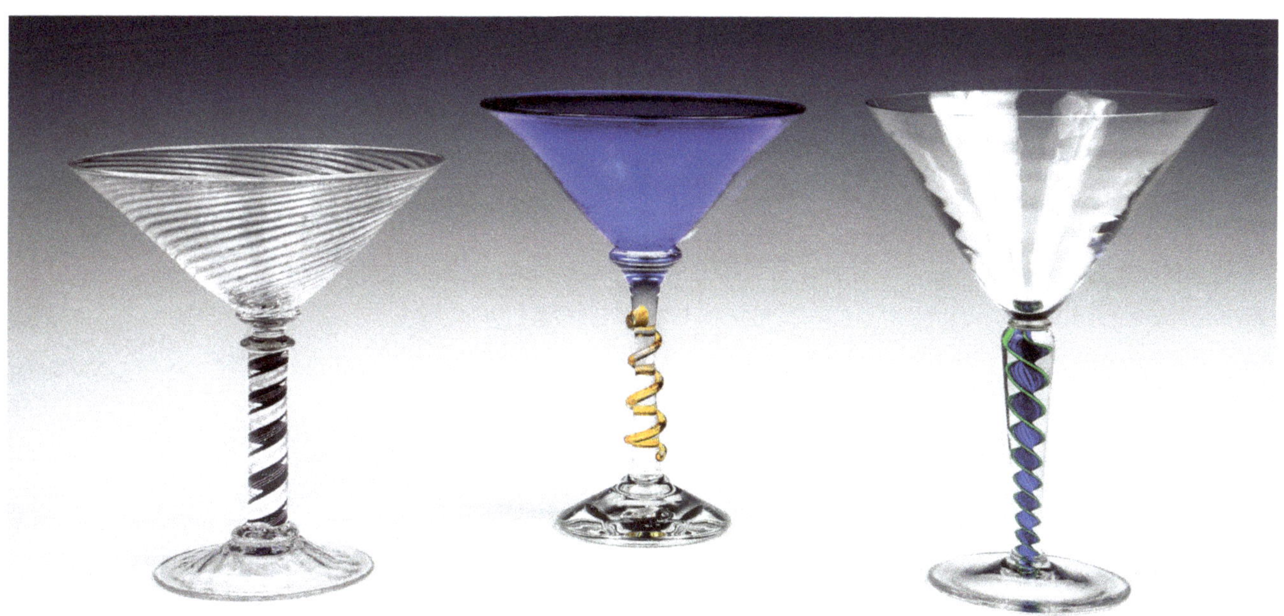

Illustration 2: More Twist Martini Glasses, including Blue Bowl with Exterior Yellow Twist. Photo by Gregory R. Staley. Julius and Ann Kaplan Collection.

I built up a collection of these glasses, along with a number of non-yellow ones. I have selected a pair of the more interesting non-yellow twist glasses to show you, as well as one rare glass which has a beautiful blue bowl with a yellow twist on the exterior of the stem (Illustration 2). Its blue bowl appealed to me since one of the stars of our Georgian glass collection had a blue bowl and foot (See Chapter 2).

9.3 | THE ORIGINAL MARTINI GLASS BY FREDERICK CARDER OF CORNING

As this collection grew, I became curious as to where and when the first American martini glass came into existence. My search to find the original ultimately led me to Frederick Carder of Corning, who designed the glasses to be used for the drinking of the American martini in 1932. These Carder designed glasses were used in many elegant bars and hotels. I was able to acquire, after much searching, three of the original Carder designed martini glasses made by Corning (Illustration 3). (See discussion of Frederick Carder, infra.)

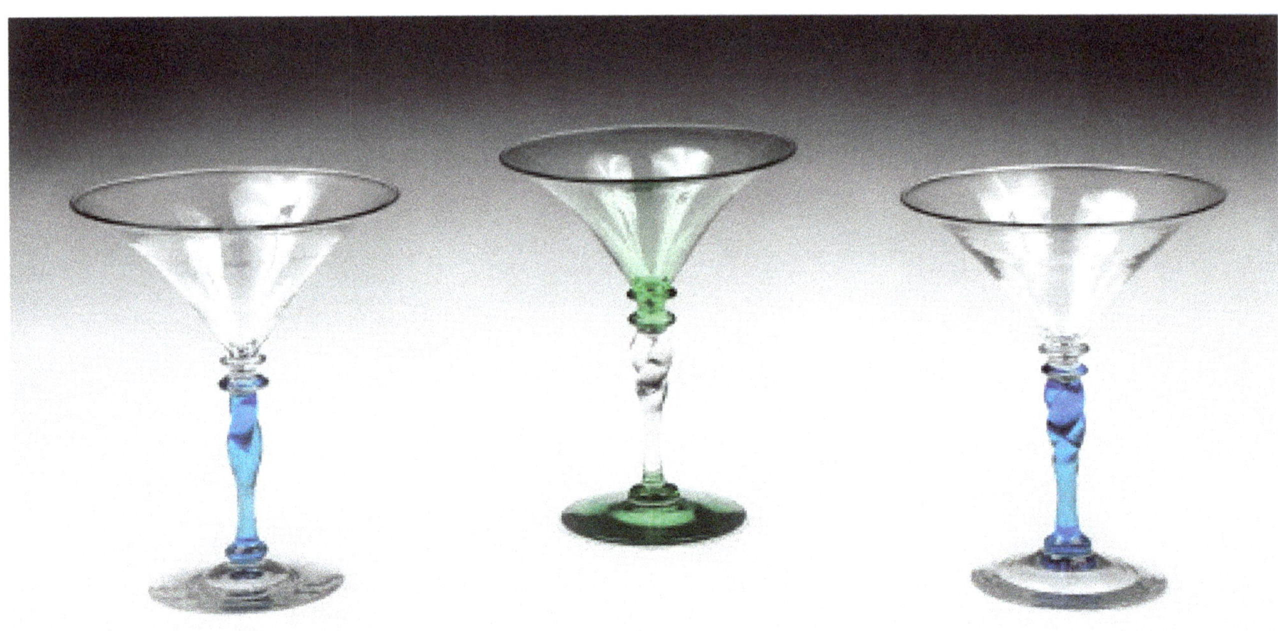

Illustration 3: Frederick Carder, The First Glasses Ever Produced for Drinking a Martini. Photo by Gregory R. Staley. Julius and Ann Kaplan Collection.

9.4 | THE FIRST GLASS FOR A MARTINI MADE IN EUROPE

Knowing that I was in search of the original American martini glass, my London glass dealer, and friend, Christopher Shepherd researched the subject from the European point of view. He finally discovered two green glasses made by Venini in Venice in the mid 1930's, which he was confident were the first glasses ever made in Europe for drinking an American martini. After a talk I gave at the Glass Circle, in London, Christopher congratulated me on my performance by filling one of the Venini glasses with vodka. Suffice it to say, after consuming all of the alcohol, I dropped the glass, and it broke. Now there is but one, and it is beautiful (Illustration 4).

A word about Venini, the venerable glass house in Murano, Venice. The business was the brainchild of Paolo Venini (1895-1959). In 1921, he and a partner opened a glass factory in Murano named Vetri Soffiati Muranesi Cappellin Cepelin Venini & C. Following a business dispute, Mr. Cappellin Cepelin

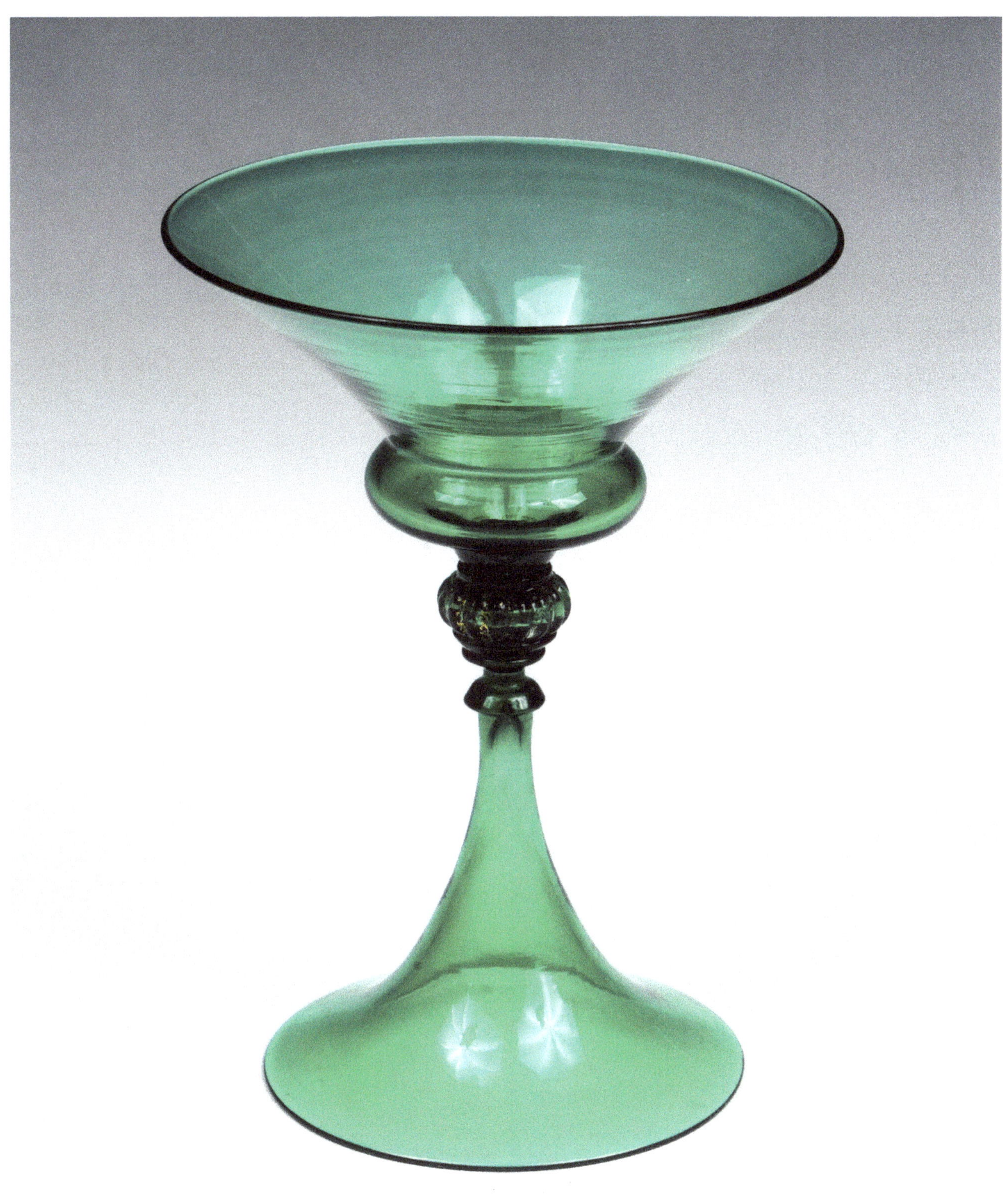

Illustration 4: Venini, The First Martini Glass Made in Europe for the American Martini. Photo by Gregory R. Staley. Julius and Ann Kaplan Collection.

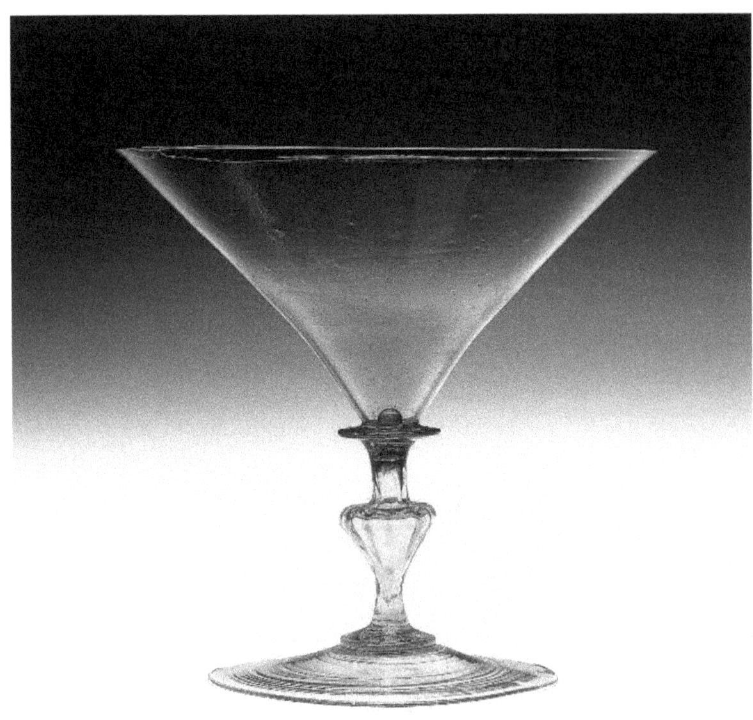

Illustration 5: Late 16th-Century Drinking Glass. Photo courtesy of Bonhams, London. Julius and Ann Kaplan Collection.

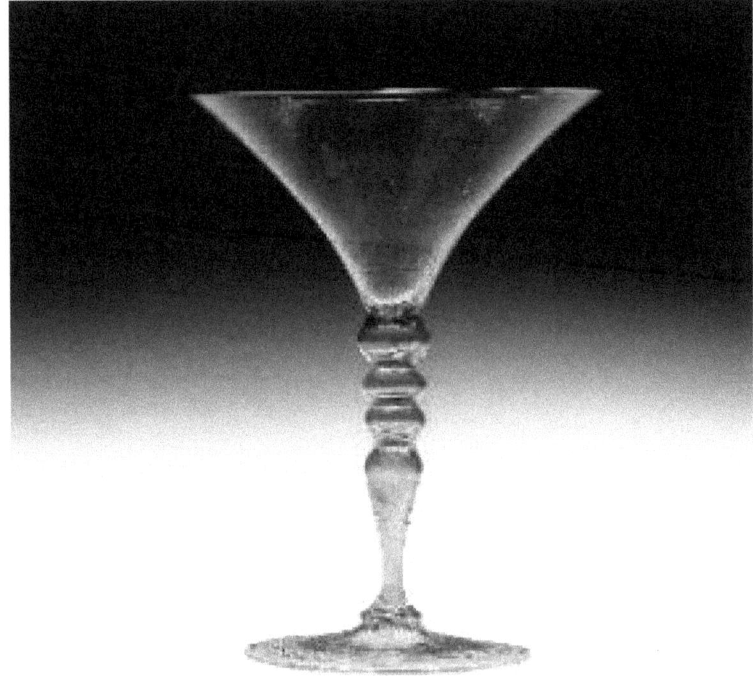

Illustration 6: Late 16th-Century (or possibly early 17th-Century) Venetian Glass. Photo courtesy of Bonhams, London. Julius and Ann Kaplan Collection.

withdrew in 1925, taking with him the firm's master glassblowers. Venini reorganized with new glass blowers. The company was ultimately renamed Venini & Co. With dramatic new designs by Venini, the firm took off, and is a high-prestige organization to this day. Indeed, Dale Chihuly went there to study glass blowing.

You may have noticed that I have often inserted the word "American" before the word "martini." This was done since Europeans have been drinking a vermouth named "Martini" for many years before the American martini was even invented. This has led to confusion in Europe between the American martini and the French vermouth. Indeed, until fairly recently, there was a perrenial problem in Europe when ordering a martini. Unless you specified that you wanted an "American martini" made from gin or vodka and vermouth, you were almost sure to be given a vermouth named Martini.

9.5 | ITALIAN RENAISSANCE "MARTINI" GLASSES

Over the years, I went to many antique shows in search of English Georgian glass. At several of these shows, I was surprised to find late 16th (which are possibly early 17th) century glasses with bowls closely resembling American martini glasses. They were made in Murano, Venice, which was even then a major glass producing center. I bought two of these late 16th-/early 17th-century glasses (Illustrations 5 and 6). I found it fascinating to think that great Italian Renaissance painters may have drunk out of these very glasses.

The Murano glass workers were prohibited by law from leaving Venice. But glass manufacturers in other parts of Europe learned of the beauty of the Venetian glasses, and the skill of the Murano glass blowers. Starting around the beginning of the 17th-century, they induced a number of Venetian workers to escape from Venice, and work for them. Many did, and the glasses they produced in Europe outside of Venice resembled the glasses made in Venice, but tended to be a bit more decorative. They are now referred to as "Façon de Venise." (Venetian fashion). I bought one Façon de Venise martini-shaped glass (Illustration 7).

Both the late 16th-century Venetian glasses and the 17th-century Façon de Venise glasses are totally unleaded and thus remarkably light weight and fragile. To hold one is to hold a feather.

9.6 | SPANISH 18TH-CENTURY (ALMOST A) MARTINI GLASS

One of my very favorite glasses is a replica of a Spanish 18th-century glass I bought in the gift shop of The Corning Museum. It is almost martini-shaped, except the rim flows open. It is such a beautiful glass that I am willing to overlook the curious shape, and accept it into my family of martini glasses as a lovely wayward child. It is a long-stemmed glass with a graceful bowl with decorative stripes throughout. I assure you that martinis taste fine in it (Illustration 8).

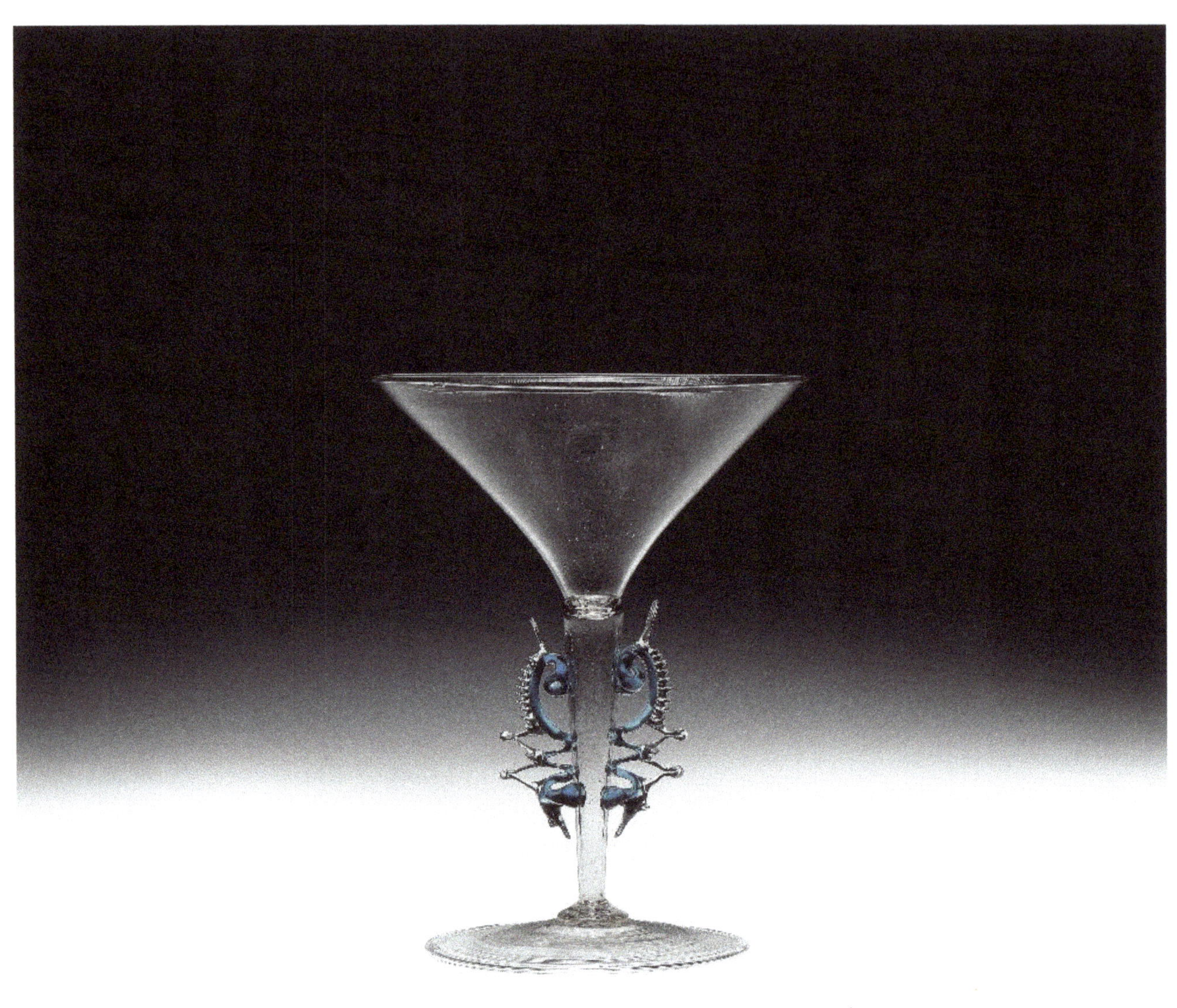

Illustration 7: 17th-Century Façon de Venise Glass. Photo courtesy of Bonhams, London. Julius and Ann Kaplan Collection.

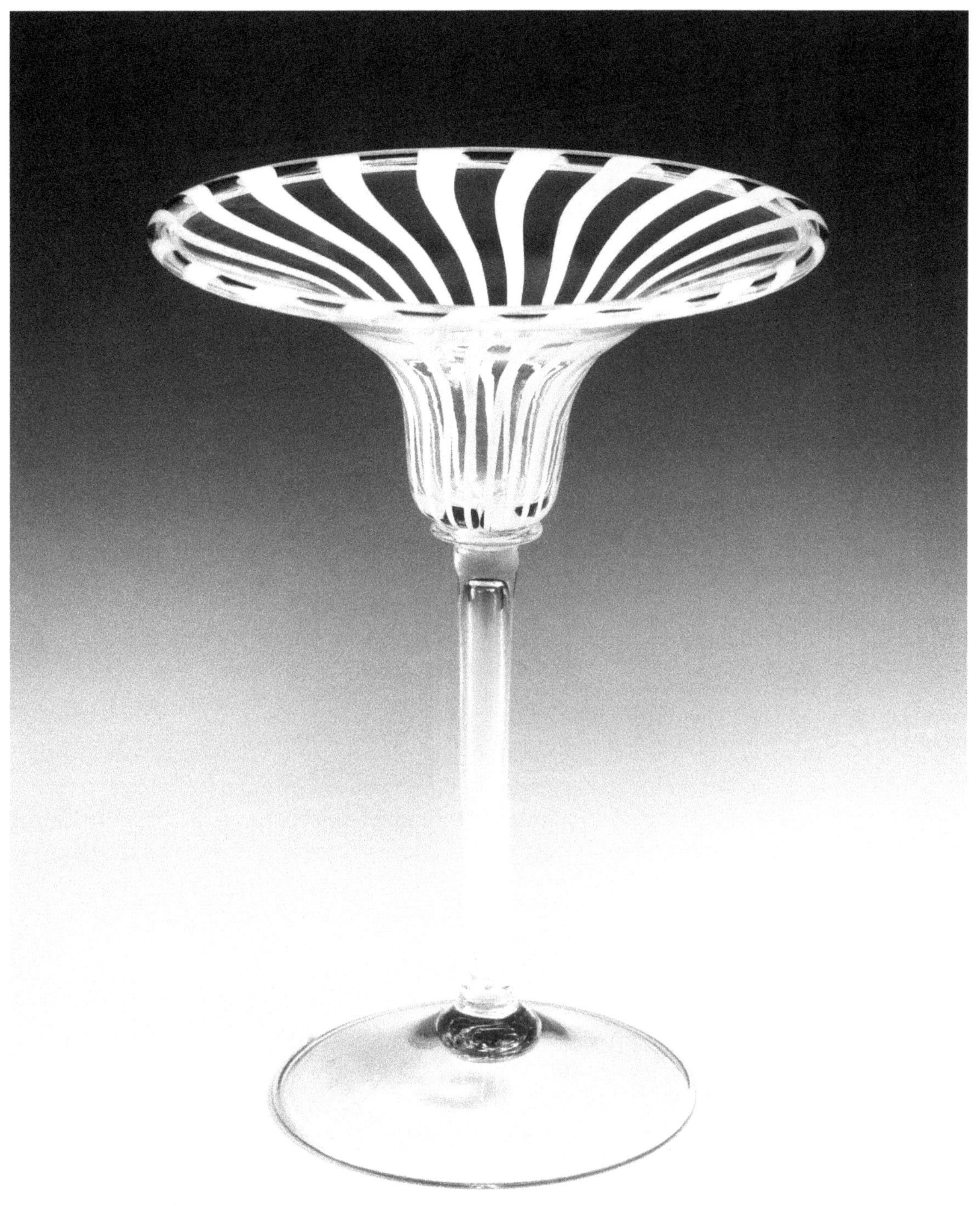

Illustration 8: 18th-Century Spanish Glass (for martinis if you wish). Photo courtesy of Bonhams, London. Julius and Ann Kaplan Collection.

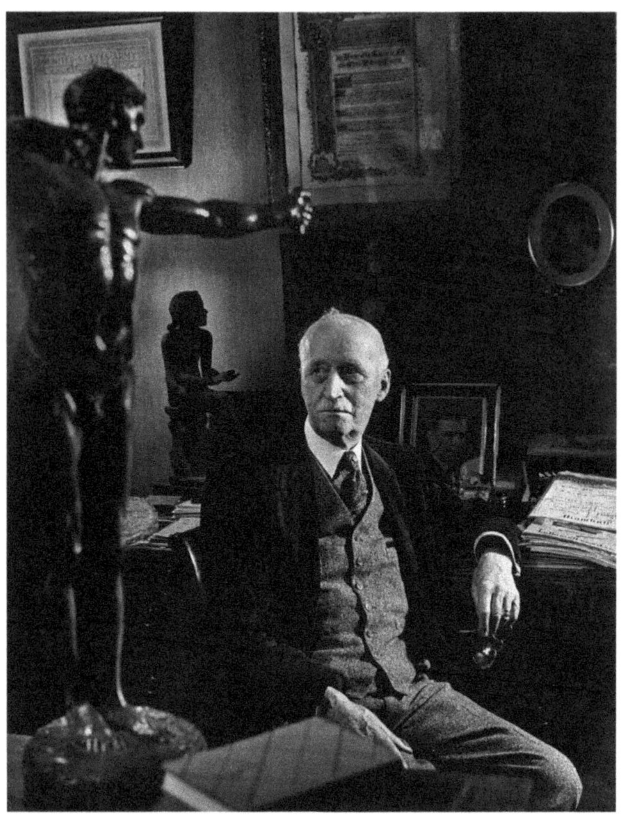

Illustration 9: Frederick Carder in his Library. Photo courtesy of the Corning Museum of Glass.

9.7 | FREDERICK CARDER

I was able to find a Corning document that described Frederick Carder. What I write now about him was taken from this document.

All American and many European martini glasses, as well as many other glass objects, owe much to Frederick Carder. He was a truly extraordinary important person. In 1879, the young English Carder became fascinated with glassmaking. In 1881, he went to work as a designer at Stevens & Williams, a large English glassmaking company, where he experimented with glass colors and design. In 1903, Carder and his family moved to Corning, New York, at the invitation of Thomas G. Hawkes, owner of Steuben Glass Works. He became the star designer at Steuben, where he worked for the next 30 years. He was so well thought of that he was given carte blanche to design all of the firm's products. In addition, he developed new colors and techniques. In 1932, Carder left Steuben to become the design director of Corning Glass Works.

Carder was the designer at Corning until he retired at the age of 96. During his 82 year career working with glass design, he designed more than 6,000 glass objects in 140 colors. The sesquicentennial of his life was commemorated in 2013, and the legacy of this gifted designer is still thriving.

In recognition of his illustrious career at Corning, a Carder Gallery was created in the Corning Museum in his honor. The Gallery contains several thousand pieces of every type of glass that Carder created—from early pieces made at Stevens & Williams to individual pieces he created in his retirement. There are also martini glasses there identical to ours.

9.8 | FREDRICK CARDER GALLERY

The Frederick Carder Gallery is visited by many thousands of people every year. I did once, in order to be sure that the martini glasses I had acquired were really the design of Frederick Carder. They are.

Referring to the many visitors to the Carder Gallery, Karol Wight, the museum's executive director said, "Their dedicated interest in the collecting and research of Carder glass is a testament to the designer's legacy."

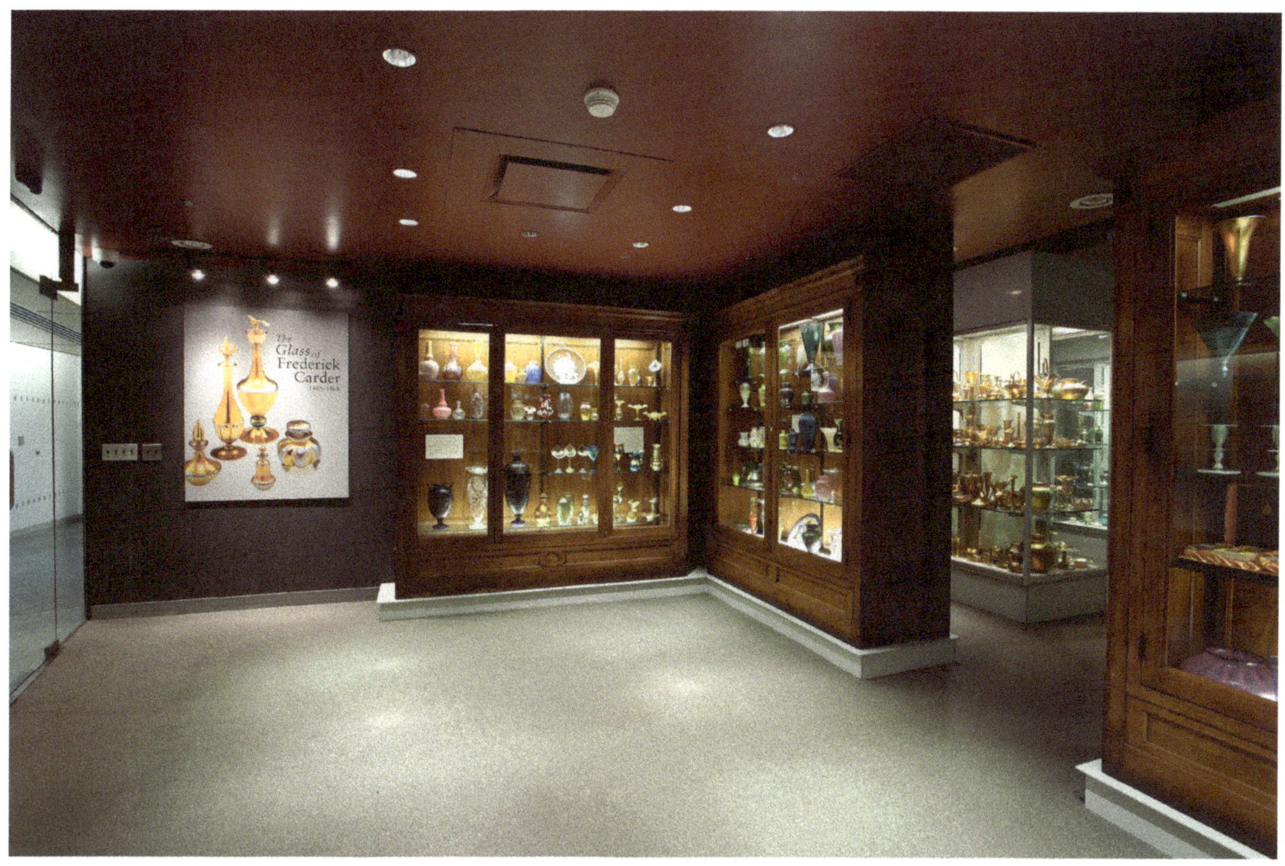

Illustration 10: The Frederick Carder Gallery, Collection of the Corning Museum of Glass, Corning, NY. Photo courtesy of the Corning Museum of Glass.

CHAPTER 10

Embassy Stemware

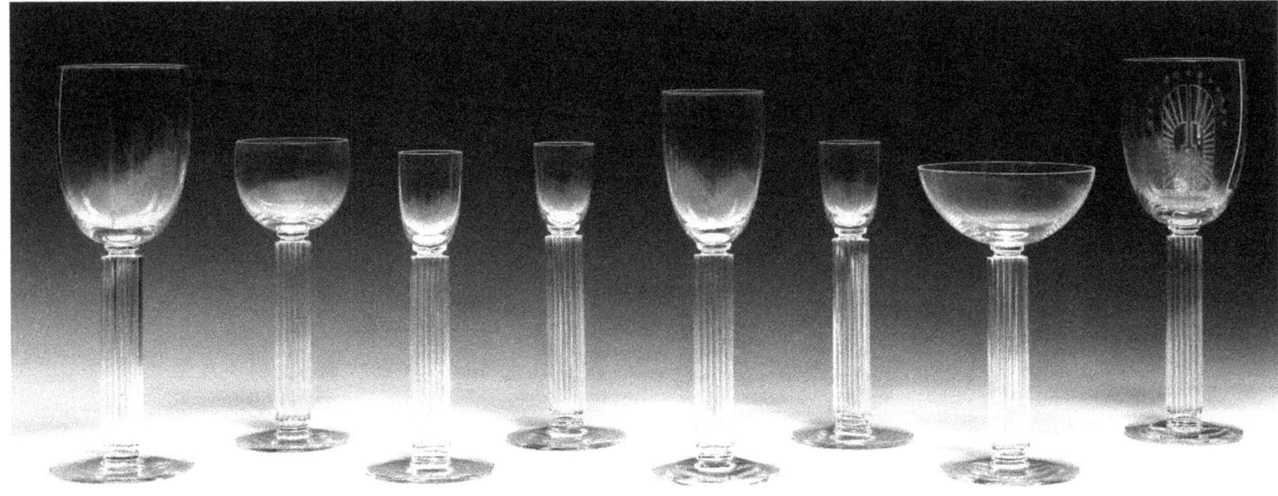

Illustration 1: The Embassy Stemwear, originally designed by Walter Dorwin Teague for the Libbey-Owens-Ford Pavillion at the 1939 World's Fair in New York. They were manufactured by Edwin W. Fuerst and are often referred to as Dorwin-Fuerst stemwear. Photo by Gregory R. Staley.

An Israeli client, Zvi Elnatan, knew that I loved glass, and, once brought me a gift of a Libbey glass designed by Walter Dorwin Teague for the Libbey-Owens-Ford Pavillion at the World's Fair in New York in 1939. It was manufactured by Edwin W. Fuerst. (The glasses are often referred to as Dorwin-Fuerst glasses.) I found it to be a very striking and beautiful design. Thereafter, whenever we went to a local glass show, and saw glasses from that set, which was most rare, we would buy them. Our collection of these glasses thus grew, but only modestly.

My friend, Dwight Lanmon, then the director of The Corning Museum of Glass noticed the set of Embassy stemware in our home, and commented favorably on them. A few months later, Dwight called me to tell me that one of the glasses from the original 1939 set, with an eagle engraved on the glass, was being sold at a small auction house in Bloomfield, Michigan. Dwight advised me that the original set had eagles engraved on all of the bowls. That set was made for, and was used at the World's Fair by, the Department of State for a diplomatic dinner it hosted at the Fair.

I have been told that the complete 1939 set with engraved eagles may now be in the White House collection. (I have not been able to confirm this.)

Upon receiving Dwight's call, I immediately telephoned my brother-in-law, Manny Sulkes, who, by happy coincidence, lived in Bloomfield, and asked him to please go to the auction and bid on my behalf for the glass with the eagle. He "won" the glass for me. With this acquisition my collection of Libbey Embassy stemware took on a new meaning. I kept my eye out for other Libbey Embassy glasses with an eagle, but, alas, I never saw another one. Here is an illustration of the Embassy stemware in our collection with the only glass with an engraved eagle on the far right. (Illustration 1).

I was pleased to learn that several important museums have examples of this Embassy glass service in their glass collections. Indeed, the British Museum is so proud of their small collection that they placed an image of it in *The British Museum: 5000 Years of Glass*, which was edited by the famous glass scholar Hugh Tate (*The British Museum Press*).

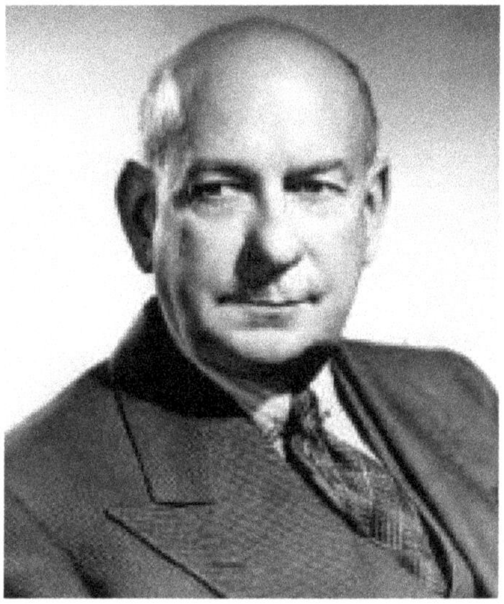

Illustration 2: Walter Dorwin Teague portrait

I learned that the designer of the Embassy stemware was Walter Dorwin Teague (1883-1960), and I offer a few comments on this remarkable designer.

Walter Dorwin Teague was often referred to as the "Dean of Industrial Design." Teague is still appreciated today for the role he played in the success of mid-century modernism. I am an aficionado of this style. Indeed, I decorated my office when I practiced law with mid-century modern furniture from Knoll. I now have the Knoll pieces in my home office.

Teague is famous for his exhibition designs for the 1939-40 New York World's Fair, including the Ford Building at the Fair, as well as the iconic Embassy stemware.

Teague's product designs, texts, photographs, and archives are found in major museums around the world. Among them are: The Metropolitan Museum of Art, New York City; Museum of Modern Art, New York City; Smithsonian Art Museum, Washington, D.C.; San Francisco Museum of Modern Art; Brooklyn Museum; Chicago Art Institute; Cleveland Museum of Art; Smithsonian Cooper-Hewitt National Design Museum; Dallas Museum of Art; Cleveland Museum of Art; Smithsonian Cooper-Hewitt National Design Museum; and the High Museum of Art, Atlanta, Georgia.

CONCLUSION

The National Museum of the Jewish People

Although not an "art object" we collected, my experience, together with that of Ori Soltes, and later Judith Barnett, in attempting to create a beautiful National Museum of the Jewish People in Washington, D.C., was certainly a search for beauty in every sense of the term, and thus an appropriate subject with which to end this book.

It all started when I joined the board of directors of the B'nai B'rith Jewish Museum late in the early 1990's. There, I met and worked with Ori Soltes, the museum director. After some years of attempting to make this little museum into a substantial Jewish museum, Ori, others, and I resigned from the B'nai B'rith Museum to attempt to create a National Jewish Museum in Washington, D.C.

Ori and I spent meaningful amounts of time together planning the museum, and searching for a site and supporters. What a pleasure it was for me to work with someone as articulate, erudite, and charming as Ori. He has a staggering depth of knowledge in the fields of art and comparative religion, as well as numerous other fields. He teaches art and religion courses at Georgetown University. He is also a linguist, speaking multiple languages. In addition, Ori is an author extraordinaire, having published many serious tomes on these and other subjects.

While we were looking for supporters of our effort to create the museum, a woman by the name of Arlette Snyder was looking for a museum to house her outstanding collection of objects related to Jews and music. They are on display in a stunning mini-museum, which is part of her home. We have collaborated productively with Arlette for years.

Despite much searching, we had difficulty finding an appropriate venue for the museum. Then, early in the year 2008, we became aware of a program of the Obama Administration to lease, on a very long-term basis, the historic Old Post Office and Clock Tower Building ("OPO") on Pennsylvania Avenue, N.W., including its substantial grounds.

The OPO is an iconic building on Pennsylvania Avenue. To be eligible to win the lease, each applicant had to submit a proposal to the U.S. Government Services Administration ("GSA") which had responsibility for leasing the OPO.

We learned that Hilton-International was planning to convert the OPO into a super luxurious Waldorf Astoria Hotel. Marriott, the world's largest hotel developer, was planning to propose a very special "6 Star" Marriott. We also heard that there was a developer who proposed to convert the OPO into a luxury Grand Hyatt Hotel. The only other hotel developer was Trump Properties, but they had no experience in D.C.

As a practical matter, we could not use the entirety of the building and its grounds for the museum. It was simply too much space and would require too much time and money to develop fully. We met with the developer who was planning to convert the OPO building into a Grand Hyatt Hotel, and learned that he did not have use for the acres of ground between the OPO and the Internal Revenue Building (IRS). That space would have been more than adequate for us to build a new edifice to house the museum. We entered into an agreement with the developer whereby he would convert the OPO into a luxury Hyatt hotel, and we would develop our museum on the grounds between the OPO and the IRS building.

Appreciating the serious competition, Ori and I were both of the view that we needed a renowned architect to design us a beautiful building. We agreed that the ideal architect would be the world-famous Daniel Libeskind. The buildings he designed included the Jewish Museum in Berlin, Germany; the extension of the Denver Art Museum; the Grand Canal Theater in Dublin; the Imperial War Museum North in Greater Manchester; the Felix Nussbaum House in Osnabruck; and, inter alia, the Danish Jewish Museum in Copenhagen. Perhaps the most meaningful assignment he received was on February 27, 2003 when he won the tight competition for the reconstruction of Ground Zero, World Trade Center site in Lower Manhattan. His Berlin Jewish Museum is the single most popular tourist attraction in all of Germany.

Ori and I met Daniel and his wife, Nina, at the OPO, late one rainy afternoon. Daniel and Nina took a stroll around the space for some minutes, and then Daniel said, "I've got an idea which I think will work." He explained that this idea called for the entrance of the museum to be directly on Pennsylvania Avenue. It would then lead back past the entrance to the IRS and the OPO to the large open area behind these buildings. The museum would have multiple levels. The roof of each level would be covered with grass, trees and plants, as well as a table and umbrella available for use by the general public. He felt that these plantings would break up the dullness of the bricks and mortar of the other buildings around the museum. It would also make the museum all the more inviting.

Daniel suggested that the museum be called the Garden of Eden Jewish Museum, a name that reflected the gardens atop each level. Attached is a rendering of the museum Libeskind designed for us, seen from its rear. It does not show the upper level gardens, although one can see parts of the greenery in the multiple gardens (Illustration 1).

I personally believed that, with the beautiful Libeskind design, and with Hyatt managing the hotel to be built within the OPO, we had an excellent chance of winning the competition, especially since we were offering GSA "two bangs for the buck"—a Grand Hyatt Hotel and a Libeskind-designed National Jewish Museum. We hired a highly regarded proposal expert, Wendy Frieman, to draft ours. Wendy enjoys an outstanding and well-deserved reputation for drafting winning proposals, and she certainly did so for us. We felt that her proposal was compelling.

But we were all trumped! The GSA, in its "wisdom," chose the plan submitted by Donald Trump. It is today the Trump International Hotel.

About two years later, I received a call from Arlette asking me if I had abandoned "our" museum project. I said that I had been absorbed in writing a book on my legal career entitled *Secrets and Suspense*, and Ori was busy writing multiple books, plus teaching and lecturing worldwide. She said that she understood, but the museum project was just too important to be put off just because we were defeated the first time around. Arlette could be compelling, and Ori and I agreed to become active again in developing a National Jewish Museum. In addition, I invited Judith Barnett to join our team. Judith is extremely bright, an experienced political fundraiser, a fine lawyer (with an international practice mainly in the Middle East), and she very much believed in the project.

We re-established our museum corporation and invited a firm of real estate brokers to help us find a new venue. We told them that our first choice would be to find a building on Pennsylvania Avenue. As if by magic, they presented us with the Newseum Building, which was just being put up for sale. The Newseum is a dynamic, interactive museum of news that allows visitors to experience the stories of yesterday and today. It is located directly on Pennsylvania Avenue at 6th Street N.W. Facing the museum, one has a perfect view of the Capitol (but a few blocks away) to one's right; a perfect view of the National Gallery of Art (East and West Buildings), just a block away, and a sweeping view of Pennsylvania Avenue, the most important street in Washington. (We Washingtonians believe it to be the most important street in the world!) It was too good to be true.

We invited our architect, Daniel Libeskind, to send one of his key people to see the venue. Carla Swickerath of the Studio Daniel Libeskind immediately came from New York to see the project. She said that Daniel knew the building well, and was most excited about it. After her review, it was decided that the building was ideal for a National Jewish Museum.

The price set for the whole building was over $300 million. But we had every hope and expectation of raising that amount, plus several hundreds of millions more for a fund to support the museums day by day operations. In Washington, D.C. virtually all museums are under the umbrella of the government of the United States, which means no entrance fees. To charge entrance fees can be the kiss of death for a museum in D.C. An example of this was the venerable, old Corcoran Gallery of Art, which charged an admission, and finally went under.

But, alas, before we could start to mobilize our financing, Johns Hopkins University stepped in with a check for $370 million, which was accepted by the owners of the Newseum.

As this book goes to press, we are still looking for an appropriate site and funding.

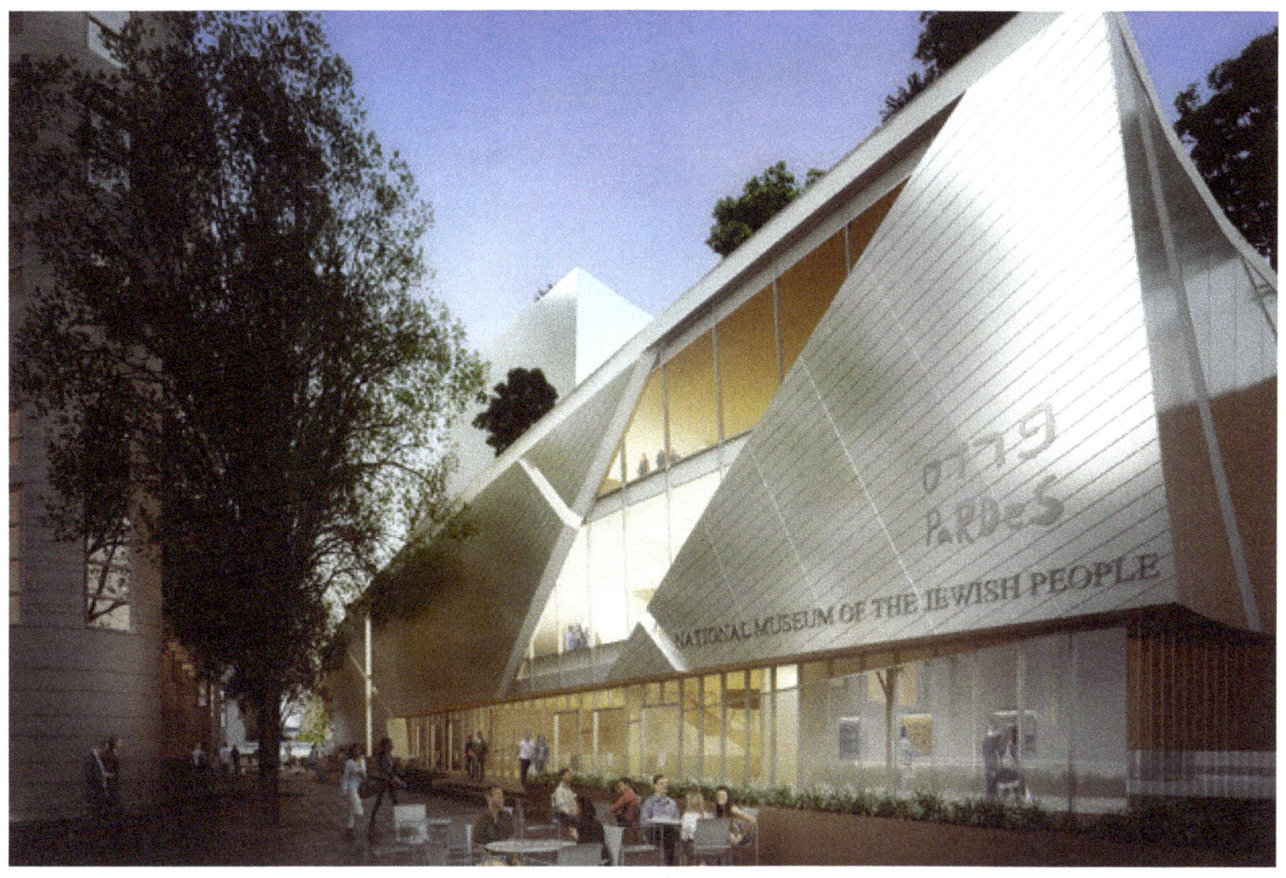

Illustration 1: Proposed National Museum of the Jewish People designed by Daniel Libeskind. Photo by Studio Daniel Libeskind.

ANNEX 1

In Memoriam

The two most influential people involved in the creation of our 18th-century glass collection were my dealers, Christopher Sheppard and John Smith. They were both extremely knowledgeable about antique glass and both were most supportive of our efforts to develop a truly outstanding glass collection. They also became friends. Alas, both have recently died: Christopher several years ago, and John several months ago.

THE LATE CHRISTOPHER SHEPPARD

Christopher Sheppard was one of the two dealers from whom I bought much of the glass in our collection. Christopher and I developed a personal and professional relationship. He was responsible for having encouraged me to acquire a number of the most important glasses in our collection, including several deemed the stars of any collection; namely, the blue glass and the Allegory of Amsterdam stipple engraved glass. Other collector friends of mine also used the services of Christopher. I start with Dr. Richard ("Rick") Mones. (See write up on Rick in Annex 2 below) He not only used the services of Christopher, but became a personal friend of Christopher and his entire family. Another member of the Sheppard Circle was Martin Wunch, who, before meeting Christopher, was primarily a collector of important early American furniture and Dutch 17th-century paintings. Yet another was Doug McCorkle. (See write up on Doug in Annex 2 below.) After being introduced by Rick to Christopher, Martin began collecting glass, including 18th-century English decanters, Renaissance glass, and even Merovingian glass. Ann and I would "break bread" with Martin and Ethel Wunch on our trips to New York for the antique shows. I was always pleased to find Rick Mones there as well. He and Martin were very close friends. They traveled frequently together, usually to shops, fairs, and auctions to pursue glass and other antiquities. There was thus one thing that we all had in common; namely, the services of Christopher Sheppard. Christopher was a friend, advisor, and glass dealer to all of us. Christopher, Rick, Martin and I would meet from time to time in New York when Christopher was there, often for the annual ceramics and glass show. Two of the things we most admired in Christopher were his encyclopedic knowledge of glass and his extraordinary keen eye. On his first visit to my home, on entering the second floor landing of our home, he looked across the landing and the dining room at one of my glass cabinets in the dining room, and asked me to allow him to examine a certain English cider glass, which was at the top of a cabinet most distant from him. I took the glass down, and he took one glance and advised me that the glass was 18th-century English, but the engraving on the glass was much more recent! Rick and Martin had a similar experience. While in Antwerp, Rick saw two early German/Dutch beakers in an antique shop. The price was reasonable so Rick took pictures of them, and sent them to Martin, who bought them. On Christopher's next visit to the Wunch apartment in New York, on entering the apartment, and still fifteen feet from the beakers, Christopher said, "Martin, where did you buy those fakes?" Martin sent the two beakers to The Corning Museum of Glass for analysis. The museum declared them fake. Martin confessed that his opinion of Christopher went up substantially when he got the museum report back. Rick concluded that Christopher had a photographic memory, and could recognize glass in the market that had been illustrated in books, catalogues, and brochures years before. (Yet another recorded feat by Christopher is set forth in Footnote 1.)

Christopher was a rotund gentleman with an immense appetite for good food and fine wines (and he would not turn down an after-dinner brandy.) He was generous to a fault when acting as a host, which he often did at his dear Brooks Club on St. James Street, or at an outrageously expensive London West End restaurant. And, on this generous note, let us now turn to Christopher's weak side. He could not manage money and was always short, using the funds from today to pay overdue bills from the past. He then started using all kinds of short cuts to pay his steady stream of creditors. Christopher was certainly one of the best, if not the best, antique glass dealer we had ever met. But unfortunately, he could not control the commercial side of his business (or his giant appetite for food and drink.) However, his strengths dwarfed these weaknesses, and we all stood with him until the very end. (These paragraphs on the late Christopher Sheppard are based in part on a short memorandum on Christopher which I asked Rick Mones to prepare.)

THE LATE JOHN SMITH

I worked with John Smith after he joined Asprey, and continued working closely with him during his entire career at Mallett's, that is, from the mid-eighties to the mid-2000's. John was a true scholar who had an encyclopedic knowledge of antique glass. John always took a personal interest in assuring that our glass collection would be outstanding. But for him, I would never have had access to some

---

1 The glass collection of Baroness Batsheva Rothschild contained a number of glass objects, including The Field Cup, a Venetian glass masterpiece of the 15th-century, which was suspected by most experts of being a 19th-century copy. Notwithstanding the views of other experts, Christopher Sheppard, after carefully examining the Cup, believed that it was "right" and he bought the Cup. Now he was confronted with the formidable task of persuading the rest of the glass world that he was correct. After many years of effort, and with the assistance of Simon Cottle, they prevailed, and now The Field Cup is proudly displayed in the Art Institute of Chicago as the 15th-century Venetian masterpiece it is.

of the gems in our Beilby Collection. It was John who led me to buy, inter alia, the rare Beilby Sugar Bowl and the unique Beilby Sweet Meat Dish. (See Chapter 2) He also encouraged us to join the Glass Circle, where he introduced us to its group of learned members. As a service to members of the Circle, John led tours to other glass producing nations. John was Chairman of the Circle for a number of years, and oversaw the evolution of the Glass Circle quarterly publication into a polished journal with articles by accomplished scholars. John's charming wife, Aileen, was also an antiquarian. She held a senior curatorial position at the British Museum. John was a Fellow of The Corning Museum of Glass. He contributed two chapters in *5000 Years of Glass*, published by The British Museum. He was a true gentleman, a serious scholar, and a dear friend.

ANNEX 2

Our Glassy Friends

May I introduce you to our other Glassy friends, who are the friends we made as direct result of collecting 18th-century English and Dutch glass. They made our journey down the Georgian Road a source of comradery, knowledge, and inspiration.

DWIGHT LANMON

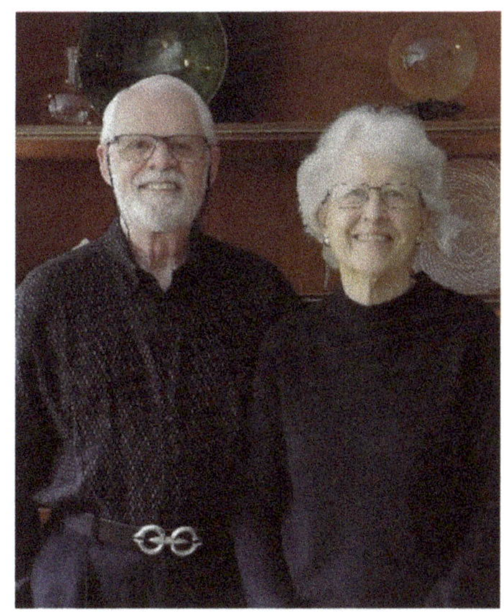

Illustration 1: Dwight and Lorri Lanmon. Photo courtesy of the Lanmons.

"It was a boyhood disease," Dwight Lanmon said of his early love of glass. "I was hunting antique shops by the time I was in high school." It is thus not at all surprising that Dwight spent 19 years working at The Corning Museum of Glass, culminating as director from 1981 to 1992. Upon completing his tenure, he said, "Glass has been at the center of my life so long, it is satisfying to have been associated with the greatest museum and library of that material."

After Corning, Dwight became the Director of Winterthur Museum, Garden and Library. After he retired to Sante Fe, he studied and collected Pueblo pottery, and wrote several books on the subject. His lovely wife Lorri was also a scholar, and taught at Cornell, *inter alia* (Illustration 1).

When we first had the distinct pleasure of meeting Dwight and Lorri, Dwight was still the Director of The Corning Museum of Glass. He was a quiet and scholarly gentleman who came to Washington, D.C. from time to time on business. Over time, we became personal friends. We took advantage of his visits to D.C. to set up dinners in his honor at our home. We invited our Washington Area circle of glass collectors and curators for these occasions. Regulars were Rick Mones, Harald Leuba and his wife Nancy Kingsbury, Gary Baker (then Glass Curator of the Chrysler Museum, Norfolk, VA), and Jean Federico, who collected American Pittsburg glass. We also repeated these dinners whenever our glass friends from London were in town. I remember like dinners for Christopher Sheppard and John Smith. Harald Leuba would frequently bring over some unusual "show and tell" glass to keep us entertained and amused.

Our dinners were warm and friendly occasions which gave us all much pleasure, and knowledge (Illustration 2).

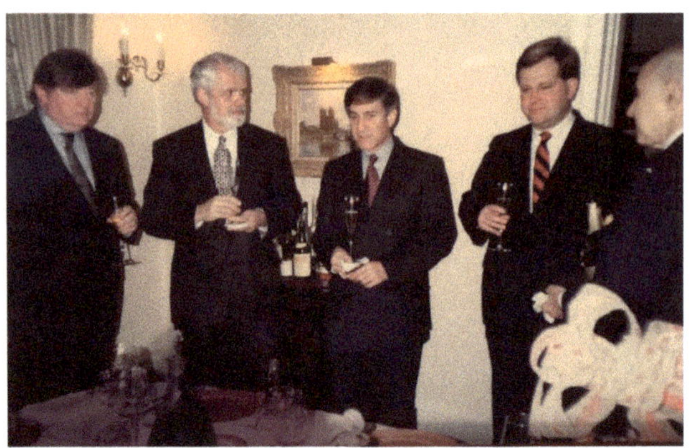

Illustration 2: A little before-dinner champagne. (Left to Right: Christopher Sheppard, Dwight Lanmon, Rick Mones, Gary Baker, and the author.)

A.C. HUBBARD

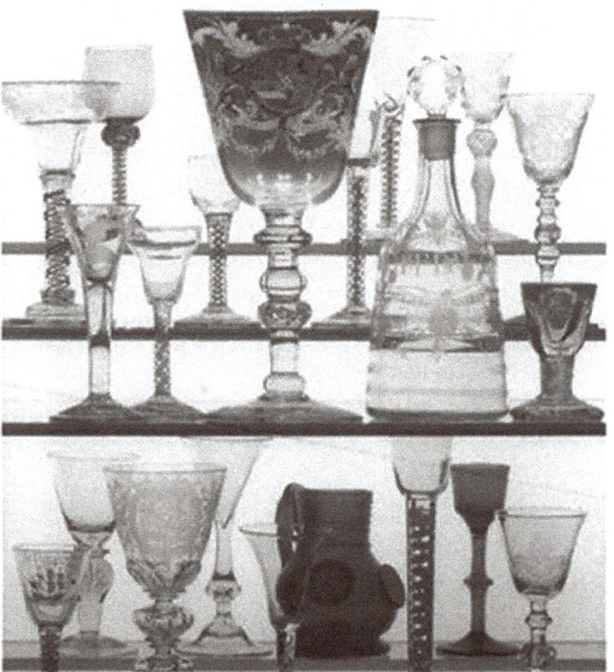

Illustration 3: A Wine-Lover's Glasses. The AC Hubbard, Jr. Collection.

A.C. built up a large and exceptionally fine collection of Georgian glass. It was beautifully displayed in his lovely home near Baltimore. Buying our Beilby glasses and color twists at auction was not always an easy task since A.C. often sought the same glasses I fancied, and fortunately for A.C., he had a pocket as deep as his love for fine Georgian glass. A.C. had Ward Lloyd, a glass expert, do an excellent book on his fabulous collection. It is entitled "*A Wine Lover's Glasses: The A.C. Hubbard Collection of Antique English Glass*" by Ward (Illustration 3). He sold his 18th-century glass collection but still owns one of the largest and best collections of early sealed wine bottles. A.C.'s collecting prowess also extended into the wine and food departments. A.C. amassed an important collection of the best of vintage wines. They are housed in a reproduction Burgundy style wine cellar in the lower level of his home. (His sister made a wonderful miniature of it, complete with wine bottles with their labels!) A.C. is a partner in several of Baltimore's best restaurants and is also the owner of Hubbard Books. But perhaps one of the greatest aesthetic contributions made by the Hubbards was through the handiwork of A.C.'s lovely wife, Penney. She creates prize winning gardens regularly on the grounds of their home, and has written an important book on the subject.

DR. RICHARD MONES

My friendship with Rick Mones and his wife Pam goes back many decades. Rick is a gentleman of great refinement and taste. He is not only a serious collector of early glass, but a scholar on the subject of 16th- and 17th-Century Dutch and German green glass with prunts. He has also collected the finest of sealed wine bottles and antique clocks. His collection also extends to the walls of his home where a fine Dutch painting of the 17th century resides. Rick, like me, often relied upon the expertise of Christopher Sheppard in buying fine glass. Rick was a regular at the dinner parties we hosted for Dwight Lanmon and others (Illustration 2). Rick has over the years shared some fine wines with me. We both fondly remember a case of simply great Puligny-Montrachet 2011. I asked Rick to provide me with a picture of the glass with which he is most proud. Here it is, the Rose Tavern bottle of the 1630's. (Illustration 4)

Rick advises that glass bottles began to be made in England in the 1630s. The Rose Tavern bottle is the earliest form and is in mint condition.

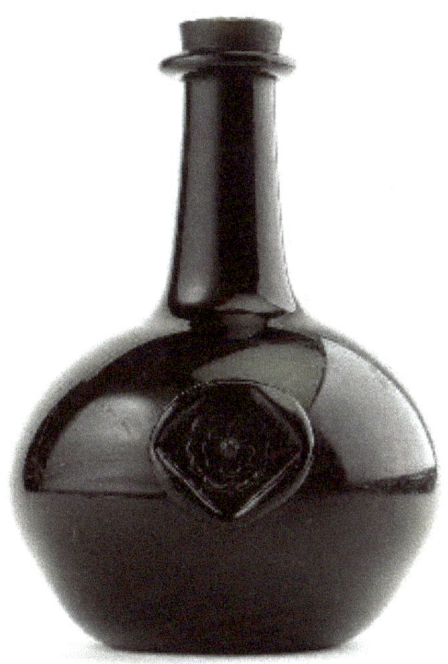

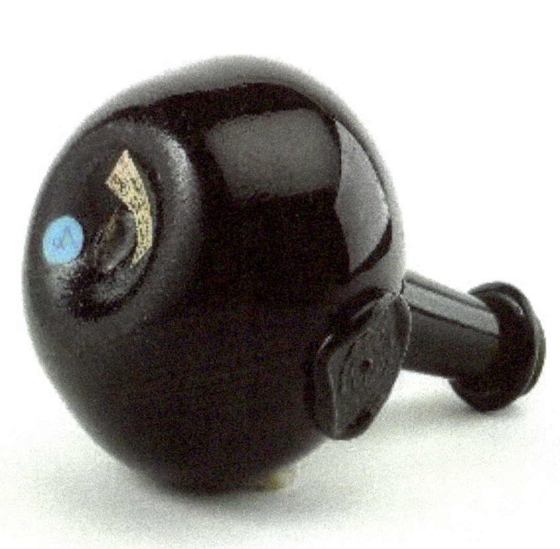

Illustration 4a and 4b: The Rose Tavern Bottle of the 1630's (Front and Bottom). Photo courtesy of Dr. Richard Mones.

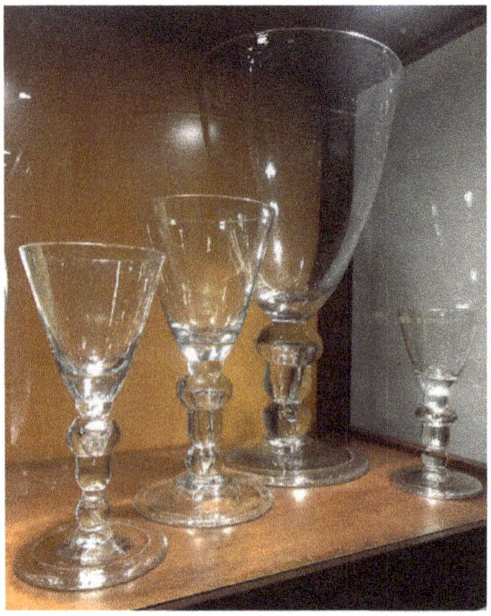

DR. DOUGLAS MCCORKLE

Doug is a resident of greater Baltimore, and a neighbor of A.C. Hubbard. His collection of Georgian glass and other objects of the period is impressive. Doug, like other of our glassy friends, was a beneficiary of the great eye of the late Christopher Sheppard. Doug, like me, also collects studio glass (Illustration 5). As you enter his home you are greeted by a whole series of lovely round sculptures by Dale Chihuly. Of very special interest is his beautiful large glass sculpture by the most prized Czech glass artists, Stanislav Libensky and Jaroslava Brychtova. Last, but not least, Doug's collection of fine wines is truly world class. So are Doug and Lynn. Doug is a Fellow of The Corning Museum of Glass.

Illustration 5: 18th-Century English baluster glasses. Photo courtesy of Dr. Douglas McCorkle.

STEPHEN POHLMANN

Stephen (a Brit who lives in Israel) is a relatively new glass friend. What a shame that I did not meet him decades ago. He is a learned gentleman and so very gracious and kind. He even read this book in an early draft and offered numerous excellent comments. His love of glass goes back at least 40 years. His father was also a glass collector. Stephen has demonstrated great taste in building up his outstanding collection of 18th-century English and Dutch glass. His collection has some exceedingly rare and beautiful glasses. In my judgement, his 18th-century stipple engraved glass by Frans Greenwood, even with a broken stem, is indeed very special. (It is also a treasured glass conspicuously missing from our collection.) His Greenwood is reproduced below (Illustration 6).

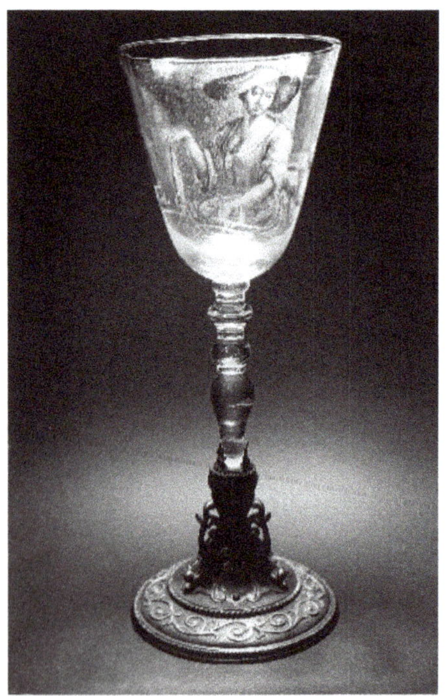

Illustration 6: Frans Greenwood. Photo courtesy of Stephen Pohlmann.

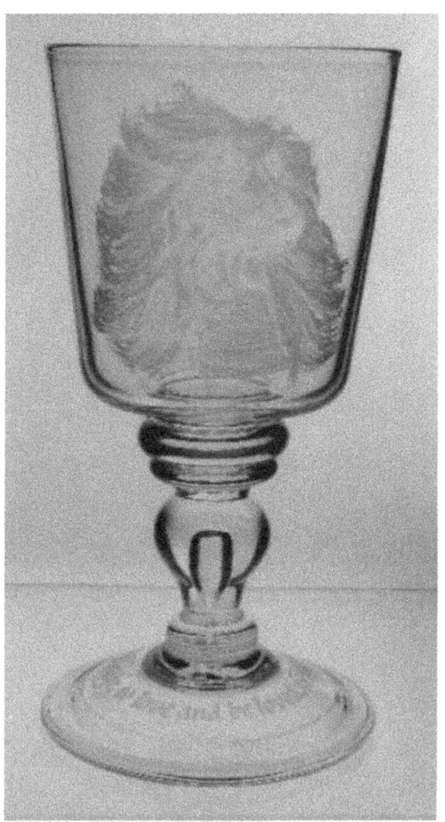

Illustration 7: Leuba's Favorite Glass. Photo courtesy of Harold Leuba.

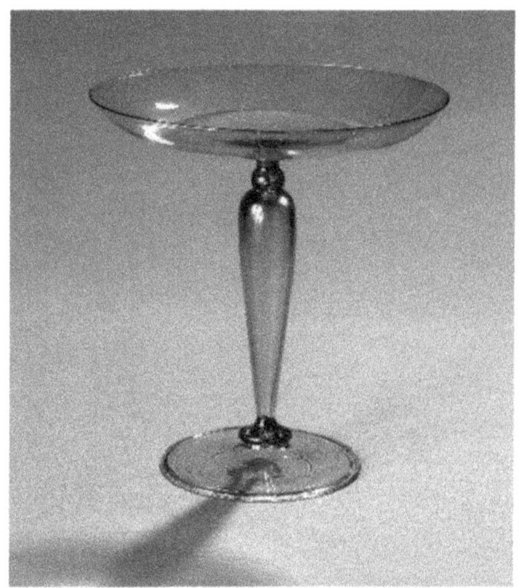

Illustration 8: Venetian Glass, 1595. Photo courtesy of Matij van Der Muelen.

HARALD LEUBA

I have already described Harald and Nancy in Chapter 2. I met Harald and Nancy Kingsbury through the good offices of the late Derek Davis of Asprey many decades ago. I have in that chapter already offered a few words about this remarkable gentleman and his wife. I there noted that they were important collectors of Georgian glass, and many other precious collectables. Harald Leuba is also a handy man *extraordinaire*. An example of his skill is the miniature English village into which he ingenuously converted his basement. A picture of one section of their incredible village made completely from scrap material is set forth in Chapter 2. Here is a picture of Harald's favorite glass (Illustration 7).

MATIJ VAN DER MUELEN

Matij is my Dutch "glassy" friend. He is a glass collector who has meticulous taste and, over the years, has assembled an outstanding collection of glass, beautifully displayed in his lovely home in Rotterdam. His substantial collection includes his first love, Venetian glass of the middle to late years of the Sixteenth century, and of course Dutch glass. He, like Robert J. Charleston, the famous glass scholar, favors Venetian glass of that period. Indeed, Matij selected as his "favorite glass" to reproduce here, the so-called Bacchus glass, named after the glass in the famous 1595 painting of Bacchus by Caravaggio in the Uffizi Museum. He advises that he most admires the simple glass without excessive adornment (Illustration 8).

I just described a remarkable group of gentlemen. And each had a spouse who shared in the wonder of collecting 18th-century English and Dutch glass. But for my interest in collecting glass, I would likely never met any of them. This, I repeat, is one of the compelling benefits of collecting.

ANNEX 3

Behind the Kaplan Collection

THE GLASS CIRCLE OF ENGLAND AND WALES

The Circle is an organization whose members number some most serious collectors, dealers, scholars, and just plain lovers of glass. Ann and I became members of the Glass Circle with the encouragement of John Smith, a former president of the Circle, and Simon Cottle of Bonham's, also a former president. The Circle meets periodically at the Art Workers Guild in London for an informal reception and lecture by a prominent glass expert. The lectures are generally excellent, and afterwards, the Circle invites the guest speaker to a near-by local restaurant to afford members an opportunity to "break bread" with the speaker. Although I do not pretend to be a glass expert, I was invited once to be the speaker since so many of the members heard of our collection, and wanted to see pictures of the glasses in it. The Circle puts out a quarterly magazine with excellent articles by experts. John Smith also frequently arranged trips for members to other countries which had a history of glass making.

OUR LIBRARY OF ENGLISH GEORGIAN AND DUTCH GLASS OF THE PERIOD

I learned early on that if one were to become truly knowledgeable in antique English and Dutch glass, one needed a basic library of books on the subject. Ann became the librarian of our glass collection and built us a comprehensive library of the important books on the subject.

THE SALE OF OUR GLASS COLLECTION

The sale took place on 28 November 2017 at Bonham's, London. Representatives of important museums were there, as were serious dealers and collectors. Every item sold, and virtually all at prices exceeding the price estimates. Bonham's prepared a truly outstanding catalogue which contributed to the great success of the sale. I thank Simon Cottle and his most talented staff for this. The sale caused me to reflect on my first encounters with Derek Davis forty some years ago when he urged me to buy only the very best, even if this meant paying a premium. He correctly observed that the most rare and beautiful glasses will normally outperform the market.

Let me not finish this discussion without noting that a serious and determined buyer named Karim Halim was a major player in the auction. He bought many of the best for his then brand-new Halim Family Museum of Time and Glass, which opened in Evanston, Illinois in September, 2017. We will thus soon be able to visit some of "our" glasses in his museum, when that part of the museum featuring Georgian glass opens. I have now visited the Halim museum and met Mr. Halim. They are both very special.

BEILBY GLASS RECOLLECTED BY SIMON COTTLE

Exquisite table-glass painted in coloured enamels by a talented family of artists based in Newcastle-upon-Tyne during the second half of the 18th century, is amongst the most renowned of all English glass. In association with the glassmakers of the town, William Beilby and his three skillful brothers, John, Ralph and Thomas and their young sister Mary, developed a unique and magnificent decorating style, using techniques previously not practiced on glass in England. Active between circa 1760 and 1778, the workshop's output was prodigious. Utilising a range of locally-made wine glasses, large goblets, decanters, flasks and bowls as their blank canvases, the Beilbys' subject matter varied widely from landscapes to birds, grapes and flowers. Most notably, the Beilby's decorated large goblets and wine glasses with impressive coats of arms and crests in polychrome enamels, enriched with opaque-white floral highlights and occasionally with gilding, to a level of quality that at least matched the finest in Europe. Their superiority in the field is not only due to their artistic talent, but also to the quality of their enamels. Their best-known white palette was used for elaborate inscriptions, delicate Rococo motifs, scenes of rural pastimes, ruined classical buildings and obelisks and bunches of grapes. The Beilby family were learned scholars with a classical education and they were also familiar with contemporary fashion and manners. They drew inspiration from the work of contemporary decorators, oil painters, watercolorists, print-makers, engravers, stained glass artists and the architects of the time. Their workshop supplied wealthy and aristocratic families with delightfully-painted and idiosyncratic crystal-clear luxury glass, intended to complement the highly decorative porcelain table services and rich interiors of the period. Glasses decorated with neoclassical ornament and Italianate landscapes were perfect for display and use within interiors reflecting the interest in neo-classicism as young aristocrats returned from their European Grand Tour travels.

There is a timeless quality to Beilby glass. Their fashionable wine glasses and goblets are supported by multi-twisted opaque-white and colour-tinted threaded stems that echo Venetian filigrana glass of the Renaissance. When painted with coats of arms, these convey a spirit of originality previously seen in German heraldic glass of the 17th-century, a unique and distinct art form hitherto unknown in Britain. The Beilbys' success has made them world famous and their achievements have placed 18th-century glass towards the forefront of British decorative arts.

Engraved glass relies on the subtleties of light for its appreciation, while colour-tinted glass derives a different brilliance from its eye-catching reedom. By contrast, Beilby reedom glass is dramatic, refined and immediate. As trained watercolour artists and copper-box enamellers, the Beilbys knew how to use colour effectively. Their deliberate choice of a single shade of colour—a luminous white—to portray and enhance their decoration was both exciting and novel in the 1760s. The difficulties of firing the enamels on to glass at a high temperature, close to its melting point should not be underestimated. The Beilbys managed to successfully blend this and the underlying clear glass so that the two layers became one. The result was enamels that remain largely intact since the day they were applied.

The Beilbys were intimately connected to London society where the nobility commissioned goblets richly painted with their coats of arms. Others were associated with the Royal Arms of George III and those of his supporters. These glasses were part of the fragile diplomacy associated with aristocrats maneuvering for power at the time and they formed exclusive gifts passed from one group to another in search of political alliances. The delightfully engraved light-baluster wine glasses with their royal coats of arms decorated in the Netherlands by Dutch artisans, gave the Beilbys the inspiration to decorate Dutch-made glasses in the same manner but in polychrome enamels. Adopting and enlivening this characteristic Dutch theme with colour was a masterstroke and opened the door for the Beilby workshop to the European market. Examples of the work of the Beilbys can be found in most of the leading international museums and art galleries where fine European glass is displayed. For example, at The Corning Museum of Glass in New York State and at the city art galleries of Toledo and Philadelphia there are significant collections of their glass. In Australia, Japan, Russia and most of the European nations, Beilby reedom glass is enjoyed and admired by museum visitors.

The Beilbys' originality continues to be unrivalled in Britain and whilst connoisseurs have marveled at the quality of their enamels, others have admired the ingenuity that enabled them to supply the London market with artistry in glass that was the height of fashion in Georgian England. By comparison with contemporary glass today, the products of the Beilby workshop stand up exceptionally well. Although the work of the Beilbys may be different in style from that of the modern glass decorator, the balance of colour to form and proportion of their glass is simply perfect. The shape of their select glasses and decanters, lends a symmetry to the enamel decoration which brings them right up-to-date in presentation.

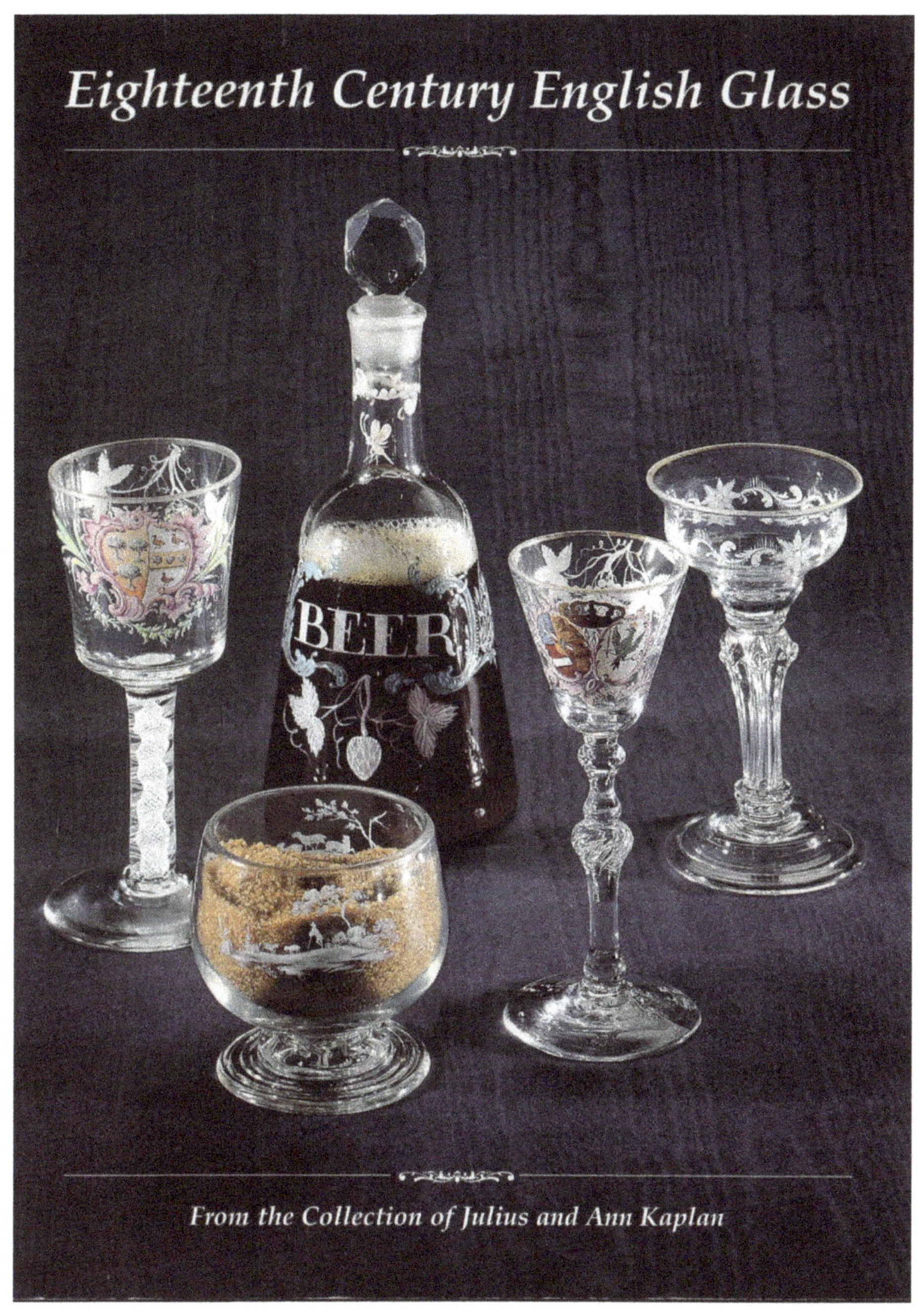

Illustration 1: Catalogue cover of *Eighteenth-Century English Glass and Related Dutch Glass: from the Collection of Julius and Ann Kaplan.*

A Short History of Eighteenth-Century English Glass by Jay Kaplan

The article by me set forth below was originally published in 1999 in The Cosmos Journal. I believe it appropriate to include it in this book since Chapter 2 of this book only discusses a small portion of English Georgian glass. This article will show the historical context of the glasses described in Chapter 2.

The well-appointed 18th-century American household was furnished for the most part with products made in America. Our affluent colonial ancestors dined at magnificent mahogany tables from New York, sat on elegant Chippendale chairs from Philadelphia, and carved and ate their turkey with cutlery and silverware from Massachusetts. However, when it came to finding glasses to drink from, Americans in those days still had to look back principally to Mother England. Proper stemware was not produced in this country until late in the century.

Fine glass was produced in substantial amounts in England during the entire 18th century. It was usually made from a lead crystal, then referred to as flint glass. George Ravenscroft, a glass maker in London, introduced the process in 1676 by mixing lead oxide and potash into a silica batch. The flint glass that resulted was acclaimed almost immediately for its beauty and clarity. Unfortunately, however, Ravenscroft's early output had a tendency to crizzle, leaving an internal network of lines that eventually caused a breakdown of the surface of the glass. But this defect was soon corrected and, by the 1680s, Ravenscroft and others were consistently producing clear, brilliant, uncrizzled glass.

English flint glass tended to be heavier, more stable, and more refractive than the unleaded soda glass then in general use on the Continent. During the Georgian period, flint glass became the predominant material in drinking-glass production throughout England, and the end products were greatly appreciated by connoisseurs. Flint glass is easily distinguished from soda glass. Besides being heavier in weight, it is also more resonant. It rings beautifully when tapped lightly with a fork, while soda glass gives off a dull thud. Leaded glass also is distinguishable by a faint grayish tinge. Both flint glass and high-quality German and Venetian soda glass sought to imitate the appearance of rock crystal, which is why we now use the word crystal for fine glassware.

Drinking glasses in those days came in many different sizes and shapes. They often had bowls, which had a small capacity by today's standards, two ounces or less. Others were enormous, and were probably used for beer or as ceremonial glasses. Whatever the size, Georgian glasses tended to be well designed, with harmonious dimensions.

English glassware in the 18th century reflected the rise of a consumer culture in England. The fashion-conscious purchaser sought an assortment of different styles and shapes for each drink served. Among the popular shapes were glasses for ale, cordials, various kinds of wine, and ratafias, an almond-based drink similar to a cordial. There were tumblers and even special toastmaster glasses. The latter had thick bowls that held a deceptively small quantity of drink, thus enabling the toastmaster to propose numerous toasts and still make it home under his own power.

By the middle of the 18th century, many items throughout the home were being made of glass. Household glassware included candlesticks, taper sticks, salvers, sweetmeat glasses, and dessert glasses for jellies, syllabubs, and possets. Decanters, in this hard-drinking era, ranged in size from a quarter-bottle capacity to a Methuselah capable of holding eight full bottles. Decanters were collected for their form, size, and style of decoration. Rarities included enameled decanters from the workshop of the Beilby family in Newcastle-upon-Tyne, and gilded examples from James Giles decorating establishment in London during the 1760s. Later, manufacturers and dealers successfully promoted the use of a distinctive decanter for each type of beverage. It became fashionable to label decanters to indicate their contents, e.g., port, sherry, madeira, claret, cyder, and even beer and ale, which, in this period, were powerful beverages more accurately described as barley wine.

CHANGING TASTES

The design of Georgian glass reflected not only the tastes of the times, the lightness of rococo superseding the heavier baroque style and motifs, but also the impact of excise tax laws. For example, in 1745 England began to tax glass on the basis of weight, a tax imposed on the manufacturer. This impelled glass manufacturers to find ways to lighten their product. One method was the elimination of the folded foot. Prior to 1745, Georgian glasses generally had been made with the base, or foot, reinforced with an extra fold or layer of metal to protect the foot from chipping. Without this reinforced base, post-1745 glasses were less expensive to make, but more vulnerable to being damaged.

One example of an early drinking glass was the baluster. The earliest of these dated back to the reign of William III and Mary, circa 1690, but the best were produced mostly during the reign of Queen Anne (1701-1716). The baluster took its name from the architectural form for the short pillar, although, in the case of the glass, the shape was usually inverted. A wide variety of stem patterns, or knops, evolved in the broad field of baluster glasses. If produced by a good maker, knops shaped as acorns, mushrooms, or cylinders are eagerly sought by collectors today. Perhaps rarest of all, the plain ovoid or egg-shaped knop is highly desirable among collectors. An air bubble was often incorporated in the knop of balusters.

With the advent of the Hanoverian monarchy in 1714, English makers began producing glasses similar to the styles being made in Germany. These glasses emerged during the reign of George I and may well reflect the influence of his court. Typically, these glasses possessed a molded pedestal stem sometimes referred to as a Silesian stem. A very small number incorporate the motto God Save King. The pedestals usually had six or eight sides, although some early four-sided ones were also made. Others were molded with diamonds or stars on the points of the shoulders. The feet are usually folded, as were the feet of baluster glasses. The Silesian stem also was found on candlesticks and sweetmeat glasses.

During the second quarter of the century, glass makers in England began to realize that the air bubble or tear in baluster glasses could be manipulated to be a central decorative feature in the stem. These manipulations took elaborate and intricate forms, and often resulted in glasses of great beauty and brilliance. Many varieties of air twists were created. They were incorporated in straight-stemmed glasses, as well as in glasses with knops. By mid-century, multi-spiral, air twist stems were extremely popular.

Before long, the air twist was overtaken in popularity by glasses with an opaque twist stem. Instead of manipulating the air bubble, manufacturers placed rods of white enamel around the inside of a cylindrical mold. The mold was then filled with molten glass, which, after cooling and reheating, could be twisted to create cotton twists of elaborate and intricate design. Opaque twist stems were used in most styles of drinking glasses, both small and large, as well as in candlesticks and sweetmeat glasses.

Around 1760, an especially attractive variation of the twist-stemmed glass emerged with the addition of color. In lieu of rods of white enamel, the glass maker now substituted, most commonly, red, green, and blue rods. These were frequently intertwined with opaque white twists, resulting in complex and very beautiful designs. Today, color twist glasses from this era are far rarer than air or opaque twist glasses. Those with brown and turquoise twists are especially rare. Yellows, though also rare, are not as difficult to find. The color twist was sometimes mixed with an air twist. Another attractive combination, though rare, is a color twist combined with both an air twist and an opaque twist. The rarest of the color twists, however, has a stem with a single color and neither an opaque nor an air twist.

In 1777, taxes once again played an important role in the development of English glassware. Parliament's approval of the Excise Act of 1777 doubled the tax rate on glass produced in England, but from 1780 onward exempted glass produced in Ireland. As a result, the Irish cut-glass industry was born. One of the early producers there was the now internationally famous Waterford manufactory. Most Irish cut glass was made for export to England and America.

The bowls of Georgian glasses were frequently decorated with engraved images. This was accomplished by using either a diamond point or, more commonly, an engraving wheel. Engraving on glass with a sharp instrument had been practiced by the Romans. Indeed, Egyptian antecedents go back as far as the 14th century, B.C., and there are references to engraved Venetian glass dating from the 16th century. By 1570, the technique had spread to England, where it was employed by both English and Dutch engravers.

The subjects of the engravings varied. Wine glasses often were decorated with representations of vines and grapes, ale glasses with barley and hops, and cider glasses with apple trees and perhaps the word CYDER. Other common 18th-century subjects included flowers and plants, busts of famous and not-so-famous persons, armorial seals of aristocratic families, hunting scenes, political slogans, animals, flags, and ships.

Bristol, famed for its glass as well as its shipbuilding, was a major center for glasses engraved with warships. The production of privateer glasses began in the late 1750s. The bowls were decorated with wheel-engraved images of the specific ships then being commissioned in Bristol for use by the English in the Seven Years War (1756-1763). Most of these privateers had bucket-shaped bowls.

GLASSES AND POLITICS

Perhaps the most famous, and controversial, of English engraved glassware is Jacobite glass: glassware that overtly or covertly supported the Stuart cause in England's Glorious Revolution of 1688-1689. This period of strife has its origins in 1669, when James, the son of Charles I of England, converted to Catholicism. In 1685, he ascended the throne as King James II and immediately started to convert his Roman Catholic faith into royal policy. This policy greatly alarmed the Protestants of England who, three years later, forced the King to flee for his life to France, replacing him with the Protestant monarchy of William III of Orange and his wife, Mary, James II's daughter.

James II spent the rest of his days attempting to recapture the throne, as did his son, James Edward Stuart, and grandson, Charles Edward Stuart. They failed, despite substantial, if often furtive, support from the Jacobites who championed their cause. Jacobite societies had to be secret since they were officially banned. Nevertheless, they met frequently and, over a bowl of water, toasted the King, often using glasses engraved with Jacobite symbols. The toast was well understood by the members as a tribute to the King over the sea, or James III, as James Edward Stuart styled himself.

The most common symbol of Jacobite support on glassware is the rose. The flower is depicted fully open and normally has two closed buds on the stem. The open flower is believed to represent the throne of England, and the two buds are interpreted to be the two Stuart sons of James III, Prince Charles Edward and Prince Henry the Cardinal Duke of York.

In addition to the symbolic flowers, Jacobite glasses frequently have words engraved on them: Fiat (meaning let it be or let it come to pass) or Redeat, Redi, or Revirescit (suggesting hope that the Prince will return). The bowls of some Jacobite glasses bear a likeness of the grandson of James II, Charles Edward Stuart, known as the Young Pretender or Bonnie Prince Charlie. But the most famous, as well as the earliest, Jacobite glasses are the Amen glasses. There are fewer than 40 known examples. Two to four verses of the Jacobite hymn and the word Amen are engraved in diamond point on their bowls.

Jacobite glasses have long been a favorite with collectors. The popularity of Jacobite glasses, in fact, drove prices so high that forgers were encouraged to produce copies. The forgeries were principally done in the 19th and 20th centuries on genuine Georgian glass. As a consequence, serious doubt has been cast on the authenticity of many putative Jacobite glasses.

Predictably, perhaps, the Protestant supporters of King William III and Queen Mary responded to the popularity of Jacobite glasses with engraved glassware of their own. The Protestant glasses usually depict an equestrian figure of William and also were frequently copied by forgers. When George I became king in 1714, thereby establishing the House of Hanover on the British throne, engraved glasses were produced that depicted a Hanoverian white horse together with a white heraldic rose.

DUTCH INFLUENCES

William of Orange was not the only Dutch connection to English glass. Dutch engravers worked on many English and English-style glasses. They tended to be more skilled than their English counterparts, which is why many English glasses were sent to Holland for engraving. Some 18th-century English glass makers may even have set up factories in the Netherlands and Norway to produce English-style flint glass. Many 18th-century glasses formerly thought to be of English origin are now thought by many experts to be of Dutch or Belgian origin.

One type of glass engraving perfected in Holland during the 18th century was diamond stippling, the use of pointillist techniques to create images on glass. The originator of stippling was Anna Roemers, who lived in Leiden in the second quarter of the 17th century. Stipple-engravers created images by making innumerable tiny dots on the bowl of the glass. Darker areas were made with dots spaced farther apart, and lighter areas with the dots closer together. The result was an image of incredible delicacy. Interestingly, the image can hardly be seen unless light is cast from above on the edge of the glass. When lighted in that way, the image is said to have been breathed upon.

Roemers stippling technique was taken up early in the 18th century by Frans Greenwood of Amsterdam (1680-1763), a gifted amateur who created beautiful images on glass. There are about 50 recorded glasses by Greenwood. Most of the stipple-engravers were, like Greenwood, amateurs. There were, however, at least two who were probably professionals and who were great masters, in any case: David Wolff (1732-1798); and an anonymous pointillist nicknamed Alias by F.G.A.M. Smit, the author of an important 20th century catalogue raisonne of Dutch stippled glass. The craftsmanship of both Alias and Wolff was immaculate. Both frequently depicted children, often together with inscriptions dealing with love, friendship, and liberty. Wolff also stipple-engraved portraits of aristocratic personages and armorials, frequently of the House of Orange. One of the most intricate and beautiful of Wolff glasses is the Personification of Amsterdam, depicting Asia and Africa paying obeisance to Amsterdam. Another important glass by Wolff pictures a house in a landscape on which is inscribed in a banderole, VRYHEIDS LUST (yearning for reedom).

No discussion of Dutch engravings on English or English-style glasses can be complete without mention of two masters of wheel-engraved glass, the Brothers Sang, Jacob Sang and Simon Jacob Sang. The Sangs originated in Brunswick, Germany, and worked in Amsterdam. An advertisement for the wares of Jacob Sang appeared in an Amsterdam newspaper in 1753. It noted that he engraved on English-style glass and that the subjects of his engraving included portraits, armorials, classical subjects, figures of all sorts, names, and inscriptions, and decorative designs of the newest fashions. Several Sang glasses, signed and dated, exist today.

THE ARTISTRY OF WILLIAM BEILBY

Rather than being engraved, some Georgian glasses were beautifully decorated with paintings, principally by an artist named William Beilby, sometimes with the assistance of his sister, Mary, and his brother Ralph. They produced their works in Newcastle-upon-Tyne, principally during the 1760s. William Beilby learned enameling and painting during the 1750s while apprenticed to a Birmingham artist named John Haseldine. In 1761, William discovered how to fire his enamel paintings onto glass so that they virtually fused with the glass. We know much of this from the diaries of Thomas Bewick, a highly regarded artist, who for several years was an apprentice in the Beilby atelier.

The most famous Beilby glasses are families coats of arms and other armorials, which often were painted in bright colors. These include royal armorials for the Dutch and English crowns, as well as armorials for important English families. A few were signed with the name of W. Beilby or Beilby Jr. Other Beilby glass was signed with a butterfly, as the American artist James Abbott McNeill Whistler did many years later in his paintings and drawings.

One of the more interesting Beilby glasses is a very handsome and tall goblet known as the Standard of Hesleyside. It carries with it an interesting story. In 1763, Edward Charlton of Hesleyside visited the Beilby workshop in Newcastle. Impressed with the quality of the workmanship he saw, Charlton commissioned William Beilby to decorate a glass that would hold a full bottle of claret. Beilby designed a goblet with a deep, round funnel bowl connected to an additional globular bowl beneath it. One side of the glass bears the inscription The Standard of Hesleyside. On the reverse side is the Charlton family arms in color with the inscription Edward Charlton Esq. 1763. According to J. Rush, who wrote about the Beilby artistry in 1987, it became the custom and a challenge... to gulp the contents [of this two-bowl glass] down without taking a breath, and drinking a full bottle of Bordeaux wine in this fashion became known as Sinking the Standard. Unfortunately, this unique glass was damaged when Charlton's drunken butler mishandled it. History does not record whether the butler himself had tried to Sink the Standard.

In addition to armorials, the Beilbys painted hunting and fishing scenes, pastoral scenes, classical ruins, exotic birds, Chinese pavilions, and beehives. Other glasses had somewhat more abstract vine-scroll and hop-and-barley motifs. In still others, the white enamel is highlighted with bluish or pink tones. The rim of the glass is frequently gilded. Among the most treasured of all Beilby glasses are those fashioned by William Beilby to commemorate the birth of the Prince of Wales on August 4, 1762. They are executed in full heraldic color, with mantling painted in white enamel and shadowing in other colors. Among the rarest Beilbys are a sweetmeat glass and a sugar bowl.

Another famous painter who decorated glass was James Giles (and his atelier). Giles gilded a variety of glass objects but was best known for his decanters, glasses, and bottles featuring portrayals of exotic birds amid slender, feathery trees. Giles also did vine trails and hop-and-barley motifs, and later added bucranium (stag head) designs to his repertoire. Although James Giles decoration of glass was highly regarded, his atelier was best known for its decoration of colored china, principally from Worcester.

Isaac Jacobs of Bristol was yet another skilled craftsman who gilded on blue (and opaque white) glass. He is perhaps best known for his blue bowls with key-fret borders, which were often signed. The bowls were brought out at the end of a meal and were used for rinsing hands and mouth, according to one account of the times.

One final type of 18th-century English glassware of interest is the rummer, a corruption of the Dutch word Roemer. This type of green-colored glass was used to drink German white wines (Hock ½ or Rhenish ½ wine, as they were called in Georgian times). The original Roemer was normally green with a prunted stem (the shape of a sliced raspberry) and a cup-shaped bowl. The Georgian version omitted the prunts and gadrooning (an abstract design), and took on the shape and design of the clear glass being produced at the time. A few of these green glasses had air twist stems and, less frequently, opaque twist stems. Very few had a green bowl and foot, with a clear opaque twist stem. Less than a dozen such glasses have survived. In general, green glass is much rarer than clear flint glass, probably reflecting a relative lack of interest by 18th-century imbibers in drinking Hock. Green decanters are even more rare. One of the rarest colored English drinking glasses of the 18th century is a glass with a blue bowl and foot, and a clear opaque twist stem.

PRESERVING THE TREASURES

Many of these works of art are greatly prized today by collectors and museums. They have gone up in value, though perhaps not as aggressively as Impressionist paintings. For a fine Georgian glass, one must count on paying anywhere from $10,000 to $25,000 and beyond for very rare and beautiful examples.

A number of museums in the United States, including The Corning Museum of Glass in Corning, New York; the Toledo Museum in Toledo, Ohio; and the Philadelphia Museum have excellent collections of English 18th-century glass. In addition, there are important private American collections, several of which are in the Washington-Baltimore area.

Recommended Readings:

Bickerton, L.M. *Eighteenth-Century Drinking Glasses: An Illustrated Guide*. Woodbridge, UK: Antique Collectors Club Ltd., 1986.

Charleston, R.J. *English Glass and the Glass Used in England*, Circa 400-1940. London: George Allen & Unwin, 1984.

Lloyd, W. *Investing in Georgian Glass*. London: Barrie and Jenkins Ltd., 1969

Julius Kaplan (Cosmos Club, 1983) is counsel to Cadwalader, Wickersham & Taft. He is a collector of Chinese ceramics, American paintings, and English glass.

Cosmos Journal, 1999

ANNEX 5

Introduction to the Catalogue of the Collection of Julius and Ann Kaplan by John Smith

Jay Kaplan started his collection of glass by buying from the long-established Asprey of London. The antique department was run by Derek Davis, an elderly second-generation glass dealer, whose father had started dealing in glass in the 1920's. Derek was known through the world as source for serious collectors and museums.

One day Derek told me that one of his enthusiastic collectors was a young American lawyer, based in Washington, D.C. Derek first met Jay in 1978 and recognized in him an active man who, obliged to travel frequently to London in the course of his legal work, sought to take advantage of these trips to pursue his interest in collecting English glass. Many of the world's best collections have been assembled by such peripatetic collectors. Jay, in turn, recognized Derek to be a serious dealer with a depth of knowledge and a wide museum clientele. Under Derek's guidance, Jay started to collect English 18th-century drinking glasses. Together they always sought quality, not quantity.

I joined Asprey in 1984. When I first met Jay in 1985, he had already formed a small, but very fine collection of 18th-century drinking glasses, the majority with twist stems. In England glass with stems decorated with threads of enamel were produced between 1755 and 1789. This method took its inspiration from Venetian latticino glass and was usually executed with white enamel. Different coloured enamel were used either in conjunction with white enamel, or occasionally with air twists. This collection has many good examples of these glasses, known to collectors as 'colour-twists', in both conventional wine glass size and also in the more unusual large size goblet. There is also a most rare 'mixed twist' glass, in which blue threads are intertwined with threads of air, and an exceedingly rare wine glass with only a blue twist.

By 1985, Derek had also introduced Jay to the work of the Beilby family. This well documented family, led by William Beilby, enameled glass in Newcastle-upon-Tyne, in the north of England, between 1762 and 1782. After the Laing Museum in Newcastle, Jay now has the best and most interesting collection of glass from this workshop, extending well beyond the drinking glasses usually seen in museums. In particular there is a sugar bowl decorated with a landscape. The bowl has only one known parallel, which is from the Jerome Strauss collection in The Corning Museum of Glass, New York. There is also a unique sweetmeat glass, once in the famous glass collection of Sir Hugh Dawson, and a rare decanter enameled in white and turquoise with the label BEER.

William Beilby went on to become a drawing master, and while he was in Newcastle, had Thomas Bewick as an apprentice. Bewick is now famous for his woodcuts of the English countryside. Examining some of Jay's Beilby glasses with rural vignettes, it is easy to see where Bewick received his training and inspiration.

Jay's collection also contains some of the very rare colored work by Beilby. He, like the best museums, is content to have restored examples in his collection if the item is of such rarity and beauty as to be unobtainable in the perfect state.

Towards the end of 1989, I left Asprey and joined Mallett where I founded a specialist glass department (although the company's records show that they had previously stocked some extraordinary fine glasses in the 1920's and 1930's.) Jay continued to be a customer and friend and bought several important items from our inaugural exhibition in May 1990 entitled 'From Restoration to Regency' which we held with Christopher Sheppard.

Jay's collection of glasses is fueled partly by his enthusiasm for good wine. He and his wife Ann have been known to hold memorable dinner parties for other serious collectors, curators and dealers, or an interesting rare wine from the Napa Valley. Guests often bring one of their new acquisitions of glass to these functions to be examined and discussed by the assembled 'glass circle.'

Jay also has a collection of ratafia glasses. Ratafia is an Italian liqueur based on almonds. It is extremely difficult to find now, although it was generally available in the 18th century, and special glasses were made for serving it.

Throughout the 90's, Jay has continued to collect English 18th-century glass, although he is now also turning his attention to the engraved glass of Holland, produced during the same period. Glass can be decorated on the surface by enameling or gilding, but the most lasting method of decorating glass is to engrave the surface. This is often done with small rotating copper wheels, which are continuously fed with wet abrasive powder. The lathe to turn the wheel is operated by a foot treadle or by water power and, in the hands of a skilled craftsman, is capable of wonderful results. Although there are glass engravers in England during the 18th century, and much commemorative glass was produced of political and social interest, the skill of English engravers did not match that of the Dutch. Today such glasses are collected for historical reasons rather than aesthetic pleasure.

The other form of engraved decoration on glass in Holland during the 18th-century was diamond point engraving. This, in turn, developed into pointillism called stipple engraving. In this technique, the surface of the glass is tapped with a diamond pointed instrument, leaving a stippled effect. This requires great draftsmanship allied to infinite patience. Only a few practitioners such as Frans Greenwood, David Wolff, and the elusive "Alius" obtained worthwhile results. This art has been revived in the 20th century by an Englishman, Lawrence Whistler. Both figurative and landscape work were produced by this technique and Jay's glass illustrated with a House in a Landscape is as good as they come, a real inspiration, as is the Personification of Amsterdam.

ANNEX 6

Author's Note

THIS BOOK IS DEDICATED TO IRVIN AND MARILYN YALOM

Irvin and Marilyn Yalom are two of my oldest and dearest friends in the world. They are both truly remarkable people. Irv is a psychiatrist and educator of great renown. He has written seminal books on group psychotherapy and existential psychotherapy. Indeed, Irvin is often deemed to be the father of group therapy and one of the parents of existential psychotherapy. In addition to his scholarly nonfiction writing, Irvin has written some best-selling fiction. His *When Nietzsche Wept* has become a classic novel.

Irvin and I grew up in Washington, D.C. in the 1930's and 40's and were brought together every weekend by our parents, who were all immigrants from Russia/Poland, and met together every Sunday for dinner and cards.

As teenagers, for several years we partnered in owning and running firework stands for a week or so before the 4th of July. Our last year was especially successful when we earned enough to pay for Irv's honeymoon trip to Europe and my purchase of an orange Plymouth convertible to take to college.

Over the years, Irv has received many awards and honors, and has given many talks. I attended but one, but I was told that it was typical. At that one, in Washington, D.C., there was a sell-out audience of well over 1000 therapists, psychologists, and others in related fields. When Irv took to the podium, everybody in the audience stood and clapped and clapped and clapped. The moderator finally had to beg the audience to stop clapping so Yalom could give his talk. Finally they did, and Dr. Yalom gave his talk. When Irvin finished, once again the entire audience stood and clapped without end. This apparently happened regularly when Irvin Yalom gave a public address.

Marilyn is also a former Washingtonian who I have known for, more or less, 66 years. She went to Wellesley, Harvard, The Sorbonne, and Johns Hopkins. She became a scholar, writer, and teacher. Marilyn was a Professor of Comparative Literature. She also served as Director of the Clayman Institute for Gender Research at Stanford University. Marilyn has also written a large number of highly acclaimed feminist (and other) books. Her books include, *A History of the Breast, A History of the Wife, Birth of the Chess Queen, The American Resting Place with photos by Reid Yalom,* and *How the French Invented Love*. Her books have been translated into 20 languages. She was decorated by the French government as an Officier des Palmes Academique in 1981.

I would not be who I am today but for Marilyn. She took me aside before I graduated from high school, and told me, in no uncertain terms, "Jay, you are not going to make the mistake that Irv made (in going to a local university). If you prefer a large school, you are going to Harvard, Yale or Princeton. If you prefer a small school, you are going to Amherst, Williams or Wesleyan. Period. No exceptions are allowed." My mother reluctantly agreed for me to go away to college. She said, "If you must follow Marilyn's suggestions, you then must go to Wesleyan." Her half- brother, Uncle Jake, lived very nearby, and all three of his children went to Wesleyan, and two of them lived very nearby. She figured that with having close family around, I would feel more secure since this would be my first time away from home.

EXPRESSION OF DEEP GRATITUDE

To my wife of 55 years, Ann Lanyon Kaplan.

I owe heartfelt thanks to my wife for her vital role, over the decades, in making the collections come to fruition, and for their display and maintenance. By way of example, I remember how much time and effort she expended in selecting just the right color of material for the backing of the glass display cases in the dining room; how she periodically polished all of the delicate miniature Hanukkah menorahs, the place cards, and every glass individually. In this book reference is made to the series of dinners held in our home for our little 'glass circle' in honor of Dwight Lanmon and others. Their success was the result of many hours of diligent preparation by Ann. She also meticulously put together our extensive library of books on glass. Indeed, her hand and heart were involved in every aspect of the creation, display and maintenance of our collections. Ann has an "eye" for art which I always relied upon fully in the selection and hanging of paintings we bought. I could not have created the Kaplan collections without her participation and support. Merci *infiniment.*

I GIVE MY DEEP THANKS TO THE FOLLOWING PEOPLE

1. **Jean Sulkes:** My sister, Jean Kaplan Sulkes, was instrumental in awakening in me at an early age a sensitivity and interest in Chinese cuisine and culture, and later in introducing me to studio glass at Habatat Galleries.

As regards Chinese art, it all started when I was a very young child! Jean took me regularly to a Chinese restaurant every Saturday for years. Jean's restaurant of choice was called Ruby Foo's which was on 13th Street, N.W. in downtown Washington, D.C. By being exposed at an impressionable age to Chinese cuisine, I not only became a life-long fan of it, but with it, I started to take an interest in Chinese culture, which led to my discovering the Freer Gallery of Asian Art at an early age. Not only did Jean and her late husband, Manny, help arouse my interest in Chinese art, but they were directly responsible for introducing me to modern studio glass.

2. Gregory R. Staley: An essential ingredient of any art book is good photographs of the art being discussed in the book. I was fortunate to find Gregory. He is a meticulous, careful photographer whose pictures speak for themselves. I thank him for the time and effort he devoted to this project, and even more importantly, for the excellent results.

3. Jessica Lynn Henke: Jessica was my editor, and was an editor par excellence. She adroitly took my rather rigid style of writing, and made it flow. And Jessica was so well organized and easy to work with.

4. Deanna Luu: Deanna was my design expert. I had no idea where one would place pictures in the midst of text, and Deanna did it admirably.

5. Jan Stewart and Debra Diamond: Both Doctors Stewart and Diamond are curators at the Freer-Sackler Museum. They both provided me with invaluable assistance. Jan Stewart read and corrected mistakes I had made in the chapter on Chinese Art. Debra Diamond studied pictures of our Indian miniature paintings and offered helpful comments.

www.ingramcontent.com/pod-product-compliance
Lightning Source LLC
LaVergne TN
LVHW060630110826
845147LV00014B/886

* 9 7 8 1 7 3 3 0 4 0 8 7 7 *